THIRD EDITION

Basic POLICE POWERS

ARREST & SEARCH PROCEDURES

THIRD EDITION

Basic
POLICE POWERS
ARREST & SEARCH PROCEDURES

EMOND MONTGOMERY
PUBLICATIONS LIMITED
TORONTO, CANADA

Gino Arcaro
NIAGARA COLLEGE

Emond Montgomery Publications Limited
60 Shaftesbury Avenue
Toronto ON M4T 1A3
http://www.emp.ca

Printed in Canada.

We acknowledge the financial support of the Government of Canada through the Book Publishing Industry Development Program (BPIDP) for our publishing activities.

Marketing director: Dave Stokaluk

Library and Archives Canada Cataloguing in Publication

Arcaro, Gino, 1957-
    Basic police powers : arrest & search procedures / Gino Arcaro.

Biennial.
3rd ed.-
Vols. for 2003-   accompanied by a copy of the Police Services Act, R.S.O. 1990, c. P-15
    as amended, 1991-2001 forming an office consolidation as of Dec. 21, 2001-; issued
    by the Queen's Printer for Ontario, c1990-.
Vols. for 2007-   published by Emond Montgomery Publications.
Includes bibliographical references and index.
Continues: Basic police procedures, ISSN 1493-2091.
ISSN 1702-3637
ISBN 978-1-55239-246-1 (2007 ; Emond Montgomery)

    1. Police—Canada.   2. Criminal procedure—Canada.   I. Title.

HV8157.A72   345.71'052   C2002-902231-2

CONTENTS

PREFACE

"Being a police officer is a privilege, not a right."

My boss, at 33 Division, Niagara Regional Police, said this to me during one of the many occasions when I was hollered at for messing up one thing or another. In his song, "Badlands," Bruce Springsteen (The Boss) was paying tribute to those who pay their dues during the daily struggle to survive in the anonymity and obscurity of front-line work. He reminded us that front-line work represents the price that has to be paid before advancing and that it serves us well. He cautioned power-mongers to *learn* from and enjoy the trials and tribulations of front-line work rather than resenting it.

My boss was paying tribute to the uniform patrol branch, the front line of policing. He was reminding me to pay my dues before getting absorbed with ambition to become a detective and to *learn* from and enjoy the struggles of front-line police work; and he was cautioning me to change my attitude or be fired.

Both bosses made sense—the front line is a place of learning.

Policing is arguably the most misunderstood job, especially by those who aspire to work in it. A variety of reasons blur and conceal the *realities* of policing and the hiring process. A healthy concept of reality is vital for successful pursuit of police employment. Ignoring reality invites failure. Consequently, the following "Immutable Realities" of policing are offered to those who are in or will be entering the police selection process:

1. "Situations which appear quite innocent, with no hostile demonstration by the person being arrested, can explode into violence, leaving the arresting officer *dead* or injured"—Alberta Court of Appeal, *R. v. Lerke (1986)*. This is the most accurate, concise description of police reality that I have ever read. Policing is one of the few jobs where being intentionally murdered is an occupational hazard. It's a risky business, one that has to be taken seriously. It's not for the faint of heart. Unfortunately, this inescapable reality is inexplicably lost on potential police recruits. The following two examples support this train of thought:
   a) During mock interviews, students are asked, "What's the worst consequence that can happen in policing?" Common answers include "losing a court case," "getting sued," and "getting fired." I have never heard the correct answer—"getting killed."
   b) During an interview by a radio talk show host about the recent murders of three police officers, I was asked by the host if a problem existed. In response to my comments, a caller stated that he did not see a problem because it was "only three deaths" and "this is not like the United States." Shocking perception!
2. Policing is not an alternative to escape the academic challenges required for employment in other careers. A parent recently told me that his son "screwed up" in high school and thought that policing would be a good career choice. The

word "vocation" is derived from the Latin word *voca*, meaning "voice" or "calling." There should be a better reason to want to be a police officer than the misguided notion that academic success is not a prerequisite for law-enforcement hiring.

3. You will not get hired as a detective, undercover officer, SWAT team member, or chief of police. Everyone hired by a police organization is assigned to the uniform patrol branch. Everyone—no exceptions. Patrol officers represent the front line. That's where you learn real policing. However, I have never heard any prospective candidate say, "I want to be a patrol officer." Instead, everyone wants to be a specialist or high-ranking officer. Commonly, people ask how the patrol branch can be avoided or bypassed. It can't. Getting promoted to a specialist branch or higher rank requires years of patrol experience—consistent performance to prove yourself. Goals will be only dreams without solid performance.

4. The world separates winners and losers. There is competition in real life. First, there is a competition to get hired; the police don't draft people like the military does. Then, there is competition for advancement after being hired. Sometimes in real life, you won't get what you want the first time, or even the second time. Sometimes it may take years. So, don't complain if you don't get hired the first time. Instead, view it as an opportunity to get better. How you handle adversity and setbacks reveals who you really are.

5. Wearing a uniform will not make you special. A uniform cannot instill courage, intelligence, or morals. If you *need* to wear a uniform, do whatever it takes to rid yourself of that need. A police uniform is not intended to fill psychological voids and emptiness.

6. You will not save the world. Instead, you will solve problems—some minor, some major.

7. If your parents, teachers, or college coordinators scare you, wait until you meet *real* bad guys. Criminals will not care about your feelings, comfort, or self-esteem. They will not try to make your life easy. Some will be nasty—they may insult you, threaten to kill you and your family, and some may even be violent toward you. The worst part is that there is no one to complain to if these things happen.

8. You won't have a stress-free day. You will be sent to a bar fight or domestic dispute where you will be required to think quickly, under pressure. You can't ask bad guys for more time to think when you are trying to figure out if you can arrest or search them. You can't ask to write a "make-up" case if you lose your court case. And you won't be given satisfaction surveys to express frustration about too much stress that bad guys might cause you.

9. Police organizations are paramilitary organizations. As a rookie, addressing an administrator with a greeting such as "What's up?" or "Hey Alice (or Ralph), how's it going?" will not be suitable or tolerated. You'll have to get used to not being on a first-name basis with your bosses.

10. A strong bench press is not enough to succeed in policing. It helps, but there are countless other traits and skills needed.

11. You won't have summers off, you might have to work on Christmas day, you will have to work the midnight shift, you might have to spend all day in courts without sleeping after a midnight shift, and you won't make $100,000 or be given a company car.

12. A fixation with guns is not normal. Firearms training is essential only because it may save you from being murdered. Don't get excited simply by carrying a gun. Get excited only by the desire to be an expert in self-defence.

13. Although there are traditional courses called "Police Powers," this does not mean you will have special "powers." Laws of arrest, search and seizure are studied. They are *not* powers—they are *solutions* to problems.

14. Television and movies are not real life. Movies like *Lethal Weapon* should never be confused with intellectually stimulating police curriculum or reality. Movies are not training videos. You can't chase cars at breakneck speeds, you can't fire rounds of bullets aimlessly while chasing people on crowded streets, and you can't create bloodbaths.

15. You can't change your past. The police prefer to hire people who have no criminal tendencies. They prefer people with proven ability to understand right from

wrong. They prefer some semblance of moral standards. They prefer to exclude substance abusers. The term "background check" understates the significance of the task. It should be renamed "A police investigation of your past behaviour." Think about this—the police can figure out who committed a murder, robbery, or other nefarious act, so trying to find out if a police candidate is a substance abuser should be relatively simple.

16. Be humble. According to a police recruiter, one of the leading factors that excludes candidates from the hiring process is arrogance.

17. Community service is not simply a resume builder. The police consider sincere volunteer work because sincere volunteer work significantly accelerates the maturation process.

18. Find a mentor. A mentor is not necessarily a friend or cheerleader who simply accepts your weaknesses. A mentor imparts wisdom, develops strengths, and eliminates your weaknesses. A mentor is a valuable gift.

19. My boss was right—being hired as a police officer is a privilege, not a right.

NEW FOR THE THIRD EDITION

The third edition of this textbook has been revised in several significant ways to make the learning process easier for all students.

DESIGN

This edition has a brand new design, one that is based on a workbook format to allow students to write answers in the book for homework assignments.

LEARNING OUTCOMES

Learning outcomes have been added for each chapter. These outcomes are specifically geared for the Police Powers course.

TEST YOURSELF

New review questions have been added at the end of a chapter to test a student's knowledge of the material.

APPENDICES

New appendices have been added on use of discretion and use of force to provide more detailed coverage of these important topics.

WEBSITE (basicpolicepowers3e.nelson.com)

A rich online resource for students and instructors, the *Basic Police Powers* website offers information on careers, study resources, and other topics of interest, created by the author himself.

INSTRUCTOR'S MANUAL/TEST BANK

This useful supplement contains lecture outlines and test questions to assist instructors in the presentation of the material in the textbook.

A NOTE FROM THE PUBLISHER

Thank you for selecting *Basic Police Powers: Arrest & Search Procedures*, Third Edition, by Gino Arcaro. The author and the publisher have devoted considerable time to the careful development of this book. We appreciate your recognition of this effort and accomplishment. We would also like to thank the students, instructors, reviewers, and police officers who have used this book in previous editions. Their comments and suggestions have been valuable to us as we prepared this new edition. Please take some time to provide your feedback by sending us an e-mail from the book's website. You may also contact the author directly at garcaro@niagarac.on.ca.

ABOUT THE AUTHOR

Gino Arcaro, B.Sc., M.Ed.

Gino is a former police officer, having worked fifteen years with the Niagara Regional Police Force, including nine years in the Uniform Patrol Branch and six years as a detective in the Criminal Investigation Branch. He has been a professor at Niagara College for twelve years, where he is the coordinator of both the Police Foundations Program and the Law and Security Program.

Gino has been a volunteer football coach for twenty-six years. He founded and coached the Niagara X-Men football team, a non-profit organization that facilitated the advancement of student-athletes to a wide range of North American universities. In 2002, Gino was hired as Offensive Coordinator at Buffalo State College, a Division III NCAA university.

Including this textbook, he has written several editions of six law enforcement books and one football book.

Unit 1

Learning Outcomes

In this unit, the student will learn

- the meaning of summary conviction, dual procedure, and indictable offences,
- to classify offences and the significance of offence classification,
- the meaning of judicial authorization,
- to define "arrest," "find committing," and "reasonable grounds,"
- to interpret and apply police officers' powers of arrest without warrant,
- to interpret and apply citizens' powers of arrest without warrant,
- to obtain a warrant in the first instance, a summons, and a bench warrant,
- the authorities to enter any place to make an arrest,
- procedures to enter a place without consent and without a warrant,
- use-of-force provisions relating to forcible entry,
- the interpretation and application of sections 10(a) and 10(b) of the *Charter,* and
- a systematic procedure for making an arrest.

CHAPTER

ONE

Classification of Offences

Learning Outcomes

The student will learn

- the meaning of "classification" of offences,
- the definitions and features of summary conviction, dual procedure, and indictable offences,
- to recognize the classification of a criminal offence, and
- how a dual procedure offence is classified permanently.

INTRODUCTION

Canadian criminal offences do not all have the same degree of severity. Some offences are more serious than others, and criminal offences are classified by severity. Understanding the classification of specific criminal offences is essential before learning to apply basic police procedures such as "arrest" and "release."

OFFENCE CLASSIFICATION

Two classifications of criminal offences exist in Canada:

1. Summary conviction
2. Indictable

Summary conviction offences are minor offences and *indictable* offences are major offences. Classification of offences is significant in relation to

1. whether an arrest without warrant may be made,
2. release of an arrested person,
3. time limit to charge an offender,
4. method of trial,
5. maximum penalty, and
6. appeal procedures.

The *Criminal Code* does not have a distinct, separate list of offences by classification. Instead, the classification of a specific criminal offence is stated in the relevant section of the statute that explains the punishment for that offence. For example, to determine the classification of "theft over $5000.00" refer to sec. 334(a) C.C., which states that a person who commits theft where the value of the property exceeds $5000.00 is guilty of an indictable offence and is liable to imprisonment for a term not exceeding 10 years. Another example is the offence of "cause a disturbance." Section 175(1) C.C. states that a person who commits this offence is guilty of an offence punishable on summary conviction.

In addition to indictable and summary conviction offences, offences may be classified as dual procedure or hybrid. Both terms are used in law enforcement and have the same meaning. They refer to offences that do not have an initial permanent classification and may be classified as either summary conviction or indictable. The rules and procedures to determine the final classification of dual procedure/hybrid offences will be explained later in this section.

SUMMARY CONVICTION OFFENCES

These offences are minor criminal offences. Summary conviction trial procedures are explained in Part XXVII of the *Criminal Code,* sections 785–840. These offences are tried in provincial court, by a judge without a jury.

A person who commits a summary conviction offence must be charged within six months. If an information has not been sworn to charge an offender within the six-month period, the offender cannot be charged.[1] Usually, the maximum penalty for summary conviction offences is a $2000.00 fine, six months in jail, or both.[2] A trial judge has no discretion to impose a greater penalty when an accused is convicted of a summary conviction offence that has a maximum penalty. However, some summary conviction maximum penalties vary, and for these, a judge can impose 18 months in jail, $2000.00 fine, or both.

The following is a list of common summary conviction offences and the section in which they are found in the *Criminal Code:*

TABLE 1.1			
indecent act	sec. 173(1)	accommodation fraud	sec. 364(1)
cause a disturbance	sec. 175(1)	transportation fraud	sec. 393(1)
trespass at night	sec. 177	indecent telephone calls	sec. 372(2)
personating peace officer	sec. 130	harassing telephone calls	sec. 372(3)
food fraud	sec. 364(1)	killing or injuring animal	sec. 445

The following is a summary conviction offence found in the *Controlled Drugs and Substances Act* (CDSA):

- possession of a Schedule II substance not exceeding the Schedule VIII amount (sec. 4(5) CDSA)

Example: Possession of marijuana, 30g or under. The maximum penalty for the summary conviction offence is $1000.00 fine, six months in jail, or both. This offence used to be a dual procedure offence under the *Narcotics Control* Act (NCA).

INDICTABLE OFFENCES

Indictable offences are major criminal offences. The *Criminal Code* establishes trial procedures for indictable offences that differ from those for summary conviction offences. The method of determining the level of court where indictable offence trials are conducted is explained at the end of this section.

There is no time limit to charge a person who commits an indictable offence. An information may be sworn any time after the offence date. However, sections 7 and 11(b) of the *Canadian Charter of Rights and Freedoms* do provide protection against unreasonable delays in prosecution. Nevertheless, a person who commits an indictable offence is never immune from prosecution, unlike a person who commits a summary conviction offence and cannot be prosecuted more than six months after the offence.

No general maximum penalty exists for indictable offences; penalties vary, ranging from two, five, ten, or fourteen years to life imprisonment. The maximum penalty is found in the relevant section of the *Criminal Code* that designates the offence.

The following is a list of common indictable offences and the section in which they are found in the *Criminal Code*:

TABLE 1.2	
first degree murder	sec. 235(1)
second degree murder	sec. 235(1)
infanticide	sec. 233
manslaughter	sec. 234
criminal negligence causing death	sec. 220
attempted murder	sec. 239
kidnapping	sec. 279(1)

continued

TABLE 1.2 continued

aggravated assault	sec. 268
sexual assault causing bodily harm	sec. 272
sexual assault with a weapon	sec. 272
aggravated sexual assault	sec. 273
forcible confinement	sec. 279(2)
robbery	sec. 343
criminal negligence causing bodily harm	sec. 221
overcoming resistance to commission of offence	sec. 246
weapons trafficking	sec. 99(1)
possession for the purpose of weapons trafficking	sec. 100(1)
importing or exporting weapons knowing it is unauthorized	sec. 103(1)
possession of firearm knowing its possession is unauthorized	sec. 92(1)
use firearm while committing an indictable offence	sec. 85
discharge firearm with intent	sec. 244
discharge air gun or pistol with intent	sec. 244.1
arson—disregard for human life	sec. 433
arson—damage to property	sec. 434
arson—damage to own property	sec. 434.1
arson—for fraudulent purposes	sec. 435
arson—by negligence	sec. 436
impaired driving causing death	sec. 255(3)
impaired driving causing bodily harm	sec. 255(2)
dangerous operation causing death	sec. 249(4)
possession of property over $5000.00 obtained by crime	sec. 355(a)
fraud over $5000.00	sec. 380(1)(a)
dangerous operation causing bodily harm	sec. 249(3)
theft over $5000.00	sec. 334(a)
break, enter with intent (house)	sec. 348(1)(a)
break, enter and commit (house)	sec. 348(1)(b)
false pretence over $5000.00	sec. 362(2)(a)
disguise with intent	sec. 351(2)
extortion	sec. 346
obstruct justice	sec. 139(2)
perjury	sec. 131

The *Controlled Drugs and Substances Act* also has indictable offences including the following:

TABLE 1.3	
possession for purpose of trafficking (Schedule I, II)	sec. 5(2)
possession of property over $1000.00 obtained by certain offences	sec. 8(1)
trafficking in substance (Schedule I, II)	sec. 5(1)
importing (Schedule I, II)	sec. 6(1)
exporting (Schedule I, II)	sec. 6(1)
production of substance (Schedule I, II)	sec. 7(1)

Schedule I substances include the most dangerous drugs and narcotics, such as

- cocaine,
- heroin, and
- phencyclidine.

Schedule II substances include cannabis (marijuana) and its derivatives.

DUAL PROCEDURE OFFENCES

Unlike summary conviction or indictable offences, dual procedure offences do not have a fixed or permanent initial classification. Instead, dual procedure is a "temporary" classification. A dual procedure offence may receive a fixed or permanent classification based on a decision made by the Crown attorney assigned to prosecute the case. Until that time, all dual procedure offences are temporarily classified as indictable. The terms "dual procedure" and "hybrid" are both used within the criminal justice system; however, the Criminal Code and other federal statutes do not use either term to designate an offence. For example, "assault" is a dual procedure offence found in sec. 266 C.C. Instead of using the phrase "dual procedure," the section states that "everyone who commits an assault is guilty of (i) an indictable offence and liable to imprisonment for a term not exceeding five years; or (ii) an offence punishable on summary conviction."[3]

Stages of Dual Procedure Classification

Although dual procedure offences are eventually designated as either summary conviction or indictable, they must have a specific classification during stages of an investigation and prosecution in order for a police officer to correctly apply basic police procedures.

The five relevant stages are

1. time of offence,
2. time of arrest,
3. time of release,
4. time that charge is laid, and
5. first appearance in court.

The first four stages occur before the first court appearance. During these four pre-court stages, as stated above, all dual procedure offences are temporarily classified as indictable. The authority for this temporary, initial classification is found in sec. 34(1)(a) *Interpretation Act*. There are no exceptions to this rule.

Therefore, all dual procedure offences are considered to be indictable at the time of arrest. This represents an advantage for police officers by expanding the number of offences that do not have a requirement of "find committing" in order to arrest without a warrant.

At the accused's first appearance in court, the Crown attorney decides upon the final classification of a dual procedure offence. There is no trial at the first appearance;

it is simply an opportunity for the accused person to enter a plea of guilty or not. The trial is scheduled for a future date.

Selecting Final Classification—Procedure

After an offender is charged with a dual procedure offence, the following general procedure occurs at the first appearance.

Step 1

The accused person is "arraigned," meaning the information is read to the accused person in open court.

Step 2

The judge asks the Crown attorney, "How do you wish to proceed?" The formal translation of this question is, "What method of trial do you wish to select?" Informally, it simply means, "How do you wish to classify the offence?" Selecting the method of trial must not be confused with the accused's election to determine the level of court where the trial will be held.

Step 3

The Crown attorney selects the method of trial; in other words, classifies the offence as summary conviction or indictable. The Crown attorney's decision is final. Neither the accused person nor the judge participates in this decision, and the decision cannot be appealed or reversed. This authority is not found in the *Criminal Code*, but in case law.[4]

Step 4

If the Crown attorney selects the offence to be summary conviction and the accused pleads not guilty, the trial must be held in provincial court.

The *Controlled Drugs and Substances Act* includes the following dual procedure offences:

TABLE 1.4	
sexual assault	sec. 271
assault causing bodily harm	sec. 267
assault with a weapon	sec. 267
assault a peace officer	sec. 270
assault	sec. 266
criminal harassment	sec. 264
dangerous operation of vehicle	sec. 249(1)(a)
possession of, over 80 mg	sec. 253(b)
theft under $5000.00	sec. 334
possession of property under $5000.00 obtained by crime	sec. 355(b)
fraud under $5000.00	sec. 380(1)(b)
false pretences under $5000.00	sec. 362(2)(b)
mischief over $5000.00	sec. 430(3)
mischief under $5000.00	sec. 430(4)

continued

TABLE 1.4 continued

break, enter with intent (place other than dwelling-house)	sec. 348(1)(e)
break, enter and commit (place other than dwelling-house)	sec. 348(1)(e)
uttering threats to cause death or bodily harm	sec. 264.1(1)(a)
uttering threats to cause damage	sec. 264.1(1)(b)
resist arrest	sec. 270
uttering threats to kill or injure animal	sec. 264.1(1)(c)
possession of prohibited or restricted weapon with ammunition	sec. 95(1)
possession of weapon obtained by offence	sec. 96(1)
making automatic firearm	sec. 102(1)
pointing a firearm	sec. 87(1)
careless use of firearm	sec. 86(1)
carrying concealed weapon	sec. 90(1)
unauthorized possession of firearm in motor vehicle	sec. 94(1)
unauthorized possession of firearm	sec. 91(1)
possession of firearm at unauthorized place	sec. 93(1)
false statement—firearm loss, theft, destruction	sec. 107(1)
tampering with serial number on firearm	sec. 108(1)
transfer firearm without authority	sec. 101(1)
losing or find firearm—fail to report	sec. 105(1)
destroying firearm—fail to report	sec. 106(1)
possession of weapon dangerous to public peace	sec. 88(1)
forgery	sec. 367
uttering forged document	sec. 368(1)
failure to comply with probation order	sec. 733.1
unauthorized importing or exporting, sec. 104(1)	
public mischief	sec. 140
fail to appear	sec. 253(a)
fail to stop at MVC	sec. 252

Table 1.5 provides a list of common dual procedure offences and the section in which they are found in the *Criminal Code*.

Step 5

If the Crown attorney selects the offence to be indictable, the accused will generally have an election regarding the level of court where the trial will be held and whether or not a jury will exist.[5]

The following is a list of common dual procedure offences and the section in which they are found in the *Criminal Code*:

Schedule III substances include:

TABLE 1.5	
possession of substance	
(Schedule I, II, III)	sec. 4(1)
trafficking in substance	
(Schedule III, IV)	sec. 5(1)
possession for purpose of trafficking	
(Schedule III, IV)	sec. 5(2)
importing, exporting	
(Schedule III, IV)	sec. 6(1)
production of substance	
(Schedule III, IV)	sec. 7(1)
possession of property	
under $1000.00	
obtained by certain offences	sec. 8(2)

- LSD
- amphetamines
- methamphetamines

    Schedule IV substances include:

- barbiturates
- anabolic steroids

Accused Person's Election

An election is defined as an option afforded to an accused person regarding the level of court where the trial will be conducted and, therefore, whether a jury will exist.[6] The three choices that an accused has are

1. Superior court, judge, and jury (preliminary hearing required),
2. Superior court, judge alone (preliminary hearing required), and
3. provincial court, judge alone (no preliminary hearing required).

    The following rules are relevant to an accused person's election.

Rule 1

Criminal trials may be conducted in either

- Superior court of criminal jurisdiction, e.g., General Division court, or
- provincial court.[7]

Rule 2

A jury trial may occur only in Superior court, not in provincial court.[8] Therefore, a Superior court trial may be tried by a judge alone or with a jury.

Rule 3

A preliminary hearing is required before a trial occurs in Superior court. No preliminary hearing precedes provincial court trials.[9]

Rule 4

All summary conviction trials must be held in provincial court.[10]

Rule 5

Superior court has absolute jurisdiction over sec. 469 C.C. offences. Section 469 C.C. lists specific indictable offences, such as "murder" and "treason," that must be tried in a Superior court composed of a judge and jury.[11] However, a Superior court judge alone, without a jury, may try a sec. 469 C.C. offence if both the accused person and the attorney general consent.[12]

Rule 6

Provincial court has absolute jurisdiction over sec. 553 C.C. offences, which includes dual procedure offences that must be tried in provincial court regardless of whether the Crown attorney selects the offence to be indictable or a summary conviction. Examples of sec. 553 C.C. offences are the five "under $5000.00" offences (theft, fraud, false pretences, mischief, and possession of property obtained by crime) and fail to comply with probation order.

Rule 7

Dual procedure offences that the Crown attorney selects as indictable (except sec. 553 C.C. offences) and indictable offences that are not sec. 469 C.C. are referred to as election indictable offences. Examples of purely indictable offences that are election indictable are "attempted murder," "robbery," and "theft over $5000.00." An accused person charged with these offences is afforded an election, meaning that he or she may choose one of the three levels of trial.

The following chart summarizes offences that allow or prohibit an election.

TABLE 1.6

NO ELECTION

1. Purely summary conviction (provincial court)

2. Dual procedure selected as summary conviction (provincial court)

3. Section 553 C.C. selected as either indictable or summary conviction (provincial court)

4. Section 469 C.C. (Superior court)

ELECTION

1. Majority of purely indictable offences

2. Dual procedure selected as indictable

Below is a summary of the classification of offences.

TABLE 1.7		
Summary Conviction	**Dual Procedure**	**Indictable**
• six-month time limit	• no time limit	• no time limit
• max. penalty six months, $2000.00, or both	• classified as indictable before court	• max. penalty 2, 5, 10, or 14 years, or life

Test Yourself

Classify the following offences by writing an "X" in the appropriate column.

Summary Conviction	Dual Procedure	Indictable
First degree murder		X
Break, enter with intent (house)		
Assault		
Mischief over $5000		
Robbery		
Trespass by night		
Sexual assault		
Perjury		
Cause a disturbance		
Trafficking substance		
Possession weapon dangerous		
Indecent telephone calls		
Theft over $5000		
Fraud under $5000		
Aggravated assault		
Food fraud		
Harassing phone calls		
Arson—damage to property		
Transportation fraud		
Assault causing bodily harm		
Indecent act		
Sexual assault with a weapon		
Forgery		
Break, enter, and commit (place not a house)		
Aggravated sexual assault		
Possession of substance (Schedule I, II, III)		
Carrying concealed weapon		
Accommodation fraud		
Fail to comply with probation order		

Summary Conviction	Dual Procedure	Indictable
Possession of stolen property, under $5000		
Personating a peace officer		
Attempt murder		
Pointed a firearm		
Weapons trafficking		
Impaired driving		
Obstruct justice		
Utter death threats		
Obstruct police		
Importing substance		
Theft under $5000		
Manslaughter		
Killing an animal		
Aggravated sexual assault		
Assault with a weapon		
Dangerous driving		
Use of firearm during commission of indictable offence		
Public mischief		
Unauthorized possession of irearm		
Over 80 mg		
Careless use of firearm		
Arson—disregard for human life		

TWO

Arrest without Warrant

Learning Outcomes

The student will be able to

- interpret sec. 495 C.C.,
- apply peace officers' power of arrest without a warrant,
- identify circumstances when a peace officer arrest without a warrant is prohibited, and
- interpret and apply sec. 494 C.C. (citizen's powers of arrest).

INTRODUCTION

Freedom and liberty are fundamental principles in a democratic society. Consequently, authority must exist in law to permit the police to arrest in specific situations. Properly applying arrest procedures is arguably the most important act that a police officer performs during an investigation. Obviously, knowing when to arrest facilitates the apprehension of offenders. However, knowing when not to arrest is equally important. An unlawful arrest may result in the following consequences:

1. Section 9 *Charter* violation—every Canadian citizen is protected against arbitrary detention or imprisonment.[13] This means that the police do not have the authority to randomly arrest or detain a person. (Random arrest means having no lawful authority to arrest.) One consequence of a sec. 9 *Charter* violation is possible exclusion of evidence obtained after the arrest.
2. Criminal liability—arresting a person intentionally, without the lawful authority that permits an arrest, may constitute a criminal offence, such as "forcible confinement." Everyone who confines, imprisons, or forcibly seizes another person, without lawful authority, may be charged with "forcible confinement," an indictable offence with a maximum penalty of 10 years in jail.[14]
3. Civil liability—an arrest made without lawful authority may result in civil action against the person who performed the arrest. Lawful authority, which permits a police officer to arrest, is found in the *Criminal Code*.

DEFINITION OF ARREST OR DETENTION

The term "arrest" is not defined in any Canadian federal statute, but in case law. "Arrest" and "detention" have essentially the same meaning. "Arrest" is defined as

1. actual restraint on a person's liberty, without that person's consent, and[15]
2. physical custody of a person with the intent to detain.[16]

Detention, as defined by the Supreme Court of Canada, in *R. v. Therens (1985)*[17] is:

1. Deprivation of liberty by physical constraint.
2. The assuming of control over the movement of a person by demand or direction of a police officer.
3. A psychological compulsion existing within a person in the form of a perception that his or her freedom has been removed.

The essential element of both arrest and detention is the actual removal of a person's freedom, or the person's belief that his or her freedom has been removed, whether or not it actually has been removed. Telling a person, "You're under arrest" and taking physical custody is only one circumstance that constitutes an arrest. Other circumstances include using words or conduct that do not include detention or the word "arrest.". A wide variety of other phrases may constitute an arrest or detention, including, "Get in the car" and "Come here, I want to talk to you." The determining factors of whether an arrest or detention has occurred include

• the intent of the officer making the demand or direction, and
• the belief of the person to whom the demand or direction is made.

An arrest or detention will have occurred if it is proven that (a) the person making the demand or detention would have prohibited the person from leaving or moving from one location to another, or (b) the person to whom the demand or direction is made reasonably believed that he or she could not have left or could not move from one location to another.

An arrest or detention does not constitute a formal charge. An offender is formally charged only when an "information" is laid and signed by a justice. An information is the name of a document used to formally charge an offender. In summary, arrest refers only to the physical custody of a person; a sworn information formally charges the person.

VOLUNTARY ACCOMPANIMENT

A person may accompany a police officer and not be under arrest, if the accompanying person consents to do so. Voluntary accompaniment does not constitute an arrest or detention; it refers to valid consent given by a person to a police officer to accompany the officer or remain with the officer for some law enforcement purpose such as questioning. Voluntary accompaniment is a procedure that may be used when no lawful authority exists in a specific situation, and the officer requires the person's presence for investigative purposes such as questioning.

Proving voluntary accompaniment requires evidence that valid consent was given by the person who accompanied the police officer. A primary element of voluntary accompaniment is evidence that the person had knowledge that he or she was free to leave at any time, and would have been permitted to leave if he or she had chosen to do so. Additionally, the person must know

1. the specific act that the officer intends to conduct (i.e., questioning),
2. the consequences that may occur (i.e., charges may result and any statement may later be used in court),
3. that consent may be refused (i.e., no obligation exists to give consent, and no consequences exist for refusing to consent), and
4. that consent may be revoked at any time (i.e., the person can change his or her mind).

The following sequence of questions/comments will achieve optimum results when used to obtain voluntary accompaniment:

Step 1

"Will you come with me (or will you meet me at the police station) for questioning about a robbery?"

Step 2

"You don't have to. The choice is yours."

Step 3

"If you do, you are free to leave at any time during the questioning."

It must be emphasized that this information should be conveyed only when no lawful authority exists to arrest the person. Voluntary accompaniment is an investigative procedure that is an alternative to arrest, when a police officer has no authority to arrest.

LAWFUL AUTHORITY TO ARREST

Two types of lawful authority to arrest exist:

1. With a warrant—This type of lawful authority represents judicial authorization, meaning that the final decision to arrest with a warrant is made by a justice, and the officer simply makes the arrest. This type of authority affects summary conviction, dual procedure, and indictable offences, and is granted when specific conditions exist and are proven.
2. Without a warrant—This type of lawful authority represents an arrest made without judicial authorization. The circumstances permitting officers to arrest without obtaining judicial authorization first are limited but do include a significant amount of authority. Authorities for both arrest with warrant and arrest without warrant are found in the *Criminal Code*. Therefore, the arrest authorities apply anywhere in Canada.

ARREST WITHOUT WARRANT—POLICE OFFICERS' AUTHORITIES

Police officers arrest offenders without a warrant more often than with a warrant. Section 495(1) C.C. establishes four lawful authorities that allow a police officer to arrest without a warrant:[18]

1. find committing a criminal offence,[19]
2. reasonable grounds that an indictable offence has been committed,[20]
3. reasonable grounds that an indictable offence is about to occur,[21] and
4. reasonable grounds that a valid warrant exists in the territorial jurisdiction in which the accused person is found.[22]

If the circumstances of any of these four authorities exist, an officer is not required to obtain judicial authorization to arrest.[23]

These authorities apply to both adult and young offenders. The sections below will interpret each authority individually, followed by explanations and examples of how to apply them.

FIND COMMITTING A CRIMINAL OFFENCE

Two elements compose this authority:

- find committing
- any criminal offence

Find committing is not defined in the *Criminal Code*; its meaning derives from case law. The definition is composed of two parts:

1. The first circumstance relates to the commission of an offence where the offender remains at the scene. Find committing is defined as seeing an offender actually commit an offence.[24] This requires witnessing the offence in its entirety,[25] which includes seeing
   a) all the elements that compose the offence, referred to as the "facts in issue," and
   b) the person who committed the entire offence.

   Find committing does not include seeing a partial offence or not seeing it occur but being told about it.[26]

2. The second circumstance relates to the commission of an offence where the offender flees from the scene. Find committing is also defined as seeing an offender actually commit an offence and pursuing him or her (a) immediately and (b) continuously until apprehension.
   a) "Immediately" means immediately after an offender has been seen committing an offence. It does not mean immediately after the offence is discovered or immediately after the commission of the offence (without having seen the offender).[27]
   b) "Continuously" is defined as without a break.[28] It means never losing sight of the offender from the time of the offence to the time of apprehension. The pursuit and apprehension must form a single transaction.[29] The concept of "never losing sight" causes some controversy, but no amount of time lapse is permitted during a pursuit in order to constitute find committing. Consequently, if the pursuer loses sight of an offender and regains sight at any time later, the pursuer is no longer found committing. Instead, the pursuer has reasonable grounds that the offender committed the offence.[30] The reason for the "no loss of sight" requirement is the possibility of human memory error regarding facial recognition of the offender. In circumstances where find committing is mandatory during an arrest, the continuous, no-loss-of-sight pursuit is significant to ensure the correct identity of the offender and to prevent the arrest of someone else.

It must be emphasized that not all of the police officer's powers of arrest are dependent on find committing. It is a requirement that applies only to this authority.

In summary, the following circumstances *do not* constitute find committing:

1. not witnessing an offence but being informed of it by a person who did witness it,
2. seeing only a partial offence, or only the outcome or result of the offence, and
3. seeing an offence being committed, pursuing the offender, losing sight for any amount of time, and finding the offender after the loss of sight.

Any Criminal Offence This authority applies to summary conviction, dual procedure, and indictable offences.

Problem-Solving Case Studies

(You are a police officer in each case. Each offender is an adult, unless otherwise indicated.)

PROBLEM 1

You are dispatched to a disturbance at a bar. Upon arrival, you see Eddie causing a disturbance inside. Can you arrest without a warrant?

_____

_____

PROBLEM 2

You are dispatched to a domestic dispute at a house. Upon arrival, you see Ward assault June inside the house. Can you arrest Ward without a warrant?

_____

PROBLEM 3

You see Wally steal a $20 000.00 car and you pursue Wally continuously until Wally stops. Can you arrest without a warrant?

_____

_____

_____

REASONABLE GROUNDS THAT AN INDICTABLE OFFENCE HAS BEEN COMMITTED

This authority is composed of three elements:

- reasonable grounds
- indictable offence
- has been committed

Reasonable Grounds This may be the most prominent and significant Canadian legal term for a police officer to learn because it applies to many police procedures. Remarkably, despite its significance, reasonable grounds is not defined in the *Criminal Code*. It is defined in case law as "a set of facts or circumstances which would cause a person of ordinary and prudent judgment to believe beyond a mere suspicion."[31]

This definition creates a standard of belief that a police officer must form, before performing the relevant act such as arrest or search. Additionally, the authority to act on reasonable grounds represents an advantage to the police officer because it permits the belief to be formed without witnessing an occurrence. Essentially, acting on reasonable grounds significantly expands the scope of authority in comparison to the requirement of find committing. However, without analyzing the definition of reasonable grounds, it may appear to be vague and lacking specific guidelines.

"A set of facts or circumstances" refers to evidence, both admissible or inadmissible.[32] The evidence may be in the form of physical objects or observations, and the amount of evidence must exceed mere suspicion in the opinion of an ordinary or prudent person. "Mere suspicion" refers to speculation or conjecture based on unsubstantiated rumour or gossip. However, "beyond mere suspicion" does not mean absolute, unequivocal knowledge that goes beyond all doubt. Instead, it refers to a belief consisting of a reasonable degree of certainty. A specific procedure about how to form reasonable grounds does not exist in statute law. The Supreme Court of Canada, in *R. v. Storrey (1990)*,[33] created the following general procedural guidelines:

1. The formation of reasonable grounds requires two tests, which refers to a decision-making process. The tests are called
   - subjective test
   - objective test

   A subjective test refers to the officer's personal belief that a set of circumstances exceeds mere suspicion. The officer conducts the subjective test by analyzing a set of circumstances and determines whether reasonable grounds exist. In other words, the subjective test is the officer's opinion that he or she has an honest belief that circumstances constitute reasonable grounds. The officer must be prepared to explain or justify the belief by explaining the basis of the opinion.

   An objective test is an opinion or belief that is made independent of the officer to determine whether reasonable grounds did actually exist. Essentially, a judge conducts the objective test to determine if the officer's belief was correct. The purpose of the objective test is to determine whether "a reasonable person placed in the position of the officer" would conclude that reasonable grounds actually existed. A judge essentially acts on behalf of the "reasonable person." In other words, the objective test determines whether the subjective test was correct. The trial judge ultimately is the person who must be convinced and makes the decision or conclusion about whether reasonable grounds actually existed.

2. The police are not required to establish a prima facie case for conviction before making an arrest; reasonable grounds does not have to prove guilt beyond reasonable doubt.

3. All available information must be taken into account and considered during the reasonable grounds formulation process. In other words, an officer cannot be selective and consider only some of the information that is available. For example, if multiple witnesses see an occurrence, and are available, the officer cannot base his or her belief only on the selected witnesses who provide positive information; information cannot be disregarded without justifiable reasons.

4. An officer is entitled to disregard only information that he or she has good reason to believe is unreliable. Witness credibility must be evaluated during the reasonable grounds formulation process. In some cases, little or no time is available to make a thorough credibility evaluation. In other cases, sufficient time is afforded to form an opinion. A witness's information may be disregarded only when the officer who receives it has a justifiable reason to believe that the witness has poor credibility.

Generally, the following specific types of evidence constitute reasonable grounds:

1. A confession made by an offender to any person, whether a police officer or a citizen. This type of evidence is the best type of reasonable grounds.

2. One credible eyewitness, meaning a person who saw the entire offence and can facially recognize the offender. Officers have no obligation to obtain corroboration (supporting evidence) to confirm one credible eyewitness.

   Forming reasonable grounds may be a simple task requiring only a matter of seconds or a complex task that requires a substantial amount of time. Each investigation involves a process unique to the circumstances of the respective case. Even so, uniform patrol officers encounter daily situations where immediate decisions are needed. An example is a domestic complaint where the victim and offender are both present.

Domestic disputes are commonly hostile, stressful situations that pose significant danger to the officer and the participants. It is not uncommon for novice, inexperienced officers to unnecessarily question the credibility or reliability of brief information reported by the victim. For example, the victim often makes a simple statement such as, "he hit me," which motivates a tirade by the offender. The uncorroborated, unsupported verbal statement made by the complainant in situations like this constitutes reasonable grounds. The offence of "assault" does not require corroboration to convict. If investigation reveals that the victim intentionally lied, the victim could be charged with public mischief. Any other evidence, such as visible injuries, simply solidify the forming of reasonable grounds.

The Supreme Court of Canada, in *R. v. Godoy (1999)*[34] ruled that the verbal statement from a woman that her husband hit her combined with the officer's observation of the victim's swollen eye constituted reasonable grounds to arrest the husband. This process and decision required only a few seconds. This case is significant to illustrate the justification to make quick decisions based on minimal evidence in potentially dangerous situations.

3. Numerous types of circumstantial evidence (which are explained in greater detail in investigation courses and textbooks).

In summary, the officer does not have to be an eyewitness. Instead, the officer may arrest without a warrant without seeing the offence occur, if evidence exists that causes the officer to believe beyond mere suspicion that the offender committed the offence. One eyewitness or a confession by the offender to a police officer or a citizen are examples of evidence that constitutes reasonable grounds. Unsubstantiated rumour, speculation, or conjecture constitute mere suspicion, which is not a sufficient belief to arrest. Hearsay evidence may be used to form reasonable grounds.[35]

CREDIBILITY—ANONYMOUS INFORMATION

As stated previously, the type or amount of evidence that constitutes a belief based on reasonable grounds is not stated in the definition of reasonable grounds. Two types of evidence that exceed mere suspicion are confessions made by an offender to any person, including a police officer or citizen, and at least one credible eyewitness. The credibility of a witness's observations is the prominent factor when basing a belief on his or her observations. Evaluating credibility is a skill that is learned through experience and by studying principles of credibility evaluation in an investigation course. Although principles of witness credibility evaluation are beyond the scope of this textbook, the issue of observations received from confidential informants is a topic that requires explanation.

Informants are an integral part of police investigations and are valuable in the formation of reasonable grounds. Informants are witnesses who have made relevant observations regarding an offence, but the police will not subpoena them to court. In order to protect the informant and to receive information from that person in the future, the police will not divulge his or her identity. Determining whether an informant's observations constitute reasonable grounds depends on the informant's credibility, and this is evaluated by using the same principles as with any other eyewitness. In some cases, the officer will know the informant by name. In other cases, the informant is anonymous and is unknown to the officer. The case study on page 22 provides guidelines regarding the use of anonymous information in the formation of reasonable grounds for the purpose of arrest without warrant.

Indictable Offence

Includes purely indictable offences and dual procedure offences. Summary conviction offences are not included in this authority.

Has Been Committed

Refers only to offences that occurred in the past. No time limit exists to make an arrest using this authority. An arrest based on reasonable grounds for indictable or dual procedure offences can occur even after six months have expired, unlike a summary conviction offence.

An officer *cannot* arrest under the following circumstances because no lawful authority exists:

1. Reasonable grounds that a summary conviction offence has been committed. An officer must find committing a summary conviction offence in order to arrest.

2. Mere suspicion that a criminal offence has been committed. No authority exists to arrest regarding any classification of offence if only mere suspicion exists. The evidence must form a belief that exceeds mere suspicion.

CASE LAW

R. V. BENNETT (1996)[36]

Issue   Does the information from an anonymous informant constitute reasonable grounds to arrest without a warrant?

Offences   "possession of narcotics" and "obstruct police"

Circumstances   A police officer received the following information from a female citizen who refused to identify herself, give her address, or her motive for reporting the information.

An informant reported that a woman was selling crack in the entrance hall of an apartment complex, and provided a detailed description of the suspect and the address of the complex. The informant also reported that the suspect had a keycase in her pocket in which the crack was hidden. The officer evaluated the informant's credibility on the basis of the precision of the information, and his prior knowledge that drug trafficking was prevalent at that apartment complex.

The officer attended at the address and saw a woman outside the building who matched the description of the suspect exactly. The officer arrested the woman for the dual procedure offence of "possession of narcotics" before searching her. When the officer prepared to search her, the woman removed a keycase from her pocket, held it in her hand, and appeared to intend to dispose of it. The officer asked her for the keycase, and she gave it to him. A quantity of crack was found inside. The officer later charged the woman with "possession of narcotics" and with "obstruct police" by attempting to hide the keycase.

Trial   The accused was found guilty of "possession of narcotics." She was also convicted of "obstruct police," but the judge ordered a stay of proceedings regarding this offence based on the principle that prevents multiple convictions.

Appeal

- The accused appealed her conviction for "possession of narcotics" to the Quebec Court of Appeal. The appeal was dismissed, and the conviction was upheld. However, the arrest was ruled to be unlawful because the circumstances did not constitute reasonable grounds. However, the seized narcotics were ruled to be admissible under section 24(2) *Charter*. The following reasons were given in the judgment:

- An anonymous "tip" is insufficient to prove reasonable grounds. The officer must also be satisfied with the reliability of the information, which must be assessed on the basis of the total circumstances.

- In this case, the officer had no means of verifying the credibility of the informant or the information.

- The officer based the arrest on the similarity between the reported description of the suspect and the description of the woman he saw at the apartment. Confirming the identity of the suspect was not the issue; instead, the suspect's involvement in drug trafficking needed confirmation and supporting evidence.

- The informant's refusal to identify herself justified the need for additional investigation. In this case the anonymous informant's report constitutes mere suspicion only.

continued

- The unlawful arrest constituted a section 9 *Charter* violation. Subsequently, the admissibility of the seized narcotics needed to be determined pursuant to section 24(2) *Charter*.

- The narcotics were admissible because the admission of them would not bring the administration of justice into disrepute.

- The admission of the evidence was allowed because the *Charter* violation was minor. The court emphasized the minor nature of the *Charter* violation by saying, "I find it difficult to imagine a more minor infringement of a right."

Additionally, the court rationalized that although the arrest was unlawful, "the officer could have believed that he was justified in placing her under arrest." Additionally, narcotics are physical evidence that existed before the *Charter* violation occurred.

COMMENTARY

This case illustrates an excellent example of the complicated nature of case law decisions rendered by appeal courts. Although the accused was convicted, this fact could be lost in the complexities of the conclusions made about the arrest. Despite the fact that the officer was correct and that the informant was accurate, the informant's report was ruled to be mere suspicion, meaning that the officer made an unlawful arrest. The reason for this conclusion must be emphasized—the informant refused to identify herself. This prevented the officer from being able to evaluate her credibility. This circumstance imposed a requirement on the officer to investigate the incident further.

An unlawful arrest does not result in automatic exclusion of evidence seized afterward. This principle will be explained later in the textbook, in the explanation of section 24(2) *Charter*. In summary, after it had been concluded that an unlawful arrest had been made, it was considered to be a minor *Charter* violation, a conclusion that strongly contributed to the admissibility of the seized narcotics.

The following case study provides excellent procedural guidelines relating to

i)   what circumstances actually constitute reasonable grounds, and
ii) whether one witness is sufficient to form reasonable grounds.

Note: The following case law decision is relevant to other police authorities that will be explained later in the textbook. The entire decision and reasons will be included, covering topics that have not been explained. References will be made in various sections of this book to the following case.

CASE LAW

R. V. GOLUB (1997)[37]

Issues

- Was the arrest lawful? Did the information obtained by the police constitute reasonable grounds that the accused committed an indictable offence? What impact does a witness's failure to remember at the trial have on reasonable grounds?

- Was the warrantless search of the house a "search incident to a lawful arrest"?

- Was a "*Feeney*" warrant required to enter and search the house?

- Did the circumstances constitute a "public safety" risk, relating to a warrantless search for firearms?

Offences   The accused was charged with multiple offences. All but one involved the possession of a sawed-off .22 calibre semi-automatic rifle.

continued

Circumstances   The accused person and his friend were in a bar at 10:30 p.m. The manager of the bar refused to serve the accused any more drinks. The accused and his friend left, and visited various bars. The accused became upset and angry. He told his friend he was having trouble with his ex-wife. He also struck his friend. The accused twice threatened to "get even" with the staff at the bar that had refused to serve him, and showed the friend an 18-inch rifle, which was concealed beneath his jacket.

The friend called the police and reported the following information to the officers:

- The accused caused a disturbance at the bar.

- The accused showed him the gun at another bar.

- The gun was described to the police as an "Uzi sub-machine gun," loaded with five clips.

- The accused was upset and agitated.

- The accused threatened to "get even" with the staff at the bar.

An investigation resulted. The police found a basement apartment rented by the accused. Initial attempts to gain entry were unsuccessful.

The Emergency Task Force (ETF) was contacted. The apartment building was evacuated at 7:00 a.m. The officer-in-charge phoned the apartment at 7:28 a.m. and spoke to the accused. The officer instructed the accused to come out the apartment door with nothing in his hands and to follow instructions from officers at the door.

At 7:35 a.m., the accused opened the door and had nothing in his hands. He was told to leave the door open, but instead, he closed the door and locked it. The accused was formally arrested about 15 feet outside the apartment door. The accused was asked if anyone else was in the apartment. He shrugged and said, "I don't think so." The officer-in-charge formed the belief that other occupants could be in the apartment and ordered the ETF to enter the apartment and search it. This order was made within seconds of the arrest. A key was used to enter. Four officers entered. The officer-in-charge testified at the trial that the intention of the search was to look for persons, not evidence, and "public safety" was definitely a concern. The ETF team was not looking for the gun upon entry, but if it was found, they were to secure it, continue the search, and turn over the scene and firearm to the investigating officers. The ETF officer-in-charge never thought about obtaining a search warrant.

One of the searching officers testified that he was to look methodically in "every room, every crevice" for other persons. The officers subsequently searched every conceivable place in the apartment where a person could possibly hide. A .22 calibre sawed-off semi-automatic rifle was found under a mattress in a bedroom. The 15-round magazine was fully loaded. Two clear boxes, each containing 100 rounds of .22 hollow-point ammunition, were beside the gun. Fifteen rounds were missing from one box. The search continued. No persons were found.

At the completion of the search, the investigating officers entered the apartment and seized the weapon and ammunition. They also searched the apartment without a warrant under the authority of the sec. 103(2) C.C., which was then in force but has been replaced with sec. 117.04(2) C.C. Consequently, two separate searches without a warrant occurred.

Trial   The rifle was excluded under sec. 24(2) *Charter* and seizure was ruled to be a sec. 8 *Charter* violation since its admission would bring the administration of justice into disrepute. The accused was acquitted.

Appeal   The Crown appealed the acquittal to the Ontario Court of Appeal. The appeal was allowed. A new trial was ordered.

COMMENTARY

Issue 1   The police relied solely on the eyewitness information provided by the accused's friend. The trial judge ruled that the observations did constitute reasonable grounds. However, the accused raised a unique issue for appeal that would have significantly impacted arrest without warrant procedures. The accused's appeal argument was that one unconfirmed eyewitness, without corroboration (supporting evidence), was insufficient to form reasonable grounds to make an arrest. The argument was

continued

based on the standards of obtaining a search warrant, where the information of an untested informant requires supporting evidence to confirm it.

The Ontario Court of Appeal rejected this argument, ruling that the information of one eyewitness is sufficient to form reasonable grounds to make an arrest without warrant. No corroboration is required to confirm the information of one eyewitness. The reasons were

1. The dynamics of an arrest situation are very different than those relating to a search warrant application.

2. An officer's decision to arrest must often be made in "volatile and rapidly changing situations."

3. The decision to arrest is based on available information, which is often less than complete or exact.

4. The law does not expect a police officer to make the same inquiry when deciding whether reasonable grounds exist as a justice is required to do when examining a search warrant application.

The court stated that the information from the accused's friend constituted reasonable grounds because the officers had a firsthand opportunity to evaluate his credibility and had no reason to ignore the information. Additionally, the court noted that not only were the police justified in acting on the information, "they would have been derelict in their duty had they not acted on it."

Finally, the court answered the question, "What impact does a witness's failure to remember at the trial have on reasonable grounds?" At the trial, in this case, the witness (accused's friend) testified that he had been too drunk on the night of the offence to remember the events. The Ontario Court of Appeal ruled that this testimony was not relevant to the existence of reasonable grounds for the arrest. No evidence existed at the trial that the witness's condition at the time of the police interview should have discredited his information. The following significant rule was made by the court:

"A failed memory several months after the events, even if legitimate, does not imply that information provided at the relevant time was unreliable."

Issue 2   The search of the immediate surroundings of a place where a person is arrested is authorized by common law and case law. The arrest in this case was made outside the accused's house, about 15 feet from his door. The entire house was searched without a warrant after the arrest. The issue on appeal was, "Was the warrantless search of the house a search incident to a lawful arrest?"

The Ontario Court of Appeal ruled that the search was a lawful incident to the arrest and did constitute a reasonable search. No *Charter* violation occurred. The following reasons were given, which provide useful procedural guidelines:

1. The search of a house as an incident to an arrest is generally prohibited, but it is authorized when "exceptional circumstances" exist.

2. "Exceptional circumstances" are defined as situations where the law enforcement interest is so compelling that it overrides the individual's right to privacy within the home.

3. The following elements contribute to a compelling law enforcement interest that constitutes exceptional circumstances:

   • the need to secure the arrested person,

   • the need to protect persons at the arrest scene, and

   • the need to preserve evidence.

4. The police interest in protecting the safety of people at the scene of an arrest is the most compelling concern at an arrest scene and one that must be addressed immediately.

5. The police cannot be asked to place themselves in potentially dangerous situations in order to make an arrest. If the police cannot protect themselves and others, they will avoid making arrests, thereby compromising law enforcement.

continued

6. The risk of physical harm to persons at an arrest scene constitutes exceptional circumstances, which justify a warrantless entry and search of the house.

7. A reasonable suspicion that "someone is on the other side of a closed door with a loaded sub-machine gun, or that someone is lying injured on the other side of that door, creates a legitimate cause for concern, justifying entry and search of the apartment for persons."

Issue 3   The arrest occurred outside the accused's home. Therefore, the *Feeney* warrant and procedure were inapplicable to the accused's arrest. Since no other person was found in the house, the court did not consider the *Feeney* case or the relevant legislation. However, it is presumed that these circumstances constituted exigent circumstances pursuant to sec. 529.3(2) C.C. that would have justified a warrantless search of a dwelling-house for a person as an exception to the *Feeney* warrant requirement.

Issue 4   A public safety risk combined with exigent circumstances justifies a warrantless search of a house for firearms under sec. 117.04(2) C.C. The suspicion by the ETF's officer-in-charge that someone else was in the apartment created a sufficient public safety risk to justify reasonable steps to investigate.
The sufficient suspicion was based on

- the witness's information,

- the accused's failure to leave the apartment door open when asked to do so, and

- the reasonable belief that there was a loaded, dangerous firearm inside the apartment.

Problem-Solving Case Studies

You are a police officer in each case. Each offender is an adult, unless otherwise indicated.

PROBLEM 4

June reports to you today that Ward assaulted her three days ago. Can you arrest Ward today without a warrant?

_____

_____

_____

_____

_____

PROBLEM 5

You are questioning Wally, with Wally's consent, about a robbery that occurred eight months ago. Wally confesses to you. Can you arrest without a warrant?

_____

_____

_____

PROBLEM 6

You see Ralph (16 years old) steal a $20 000.00 car. You pursue Ralph, but you lose sight of him. You see Ralph 24 hours later. He is walking on a sidewalk and you recognize him. Can you arrest Ralph without a warrant?

_____

_____

_____

_____

_____

PROBLEM 7

Wally reports the following to you right now: Wally met Eddie at a bar last night at 11:00 p.m. Eddie confessed to him that he committed "break, enter and theft" at a house situated at 10 King St., seven days ago. Can you arrest Eddie without a warrant?

_____

_____

_____

_____

PROBLEM 8

June reports to you right now that she saw Eddie commit an "indecent act" on King St. one hour ago. Can you arrest Eddie without a warrant?

_____

_____

_____

_____

_____

_____

_____

PROBLEM 9

June reported to you yesterday at 5:00 p.m. that she received three obscene phone calls between 1:00 and 4:00 p.m. You develop a suspicion that Eddie, a next-door neighbour, committed the offences. The suspicion is based merely on unsubstantiated speculation. You interrogate Eddie today, with Eddie's consent. Eddie confesses that he committed the offences. Can you arrest Eddie without a warrant?

_____

_____

_____

PROBLEM 10

You are investigating an "attempted murder" that occurred five hours ago. Ward is the victim. You form a suspicion that Eddie may be the offender, based merely on unsubstantiated speculation. Can you arrest Eddie for suspicion of "attempted murder" or for the purpose of questioning him in order to form reasonable grounds?

_____

_____

_____

_____

_____

_____

_____

_____

REASONABLE GROUNDS THAT AN INDICTABLE OFFENCE IS ABOUT TO OCCUR

Three elements compose this authority:

* reasonable grounds,
* indictable offence, and
* about to occur.

Reasonable Grounds

One credible eyewitness, a confession made by the offender to anyone, or any circumstances that exceed mere suspicion constitute reasonable grounds.

Indictable Offence

Includes purely indictable and dual procedure offences. Summary conviction offences do not apply to this authority.

About to Occur

This term is not defined in the *Criminal Code*. It means that an offence has not been committed but may be committed in the near future. The person who is about to commit an indictable offence cannot be charged because no offence will have occurred.

This authority allows a police officer to prevent the commission of an indictable or dual procedure offence. Officers cannot prevent a summary conviction offence from occurring by means of arrest because no authority exists to arrest a person on reasonable grounds that a summary conviction offence is about to occur. Consequently, summary conviction offences may be prevented only by alternate means, such as using one's communication skills.

Section 503(4) C.C. governs the length of detention and the release procedures regarding an arrest made with this authority. The arrested person must be released unconditionally as soon as practicable after the officer is satisfied that the continued detention of the arrested person is no longer necessary to prevent the commission of an indictable offence (by the arrested person). An information to charge the arrested person will not be laid because no offence will have been committed.

Problem-Solving Case Studies

You are a police officer in each case. Each offender is an adult, unless otherwise indicated.

PROBLEM 11

You see an intoxicated person walking toward his car. This person insists to you that he is driving home. Can you arrest?

_____

_____

_____

PROBLEM 12

You arrive at a dispute between two people. One person becomes hostile and indicates, by means of words and/or conduct, that he may assault the other person. Can you arrest?

_____

_____

_____

Note: If no offence actually occurs, and an officer arrests a person to prevent an offence from being committed, the arrested person may be detained only until the reasonable grounds no longer exist. The arrested person must be released when the detention is no longer needed to prevent the commission of the indictable offence.[38] For example, in Problem 11, reasonable grounds no longer exist when the intoxicated person becomes sober. At this time, the arrested person must be released unconditionally, meaning that no charge will be laid.

This particular arrest-without-warrant authority does not frequently apply because many "about to commit" circumstances also constitute actual offences. For example, in Problem 11, if the intoxicated person is standing near the driver's door while holding the car keys, he may be charged with "care or control of a motor vehicle while impaired," which is a dual procedure offence. Although the intoxicated person is about to commit "impaired driving," he has already committed "care or control while impaired."

In Problem 12, if the person makes a threatening act or gesture, the offence of "assault" has been committed.[39] Also, if the person makes a verbal statement threatening to cause bodily harm, the offence of "uttering threats" has been committed.[40]

Other circumstances pose problems to police officers requiring a decision about whether to arrest a person before the actual offence occurs. The following problem illustrates this.

PROBLEM 13

Eddie tells Wally that he intends to commit robbery at a specific store, or commit a break and enter at a specific place. Wally reports this to you. What are your alternatives?

_____

_____

_____

The three alternatives you may exercise are as follows:

1. If the suspect is arrested because he is about to commit "robbery" or "break and enter," the suspect will be deterred from actually committing the offence at least until after his or her release. There is no assurance that the suspect will be deterred indefinitely. Additionally, the length of detention is limited. The suspect must be released when the reasonable grounds no longer exist.

2. Attempting to commit a specific indictable offence, such as "attempted break and enter," is an indictable offence.[41] An attempt is defined as "having the intent to commit an offence, and, doing or omitting to do anything for the purpose of carrying out the intention, whether or not it was possible under the circumstances to commit the offence."[42] The elements of an attempt are

   a) preparation that is fully complete and ended, and
   b) the "next step" done by the offender to commit the offence, and
   c) with the intention of committing the offence.[43]

   Mere preparation alone does not constitute an offence.[44] Mere preparation refers to the preparation without any other overt act done to commit the offence. Consequently, a person about to commit an indictable offence may possibly have committed an "attempt to commit an indictable offence" for which he or she may be charged.

3. "Conspiracy to commit an indictable offence" is a separate indictable offence.[45] Conspiracy is defined as "an agreement by two or more persons to commit a criminal offence."[46] An overt act, meaning the next step to commit the offence, does not have to be proven.[47] However, only one person's intention does not constitute a conspiracy.

In summary, when reasonable grounds exist, most arrests without warrant are made in relation to indictable offences that have been committed, as opposed to those about to be committed. Very few "about to commit" circumstances constitute offences.

REASONABLE GROUNDS THAT A VALID WARRANT EXISTS IN THE TERRITORIAL JURISDICTION IN WHICH THE ACCUSED PERSON IS FOUND

Three elements compose this authority:

- reasonable grounds,
- valid warrant exists, and
- in the territorial jurisdiction in which the accused is found.[48]

To understand the reason that this authority is listed in the arrest without warrant section, the provisions of sec. 29(1) C.C. must be examined. According to this section of the *Criminal Code*, when a police officer arrests with a warrant, the officer is required to have possession of the warrant at the time of the arrest.[49] Warrants are usually stored in the central records department at a police station. Therefore, when an officer checks a person on CPIC, the police computer data system, and is informed that a warrant exists for the arrest of this person, the officer is not likely to have possession of the warrant and therefore cannot fulfill the "possession" requirement of sec. 29(1) C.C..

To deal with this dilemma, sec. 495(1)(c) C.C. allows an officer to arrest without having possession of the warrant if the following conditions exist:

Reasonable Grounds

A CPIC message stating that a person is wanted constitutes reasonable grounds that a warrant exists.

Valid Warrant Exists

An arrest warrant must be signed by a justice, defined as a justice of the peace or a provincial court judge.[50] Most justices have authority throughout their respective province. Therefore, an arrest warrant signed by a justice in a particular city is valid throughout that respective province, if the justice has authority throughout the province. For example, an arrest warrant signed by a justice in Toronto is valid anywhere in Ontario. The CPIC message will state the city where the arrest warrant was signed.

In the Territorial Jurisdiction in Which the Person Is Found

This refers to the legal authority or power of a court to conduct a proceeding in a particular city or region[51] where the officer has found the suspect, e.g., Niagara Region. A CPIC message regarding arrest warrants usually includes the following information:

e.g., Wanted—(offence)—(city where warrant was signed and issued)

e.g., Wanted—"theft over $5000.00"—Calgary.

"Wanted" constitutes reasonable grounds that the warrant exists. The city where the warrant was issued informs the officer that the warrant is valid anywhere in the province in which the city is situated. If the suspect is found anywhere in that province, a police officer may arrest the suspect without having possession of the warrant at the time of the arrest.

Problem-Solving Case Studies

You are a police officer in each case. Each offender is an adult, unless otherwise indicated.

PROBLEM 14

You stop Wally in St. Catharines, Ontario. A CPIC check reveals the following message: Wanted—"robbery"—Toronto. Can you arrest Wally without having possession of the warrant?

_____

_____

_____

PROBLEM 15

You stop Eddie in Calgary, Alberta. A CPIC check reveals the following message: Wanted—"assault"—Edmonton. Can you arrest Eddie without having possession of the warrant?

_____

_____

_____

_____

The following three general rules apply to the authority to arrest based on reasonable grounds that a valid warrant exists in the territorial jurisdiction where the accused person is found.

Rule 1

An arrest warrant may be issued for any criminal offence, *including summary conviction*. An arrest warrant for a summary conviction offence is valid throughout the province in which it was issued. For example, if an officer finds a person in Toronto and learns that a valid warrant, issued in Toronto, exists for a summary conviction offence, the officer may arrest without having possession of the warrant. This authority must not be confused with a situation where no warrant has been issued, yet reasonable grounds exist that a summary conviction offence occurred. No "arrest without warrant" may be made in this circumstance.

PROBLEM 16

You stop Wally in Edmonton, Alberta. A CPIC check reveals the following message: Wanted—"trespass by night"—Calgary. Can you arrest without having possession of the warrant?

_____

_____

Rule 2

An "out-of-province" arrest warrant is not valid at the place where the accused person is found by police at the time the CPIC message is received. However, if the arrest warrant is for an indictable or dual procedure offence, an officer may arrest (without warrant) using the authority that reasonable grounds exist that an indictable offence has occurred.

PROBLEM 17

You stop June in Halifax, Nova Scotia. A CPIC check reveals the following message: Wanted—"assault"—Montreal. Can you arrest June?

_____

_____

Rule 3

A police officer has no authority to arrest a person regarding an "out-of-province" summary conviction offence. This type of warrant is not valid in the territorial jurisdiction where the accused person is found, and an officer has no authority to arrest on reasonable grounds for a summary conviction offence.

PROBLEM 18

You stop Eddie in Regina, Saskatchewan. A CPIC check reveals the following message: Wanted—"indecent act"—Montreal. Can you arrest Eddie?

_____

_____

ARREST PROHIBITED

The provisions of sec. 495(2) C.C. prohibit an officer from arresting an offender under certain circumstances. Although these provisions will be explained in greater detail in Unit Two, briefly, they state that a police officer shall not arrest without a warrant if

- the offence is summary conviction or dual procedure, and
- an arrest is not necessary in the public interest, meaning that:

    a) the identity of the offender is known, and

    b) no evidence needs to be secured or preserved, and

    c) no reasonable grounds exist that the offender will repeat the offence, and

    d) no reasonable grounds exist that the offender will fail to appear in court.

    If these four requirements are fulfilled, the offender poses no threat or risk to the public, and an officer is prohibited from arresting or taking custody of the offender. Instead, an officer may charge the offender only by laying an information and compelling him or her to appear in court by serving either

1. an appearance notice,[52] or
2. a summons.[53]

Problem-Solving Case Studies

You are a police officer in each case. Each offender is an adult, unless otherwise indicated.

PROBLEM 19

Five days ago, June reported a "mischief under $5000.00" to you. Today, you form reasonable grounds that Eddie committed the offence. You also determine the following during the investigation:

- Eddie's correct identity is known.
- All necessary evidence is secured, and no other evidence needs to be preserved.
- No reasonable grounds exist that indicate that Eddie will repeat this offence or any other offence.
- No reasonable grounds exist indicating that Eddie will fail to appear in court.

Can you arrest Eddie without a warrant, and, if not, what can you do?

_____

_____

_____

_____

_____

PROBLEM 20

You form reasonable grounds today that Eddie committed "assault" five days ago. How will you determine whether to arrest Eddie without a warrant?

_____

_____

_____

_____

BREACH OF THE PEACE

A fifth lawful authority to arrest without a warrant is established in sec. 31(1) C.C. This authority is called "breach of the peace." It allows a police officer to arrest without a warrant if the following conditions exist:

1. The officer must first witness the breach of the peace, which is defined as "the violation of the peace, quiet, and security to which one is legally entitled."[54]
2. After the breach of the peace is witnessed, the officer may arrest anyone who

   - is found committing the breach of the peace, or
   - is about to join in the breach of the peace, or
   - is about to renew the breach of the peace.[55]

The important element of this authority is that the officer must first see it happen. Once that occurs, the officer may prevent other persons from joining in or renewing it, but only after the breach occurs. Breach of the peace is not an offence; it is a procedure. Persons arrested for breach of the peace will not be charged. An information cannot be sworn because no offence occurred. The arrested person will simply be released unconditionally, meaning without charges, when peace has been restored and the person is no longer likely to repeat the breach.

"Cause a disturbance," a summary conviction offence, and "breach of the peace" are similar except for one element. An officer may arrest and charge for "cause a disturbance" only if the disturbance occurs in a public place. A person cannot be charged or arrested for "cause a disturbance" in a dwelling-house.[56] On the other hand, "breach of the peace" may occur anywhere. Consequently, an officer may arrest for "breach of the peace" in a dwelling-house or in a public place.

"Breach of the peace" is most commonly used to arrest a person in a dwelling-house when a disturbance is created and no criminal offence, such as "assault" or "uttering threats" has occurred.

Problem-Solving Case Study

You are a police officer in this case. The offender is an adult.

PROBLEM 21

You attend at a dwelling-house regarding a domestic. Two occupants, Ward and June, are present. Ward is drunk. You see him screaming and shouting at June, preventing her from enjoying the peace, quiet, and security to which she is entitled. No assault or threats have been committed by Ward. What can you do in this case?

_____

_____

_____

ARTICULABLE CAUSE—POLICE AUTHORITY TO DETAIN

Section 495 C.C. does not authorize police officers to arrest on a belief based on mere suspicion that a person has committed a criminal offence. However, a common problem occurs during investigations, particularly during the preliminary stage shortly after the offence happens. Because of the limited time to obtain and evaluate information, mere suspicion is the only belief that exists when a suspect is found. The police have a duty to investigate the suspect's involvement, but they have no statutory authority to arrest or detain a suspect without reasonable grounds to believe that the person has committed an indictable offence. In other words, the *Criminal Code* and no other statute gives the police authority to detain a person for the purpose of elevating mere suspicion to reasonable grounds through investigation so that a lawful arrest may be made.

One method of investigating a suspect on mere suspicion for purposes such as questioning is by obtaining consent. Consent to questioning constitutes voluntary accompaniment, which is not a detention.

The second possible method is a little-known but significant authority that allows the police to detain a suspect for investigative purposes when "articulable cause" exists. This authority is found in common law and has been confirmed by various case law decisions. It is a valuable problem-solving procedure that may be used in situations where only mere suspicion exists and a suspect is found.

The case law "articulable cause" authority is not specific. It is a general authority that includes some vague principles. Case law decisions have provided valuable interpretation and procedural guidelines. The prominent contemporary case that gave the most valuable interpretation was made by the Ontario Court of Appeal in *R. v. Simpson (1993).*[57]

The British Columbia Court of Appeal (B.C.C.A), in *R. v. Ferris (1998),*[58] adopted the Simpson decision and ruled on two other cases relevant to articulable cause:

- *R. v. Yamanaka (1998),*[59] and
- *R. v. Lal (1998).*[60]

The Supreme Court of Canada, in *R. v. Godoy (1999),*[61] applied the principles of articulable cause, which arguably makes the authority part of a binding decision that applies throughout Canada.

Some of these cases will be explained to show how the articulable cause authority can be used by a patrol officer during daily investigations.

ARTICULABLE CAUSE AUTHORITY

The Ontario Court of Appeal, in the *Simpson* case, made the following rule:

> the police have authority to detain persons for investigative
> purposes without making an actual formal arrest, if the
> detaining officer has "articulable cause" for detention.

The court stated that the "articulable cause" authority originates in common law. Several Supreme Court of Canada decisions were cited in the *Simpson* case that explained a general case law authority to detain for investigative purposes where reasonable grounds are absent to make a lawful formal arrest. The relevant Supreme Court of Canada cases are

- *R. v. Dedman (1985),*[62]
- *R. v. Waterfield (1964),*[63]
- *R. v. Knowlton (1978),*[64] and
- *R. v. Stenning (1979).*[65]

DEFINITION

The term "articulable cause" is not found in any Canadian statute and is rarely, if ever, spoken in law enforcement. It is an American phrase adopted by the ONT. C.A., B.C.C.A., and apparently confirmed by the Supreme Court of Canada

"Articulable cause" is defined in case law by the ONT. C.A. as

> a constellation of objectively discernible facts which give the detaining
> officer reasonable cause to suspect that the detainee is criminally
> implicated in the activity under investigation.[66]

In other words, it means mere suspicion that a person has committed an offence is based on a set of clear facts. A "hunch" based entirely on intuition gained by experience does not constitute articulable cause even if the "hunch" proves to be correct. This means that a "guess" that is later proven accurate is not articulable cause because there is no factual basis for the belief.

PROCEDURES

The B.C.C.A. in *R. v. Lal (1998)*[67] referred to a Supreme Court of Canada guideline in *R. v. Debot*[68] to establish two general principles about forming a belief:

- "conclusory statement," and
- "totality of the circumstances."

A "conclusory statement" refers to information from a source that is a mere statement that forms a conclusion without any facts that led to the conclusion. An example is information from a confidential informant that a person is "carrying on a criminal activity." This is a mere statement that includes no facts. A conclusory statement will not be sufficient to constitute articulable cause.

"Totality of the circumstances" refers to a combination of all the factors and information that compose a belief. It refers to more information and facts than a simple conclusory statement. The totality of the circumstances will constitute articulable cause if the information received was

- compelling,
- credible, and
- corroborated (supported by other information or by police investigation).

The amount of information needed to form articulable cause, or mere suspicion in other words, is far less than that required for reasonable grounds. Consequently, proving reliability of the information that led to articulable cause needs less proof in comparison to doing the same for reasonable grounds. The standards are less demanding for articulable cause than for reasonable grounds.

When a detention, based on articulable cause (mere suspicion), results in a charge, the first step in a prosecution is to prove that articulable cause existed. Successfully proving this does not automatically justify the detention because not all types of suspicions authorize the detention of a suspect. The next step is to prove that the type of suspicion justified a detention. There are two general types of suspicions that both form articulable cause. Only one type justifies a detention. The other does not:

1. A reasonably based suspicion that a person committed some property-related offence at a "distant point in the past" constitutes articulable cause, but it does not justify a detention for questioning.
2. A reasonable suspicion that a person has just committed a violent crime and is in the process of fleeing from the crime scene also constitutes articulable cause, but this type may justify a detention to quickly confirm or refute the suspicion.

When articulable cause does justify a detention, what investigative procedures may be conducted? Generally, the police may

- ask for identification,
- briefly question the suspect, or
- search the suspect.

The police cannot, generally

- physically restrain the suspect, or
- conduct an extensive interrogation.

These are general procedural guidelines created by the Ontario Court of Appeal in the *Simpson* case. The B.C.C.A. adopted them in the *Ferris* case. The following analysis of four case law decisions provides examples of

- what specific circumstances do and do not constitute articulable cause to justify a detention, and
- the diverse range of investigative procedures that may be conducted when a detention is justified.

R. V. SIMPSON (1993)[69]

The *Simpson* case provides an example of circumstances that do not constitute articulable cause. A police officer stopped a car that had been at a suspected "crack house." The officer's suspicion of drugs being in the car was based on an internal police memorandum written by another police officer. The information originated from an unknown source, and it was unknown how old or new the information was. The officer knew nothing about the driver or passenger other than that they had visited the house. The officer asked the occupants to get out of the car. Questions about identification and past record were asked and answered. The accused stated that he had been in trouble for theft and "a knife" but that he did not have possession of the knife currently. The officer saw a bulge in the accused's pocket and asked what was in the pocket. The accused replied, "Nothing." The officer asked the accused to remove the item. As the accused began to do so, the officer grabbed the accused's hand and removed a bag of cocaine.

The Ontario Court of Appeal ruled that the officer had no articulable cause for detention. The court made the following significant rulings:

1. "Attendance" at a location believed to be the site of ongoing criminal activity is a factor that may contribute to the existence of "articulable cause."
2. However, where this is the sole factor and the information is of unknown age and reliability, no articulable cause exists.

The cocaine was excluded under sec. 24(2) *Charter* because of the severity of the *Charter* violations committed. If the court had perceived the *Charter* violations as being less severe, the drugs may have been admissible.

In summary, the following are the significant elements of the decision:

• The court stated that until Parliament makes statutory amendments, the case law authority for the police to detain persons for investigative purposes when mere suspicion exists will be regulated by the case law guidelines found in *R. v. Waterfield (1964)*.
• The "articulable cause" authority is supported by case law. The existence of articulable cause does not automatically justify a detention.
• The existence of articulable cause justifies a brief detention to ask for identification, but does not justify any physical restraint or extensive interrogation. Therefore, refusal to produce identification is not an offence and does not justify physical detention.

R. V. FERRIS (1998)[70]

The British Columbia Court of Appeal, in *R. v. Ferris (1998)*, agreed with the Ontario Court of Appeal that investigative detentions based on articulable cause are lawful. The circumstances of that case are as follows:

The accused was charged with possession of cocaine for the purpose of trafficking. The accused was a passenger in a car that was followed by the police. A routine computer check by the officers revealed that the plates on the car had been reported stolen. Three occupants were in the car.

The officers formed a belief that

• the car itself was likely stolen,
• it may have been used in a violent crime, and
• the occupants may be armed.

The officers stopped the car. The driver opened his door and immediately ran. One officer pursued him. The remaining officer approached the stopped car with his gun drawn. The accused was seated in the front passenger seat. Another occupant sat in the back. The occupants were told to get out of the car. The officer told the accused that she was "under investigation for possession of stolen property" and then handcuffed her behind her back. A "pat down" search was conducted. Upon request, the accused identified herself verbally and stated that her identification was inside a waist pack that she was wearing. The officer searched it for I.D. and weapons. Two ounces of cocaine were found and seized. The accused was arrested and informed of her right to counsel.

The B.C.C.A. made the following rulings:

1. A common law police authority does exist to detain a person during the course of a police investigation.
2. The stolen plates indicated an intention to avoid identification and detection. Combined with the driver's fleeing from the car, it was reasonable to suspect that the occupants had committed some type of crime.

3. It was "beyond dispute" that articulable grounds existed to detain the passengers to determine what criminal activity was occurring.
4. The police were justified to search for weapons in this case.
5. A search for weapons as an incident to detention is justified if the police believe that the person detained is carrying a weapon. In proper circumstances, the police have authority to search for weapons as an incident to an investigative stop. A search in these cases must be proven to have been reasonably necessary, which it was in this case.
6. The scope of the search was reasonable. Both the "pat down" and search of the waist pack were justified by the circumstances of this case. A reason given was that the police were conducting a spontaneous investigation as opposed to a planned investigation.

Two other recent cases illustrate examples of circumstances that constitute articulable cause to detain for investigative purposes:

R. V. YAMANAKA (1998)[71]

Offence   Possession of instruments for the purpose of breaking into a coin-operated device

Circumstances   At 5:30 a.m., the police received several 911 calls about possible gunfire on a specific street. Two officers were separately dispatched. The first officer saw the accused standing near a parked car and accepted his explanation that the car had broken down after backfiring. The second officer looked in the car and saw drywalling equipment. He noticed that the accused was closely holding a gym bag. He became suspicious about the explanation and suspected the accused caused the reported gunfire. This officer asked to look in the gym bag for firearms. The accused agreed, and the officer found the instruments. The officer later testified that he would have searched for firearms regardless of whether consent was given.

B.C.C.A. Ruling   The accused was convicted at his trial, and the British Columbia Court of Appeal dismissed the accused's appeal. The court made the following rulings:

1. The principles of the *Ferris* case governed this case.
2. The circumstances constituted articulable cause to both
   - temporarily detain the accused for the purpose of investigating the gunfire complaint, and
   - search the accused for weapons.

The justification for searching was stronger in this case than in the *Ferris* case because of the gunshot complaints. It did not matter that the first officer believed the accused's original explanation; the second officer was not bound to make the same conclusion.

The court also made an interesting comment. The Crown conceded at the trial that the accused had not given genuine consent, "although anyone but a lawyer or a judge would probably think he did." Genuine consent was not essential to the lawfulness of the search.

R. V. LAL (1998)[72]

Offences   1.   Possession of a concealed weapon
              2.   Possession of an unregistered restricted weapon

Circumstances   Two brothers had been killed as part of a gang-related feud regarding drug trafficking. Officers were assigned to protect the home of the remaining family members.

One of the officers received information from his superiors over a computer terminal that the occupants of a specifically described car (including plate number) were to be considered armed, dangerous, and a threat to the house being guarded. Five days later, the officers saw the car and stopped it two blocks from the guarded house. The officer stood behind the car with his gun drawn. The driver held documents out the window of the driver's door while his hand shook vigorously.

The driver was asked to step out, and he was searched. The officer unbuckled a pack that the accused was wearing around his waist. The pack fell to the ground because of its heavy weight. The pack was opened, and a loaded semi-automatic pistol was found and seized. The accused was arrested.

At the trial, the officer testified that

- He had "no idea of the source of that information or of the reliability" other than it was sent by his corporal, who was not called to testify.
- The accused had no criminal record and was unknown to the police.
- His reasons for the search were concern that the accused possessed a firearm, and to protect his own safety and that of the family he was guarding.

B.C.C.A Ruling

The accused was convicted at his trial, and the British Columbia Court of Appeal dismissed his appeal. The following rulings were made:

There are two general methods of forming a belief:

- "conclusory statement," and
- "totality of the circumstances."

A conclusory statement refers to information from a source that is simply a conclusion without the facts that led to the conclusion. There are no reasons or supporting details that show how the conclusion was reached.

Totality of the circumstances refers to a combination of all the factors that compose an officer's belief. There are three general factors that a judge will consider:

- Was the information that was received compelling?
- If the information was based on a "tip" originating from a source outside the police, was that source credible?
- Was the information corroborated (supported) by police investigation?

The "totality of the circumstances" refers to more information than a simple conclusory statement.

A mere conclusory statement will not constitute articulable cause. Additional independent circumstances must support the belief. Articulable cause must be based on the "totality of the circumstances." The standard of mere suspicion (articulable cause) is "less demanding" than for reasonable grounds. Therefore, proving reliability of information that led to articulable cause also is less demanding than proving reliability for reasonable grounds information.

In this case, the information that caused the officer to detain the suspect and conduct the search was analyzed by the court as follows:

- The information received by the corporal was largely conclusory but it did contain some detail.
- This car was "said to be connected in *some way*" with two murders and later found two blocks from the victims' family. Combining these facts constituted articulable cause based on the totality of the circumstances. The officer had mere suspicion that permitted him to make an investigative stop of the car. The totality of the circumstances eliminated the possibility of a coincidence. Therefore, the *detention* was lawfully based on articulable cause.
- The search for weapons was justifiable under the circumstances because articulable cause existed to stop and detain the accused, and there was a suspicion of further violence.

Note: The *Lal* decision has been appealed to the Supreme Court of Canada. No decision had been made at the time of publication.

CITIZENS' POWERS OF ARREST

Police officers are commonly called upon to take custody of a person arrested by a citizen. An officer must be cognizant of citizens' lawful authorities to arrest without warrant, in order to determine whether the detention of the arrested person may be lawfully continued.

Citizens' arrest authorities are more restrictive than those granted police officers. Sec. 494 C.C. lists the authorities as they apply to both adult and young offenders.

Although police officers are included in the term "anyone" in sec. 494, sec. 495 specifically defines the authorities available to police officers. This is why the term "anyone" in sec. 494 is commonly applied to citizens.

The term "citizen," although not defined in the *Criminal Code,* is anyone who is not a peace officer, and includes

- security guards,
- private investigators,
- any member of private policing,
- municipal by-law officers,
- auxiliary members of a police service,[73] and
- hotel security (bouncers).

ARREST WITHOUT WARRANT—CITIZENS' AUTHORITIES

Citizens are authorized to arrest, without warrant, under the following circumstances:

1. finds committing an indictable offence,[74]
2. owner or person in lawful possession of property, or person authorized by the owner, finds committing a criminal offence on or in relation to that property,[75] and
3. sees a person believed to be escaping from and freshly pursued by persons who have lawful authority to arrest, and believed to have committed a criminal offence.[76]

FINDS COMMITTING AN INDICTABLE OFFENCE

This authority allows a citizen to arrest an offender who has committed an indictable or dual procedure offence if the citizen sees the entire offence occur and apprehends the offender immediately, or sees the entire offence occur and pursues the offender without losing sight of him or her until apprehension occurs. An arrest cannot be made on reasonable grounds that an offence occurred, meaning without the citizen actually witnessing the entire offence.

This type of citizen may be the owner of property or a non-owner. The arrest may occur anywhere: in a public place or in a private dwelling-house. Summary conviction offences are not included in this authority.

OWNER OR PERSON IN LAWFUL POSSESSION OF PROPERTY, OR PERSON AUTHORIZED BY THE OWNER, FINDS COMMITTING A CRIMINAL OFFENCE ON OR IN RELATION TO THAT PROPERTY

This authority is restricted to a specific type of citizen and to a specific geographic location. The specific types of citizens are

1. owner—person who actually owns the property,
2. person in lawful possession—not the owner, but has possession and control of the property with the owner's lawful consent, and
3. person authorized by the owner—a person who has control of the premises and can regulate access of persons onto the property. The best example is an employee.

Property includes houses, buildings, and motor vehicles. The location is restricted to "on or in relation to" that property. Off the owner's property is not included in this authority.

This authority extends the applicable offences to any criminal offence. *Summary conviction offences are included only for this authority.* An arrest may be made only if the person finds committing, not on reasonable grounds. A citizen cannot arrest if he or she did not witness the offence being committed.

SEES A PERSON BELIEVED TO BE ESCAPING FROM AND FRESHLY PURSUED BY PERSONS WHO HAVE LAWFUL AUTHORITY TO ARREST, AND BELIEVED TO HAVE COMMITTED A CRIMINAL OFFENCE

The circumstances of this authority rarely occur. Caution must be used when interpreting this authority. The section refers to a citizen's belief based on reasonable grounds, but it does not mean that a citizen may arrest exclusively on the reasonable grounds that an offence has occurred.

This authority essentially permits a citizen to help another person apprehend a fleeing offender, without having seen the offence occur. If a citizen sees a person pursuing another, the citizen may arrest the fleeing offender only if the citizen reasonably believes that

- the pursuer has lawful authority to arrest, and
- the fleeing person has committed a criminal offence.

Although the citizen does not have to see the criminal offence occur, an arrest cannot be made unless the citizen sees the fleeing offender pursued by a person who has lawful authority to arrest.

Citizens have no lawful authority to arrest in the following circumstances:

- reasonable grounds that an indictable, dual procedure, or summary conviction offence has occurred,
- reasonable grounds that a person is about to commit an indictable, dual procedure, or summary conviction offence, and
- a non-owner finds committing a summary conviction offence on public property.

Problem-Solving Case Studies

You are a police officer in each case. Each offender is an adult, unless otherwise indicated.

PROBLEM 22

Ward is a security guard working in a department store. He sees Eddie commit "theft under $5000.00" by stealing an item. Eddie leaves the store without paying for the item. Ward follows Eddie, never loses sight of him, and approaches Eddie in the parking lot. Can Ward arrest Eddie without a warrant?

_____

_____

_____

PROBLEM 23

Wally is assaulted by Eddie. The assault occurs on the sidewalk of Rice Rd. Can Wally arrest Eddie?

_____

PROBLEM 24

Ward is walking his dog on the sidewalk of King St. He sees Eddie on the roadway of King St. committing "cause a disturbance." Can Ward arrest Eddie?

_____

_____

PROBLEM 25

Ward is a bouncer at a privately owned bar. He sees Eddie, a customer inside the bar, commit "cause a disturbance." Can Ward arrest Eddie?

PROBLEM 26

Eddie is drunk and driving on Lincoln St. He stops at Wally's house and, after Wally enters the front seat of the car, Eddie drives away from the house. Wally then realizes that Eddie is intoxicated while he is driving. Can Wally arrest Eddie?

PROBLEM 27

Ward is driving his car on Barton St. and stops for a red light. He sees Eddie, a pedestrian, walk toward his (Ward's) car then smash the passenger window. Can Ward arrest Eddie?

PROBLEM 28

June owns a house on Parkdale Avenue. She is home alone at 11:00 p.m. She sees Eddie commit "trespass by night" in her backyard. Can June arrest Eddie?

PROBLEM 29

June is a private investigator, working in a department store. She is investigating a "theft over $5000.00" incident that occurred seven days ago. She interrogates Eddie, an employee, right now with Eddie's consent. Eddie confesses that he committed the offence. Can June arrest Eddie?

PROBLEM 30

June is a security guard at a community college. Clarence reports to her right now that he saw a man commit "mischief under $5000.00," 15 minutes ago, by breaking a glass door in the college. The offender left the scene immediately. Clarence is in June's office reporting the offence as Eddie walks past the office. Clarence recognizes Eddie as being the man who broke the window and informs June.

a) Can June arrest Eddie?

_____

_____

_____

_____

b) Can Clarence arrest Eddie?

_____

_____

_____

c) June and Clarence call the police. Cst. Friendly arrives. Clarence reports his observation. Can Cst. Friendly find Eddie and arrest him without a warrant?

_____

_____

PROBLEM 31

Ward is at his house right now. He hears a news broadcast that Eddie is wanted for "robbery." Eddie arrives at Ward's house 15 minutes later to visit. Can Ward arrest Eddie?

PROBLEM 32

June is a security guard at a community college. Clarence reports the following to her right now. Eddie told Clarence one hour ago that he intended to steal a college van that is currently parked near the main building. Eddie is in a class right now. Can June arrest Eddie to prevent the offence of "theft over $5000.00?"

BREACH OF THE PEACE

Sec. 30 C.C. establishes an additional authority for citizens to arrest. A citizen may arrest a person who commits "breach of the peace." The rules of this authority are the same as those for police officers regarding "breach of the peace" and are detailed in sec. 31 C.C. Although the citizens' and police authorities are found in different sections of the *Criminal Code,* "breach of the peace" is not a criminal offence in either section. It is simply a procedure.

The conditions for citizens to arrest regarding "breach of the peace" are

a) must witness a breach of the peace, and
b) may arrest:
  • anyone committing it, or
  • anyone about to join in the existing breach of the peace, or
  • anyone about to renew the breach of the peace
c) for the purpose of interfering to prevent the continuance or renewal of the breach of the peace.[77]

CITIZEN'S DUTY AFTER AN ARREST

Sec. 494(3) C.C. creates a mandatory obligation for a citizen who makes an arrest to "deliver" the arrested person "forthwith" to a peace officer.[78] Forthwith is defined as immediately or as soon as practicable.[79] The significance of this provision is

1. A citizen has no discretion to release an arrested person without notifying and giving custody of the arrested person to an officer.

2. Failure to deliver an arrested person to a police officer and subsequent release by a citizen may constitute the offence of "obstruct justice."[80] This offence may be committed in a variety of ways, including intentionally allowing an offence to go unreported to the police, thereby allowing an offender to go undetected and escape prosecution.[81]

3. If a citizen arrests an offender but does not wish to have the offender charged, the citizen must call the police, and the officer will decide upon the action to be taken afterward. The officer will decide which method of release will be used.

An officer who receives custody of a person arrested by a citizen must interview the citizen and analyze the circumstances to determine whether the officer has lawful authority to continue the detention.

TABLE 2.1

SUMMARY OF POLICE/CITIZEN ARREST AUTHORITIES

A police officer
MAY ARREST

i) find committing
  - indictable, or
  - dual procedure, or
  - summary conviction

ii) reasonable grounds that
  - indictable, or
  - dual procedure is about to occur

iii) reasonable grounds that valid warrant exists in territorial jurisdiction where accused is found

iv) find committing
  - breach of the peace

A police officer
CANNOT ARREST

i) reasonable grounds that
  - summary conviction has occurred

ii) reasonable grounds that
  - summary conviction is about to occur

iii) mere suspicion that
  - indictable, or
  - dual procedure, or
  - summary conviction has or is
  about to occur

A citizen
MAY ARREST

i) find committing
  - indictable, or
  - dual procedure

ii) reasonable grounds that a person escaping from and pursued by a person who may lawfully arrest, and the offender has committed
  - indictable, or
  - dual procedure, or
  - summary conviction

iii) owner, or person authorized, on or in relation to property, finds committing
  - indictable, or
  - dual procedure, or
  - summary conviction

iv) find committing
  - breach of the peace

A citizen
CANNOT ARREST

i) reasonable grounds that
  - indictable, or
  - dual procedure, or
  - summary conviction has occurred

ii) reasonable grounds that

continued

TABLE 2.1 continued	

iv) warrant not valid in territorial jurisdiction where accused person is found
 	
v) reasonable grounds
 	
  • breach of the peace has been committed
	• indictable, or
	
	• dual procedure, or
	
	• summary conviction is about to occur
	
	iii) reasonable grounds
	
	  • breach of the peace has been committed
	
	iv) non-owner finds committing
	
	  • summary conviction

Test Yourself

You are a police officer in each case.

1. Wally (25) reports to you right now that Eddie (27) pointed a firearm at him 20 minutes ago. Eddie left the scene and is at his house. You attend there, and he answers the door. Explain in detail

   • whether you can arrest him without a warrant, and
   • the precise reasons for your answer

   _____

   _____

   _____

   _____

   _____

   _____

   _____

   _____

   _____

   _____

   _____

   _____

   _____

   _____

   _____

   _____

2. June (30) reports to you right now that she saw Eddie (27) commit trespass by night at her house 20 minutes ago. Eddie left prior to your arrival. You attend at his house and find him there 30 minutes later. Can you arrest him without a warrant? Explain your reasons in detail.

_____

_____

_____

_____

_____

_____

_____

_____

_____

_____

_____

_____

_____

3. Ward (30) reports that he saw Eddie (27) commit theft under $5000 eight months ago. You go to Eddie's house and find him. Can you arrest him without a warrant? Explain your reasons in detail.

_____

_____

_____

_____

_____

_____

_____

_____

_____

_____

4. You stop a car on King St. at 1:45 a.m. The driver is Wally (24). A CPIC reveals the following message: Wanted—Robbery—Montreal. Can you arrest him without a warrant? Explain your reasons in detail.

_____

_____

_____

_____

_____

_____

_____

_____

_____

_____

_____

_____

_____

5. Wally (24) reports to you right now that Eddie (27) committed assault with a weapon three weeks ago. You find Eddie 20 minutes later. Can you arrest him without a warrant? Explain your reasons in detail.

_____

_____

_____

_____

_____

_____

_____

_____

_____

_____

_____

_____

_____

_____

_____

_____

_____

_____

_____

THREE

Arrest with Warrant

Learning Outcomes

The student will be able to

- identify the elements of an arrest warrant,
- obtain an arrest warrant, and
- execute an arrest warrant.

INTRODUCTION

An arrest with warrant represents an arrest with judicial authorization. This type of arrest is authorized by a justice, defined as a justice of the peace or a provincial court judge.[82] The decision to arrest is made by the justice.

An arrest warrant is not automatically issued or granted simply because a request is made by an officer. A police officer must apply for an arrest warrant. A procedure is required to obtain an arrest warrant, and specific evidence must be proven by the officer applying for the warrant. These procedures apply to both adult and young offenders.

ELEMENTS OF AN ARREST WARRANT

The term "arrest warrant" is defined in sec. 493 C.C. as a warrant described in Form 7.[83] Form 7 is a document entitled "warrant for arrest" and is described in Part XXVIII of the *Criminal Code,* under sec. 841 C.C.[84] It is a written order that must include specific information, and is composed of the following elements:

- it commands a peace officer,
- to arrest forthwith,
- the person named on the warrant,
- for the specific offence(s) committed,
- bring the accused to a justice after the arrest is made, and
- obtain a justice's signature.

Each element has a significance and meaning:

Commands a Peace Officer

Arrest warrants are directed to peace officers only, not citizens. The document "commands" the officer to arrest, thereby removing discretion; the officer must arrest.

To Arrest "Forthwith"

Forthwith is not defined in the *Criminal Code.* No specific time limit is attached to the meaning. Various case law sources define forthwith as meaning "as soon as practicable."

The Person Named

The name of the accused person must be stated on the document.

Specific Offence

The offence(s) with which the accused is charged must be named.

Bring the Accused to a Justice

After the arrest is made, the accused must generally be returned to a justice. The arresting officer cannot release the accused person. The accused must be brought to a police station and then to a justice to determine whether the accused will be released or detained. An exception does exist, which will be explained in Unit Two.

Signature of the Justice

This represents the judicial authorization. No one other than a justice may sign it.

The following general sequence explains the role of the justice and the police in relation to arrest warrants:

- the justice authorizes the arrest,
- the police arrest the accused, and then
- the accused is brought back to a justice.

Generally, the police have no other role after the authorization is received, other than to bring the accused to a justice. An exception exists if the arrest warrant is endorsed by the justice for release by the police in certain circumstances that are explained in Unit Two.

TYPES OF ARREST WARRANTS

Two types of arrest warrants will be examined:

1. warrant in the first instance,[85] and
2. bench warrant.[86]

WARRANT IN THE FIRST INSTANCE

This term refers to a warrant issued to arrest an offender who has committed and has been charged with any criminal offence. Therefore, this type of warrant may be issued regarding indictable, dual procedure, and summary conviction offences. Because an officer is authorized to arrest for a summary conviction offence if the offender is found committing the offence, it is often forgotten that an arrest warrant may also be issued for a summary conviction offence.

GENERAL RULES

The following are rules governing a warrant in the first instance.

Rule 1

A criminal offence must occur before the warrant may be issued. The warrant cannot be issued to arrest a person who is about to commit a criminal offence. Consequently, a warrant may not be issued to arrest a person to prevent the commission of a criminal offence.

Rule 2

Reasonable grounds must exist that the accused committed a specific criminal offence before a warrant may be issued.

Rule 3

The warrant cannot be based only on a suspicion that the accused might have committed the offence.

Rule 4

An offender must be charged first before a warrant in the first instance may be issued. An arrest warrant cannot be issued without swearing an information first to charge the offender with an indictable, dual procedure, or summary conviction offence.[87]

Rule 5

After the information is laid, the issuance of the warrant is not automatic. This means that a mere request by a police officer is insufficient reason for an arrest warrant to be issued. An officer must follow a specific procedure to prove that the accused's arrest is necessary in the public interest.[88] If the police fail to prove this, a summons will be issued instead of a warrant.

HOW TO OBTAIN THE WARRANT—PROCEDURE

The procedure to obtain a warrant in the first instance is derived from the provisions of sec. 507 C.C. and sec. 788 C.C.

Step 1

Form reasonable grounds that a specific person has committed either an indictable, dual procedure, or summary conviction offence.

Step 2

Appear before a justice for the purpose of swearing an information. Anyone, a citizen or a police officer, may do this.[89]

Step 3

Prove to the justice the reasonable grounds for believing that the offender(s) committed the offence.[90] This specific procedure is explained in Unit Three of this textbook.

Step 4

If reasonable grounds is proven and the justice signs the information, the accused is then formally charged with the specific offence.

Step 5

After the accused is formally charged, a decision must be made by the justice regarding which method (which document) to use to compel the accused to court. Two possibilities exist: (a) summons, or (b) warrant in the first instance. The determining factor is whether evidence exists that the accused's arrest is necessary in the public interest.

Step 6

The next step is to introduce any evidence relevant to this issue.

Step 7

If no evidence exists that it is necessary in the public interest to issue a warrant for the arrest of the offender, the justice will issue a summons to compel the offender to court.[91] This means that the police officer has failed to introduce any/sufficient evidence to convince the justice that the offender may repeat an offence or may fail to appear in court. By issuing a summons, the justice is satisfied that the accused should not be arrested because he or she represents no danger or risk to the public. The summons will then be served to the accused and the accused will not be in custody for any period of time before the trial.

Step 8

If the person who lays the information proves reasonable grounds that it is necessary in the public interest to issue a warrant, then a warrant in the first instance will be issued for the offender's arrest. This means that sufficient evidence was introduced to convince the justice that the accused may repeat an offence or may fail to appear in court. Examples of evidence that may successfully prove "necessary in the public interest" include the accused's history, current conduct, and personal status, such as

- past criminal record,
- accused's history of violence,
- accused's tendency to repeat offences, including offences committed that resulted in no charges laid,
- any past history or record of failure to appear in court,
- threats made by the accused to the victim or witnesses,
- severity of the offence committed,
- no fixed address,
- no means of income,
- no family, and
- nothing to hold the accused to the community.

MULTIPLE OFFENDERS

Where more than one offender commits one offence, the determination of whether a warrant or summons will be issued is made separately. The reason is that the factors used to determine whether the warrant is necessary in the public interest apply to each separate offender; the factors may not be the same for each offender.

Consequently, evidence pertaining to "necessary in the public interest" must be introduced for each individual, not for the entire group.

FIGURE 3.1   Warrant in the First Instance—Procedure

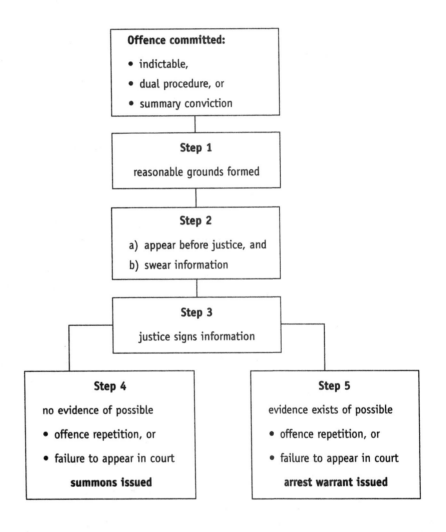

Problem-Solving Case Study

You are a police officer in this case. The offender is an adult.

PROBLEM 33

Yesterday, you attended at Wally's residence in response to a call. Wally was found unconscious and had suffered serious injuries. The offender had left prior to police arrival. Statements obtained from witnesses who were present and from Wally after he regained consciousness constitute reasonable grounds that Eddie committed "aggravated assault."

a) Can you arrest Eddie today, without a warrant?

_____

_____

_____

b) Is it possible for you to obtain an arrest warrant?

_____

_____

_____

c) Can an arrest warrant be obtained in this case without first swearing an information?

_____

d) You appear before a justice to swear an information. What do you have to prove to convince the justice to sign the information?

_____

_____

e) If you successfully prove the reasonable grounds but prove nothing else, will the arrest warrant be automatically issued?

_____

f) What do you have to prove in order for the justice to issue an arrest warrant?

_____

g) Do you have to complete any other document to apply for an arrest warrant?

_____

_____

_____

ARREST WITHOUT A WARRANT V. OBTAIN JUDICIAL AUTHORIZATION

The circumstances in Problem 33 give an example of an investigation where an officer must decide whether to arrest without a warrant or obtain judicial authorization to arrest with a warrant. The decision is required only in relation to situations where reasonable grounds are formed that an indictable or dual procedure offence has been committed. An officer is allowed to arrest without a warrant but also has the alternative of obtaining an arrest warrant. What factors would an officer consider? If the officer believes that the evidence obtained exceeds mere suspicion and is confident about the accuracy of the reasonable grounds, an arrest without warrant gives him or her the advantage of expediting the arrest and bypassing the procedure required to obtain a warrant. The disadvantage of arresting without a warrant is that other officers may not know that a specific offender is wanted. This may pose a risk if the offender is a danger to the public and the arrest without warrant is not completed quickly, or if the offender cannot be found immediately.

Consequently, an officer may choose the alternative of seeking judicial authorization and obtaining an arrest warrant for the following reasons:

1. Uncertainty as to whether the existing evidence constitutes reasonable grounds. A justice will make that decision after an arrest warrant is issued.
2. A CPIC entry (that the accused is wanted) is made. A greater number of officers will then have knowledge of this. If no warrant is issued, an officer may stop the offender, do a random check, and because there is no CPIC entry, not know that another officer has formed reasonable grounds to arrest the offender.

Additionally, if the offence is summary conviction, and the officer forms reasonable grounds that a summary conviction offence has been committed, the officer cannot arrest without a warrant. The only alternative is to swear an information within six months of the offence date. If the officer proves that an arrest warrant is necessary in the public interest, then a justice may issue an arrest warrant even though the offence is summary conviction.

Problem-Solving Case Study

You are a police officer in this case. The offender is an adult.

PROBLEM 34

You form reasonable grounds today that Eddie has committed an "indecent act" three times during the past week.

a) Can you arrest without a warrant?

_____

_____

b) Is it possible to obtain an arrest warrant?

_____

_____

BENCH WARRANT

This term is commonly used in reference to an arrest warrant issued by a justice in the following specific circumstances[92]:

1. Accused person fails to appear in court: "Fail to appear in court" is a dual procedure offence. A bench warrant may be issued by a judge when an accused person fails to appear in court.[93] The bench warrant may be issued without an information being sworn first.[94]
2. An accused is charged and a summons is issued. At a later date, evidence exists that a warrant is necessary in the public interest.[95] This allows a justice to cancel the summons and replace it with an arrest warrant. For example, the summons would have been initially issued because no evidence existed at that time that an arrest warrant was necessary in the public interest. After the summons was issued and before the accused person's court date, evidence may arise that the accused poses a danger to the public. An officer may appear before a justice, state the evidence, and the justice may replace the summons with an arrest warrant.
3. A summons is issued for an accused person, but the accused person cannot be served because he or she is evading service of the summons upon him or her.[96] The term "evading service" is not defined in the *Criminal Code*. Consequently, there are no specific number of attempts that constitute evading service. Proving evasion requires evidence of numerous attempts and evidence that the accused is intentionally evading service. A simple example of evidence that proves the accused's intent to evade service is a verbal statement made by the accused to another citizen

that he or she is avoiding the police and service of the summons. It is important to document the circumstances surrounding the attempt(s) to serve the summons for future use if an arrest warrant is to be sought. The following notes demonstrate this point:

a) Make numerous attempts to personally serve the summons at the accused's home, place of work, and any other relevant places.
b) Record the time of each unsuccessful attempt in your notebook.
c) Interview family members and people familiar with the accused to obtain information about the accused person's intention. Effective methods of helping prove intentional evasion of service are

- Phone the accused to arrange service. Failure to attend the appointment is circumstantial evidence of intentional avoidance.
- Ask family members or friends to inform the accused that you are attempting to serve the accused. Interview these people later so that relevant information may be received that the accused is intentionally avoiding service of the summons.

d) Appear before a justice with the summons. Explain the number of attempts made to serve the summons and relevant evidence that proves intentional evasion of service. If the justice is satisfied that the accused is evading service, the summons will be replaced with an arrest warrant. If the justice is not satisfied, make additional attempts to serve the summons and then, if necessary, appear again before a justice to prove evasion of service.

4. Reasonable grounds exist that an accused
   a) Has contravened or is about to contravene a summons, appearance notice, promise to appear, undertaking, or recognizance. Proving this requires evidence that

   - a document was served to compel his or her court appearance, and
   - reasonable ground exists that the accused will fail to appear. An example is a verbal statement made by the accused, to anyone, stating the intent to fail to appear.

   b) Has committed an indictable offence while awaiting a trial, after the accused was given a summons, appearance notice, promise to appear, undertaking, or recognizance.[97] Proving this requires evidence that

   - A document was served to compel a court appearance, and
   - The accused committed any indictable offence before the trial.

   The difference between this bench warrant and a warrant in the first instance is that the justice may issue a bench warrant without an information being sworn first.[98]

5. An accused fails to appear for the purpose of being fingerprinted and photographed, at a specific time and place stated on a summons, appearance notice, promise to appear, or recognizance.[99] A police officer may compel a person arrested for a dual procedure or indictable offence to attend at a specific police station, or at a specific date and time. The *Identification of Criminals Act* provides this authority. Failure to attend for fingerprints and photographs is a dual procedure offence.[100]

6. A witness
   a) Who will fail to appear in court if a subpoena is issued. This refers to a situation where an officer appears before a justice for the purpose of obtaining a subpoena to compel a witness to a trial and proves that reasonable grounds exist that the witness will fail to appear at trial. If this is proven, an arrest warrant is issued instead of a subpoena.[101] An example of reasonable grounds is a verbal statement made by the witness to anyone, before a subpoena is issued, stating the intent to fail to appear.
   b) Who had a subpoena issued for him or her, and an officer later proves that the witness is evading service of the subpoena. If this is proven, an arrest warrant will replace the subpoena.[102]

c) Who has been served with a subpoena and later fails to appear or remain at the trial. If this occurs, the Crown attorney must prove that the subpoena was properly served to the witness and that the witness will likely give relevant evidence. The trial judge may issue an arrest warrant if these circumstances are proven.[103]

TO SUMMARIZE

A bench warrant may be issued by a justice without an information being sworn first if the accused person

1. fails to appear in court,
2. intentionally evades service of a summons,
3. is served with a document that compels a court appearance and reasonable grounds develop that the accused will repeat the offence or fail to appear, and
4. fails to appear for photographs and fingerprints.

or if the witness

1. demonstrates (reasonable grounds exist) that he or she will fail to appear if the subpoena is issued, i.e., instead of the subpoena,
2. intentionally evades service after the subpoena is issued, i.e., replaces the subpoena, or
3. fails to appear in court after the subpoena is issued and served.

CONTENTS OF AN ARREST WARRANT

Every arrest warrant must include the following information:

1. Name or description of the accused.
2. The offence that the accused committed, briefly set out. This means that the short-form name of an offence (e.g., break and enter) may be used instead of the longer, formal working that is used on the information.
3. An order that the accused be arrested forthwith and be brought before a justice, either the justice who issued the warrant or another justice who has jurisdiction in the same territorial division.[104]

Additionally, the warrant must be signed by a justice after the warrant is completed. A warrant cannot be signed when it is blank.[105] All warrants must be directed only to peace officers within the same territorial jurisdiction of the justice. Most justices have jurisdiction throughout the respective province where they are situated. Therefore, an arrest warrant is usually valid throughout the province, and any police officer within that province may arrest.[106]

Warrants are not directed to citizens. Consequently, citizens cannot arrest with a warrant.

TIME LIMIT

No time limit exists in the *Criminal Code* regarding the validity of an arrest warrant. It is valid, or remains in force, until the arrest warrant is executed, meaning that the warrant is carried out and the accused is arrested.[107]

An additional time limit, which is controlled by the Crown attorney, is imposed on the validity of an arrest warrant. An information, after it is signed by a justice, is owned by the Crown attorney, who may withdraw the information any time before the trial. If the Crown attorney decides not to prosecute the offender and withdraws the information, the arrest warrant becomes invalid. Therefore, the time limit of an arrest warrant is until it is executed or until the Crown attorney withdraws the information.

EXECUTION OF AN ARREST WARRANT

Executing a warrant means to carry it out or to complete the task required by the warrant. The answers to the following questions and answers demonstrate the rules that apply to the execution of a warrant:

Rule 1

A warrant may be executed anywhere.

Rule 2

A warrant may be executed at any time, on any day, including a holiday.[108]

Rule 3

The officer who executes the warrant has a duty under sec. 29(1) C.C. to have possession of the warrant, when feasible, and produce it when requested to do so.[109] An officer will have possession of the warrant when he or she intends to execute it at a specific time and place. However, it is common for an officer to stop persons and conduct routine CPIC checks. In some cases, this check reveals that a warrant exists, but the officer does not have possession of the warrant. Section 495(1)(c) C.C. creates a temporary exception to sec. 29(1) C.C. by allowing an officer to arrest without having possession of the warrant. If the accused is arrested, and the officer does not have possession of the warrant, the warrant must be retrieved from central records and produced for the accused while he or she is at the police station. Although production is necessary only when a request is made, production of the warrant should be made to accused persons in all cases to prevent unnecessary violations of sec. 29(1) C.C. Production includes reading the contents of the warrant to the accused, which informs him or her of the reason for the arrest, a statutory requirement. The warrant is considered to have been executed when production is made.

A copy of the warrant does not have to be given to the accused, and one should never be given in order to prevent the unlawful use of a copy of a warrant.

AFTER EXECUTION

After an accused person is arrested with a warrant, the accused must be brought to a justice for a bail hearing.

The significance is that the arresting officer or the officer-in-charge of the police station generally cannot release the accused. An exception exists to the rule, however. A justice may make an endorsement on a warrant that permits release if the offence is not a sec. 469 C.C. indictable offence, e.g., murder. This endorsement allows the officer-in-charge to release the accused if certain release provisions are fulfilled (see Unit Two). This may eliminate the need to bring the accused before a justice for a bail hearing.[110]

EXECUTING IN-PROVINCE AND OUT-OF-PROVINCE WARRANTS

Police officers commonly find persons in one city who are wanted in another. The cities may be in the same province or in different provinces. The officer must determine where the arrest warrant was issued to determine what procedure to use. Different procedures are used for in-province and out-of-province arrest warrants because a warrant is valid throughout the province where the justice has jurisdiction. Although this jurisdiction usually includes the entire province, the warrant is not valid outside that province.

Before learning the procedures, the following general rules must be understood:

Rule 1

An arrest warrant signed by a justice is valid only in the province where the justice has jurisdiction. For example, an arrest warrant signed by a justice in Toronto is usually valid anywhere in Ontario.

Rule 2

An arrest warrant signed in a particular province is invalid in all other provinces. For example, an arrest warrant signed by a justice in Toronto is invalid in all provinces outside Ontario.

Rule 3

An out-of-province arrest warrant requires the endorsement (signature) of a justice who has jurisdiction where the arrest is made. For example, if a police officer in Vancouver arrests an accused person who is wanted on an arrest warrant signed by a justice in Ontario, the arrest warrant must be endorsed by a justice who has jurisdiction in British Columbia.[111]

Rule 4

A CPIC message stating that a person is wanted regarding an arrest warrant represents reasonable grounds that a warrant exists and that the person committed the offence for which the arrest warrant was issued. For example, a police officer in Vancouver stops a person in that city. A CPIC message reveals that the person is wanted for "robbery" in Toronto. Reasonable grounds exist that the person committed the indictable offence of "robbery," and the officer may arrest without having the warrant. The warrant is invalid in Vancouver. An endorsement by a Vancouver justice will make the warrant valid.

Rule 5

Arrest warrants have a radius specified referring to the maximum distance where a Crown attorney will authorize transportation to take custody of the prisoner and return him or her to the location where the offence was committed. The radius does not increase or decrease the area where the warrant is valid. Examples of radius include

- Specific number of kilometres. For example, a CPIC message may state: Wanted— "theft under $5000.00"—Toronto, radius 200 km. The Crown attorney will authorize transportation and return of the accused only if the accused is arrested within a 200 km radius of Toronto. However, the warrant is valid anywhere in Ontario. The radius does not diminish the area of validity. The 200 km radius informs the arresting officer that transportation and return of the accused will not be authorized if the arrest is made beyond the 200 km radius. The Crown attorney usually decides the specific number of kilometres.
- Province-wide. This radius informs an officer that transportation will be authorized to return an accused person from any area of arrest within the province.
- Canada-wide. This radius informs an officer that the Crown attorney has authorized transportation and return of the accused from anywhere the accused is arrested in Canada. However, a Canada-wide radius does not extend the area of validity; the warrant remains valid only in the province where the justice signed it. If the arrest is made anywhere in Canada, outside the province where it was signed, the warrant requires an endorsement by a justice where the arrest is made.

Rule 6

A trial must be held in the city/jurisdiction where the offence occurred.

IN-PROVINCE WARRANT

Officers who find a person in a city and learn that the person is wanted in another city in the same province may arrest the person regardless of whether the offence is summary conviction, dual procedure, or indictable. The reason is that the arrest warrant is valid throughout the province where the justice signed it, if the justice has provincial jurisdiction.

The following examples explain how to apply this rule:

Example 1 A police officer in Toronto stops a person, and a CPIC check reveals that the person is wanted for "robbery" in Hamilton. To determine whether an arrest is justified, the officer needs to analyze the CPIC information. "Wanted" means that reasonable grounds exist that a warrant exists and that the accused committed the offence stated in the message. "Robbery" is classified as an indictable offence. Hamilton police service notifies the officer that the warrant is valid where he or she has stopped the accused, which is in Toronto in this case. The officer may arrest in this case and be justified using either of the two following authorities:

1. The warrant is valid in Toronto.
2. Reasonable grounds exist that the person has committed an indictable offence.

Example 2   A police officer in Windsor, Ontario, stops a person, and a CPIC message states that he or she is wanted for "indecent act" in Toronto. "Indecent act" is classified as a summary conviction offence. "Wanted" means that reasonable grounds exist that a warrant exists and that the person committed the offence. "Toronto" informs the officer that the warrant is valid in Windsor. The officer may arrest without having possession of the warrant because reasonable grounds exist that a valid warrant exists in the territorial jurisdiction where the accused person is found. This particular example often causes confusion because many students focus only on the fact that the offence is classified as summary conviction and that no authority exists to arrest on reasonable grounds. When analyzing a case study, students must recognize whether any authority exists to arrest, without emphasizing only one specific authority.

Procedure after Arrest

In both of the above examples, a procedure must be followed that applies the general rules that were previously mentioned. An emphasis must be placed on the fact that the arrest warrant does not have to be endorsed by another justice because it is valid throughout the province in which it was signed. The procedure is as follows:

Step 1

The arresting officer should transport the accused person to the police station in the city where the arrest is made.

Step 2

The arresting officer notifies the police service that holds the warrant that the accused is in custody.

Step 3

The officers from the city where the warrant is held and was issued travel to the city where the accused is detained, bringing the original arrest warrant.

Step 4

After arrival, the officers holding the original warrant then execute the warrant at the police station where the accused is detained. Execution requires possession and production of the warrant. The warrant does not have to be endorsed by a justice in the city where the accused person is detained because the warrant is valid throughout the province.

Step 5

The accused is then transported to the city where the warrant was issued. The accused is generally brought to a justice for a bail hearing. Other possible release procedures may apply, which will be explained in Unit Two. The trial will be conducted in the city/jurisdiction where the offence occurred.

OUT-OF-PROVINCE WARRANT

The procedures relating to out-of-province arrest warrants are predicated on the classification of the offence for which the accused person is wanted. Determining whether an arrest may be made regarding an out-of-province arrest warrant depends on whether the CPIC message states that the accused is

1. wanted for a summary conviction offence, or
2. wanted for an indictable or dual procedure offence.

Wanted for a Summary Conviction Offence

If a police officer stops a person, and a CPIC message states that the person is wanted regarding an out-of-province warrant for a summary conviction offence, no arrest may be made for the following reasons:

- The warrant is not valid in the province where the officer stopped the person.
- A police officer cannot arrest for summary conviction offences based on reasonable grounds.
- The officer did not find the offence being committed.

Although no arrest may be made in this situation, the warrant remains in effect. The accused may be arrested in the future in the province where the warrant is valid.

Wanted for an Indictable or Dual Procedure Offence

A warrant for an indictable or dual procedure offence is not valid outside the province where it was issued. However, this type of warrant permits the police to arrest by means of another authority. An out-of-province warrant for indictable or dual procedure offences represents reasonable grounds that the accused committed the offence, which authorizes the arrest on that basis. After the arrest is made, the accused is brought to the police station in the city where the arrest occurred. The accused must be ultimately returned to the city/jurisdiction where the offence occurred for court.

To accomplish this, the warrant must be made valid in the province where the accused is detained. This requires officers from the province where the warrant was issued to travel to the province where the accused is detained, with the original warrant. The warrant is then brought to a justice where the accused is detained. The justice endorses the warrant by signing it, which signifies two things: (a) it makes the warrant valid in the province where the accused is detained, in order for it to be executed, and (b) it temporarily makes the out-of-province officers peace officers in the province where the accused is detained. Otherwise, the out-of-province officers are citizens in the province where the accused is detained. The procedure used to execute an out-of-province warrant is explained in the following example:

Situation

You stop Eddie in Toronto. A CPIC message reveals the following: Wanted—"attempt murder"—Calgary, radius Canada-wide. What procedure will be followed to execute this out-of-province warrant?

Step 1

The Calgary warrant is invalid in Toronto. However, you have reasonable grounds to believe that Eddie committed the indictable offence of "attempt murder." Therefore, you may arrest Eddie without a warrant.

Step 2

Eddie is transported to a Toronto police station and detained there. You notify the Calgary police service of the arrest. Calgary officers will attend Toronto to pick up Eddie. The Toronto police cannot transport Eddie to Calgary.

Step 3

Eddie must be brought before a justice in Toronto, without unreasonable delay within 24 hours after the arrest.[112] If a justice is not available within 24 hours, Eddie must be brought before a justice as soon as possible. The only purpose for bringing Eddie before a justice is to prove the reasonable grounds for making the arrest.[113]

Step 4

When Eddie is before a Toronto justice, you must prove that reasonable grounds exist that Eddie committed the alleged offence.[114] Reasonable grounds may be proven by submitting a copy of the CPIC message or a copy of the information and the warrant from Calgary. Testimony about any conversation with Calgary officers may be used as supporting evidence. If you fail to prove reasonable grounds that Eddie committed the offence, he must be released.[115]

Step 5

If you successfully prove reasonable grounds, Eddie may be detained in Toronto for a period of up to six days. The Calgary police must attend Toronto within six days, to execute their warrant and return Eddie to Calgary.[116] Additionally, the Calgary police may bring an affidavit that proves the signature of the Calgary justice who signed the warrant.[117]

> **Note:** If the Calgary police fail to execute the warrant within six days, Eddie must be released.[118] However, Eddie remains charged, and the warrant will remain in existence in Calgary. If Eddie is released after six days, reasonable grounds will still exist that he committed an indictable offence. Nothing prevents another arrest. Upon arrest, you must repeat the procedure by bringing Eddie before a justice and obtaining another detention order of up to six days.

Step 6

Upon arrival in Toronto, the Calgary officers must appear before a Toronto justice and present the arrest warrant to the justice. The Calgary officers must prove the signature of the Calgary justice by

- an affidavit of the signature of the Calgary justice, or
- sworn evidence under oath by the Calgary officer, if the officer can testify that he or she knows the signature is valid.[119]

Step 7

The Toronto justice endorses the Calgary warrant. The endorsement signifies two things:

- the Calgary officers are authorized to act as peace officers in Toronto for the purpose of executing the warrant, and
- the warrant becomes valid in Toronto. It may be executed in Toronto and Eddie may be returned to Calgary.[120]

Step 8

The Calgary officers return Eddie to Calgary and bring him before a Calgary justice.[121] The trial will be conducted in Calgary; it may not be conducted in Toronto.

TO SUMMARIZE

The following is a summary of the responsibilities of the officers involved in the execution of an out-of-province arrest warrant. Two officers are involved:

1. the arresting officer (outside the province where the warrant was issued), and
2. the executing officer (in the province and jurisdiction where the warrant was issued).

Arresting officer's responsibilities

1. ensures that the CPIC message states that the accused is wanted for an indictable or dual procedure offence (do not arrest if summary conviction),
2. transports the accused to the police station in the city where the arrest was made,
3. brings the accused before a justice within 24 hours after the arrest is made, or as soon as practicable, and

4. proves to the justice that reasonable grounds exist that the accused committed the offence.

Executing officer's responsibilities

1. obtains an affidavit to prove the signature of the justice who issued the warrant,
2. within six days of the arrest, brings the arrest warrant and affidavit to a justice in the place where the accused is detained,
3. attends before a justice where the accused is detained,
4. proves the signature on the arrest warrant by means of the affidavit or, alternatively, swears under oath to prove that the justice signed the warrant,
5. takes custody of the accused once the justice endorses the warrant,
6. returns the accused to the city where the offence occurred and the warrant was issued, and
7. brings the accused to a justice within 24 hours or as soon as practicable.

Problem-Solving Case Studies

You are a police officer in each case. Each offender is an adult, unless otherwise indicated.

PROBLEM 35

You stop George in Winnipeg. A CPIC message reveals: Wanted—"indecent act"—Halifax. Can you arrest?

_____

_____

PROBLEM 36

You stop Wally in Calgary. A CPIC check reveals the following: Wanted—"trespass by night"—Edmonton.

a) Can you arrest?

_____

_____

b) An Edmonton officer travels to Calgary with the warrant to execute it. Does the warrant require an endorsement?

_____

_____

Test Yourself

1. You arrive at a scene of a stabbing. Wally (24) reports that Eddie (27) tried to kill him by stabbing him with a knife eight minutes ago. Eddie left prior to your arrival. An eight-hour search for Eddie is unsuccessful. Explain in detail how you would obtain an arrest warrant for Eddie.

_____

_____

_____

_____

_____

_____

_____

_____

_____

_____

_____

_____

_____

_____

_____

_____

_____

_____

_____

_____

2. You stop a car in Hamilton, Ontario, at 2:00 a.m. Wally (24) is the driver. He is wanted in Vancouver for robbery. You arrest him.

Explain in detail

a) your responsibilities and procedures to follow, and
b) how the out-of-province warrant will be executed.

_____

_____

_____

_____

_____

_____

_____

_____

_____

_____

_____

CHAPTER FOUR

Location of Arrest—Forcible Entry

Learning Outcomes

The student will be able to

- enter a place by "consent,"
- interpret sections 529-529.4 C.C., and
- apply for, obtain, and execute a *"Feeney"* warrant.

INTRODUCTION

After learning when a lawful arrest may be made, you must learn specific procedures to know where to make an arrest. "Where" refers to the place that a police officer may enter to make an arrest.

An offender may be found in a variety of places when police have lawful authority to arrest. Types of places include

- street and sidewalk,
- motor vehicle,
- business premise,
- school,
- office,
- bar, and
- dwelling-house.

In some cases, the police will be allowed to enter a place by consent or invitation. When consent is not given to enter, the issue of forcible entry to make a lawful arrest becomes relevant. Before 1997, no statutory provisions existed in the *Criminal Code* relating to entry into places, such as dwelling-houses, for the purpose of making an arrest. Procedures and authorization to forcibly enter a dwelling-house were found in case law. However, in 1997, the Supreme Court of Canada made a landmark decision in *R. v. Feeney*, relating to forcible entry into a dwelling-house to make an arrest. In response to that case, *Bill C-16* amended the *Criminal Code* by adding provisions in sections 529, 529.1, 529.2, 529.3, and 529.4, which include new warrants to enter a dwelling-house for the purpose of making an arrest.

FACTORS

Two factors must be considered relating to how to enter a place to make an arrest:

1. type of place, and
2. existence or absence of consent.

TYPE OF PLACE

The types of places where an arrest is made can be categorized in two groups:

1. dwelling-house, and
2. any place other than a dwelling-house.

Dwelling-house is defined in sec. 2 C.C. as "the whole or any part of a building or structure that is kept or occupied as a permanent or temporary residence, and includes

- a building within the curtilage of a dwelling-house that is connected to it by a doorway or by a covered and enclosed passageway, and
- a unit that is designed to be mobile and to be used as a permanent or temporary residence and that is being used as such a residence."[122]

The key element that qualifies a place as a dwelling-house is its use as a "permanent or temporary residence." If the place in question is "kept or occupied" for that purpose, the place is considered to be a dwelling-house. The following places are dwelling-houses if currently being used as a temporary or permanent residence:

- house or apartment,
- garage attached to a house,
- motel room or rented room,
- tent, or
- a mobile unit designed to be used as a permanent or temporary residence such as a trailer.

"A place other than a dwelling-house" refers to any public location or privately owned building that is not kept or occupied as a permanent or temporary residence.

In other words, if the place is currently not being used as a residence, it is not a dwelling-house. For example, the following places are obviously not a building and require no entry. However, they are still considered a "place":

*   business premises,
*   detached garage,
*   office,
*   school,
*   bar and licensed premises,
*   mobile unit that is not designed to be used as permanent or temporary residence, and
*   street and sidewalk.

CONSENT

The second relevant factor regarding entry to make an arrest is consent. No Canadian statute defines consent or creates procedural guidelines to obtain valid consent. Valid consent is defined in case law as a "voluntary and informed decision to permit the intrusion of the investigative process upon his constitutionally protected rights."[123]

The key elements of the consent definition are

1. informed decision. The person making the decision must be informed of sufficient facts and must have adequate knowledge of exactly what has been decided.
2. the decision must be voluntarily made. No person is obliged to give consent to permit entry into a place. Every person has the choice to give or refuse consent.

Although case law consent guidelines exist, there is no procedural guideline that explains specifically how to obtain consent to enter a place to make an arrest.

The Supreme Court of Canada, in *R. v. Borden (1994)*[124] and the Ontario Court of Appeal, in *R. v. Wills (1992)*[125] established procedural guidelines that form elements of valid consent. Both cases relate specifically to search and seizure but also apply to all investigative procedures involving consent. Each element is explained in Chapter 16.

The most important elements of valid consent to be proven regarding entry into a place to make an arrest are

1. Consent must be expressed or implied. Entry into a business premise is usually made by implied consent. Entry into houses requires a clear, unmistakable invitation to enter, without any ambiguity.
2. Consent must be voluntary. Voluntary means free from inducements ("inducement" is defined as a threat or promise).
3. Reason for entry must be clear. The person giving consent must have knowledge of the specific act to be conducted. Consequently, for example, the police officer must state that the reason is to arrest the suspect in the matter.
4. Identification as a police officer (a badge) must be produced. Proving that an "invitation to enter" constituted "valid consent" requires effective notebook recording and court testimony. Recording verbatim conversation is crucial to proving consent. Paraphrasing should be avoided. Paraphrased testimony usually is insufficient evidence.

WHO MAY GIVE CONSENT

The last factor that must be considered during consent procedures is determining whether a occupant of a place has lawful authority to give consent. Any of the following occupants of a place may lawfully give consent, or invite the police to enter a place:

*   owner,
*   lawful possessor of the place,
*   person authorized by the owner, and
*   a person who has control of the place by having the authority to regulate access into the place. "Regulating access" refers to the authority to permit entry, prohibit entry, or remove persons from the place.[126] Conversely, persons who cannot give consent are guests or visitors.

TO SUMMARIZE

Entry by consent constitutes entry without judicial authorization, or in other words, warrantless entry. *Bill C-16* introduced new *Criminal Code* provisions that create warrants to enter dwelling-houses for the purpose of making an arrest. Consequently, when the police enter a house by consent or invitation, they have the onus to prove beyond reasonable doubt that consent was valid. Properly obtained consent negates the requirement to obtain prior judicial authorization, in the form of a warrant, to enter. Unlawful, warrantless entry into a house to make an arrest constitutes a *Charter* violation, which may result in the exclusion of evidence obtained after the violation. However, the new *Criminal Code* warrants apply only to dwelling-houses, not to buildings and places that are not dwelling-houses. Entry into places that are not dwelling-houses is made without a warrant.

The next topic relates to entry into dwelling-houses without consent, where a warrant is required, and the circumstances that authorize forcible entry.

WARRANTS TO ENTER A DWELLING-HOUSE

Before 1997, no warrants existed in the *Criminal Code* to authorize entry into a house for the purpose of making an arrest. The authority to enter a house for that purpose, without consent, was found in two Supreme Court of Canada case law decisions that established procedural guidelines explaining how to enter a house without a warrant. The key point is that all entries into houses to make arrests before 1997 were made without a warrant because no warrant existed.

The Supreme Court of Canada, in *R. v. Feeney (1997)* made a landmark decision relating to warrantless entry into a house for the purpose of making an arrest. In response to *Feeney*, *Criminal Code* amendments were made. Understanding the new provisions requires an explanation of the authorities that existed before the *Feeney* case, because the principles and procedures of the law prior to *Feeney* are relevant to the new *Criminal Code* provisions.

AUTHORITY TO ENTER (BEFORE *FEENEY*)

The issue of entering a house to make an arrest has two relevant tenets of Canadian law:

1. a person's house is his or her castle, and
2. no offender is immune from arrest by taking refuge in a certain place.

Before the *Feeney* case, and the *Criminal Code* provisions made in response to it, the authority to enter a house without a warrant was governed by two case law decisions made by the Supreme Court of Canada:

- *Eccles v. Bourque (1974),*[127] and
- *R. v. Landry (1986).*[128]

The procedural guidelines created by these cases are still relevant to the new *Criminal Code* amendments because

- terms used in the new amendments are defined in these cases,
- some of the procedures are similar to the authority found in sec. 529.4 C.C., and
- the procedures still apply to places that are not dwelling-houses.

FORCIBLE ENTRY—PROCEDURE

Generally, forcible entry without a warrant or consent was justified if two beliefs were formed, an announcement was made, or when an exception existed to making the announcement. The specific step-by-step procedure was as follows:

1. The starting point was to form the first belief based on reasonable grounds. One of the following beliefs had to exist:

   a) that a valid arrest warrant existed to arrest the offender. This belief was established by a CPIC message, by being informed of its existence by another officer, or by personal knowledge of having been present when the arrest warrant was issued.

b) that an indictable offence had been committed. This belief may have been based on the observations of a police officer, or the observations of an eyewitness, as reported to the officer during an investigation. The offence may have been indictable or dual procedure. In this case, the offence has ended; it was committed at any time in the past.

c) that an indictable offence was about to occur. This authority allowed a police officer to prevent the commission of an indictable or dual procedure offence. The most common offences relevant to this authority were assault-type offences. Reasonable grounds of this belief was commonly formed by an officer attending at a house in response to a call for assistance, and making aural or visual observations. Examples include hearing or seeing

- a person making a request for help, or
- a person threatening to harm another, or
- a person telling another to stop hitting him or her, or to put down a weapon, or
- sounds that indicate or suggest that violence is occurring inside that place, or
- windows and open doors affording a view inside the place, allowing the officer to see that violence is about to occur, or
- previous information received from an eyewitness—a victim or another eyewitness may phone the police and report circumstances that will form the belief that an offence is about to occur.

These circumstances may then be conveyed by means of a radio broadcast, which when heard by the attending officer, will then form the basis of belief.

In summary, a police officer was authorized to enter a house upon arrival if the reasonable belief suggested that someone inside that place was about to become a victim of a crime. In other words, if, when approaching a house or standing outside a door, evidence was seen or heard that suggested that some person inside was being injured or was about to suffer injury, no hesitation was needed to enter to protect a life. The reasonable belief justified entrance.

2. The second belief then needed to be formed. Reasonable grounds had to be formed that the offender is currently in the house or place. A belief that the offender was or may be in the place was insufficient. Reasonable grounds that the offender is currently in the house may be established by

- seeing the offender entering the house or place, or
- seeing the offender in the house, or
- being informed by an eyewitness that the offender is in the house, or
- recognizing the offender's voice and having familiarity with his or her voice.

Mere suspicion, based on speculation or conjecture, that the offender was inside the house was insufficient evidence to force entry. This prevented unrestricted police entry into a house.

3. Making a proper announcement prior to entering was the next step after forming the required belief. A proper announcement required giving three notices:

- presence (knocking or ringing doorbell),
- authority (identifying oneself), and
- purpose (state reason for entry).

Forced entry was not justified at this stage, after the three notices were given. After the three notices were given, entry had to be requested, and the request had to be denied. Forced entry was justified after the denial.

4. The existence of exigent circumstances justified forced entry without a proper announcement being made, in order to protect persons, including the officer, and/or the loss of property. Evidence of exigent circumstances includes

a) presence of weapons or violence, for example:

- information from a witness that the offender has weapons inside the house, or
- personal observation that the offender is armed, or
- hearing anything that indicates violence is occurring inside the house.

These circumstances will cause a reasonable belief that a person, including the officer, may suffer injury or may die. Making a proper announcement would not be safe or prudent when these circumstances exist. *Personal safety and protecting other persons' lives supersedes everything else in law enforcement.* It must be emphasized that reasonable grounds do not require overwhelming evidence that proves, beyond all doubt, the existence of weapons. If the belief is reasonable, an officer will not be criticized or suffer consequences for entering forcibly without consent and without a proper announcement.

b) personal observation that evidence is being destroyed, lost, altered, or moved. An example is the destruction of narcotics. If an officer, through a window, sees the offender running to the bathroom, the offender may be attempting to dispose of drugs. Entry without a proper announcement would be justified.

c) pursuing an offender and the offender enters a house, or any other place during the pursuit. This circumstance is called "hot pursuit." If an officer is pursuing the offender in this situation, the officer may enter the house immediately without consent and without making a proper announcement.

EXISTING LAWS

Section 495 C.C. creates a police officer's powers of arrest, without warrant, but does not establish guidelines or procedures regarding forcible entry into a dwelling-house, without a warrant, to arrest an offender. A warrantless arrest must include subjective

CASE LAW

R. V. FEENEY (1997)[129]

The following is an explanation of the circumstances of the investigation, an analysis of the laws that existed at the time of the offence, and the reasons for the landmark decision made by the Supreme Court of Canada regarding the authority to enter a house.

Offence   The offence relating to the *Feeney* case was murder.

Circumstances   The body of an 85-year-old man was found in his home, at 8:20 a.m. He had suffered five blows to the head with an iron bar or similar object. The exact time of death could not be determined. The victim had last been seen alive the previous evening. During the preliminary investigation, police found blood splattered inside the victim's house and a pack of Sportsman cigarettes at the crime scene. Upon information received, three officers attended at the scene of a motor vehicle collision about a half-kilometre from the victim's house. At the scene, the victim's pickup truck was found in a ditch. A female witness informed officers that the truck was in the ditch at 6:45 a.m. She identified the suspect by given name only and advised that she had seen him walking along a road a few minutes earlier where the victim lived, carrying a bottle of beer or cup of coffee. The suspect's residence was known to be a trailer situated on another person's property. Upon arrival at the property where the suspect lived, a witness informed the police that the suspect had stolen a truck from the property where the trailer was situated and that the suspect returned home at 7:00 a.m. He had been drinking and was currently sleeping in a trailer behind the residence.

The officer-in-charge of the investigation went to the trailer, knocked on the door, and identified himself by saying, "Police." After no answer was received, the officer entered the trailer, went to the suspect's bed, shook the suspect's leg, and said, "I want to talk to you." The officer asked the suspect to get out of bed and move to the front of the trailer in better light. The officer saw blood splattered all over the front of the suspect, read the right to counsel, and cautioned the suspect. The right to counsel

continued

did not include reference to a toll-free number. The officer arrested the suspect and asked whether he understood his right to counsel. The suspect did not initially respond. When asked again, the suspect answered, "Of course, do you think I'm illiterate?" Immediately afterward, the officer asked the suspect how he got the blood on him. The suspect answered that he had been hit in the face with a baseball bat the day before. The officer seized a pair of blood-stained shoes, a package of Sportsman cigarettes, and the blood-stained T-shirt worn by the suspect.

At 12:17 p.m., the suspect left a message for a lawyer to call the police station. At 12:33 p.m., a breath sample was taken. The suspect was not informed that he did have a choice about whether to give the breath sample in that situation. The suspect was detained in a cell. At 10:00 p.m., two detectives began interrogating the suspect. The suspect stated, "I should have a lawyer," but the questioning continued. The suspect confessed that he struck the victim and stole cigarettes, beer, and cash from the victim's house. He put the cash under his mattress in his trailer. A search warrant was obtained to search the suspect's trailer and to seize the money beneath the mattress. A second interrogation occurred at 3:05 a.m. It lasted for 1 1/2 hours. The suspect still had not spoken to a lawyer. Two days after the arrest, the suspect was fingerprinted at 9:25 a.m. and again at 9:54 a.m. The suspect spoke to a lawyer for the first time between the fingerprinting sessions.

and objective grounds. Section 495(1)(a) C.C. creates the subjective requirement, referring to the condition that the individual police officer must believe that reasonable grounds exist that the offender committed an indictable offence.

The objective requirement was added by the Supreme Court of Canada in *R. v. Storrey (1990)*. This refers to a conclusion that must be made by a judge that reasonable grounds actually did exist to believe that the offender committed an indictable offence. The test used to draw this conclusion is, "Would a reasonable person, standing in the shoes of the officer, believe that reasonable grounds existed?" In other words, the objective test is an evaluation of what a reasonable person would believe given the officer's same knowledge. A problem exists when an offender, whom the police believe on reasonable grounds has committed an indictable offence, is in a house and the police are not given consent to enter. A search warrant to search a place for an offender cannot be obtained because no such warrant exists; search warrants may be obtained to search for physical items only. The *Criminal Code* has no provision that establishes a search warrant to search any place for an offender.

The Supreme Court of Canada, in *Eccles v. Bourque (1975)*, authorized police officers to forcibly enter a dwelling-house without consent to make an arrest with a warrant, if reasonable grounds existed that the accused person was in the house and proper announcement preceded the entry. In *R. v. Landry (1986)*, the Supreme Court of Canada authorized the police to enter a house without permission to make an arrest without a warrant, if the requirements of sec. 495 C.C. and those in *Eccles v. Bourque* are met. The Supreme Court made the *Landry* decision because the *Criminal Code* does not provide for a warrant to search a place for an offender, and to prevent offenders from hiding inside a house to avoid arrest. Therefore, a combination of these three case law decisions and sec. 495 C.C. establish the following rule:

A warrantless arrest following forcible entry into a house is lawful if

- subjective and objective reasonable grounds exist that the offender committed an indictable offence; and
- reasonable grounds exist that the offender is inside the house, and
- proper announcement is made before entering; and
- before forcing entry, admissions into the house must be requested and denied; or
- if exigent circumstances exist, a proper announcement and request for admission are not required.

In *Feeney*, the accused was convicted of second-degree murder after a jury trial in the Supreme Court of British Columbia. He appealed to the British Columbia Court of Appeal, who unanimously dismissed the appeal.

The accused appealed to the Supreme Court of Canada, who allowed the appeal in a 5:4 decision and ordered a new trial. The three questions surrounding the accused's appeal to the Supreme Court of Canada were

- Did the police violate sec. 8 *Charter* during their investigation?
- Did the police violate sec. 10(b) *Charter*?
- What evidence, if any, should be excluded under sec. 24(2) *Charter*?

The primary issue raised in the appeal was the authority of the police to enter a private dwelling-house to make an arrest without a warrant. Justice Sopinka wrote a lengthy judgment for the majority. The dramatic conclusions may have significant impact on the procedures used by officers in the future. In this case, Justice Sopinka ruled that reasonable grounds existed that the accused was in the trailer, based on the information received by the police; however, subjective grounds did not exist.

This conclusion was based on two factors:

- the testimony of the officer-in-charge of the investigation—that he did not believe he had reasonable grounds to arrest the accused when he entered the trailer, and
- the officer did not arrest the accused immediately upon entering the trailer. Instead, the arrest was made after the blood stains were seen on the accused's shirt.

Objective grounds did not exist in this case for the following reasons:

- the absence of subjective grounds implies the absence of objective grounds, unless the officer has an unreasonably high standard; and
- the objective requirement created by *Storrey* is in addition to the subjective requirement created by sec. 495 C.C.

The objective test does not replace the subjective test. Therefore, if reasonable grounds did in fact objectively exist, despite the absence of the officer's belief that reasonable grounds did not exist, the objective requirement is not met. If the officer did not believe that reasonable grounds existed, but the belief was wrong because reasonable grounds objectively did exist, then the final conclusion will be that reasonable grounds did not exist, unless it is determined that the officer's standard of determining reasonable grounds was unreasonably high.

Four prominent facts composed the evidence known to the police prior to entering:

- the deceased person's truck appeared to have been stolen before it had been involved in the collision,
- the accused had been seen walking near the scene of the accident,
- a witness assumed that the accused had driven the deceased person's truck because the accused had been involved in a collision at the same location while driving another vehicle earlier, and
- an occupant at the accused's residence told the police that the accused returned home at 7:00 a.m. after drinking all night and had earlier been involved in a collision, while driving another vehicle, at the site where the victim's vehicle was found.

This evidence did not constitute reasonable grounds to arrest the accused for murder; it constituted mere suspicion only. Consequently, when the officer entered the trailer, the subjective and objective belief was predicated on mere suspicion.

NEW LAWS

The *Landry* authority to forcibly enter a house to arrest a person without a warrant no longer applies. The police must now obtain a warrant before forcibly entering a house to arrest an offender for an indictable offence, and the following new procedures apply: a warrant must be obtained first. Justice Sopinka stated that the police must obtain judicial authorization for the arrest by obtaining a warrant to enter the dwelling-house for the purpose of arrest, the warrant must be obtained on the basis of reasonable grounds that the offender committed the offence, and, if he or she is inside the house, a proper announcement must be made before entering.

An exception occurs when an officer is in "hot pursuit" of an offender. The court did not fully address an exception for exigent circumstances, stating that there was no need for this issue to be decided in the *Feeney* case, since exigent circumstances did not exist.

This new law creates confusion about two prominent issues:

- Since the *Criminal Code* does not provide for a search warrant to search a house for offenders, what document must be used as the warrant?
- What are the police expected to do in emergencies when they are called to a house and hear circumstances that indicate an indictable offence is being committed inside the house?

In response to the first question, Justice Sopinka stated that, "If the *Code* currently fails to provide specifically for a warrant containing prior authorization, such a provision should be read in. While the absence of such a provision could have a profound influence on the common-law power of arrest, its absence cannot defeat a constitutional right of the individual. Once a procedure to obtain prior authorization is created, the concern that suspects may find permanent sanctuary in a dwelling-house disappears."

Regarding the second question, Justice Sopinka "refrained" from deciding whether an exigent-circumstances exception exists to the new warrant requirement. Exigent circumstances include an emergency where the safety of the police or public is in question, or where the possibility exists of destruction of evidence. According to Justice Sopinka, exigent circumstances did not exist in the *Feeney* case because "the situation was the same as in any case after a serious crime has been committed and the perpetrator has not been apprehended." In his opinion, the safety of the public and of the police was not in jeopardy. Regarding the blood stains, the Justice stated that the police had "no knowledge of evidence that might be destroyed."

Justice Sopinka did not agree with a unanimous decision by the British Columbia Court of Appeal, in which Justice Lambert wrote, "The police were facing a situation which could be classified as an emergency, or as exigent circumstances which would require immediate action, and that in addition they were facing circumstances where the possibility of the destruction of evidence, particularly evidence in relation to blood stains, was a real one and had to be addressed."

RIGHT TO COUNSEL—SEC. 10(B) *CHARTER*

The majority ruled that the police violated the accused's sec. 10(b) *Charter* right to counsel. The reasons for this ruling were "the right to be informed of the right to counsel begins immediately upon arrest or detention." According to *R. v. Therens (1985)*, detention occurs when a police officer assumes control over the movement of a person by demand or direction. In this case, detention began when the police officer shook the accused's leg and told him to get out of bed. The accused should have been informed of the right to counsel at that time. Instead, the right to counsel was read after the accused moved to the lighted area where the blood stains were seen.

The accused was not given a reasonable opportunity to exercise his right to counsel. He was not given access to a telephone before he was questioned inside the trailer about the blood on the shirt and shoes. Consequently, the statement in the trailer occurred after a sec. 10(b) *Charter* violation.

SEARCH WARRANT—SEC. 8 *CHARTER*

The majority ruled that the search of the trailer with a warrant constituted a sec. 8 *Charter* violation. The reasons were

- the police learned about the shirt and shoes as the result of the initial search and interview inside the trailer,
- the location of the stolen money was learned as the result of the interrogation at the police station, and
- all of the evidence was obtained after a *Charter* violation had been committed.

FINGERPRINTS—SEC. 8 *CHARTER*

The accused's fingerprints were found on the victim's refrigerator and on an empty beer can found inside the victim's truck. Taking fingerprints from an accused constitutes a search and seizure related to the accused person's body. The Supreme Court of Canada in *R. v. Beare (1988)* ruled that taking fingerprints from an offender following a lawful arrest is reasonable and does not constitute a *Charter* violation. However, the majority ruled that since the arrest in this case was unlawful and involved a number of *Charter* violations, the taking of the accused's fingerprints constituted a sec. 8 *Charter* violation.

ADMISSIBILITY OF EVIDENCE—SEC. 24(2)

The final issue related to the admissibility of the evidence obtained by the police, including the shirt, shoes, cigarettes, fingerprints, and statements made inside the trailer and at the police detachment. Admissibility of evidence is determined by applying sec. 24(2) *Charter*. The prominent element of sec. 24(2) *Charter* is whether the admission or exclusion of evidence obtained after the commission of a *Charter* violation will bring the administration of justice into disrepute. The Supreme Court of Canada, in *R. v. Collins (1987)*, established general policies that must be used to determine whether evidence will be admitted or excluded. "Disrepute" was defined as a concept that involves some element of community views. A "reasonable person test" was established as the standard used to make the determination regarding the reputation of the administration of justice. The test involves the perception of a reasonable person, defined as an average person within a reasonable community. Included in the factors created by the *Collins* case, but not exclusively, were elements that pertained to the fairness of the trial. The majority of the Supreme Court of Canada in *R. v. Stillman (1997)* refined and clarified the trial fairness factor by summarizing the following rule:

- Each piece of evidence must be classified as conscriptive or nonconscriptive.

Conscriptive evidence refers to evidence that the accused is compelled to incriminate himself with at the behest of the state by means of a statement, the use of the body, or the production of bodily samples. Nonconscriptive evidence refers to evidence that the accused was not compelled to participate in the creation or discovery of, such as physical items.

The Crown has the onus to prove on a balance of probabilities that conscriptive evidence would have been discovered by nonconscriptive means. Failure to do so will result in the determination that conscriptive evidence will render the trial unfair. As a general rule, this evidence will be excluded without consideration of the seriousness of the breach or the effect that exclusion will have on the reputation of the administration of justice.

If the Crown successfully proves that conscriptive evidence would have been discovered by nonconscriptive means, the admission of it will generally not render the trial to be unfair.

The shirt, shoes, cigarettes, and money were not conscriptive evidence. However, the seizure of these items occurred after serious *Charter* violations. The police "showed little regard for his sec. 10(b) rights." Consequently, these items were excluded under sec. 24(2) *Charter*. The statements and fingerprints were conscriptive evidence. They were excluded because their admission would adversely impact the fairness of the trial, thus harming the reputation of the administration of justice. In summary, the majority set aside the conviction and ordered a new trial.

Dissenting Justice L'Heureux-Dubé and three other justices opposed the ruling, stating that the arresting officer did have reasonable grounds to believe that the accused committed the murder. The Supreme Court of Canada decision in *R. v. Silveira (1995)* was referred to as an example that a private dwelling-house does not offer immunity from a police investigation.

Justice Dickinson quoted from *Eccles v. Bourque* that "the criminal is not immune from arrest in his own home nor the home of one of his friends." The entry into the trailer was considered lawful. The search warrant was properly issued. The fingerprinting was an incident of a lawful arrest and did not violate the *Charter*. The accused was properly informed of the right to counsel. The police have no obligation "to assure themselves positively that an accused understands what his right to counsel entails. It was recognized very early in *Charter* jurisprudence that placing this burden on the police would be prohibitive and would inhibit legitimate police investigative techniques." The police did not violate sec. 10(b) *Charter* by questioning the accused because he did not invoke his right to counsel. In this case, the police had no indication from the accused that he wanted to speak with a lawyer. Finally, the dissenting minority "commended" the police for acting quickly to prevent further violence after a "savage, physical beating inflicted on a helpless victim for no apparent reason."

TRANSITION PERIOD

The Supreme Court of Canada, upon realizing its judgment would require legislative changes to uphold its own decision in this matter, granted a six-month transition period on June 27, 1997, to determine the document that will be used as authorization to enter a house to arrest an offender and who will have jurisdiction to issue it. The requirements created by the *Feeney* decision were stayed for the time period beginning May 22 and ending November 22, 1997. During this time, the procedures established in *Landry* still applied to circumstances where forcible entry into a dwelling-house is necessary to arrest an offender without a warrant.

CRIMINAL CODE AMENDMENTS—*FEENEY* WARRANTS

Bill C-16 created *Criminal Code* amendments in response to the *Feeney* decision. The new provisions begin at sec. 529 C.C. under the title "Powers to Enter Dwelling-Houses to Carry out Arrests." The relevant provisions and titles are

- sec. 529 C.C.—Including Authorization to Enter in Warrant of Arrest,
- sec. 529.1 C.C.—Warrant to Enter Dwelling-House,
- sec. 529.2 C.C.—Reasonable Terms and Conditions,
- sec. 529.3 C.C.—Authority to Enter Dwelling-House without Warrant, and
- sec. 529.4 C.C.—Omitting Announcement before Entry.

The first two provisions create judicial authorization for entry in the form of two types of warrants that have become informally known as "*Feeney*" warrants. Additionally, the new provisions include the authority to enter houses without a warrant when exigent circumstances exist. The warrantless entry authority is similar to the procedures created by the *Eccles v. Bourque* and *R. v. Landry* decisions, which composed the laws prior to the *Feeney* decision.

TYPES OF WARRANTS

The *Criminal Code* creates two types of warrants that represent judicial authorization to enter a dwelling-house to make an arrest:

1. an ordinary arrest warrant that includes written authorization to enter a house to make the arrest. This provision is found in sec. 529 C.C.
2. a warrant to enter a dwelling-house. This provision is found in sec. 529.1 C.C. It is a separate document from an arrest warrant and any other document.

ARREST WARRANT

This document is Form 7 and is illustrated in sec. 841 C.C. Its principal function is providing judicial authority to arrest the person named on the warrant. This amendment now permits the justice to add a paragraph, shown in sec. 841 C.C. on Form 7, that authorizes police officers to enter a specific dwelling-house for the purpose of arresting the person named on the warrant.

Consequently, when the justice includes the paragraph authorizing entry, the single document known as an "arrest warrant" authorizes two procedures:

- arrest of the offender and
- entry into the house.

The obvious advantage of using the provision is eliminating the need to acquire a separate, additional document to authorize the entry. Only one document needs be obtained under this provision. The inclusion of the paragraph authorizing entry cannot be automatically made. The officer who requests the inclusion of that authority must apply for it by completing a document called an *Information to Obtain*. The purpose of this application is to prove, under oath, that reasonable grounds exist that the person named on the warrant will be present in the dwelling-house at the time of entry.

If reasonable grounds are successfully proven that the person named on the warrant will be in a specific dwelling-house, the justice will add the written authority on the warrant to enter the house. However, officers are bound by sec. 529(2) C.C. to ensure that reasonable grounds continue to exist immediately before entering the house. Section 529(2) C.C. stipulates that the included authority to enter the house "is subject to the condition that the peace officer may not enter the dwelling-house unless the peace officer has, immediately before entering, reasonable grounds to believe that the person to be arrested or apprehended is present in the dwelling-house." Consequently, the police have the onus to re-evaluate the reasonable grounds immediately before executing the warrant and entering the house. If the reasonable grounds continue to exist, entry may be made. However, if the reasonable grounds no longer exist immediately before entry, the included written authorization is cancelled and entry is prohibited; the document reverts to only judicial authorization to arrest.

Therefore, when an arrest warrant is used to enter a house and entry is made with a subsequent arrest of the offender, the police must prove two separate reasonable grounds of belief that the offender was currently in the house:

- at the time the information to obtain was presented to the justice, and
- at the time immediately before entering.

PROCEDURE

Step 1

Form reasonable grounds that the offender has committed any classification of offence.

Step 2

Form reasonable grounds that the offender is currently in a specific dwelling-house.

Step 3

Complete two documents privately, not in the justice of the peace's presence:

- an "information" to charge the offender, and
- an Information to Obtain—this document is Form 1 and is illustrated in sec. 841 C.C.

The "Information to Obtain" is the application to gain authority to enter the dwelling-house included on the arrest warrant, and it must include the following content:

- name of the accused,
- name of the offence,
- specific address of the house, and
- that the accused is currently in the house.

What circumstances constitute reasonable grounds? The definition of reasonable grounds must be referred to. The definition does not state specific circumstances that actually constitute reasonable grounds; reasonable grounds is a belief that exceeds mere suspicion. Examples of circumstances that usually constitute reasonable grounds include

- a credible eyewitness (citizen or police) who saw the offender inside the house or saw him enter the house,
- the accused's admission, such as informing another person by telephone that he is inside the house, and
- circumstantial evidence that exceeds mere suspicion.

The reasonable grounds narrative must be in writing on the Information to Obtain. The quantity of the content usually requires additional pages that are entitled

"Appendix A." A detailed explanation about completing an Information to Obtain is found in Unit Four—Search and Seizure.

Only one dwelling-house may be named on the Information to Obtain. The reasonable grounds must correspond specifically to the accused's presence in one house. An application cannot be made to search multiple houses. If the circumstances indicate that the accused may be in one of several houses, the application will be denied because only mere suspicion exists about the accused's actual whereabouts.

The place named on the information must be a dwelling-house. Any other type of place cannot be named because no warrant is needed for places that are not dwelling-houses. Finally, the Information to Obtain must be written without any assistance from the justice.

Step 4

After both documents are completed, appear before a judge or justice. A justice is a provincial court judge or a justice of the peace (JP). The appearance is made out of court.

The first document presented is the information to charge the offender. The reason is that an arrest warrant must exist before an application is made to enter a house. The first step in obtaining an arrest warrant is laying the information to charge the offender.

Step 5

Prove reasonable grounds that the accused committed the offence. This procedure is called an "*ex parte* hearing," which is explained in Unit Three of this textbook. This step relates to the information.

Step 6

If reasonable grounds are proven, the justice signs the information. The accused is formally charged at this time.

Step 7

The justice decides what method to compel the accused to court. As explained in the previous section, the officer must introduce evidence that proves reasonable grounds that an arrest warrant is necessary in the public interest. Failure to prove this element results in the issuance of a summons, not an arrest warrant.

Step 8

After the officer proves that a warrant is necessary in the public interest, the justice issues an arrest warrant. The justice, not the officer, completes the warrant.

Step 9

Present the Information to Obtain to the justice and swear the contents under oath. The JP reads the sworn written contents and decides whether reasonable grounds exist that the accused is currently in the house.

Step 10

If the justice concludes that reasonable grounds exist, he or she will include an additional paragraph on the arrest warrant itself that authorizes entry into the specific house. The contents of the authorization are found in sec. 841 C.C. on Form 7. A separate document is not issued. If the justice concludes that reasonable grounds do not exist, the authorization will not be included. Entry into the house will not be authorized without consent. The arrest must be made at another location, or consent must be obtained to enter.

WARRANT TO ENTER DWELLING-HOUSE

This is an alternative means to enter a house to make an arrest. It is a separate document in addition to an arrest warrant. The document is Form 7.1 and is illustrated in sec. 841 C.C.

A judge or justice may issue this warrant authorizing a peace officer to enter a specific dwelling-house to arrest a person "identified or identifiable" by the warrant. An application must precede this warrant (by the submission of an Information to Obtain under oath) to prove reasonable grounds that the accused person "is" or "will be" present in the dwelling-house. Additionally, it must be proven that lawful authority exists to arrest the accused person with or without a warrant. An arrest warrant may or may not be obtained before applying for a separate warrant to enter a house. In other words, obtaining an arrest warrant is not necessary to obtain a separate warrant to enter a house. This provision allows the issuance of the warrant to enter if reasonable grounds are proven that the accused has committed an indictable or dual procedure offence, authorizing an arrest without a warrant.

The type of lawful authority to arrest must be proven on the Information to Obtain. When this type of warrant is used to enter, no requirement exists to re-evaluate the reasonable grounds for believing that the offender is in the house immediately before entry. This nonrequirement contrasts with the required procedure (before entry) of an arrest warrant.

PROCEDURE

Step 1

a) Form reasonable grounds to arrest an offender, without a warrant, for an indictable or dual procedure offence; or

b) obtain an arrest warrant for any classification of offence.

Step 2

Complete an Information to Obtain containing the same requirement as the previous type of authorization to enter plus an explanation that proves the lawful authority to arrest the offender.

Step 3

Appear before a justice and swear the Information to Obtain under oath. The justice analyzes the contents and decides whether reasonable grounds exist that the offender is currently in the specifically named dwelling-house and if lawful authority to arrest is proven.

Step 4

If the justice concludes that both requirements are proven, he or she will issue a warrant to enter the specifically named dwelling-house, on Form 7.1.

MANNER OF ENTRY

The "manner" refers to the procedures used to physically enter. They are addressed in sec. 529.2 C.C. This provision creates a mandatory obligation upon the justice to include, on either warrant, "any terms and conditions that the Justice considers advisable to ensure that entry into the dwelling-house is reasonable in the circumstances."

The use of the word "shall" in this provision, means that the justice must include reasonable terms and conditions of entry on both types of warrants. In other words, the absence of terms and conditions on either type of warrant violates sec. 529.2 C.C.

The section does not specify the precise terms and conditions regarding the manner of entry. The phrase "any terms and conditions" suggest a wide latitude of discretion that the justice may use regarding the manner of entry. However, common law requirement of prior announcement provides the guidelines regarding the manner of entry. Proper prior announcement is made by giving three notices:

- presence (knock or use doorbell),
- authority (identify as police officer), and
- purpose (state reason for entry).

Forced entry is not justified at this stage. After the three notices are given, entry has to be requested and the request has to be denied. Forced entry is justified after the denial occurs.

Section 529.2 C.C. states that the imposition of "any" reasonable terms and conditions is "subject to sec. 529.4 C.C.," which creates an exception to making a proper prior announcement. Under sec. 529.4 C.C., the justice who authorizes a peace officer to enter a house by means of either type of warrant may authorize that the entry be made without making a proper prior announcement if reasonable grounds are proven on the Information to Obtain that create a belief that a prior announcement would cause either of the following:

- expose the officer or any person to imminent bodily harm or death, or
- result in the imminent loss or destruction of evidence relating to the commission of an indictable offence.

Either of these circumstances constitute exigent circumstances. After reasonable grounds are proven on the Information to Obtain that bodily harm, death, or loss of evidence will reasonably occur if a prior announcement is made, the justice may include on the warrant the authority to enter the house without prior announcement as a term and condition required under sec. 529.2 C.C.

If the authority to enter without prior announcement is included on either type of warrant, that authority does not automatically extend to the time of execution. Section 529.4 C.C. imposes an onus on the police to re-evaluate the reasonable grounds for believing the exigent circumstances, or imminence of bodily harm, death, or loss of evidence immediately before entering. Entry without prior announcement is permitted only if the reasonable grounds of exigent circumstances exist immediately before entering the house. If the reasonable grounds no longer exist, the justice's authorization to enter without prior announcement is cancelled; entry without prior announcement cannot be made.

Consequently, the police must make a proper prior announcement before entering when the reasonable grounds and the belief changes from the presence to the absence of exigent circumstances.

In summary, when authorization is given by a justice to enter without prior announcement and entry is forcibly made in that manner, the police will have to justify and prove that two separate reasonable grounds for belief existed of exigent circumstances:

- at the time that the Information to Obtain is presented to the Justice, and
- at the time immediately before entry.

WARRANTLESS ENTRY INTO HOUSE

Section 529.3(1) C.C. creates authority for the police to enter a house without a warrant for the purpose of making an arrest if exigent circumstances exist. A warrantless entry is justified under either of the following conditions:

- the police officer has reasonable grounds to believe that the person is present in the dwelling-house,
- the conditions exist for obtaining a sec. 529.1 C.C. warrant to enter, or
- exigent circumstances exist that make it impracticable to obtain a warrant.

Exigent circumstances are defined in sec. 529.3(2) C.C. as circumstances in which a police officer

- has reasonable grounds to suspect that entry into the dwelling-house is necessary to prevent imminent bodily harm or death to any person; or
- has reasonable grounds to believe that evidence relating to the commission of an indictable offence is present in the house and that entry into the house is necessary to prevent imminent loss or destruction of the evidence.

After the conditions that justify a warrantless entry exist, an officer must follow the procedural rules established in sec. 529.4(3) C.C. regarding the manner used to physically gain entry. Specifically, the primary issue is whether or not a prior announcement is required. Section 529.4(3) C.C. creates two alternatives; the making of a prior announcement is determined by the effect that the announcement will have on either the protection of persons or evidence.

RULES THAT APPLY TO A WARRANTLESS ENTRY

An officer must make a prior announcement if no reasonable grounds exist immediately before entry to suspect that prior announcement will expose any person, including the officer, to imminent bodily harm or death, and no reasonable grounds exist to believe that prior announcement would result in imminent loss or destruction of evidence relating to any indictable offence. Prior announcement may be omitted if, immediately before entry, reasonable grounds exist to

- suspect that prior announcement will expose any person, including the officer, to imminent bodily harm or death; or
- believe that prior announcement would result in imminent loss or destruction of evidence relating to any indictable offence.

Emphasis is required on the distinction between reasonable grounds to "suspect" and "believe." The standard of reasonable grounds relating to the protection of life is lower than the standard needed for the protection of evidence.

HOT PURSUIT

The Supreme Court of Canada, in *R. v. Macooh (1993)*[130] defined "hot pursuit" as the continuous pursuit of an offender, conducted with reasonable diligence, so that the pursuit and capture along with the commission of the offence may be considered as forming part of a single transaction. Hot pursuit begins with the commission of any classification of offence. A police officer finds the offence being committed, the offender flees, and the officer pursues continuously until apprehension.

The Supreme Court of Canada, in *R. v. Feeney*, recognized hot pursuit of an offender who enters a house as constituting exigent circumstances to enter the dwelling-house without a warrant.

EXECUTING AUTHORITY TO ENTER

Executing an authority means to carry it out. The execution of the warrants to enter and the authority to enter without a warrant include procedures relevant to

- method of entry, i.e., forcible (explained previously),
- when the warrant must be executed (time),
- what documents to bring, and
- what "other" items can be seized.

USE OF FORCE

The *Criminal Code* sections authorizing powers to enter a dwelling-house do not specify the exact circumstances that justify use of force to enter or the degree of force allowed under justifiable circumstances. The use of force and the degree of force that can be used are governed by the combination of the following factors:

1. the terms and conditions authorized on a warrant,
2. the effect that prior announcement will have on life or evidence, when a warrantless entry is justified, and
3. sec. 25-28 C.C. These provisions are entitled "Protection of Persons Administering and Enforcing the Law." They explain the guidelines and general principles regarding the circumstances that justify the use of force and the degree of justifiable force that may be used.

Section 25 C.C. justifies use of force when a police officer is authorized by law to do anything in the administration or enforcement of the law. This provision includes case law authorization to enter dwelling-houses, or any other place, without a warrant.

The degree of force that may be used is stated in general terms by the combined effect of sections 25(1) & 26 C.C. Specific guidelines are not stated. Section 25(1) C.C. states that "as much force as is necessary for that purpose" may be used. Section 26 C.C. imposes a limit of force that may be used, stating that excessive force cannot be used and may result in criminal liability. Determination of whether the force used is considered excessive or not will be made "according to the nature and quality of the act."[131] Consequently, the degree of force that may be used varies in each case, and common sense will be a proper guide. The nature of force used is that which is necessary to accomplish the intended goal of gaining entry.

Finally, when can force be used, and at what point in the procedure? The Supreme Court of Canada in the previously noted case law decisions did not impose a waiting period, when the required conditions exist, to enter. Therefore, force may be used immediately after a request to enter is denied, or after exigent circumstances are proven to exist and entrance cannot be gained without force, e.g., the door is locked. Any hesitation may be detrimental to personal safety or to the lives of persons inside the house.

4. Section 8 *Charter.* The key element of this provision is reasonableness. This provision governs the entire execution of a warrant. The use and degree of force must be reasonable under the circumstances, but no specific procedures are provided in sec. 8 *Charter.*

TIME OF EXECUTION

Generally, a justice writes one date on the warrant, the date of issuance. The authorization to enter is valid for that day, but, if the authorization is an arrest warrant, the police must re-evaluate the reasonable grounds to believe that the offender is in the house immediately before entry. Consequently, the entering officer(s) must prove that reasonable grounds existed at the time the Information to Obtain was presented to the justice and also at the time immediately before entry.

A separate warrant to enter a house does not have the requirement to re-evaluate the reasonable grounds immediately before entry.

However, the execution of both warrants is governed by sec. 8 *Charter.* The entry must be reasonable, meaning that if the belief about the offender being in the house changes before entry, the warrant cannot be executed (e.g., if the circumstances indicate that the offender is no longer in the house).

DOCUMENTS

Section 29(1) C.C. imposes an obligation for the police to "have" the warrant, where it is feasible to do so, and produce it when requested, during execution of any warrant. Therefore, the officer must comply with two obligations:

- possession of the warrant, and
- production of the warrant, when requested.

No obligation exists to give the accused or any occupant an original or photocopy of any document.

SEIZURE OF EVIDENCE

Both types of *Feeney* warrants and the authority for warrantless entry authorize entry into a house and a search only for the purpose of making an arrest. They do not authorize the search for and seizure of physical items that constitute evidence.

However, search and seizure authorities exist that permit the seizure of evidence inside the house:

- sec. 489(2) C.C.,
- plain-view doctrine, and
- search incident to an arrest.

All three search and seizure authorities are explained in Unit Four of this textbook. The following is a summary of the three authorities:

1. Sec. 489(2) C.C.: This provision gives the police authority to seize an item without a warrant if the officer

   a) is lawfully present in a place with or without a warrant, and
   b) believes on reasonable grounds that the item will afford evidence to any criminal offence, including items that have been obtained by or used in the commission of a criminal offence. The offence may be the one for which the offender will be arrested or any unrelated offence.

   Being lawfully in a place includes entering a house by

   - either *Feeney* warrant,
   - warrantless authority under sec. 529.3 C.C., or
   - consent.

   Section 489(2) C.C. does not state the means by which the evidence may be found. No reference is made to the act of searching for the item. The absence of the specific authority to search for items suggests that only items in plain view may be seized.

2. Plain View Doctrine: This case law authority authorizes the police to seize any item found in plain view when lawfully on any premises by means of a warrant, without a warrant, or consent. Plain view refers to the inadvertent finding of an item. Inadvertent means that the item was not found as the result of a physical search, and the police had no prior knowledge that the item was in the place.[132]

3. Search Incident to an Arrest: This is a common law authority that permits the police to automatically search

   a) the arrested person[133] after the person has been lawfully arrested inside a house or any other place and
   b) the immediate surroundings.[134]

   The arrested person may be searched immediately. This means that reasonable grounds do not have to be formed, prior to the search, that the offender has an item that may be seized. Any item may be seized from the offender that

   a) is evidence to any offence, whether or not related to the offence for which the offender was arrested, or
   b) may cause injury to any person, including the offender, or
   c) may help the offender escape.

   Afterward, the "immediate surroundings" of the place where the offender was arrested may be searched without a search warrant. The immediate surroundings include the entire room where the arrest was made. However, it does not include the entire house or premises.[135]

SUMMARY

Despite the controversy surrounding the *Feeney* ruling and subsequent *Criminal Code* amendments, the laws relating to entry into a dwelling-house have not been drastically altered. Warrantless entry into a house to make an arrest is still authorized when exigent circumstances exist, i.e., the same as in pre-*Feeney* laws. The only change is the requirement to obtain judicial authorization to enter a house when exigent circumstances are absent. The *Feeney* amendments should be viewed as being long-needed structured procedures that permit warrantless entry when emergencies exist.

Two important rules must be emphasized relating to the *Feeney* amendments. The *Feeney* laws do not apply in the following circumstances:

- when the offender is outside the dwelling-house, and
- when the offender is in any place that is not a dwelling-house.

911 RADIO BROADCASTS/PROTECTING LIFE

Uniform patrol officers receive a myriad of radio broadcasts, creating countless unique problems that must be solved with immediate decisions. "Unknown problem" and "911" radio broadcasts provide limited or no information to form beliefs. Upon arrival at the scene, decisions must be made regarding entry into dwelling-houses while obvious potential personal or public danger exists.

A useful set of procedural guidelines are found in the following case study, pertaining to disconnected 911 calls, where the protection of life and prevention of death or injury are the primary issues.

CASE LAW

R. V. GODOY (1997)[136]

The *Feeney* provisions are relevant to entering a dwelling-house to arrest an offender. The *Godoy* case deals with a different issue—entering a house to protect life and prevent death or injury. In emergency cases where a person requires immediate assistance in a dwelling-house, police officers are reliant upon the content of a radio broadcast to form reasonable grounds and make decisions about entering a house to protect potential victims inside the house. Sufficient information reported by a complainant to the dispatcher facilitates the responding officer's decision. However, in some situations a complainant may only be able to dial 911 without verbally conveying information. Consequently, the responding officer may have only a disconnected 911 telephone call to make a decision about entering a house. No authority is found in statutory law. No case law decisions are directly related to this issue.

Officers relied on a combination of the common law authority to protect life to enter the house and the principles established by the Supreme Court of Canada in *R. v. Landry*. Although this issue appears to be a simple common-sense topic, the Ontario Court of Appeal, in *R. v. Godoy (1997)*, made a significant ruling relating to police authority to enter a dwelling-house to investigate the nature of an unknown problem following a disconnected 911 call.

Issue   Does a disconnected 911 call constitute reasonable grounds to enter a dwelling-house without a warrant and without consent, to protect life, prevent death, or prevent serious injury?

Offences   "assaulting a peace officer with intent to resist arrest" and "assault"

Circumstances   Officers received a radio broadcast of an "unknown problem" at an apartment, originating from a 911 call where the phone was disconnected before the caller spoke. This type of call represents the second-highest priority to the police, second only to a call of an "officer down."

Four officers responded to the apartment. They listened at the door before knocking and heard nothing. After knocking on the door, officers waited a few minutes until the door was partially opened by a person, later identified as the accused, who asked, "What do you want?" An officer asked, "Something has occurred here. Is everything all right?" The accused responded, "Sure, there is no problem." An officer stated, "Well perhaps there is a problem here, and we'd like to find out for ourselves if there is a problem inside the apartment."

The accused tried to close the door. An officer prevented the closing of the door with his foot and entered, followed by the other officers. One officer heard a woman sobbing. The woman was found in a bedroom. Her left eye was swollen and beginning to close from the swelling. She informed the officer that the accused had hit her. The accused was arrested on the basis of the complainant's information and the officer's observation of the injury. The accused resisted the arrest and a struggle ensued. During the struggle, the accused bent an officer's finger and broke it. The accused was charged with assaulting the woman and assaulting the officer with intent to resist arrest.

continued

Trial   The trial judge acquitted the accused of both charges. The reasons were

- the accused testified that the victim had slipped and fallen against some furniture, and

- the officers' entry into the apartment was unauthorized, which rendered all subsequent police action illegal. The trial judge ruled that a mere 911 call and a denial of entry did not constitute reasonable grounds to enter without a warrant, as required by case law. Oddly, the judge stated, "I have no doubt that the police officers in this case were acting in what they thought were the best interests of (the complainant) and the question of what would have been sufficient to allow them to enter is difficult to answer, but based on the facts of this case when the accused denied entry to the police officer, which I find as a fact, the police officers were not acting lawfully at the time of the arrest of the accused and therefore cannot be said to have been in the execution of their duty."

The Crown appealed this decision to a Summary Conviction Appeal Court.

Summary Conviction Appeal Court   The appeal was allowed. The 911 call and denial to enter did constitute reasonable grounds to enter. The appeal judge stated, "One can only speculate as to what the response would have been had the police taken 'no' for an answer only to have it reported later that a homicide had taken place."
The accused appealed to the Ontario Court of Appeal.

Ontario Court of Appeal   The court unanimously dismissed the accused's appeal for the following reasons:

- the police had no intention of arresting anyone when they entered the apartment,

- the reason they entered was to determine the origin and reason for a properly interpreted distress call, and

- they considered it their duty to respond.

Section 42(1) of the *Police Services Act* of Ontario explains the duties of a police officer to be

- preserving the peace,

- preventing crimes and other offences, and

- providing assistance and encouragement to other persons in their prevention.

Assisting crime victims, sec. 42(3), states that a police officer has the powers and duties ascribed to a constable at common law.

The Supreme Court of Canada, in *R. v. Dedman (1981)*, stated that "at common law, the principal duties of police officers are the preservation of the peace, the prevention of crime, and the protection of life and property." Based on the Supreme Court of Canada's statement, the Ontario Court of Appeal emphasized that a police officer's duty to protect life is a "general duty."

A disconnected 911 call does not constitute reasonable grounds that an indictable offence has been committed. However, it does constitute reasonable grounds to believe that an emergency existed in the apartment and that the caller was in distress. Although the reason for the call was unknown, the police were clearly obliged to investigate further.

No time existed to obtain a warrant to enter, and no warrant exists that may be obtained to enter under these circumstances.

By making a 911 call, an occupant has asked for help and is asking for direct intervention. A compelling public interest exists in prompt and effective police response to a 911 call. The common law is flexible to recognize modern circumstances. Where human life and safety are at stake, it is in the public interest that the police enter the dwelling-house rather than leave and find out later that an avoidable death had occurred.

In summary, the court concluded that the forced entry in response to a disconnected 911 call was a justifiable use of police powers. The officers had authority to enter the apartment without a warrant and without consent, and they were acting in the lawful execution of their duties when the officer was assaulted.

The accused, in *R. v. Godoy*, appealed to the Supreme Court of Canada, which dismissed the appeal and ordered a new trial in provincial court. The Supreme Court

continued

of Canada, in ruling that the Ontario Court of Appeal had correctly concluded that the warrantless entry into the house, in this case, was a justifiable use of police powers, established an authority that allows police officers to enter a dwelling-house to investigate the extent of a 911 call. The following reasons and explanations were given that establish procedural guidelines relating to 911 calls:

1. The police clearly have the authority to investigate 911 calls, which justifies their presence on the person's property outside the house. Whether forcible warrantless entry into house can be made depends on the circumstances of the 911 call.

2. A disconnected 911 call, resulting in an "unknown problem" call, extends the police duty to ascertain the reason for the call, and constitutes reasonable grounds to believe that "the caller is in some distress and requires immediate assistance," which equates to exigent circumstances.

3. When the accused told the police that there was "no problem," the police had common law authority to enter the house to verify that there was in fact no emergency. Accepting the accused's statement that there was "no problem" would have been insufficient to satisfy their common law and statutory duty to protect life and safety.

4. The accused's attempt to close the door on the police provided additional justification for forcible entry without a warrant.

5. The privacy of the accused person at the door is secondary to the interest of any person inside the house.

6. After the police entered the house, hearing the wife's crying justified the search of the house to find her.

7. The *Feeney* case and relevant *Criminal Code* provisions do not apply to this case because the *Feeney* procedures apply to entry into a house for the specific purpose of making an arrest.

8. The wife's condition combined with her statement constituted reasonable grounds to arrest the accused.

In summary, this case establishes the following procedural guidelines:

1. A disconnected 911 call, or a radio broadcast stating "911-unknown problem," justifies

   * presence on the property,

   * warrantless, forcible entry into a house, and

   * search for injured persons.

2. A person who answers the door, and informs the police that there is no problem inside, cannot prevent entry into the house. Taking the word of the person who answers the door that there is "no problem" inside, and not entering the house to investigate further, constitutes a neglect of duty.

3. A disconnected 911 call authorizes warrantless entry into a house to search for injured persons who may then provide information to form reasonable grounds to make an arrest.

4. A disconnected 911 call allows an officer to form reasonable grounds to believe that the caller is in some distress and requires immediate assistance. This constitutes exigent circumstances, which would justify a forcible, warrantless entry without making a prior announcement.

Test Yourself

1. Wally (24) reports that Eddie (27) committed assault bodily harm 15 minutes ago. Eddie left the scene 10 minutes ago. You attend at Eddie's house 20 minutes later. Eddie looks through the window in the door. The door is locked. You see Eddie. You ask him to open the door. Eddie replies, "No," and walks away from the door.

Explain in detail the procedure you would use to enter the house and arrest Eddie.

_____

_____

_____

_____

_____

_____

_____

_____

_____

_____

_____

_____

_____

_____

_____

_____

_____

_____

_____

_____

_____

_____

_____

2. While on patrol at 10:30 p.m., you receive a call to attend a house at **6000 King St.** regarding a break and enter in progress. Upon arrival, you find June (30) outside in front of the house. She reports the following:

- She owns the house.
- Her sister and 4-year-old son are inside visiting.

- June's ex-boyfriend Ward (32) broke into the house four minutes ago.
- He punched June. June escaped and ran out of the house.
- June's sister and her child are still inside the house.
- You hear both the sister and the child screaming.

Explain what you would do and the reasons according to the relevant laws.

_____

_____

_____

_____

_____

_____

_____

_____

_____

_____

_____

_____

_____

_____

_____

_____

_____

_____

_____

_____

_____

_____

_____

_____

_____

_____

_____

_____

CHAPTER

FIVE

Making an Arrest

Learning Outcomes

The student will be able to

- interpret Section 10 (A) and 10 (B) of the *Charter*,
- apply Section 10 (A) and 10 (B) of the *Charter*, and
- prevent *Charter* violations during an arrest.

INTRODUCTION

Now that you have learned *when* and *where* a lawful arrest may be made, the final topic is how a lawful arrest may be made. *How* to make an arrest refers to a systematic step-by-step procedure that ensures the optimum outcome—preventing *Charter* violations that may result in the exclusion of evidence. These procedures are not systematically listed in one specific source of law. The list is composed of procedures derived from a number of authorities, or sources of law, such as the *Criminal Code,* case law, and the *Canadian Charter of Rights and Freedoms,* referred to as the *Charter.*

The *Charter* creates general provisions regarding informing an arrested person of the reason for the arrest and the right to counsel. However, these provisions are not specific and do not establish every procedure and guideline. Case law decisions, particularly those made by the Supreme Court of Canada, establish mandatory procedures that must be followed after an arrest is made.

Each step in the procedure will include the authority that creates it. For example, if a statute such as the *Criminal Code* or the *Canadian Charter of Rights and Freedoms* establishes the procedure, it will be referred to as a "statutory requirement," meaning it is mandatory because a specific law requires it. Another may be a case law requirement or authority, which means it is also required by law. If a procedure is simply a recommended one, it will be described as a nonstatutory or non–case law requirement.

RELEVANT *CHARTER* PROVISIONS

Before the procedures used to make an arrest are explained, the relevant *Charter* provisions will be interpreted. The *Charter* is a federal statute that supersedes all other Canadian laws. Its provisions are valid everywhere in Canada, and two sections of the *Charter,* 10 and 24, are relevant to arrest.

Section 10 *Charter* creates two general procedures in subsections 10(a) and 10(b) *Charter.* Section 10(a) *Charter* relates to the reason for an arrest, and sec. 10(b) *Charter* relates to the right to counsel.

SECTION 10(A) *CHARTER*

This provision guarantees that everyone has the right, upon arrest or detention, to be informed promptly of the reasons for the arrest or detention. This establishes only a general guideline. Case law decisions have established additional mandatory procedures that are not printed in the section. The respective cases must be referred to in order to determine those procedures.

SECTION 10(B) *CHARTER*

This provision guarantees that everyone has the right, upon arrest or detention, to retain and instruct counsel without delay, and to be informed of that right. Again, this creates only a general base guideline. Supreme Court of Canada decisions have added components that create mandatory procedures that are included in sec. 10(b) *Charter* but are not printed in that section.

Consequently, it is a *statutory requirement* to inform an arrested person of both the reason and right to counsel. Failure to properly inform an arrested person of the reason for the arrest and of the right to counsel constitutes a *Charter* violation. The consequence of a *Charter* violation is the *possible* exclusion of evidence obtained after the violation is committed.[137] This means that any type of evidence, such as physical items, a confession, breath samples, or blood samples, obtained after a sec. 10(a) or 10(b) *Charter* violation, will not be automatically excluded from the trial. In other words, if the police fail to give a proper reason for the arrest or improperly inform the arrested person of the right to counsel, any evidence obtained afterward will not be automatically inadmissible.

This represents a significant advantage for police officers because

1. Evidence obtained after a *Charter* violation may be admissible at the trial, despite a *Charter* violation caused by an improper procedure, and

2. evidence that existed before the commission of the *Charter* violation is unaffected by the *Charter* violation. This means that a *Charter* violation cannot possibly negate evidence obtained before the violation, including seized items or witness observations.

Section 24(2) *Charter* is the provision that determines admissibility of evidence that is obtained *after the police commit a* Charter *violation*. This provision states that evidence obtained after a *Charter* violation must be excluded only if the admission of the evidence would bring the administration of justice into disrepute. This means that the evidence will be admissible only if the criminal justice system would acquire a poor reputation were the evidence to be admitted at the accused's trial. Conversely, the evidence must be admissible if the exclusion of it would cause the criminal justice system's reputation to suffer. The trial judge has discretion to rule that the evidence is admissible or inadmissible.

A Supreme Court of Canada decision, in *R. v. Collins (1987)*,[138] established additional guidelines for trial judges to consider when determining the admissibility of evidence obtained after the commission of a *Charter* violation:

1. Physical items should usually be admissible, even if the item was seized after a *Charter* violation.
2. Evidence that originates from the accused person, e.g., a confession, or bodily substances including blood or breath samples, should usually be inadmissible.

However, neither principle requires automatic exclusion or admission at the trial. A detailed explanation of sec. 24(2) *Charter* is found in the "Search and Seizure" unit of this textbook.

COMMENTARY

The principles of sec. 24(2) *Charter* and the *Collins* ruling have a profound significance on the procedures that must be used to make an arrest. After learning the procedures explained in this section, students will be cognizant of the fact that, to comply with all *Charter* provisions, an arrested person must be informed about a myriad of information at the time of arrest. The procedures that will be explained in this section represent the best method to achieve the optimum result, which is the prevention of *Charter* violations. Although one should obviously strive to use the best method at the time of each arrest, students must also be aware of the fact that the time of an arrest may be hectic, chaotic, and pose a risk to the arresting officer's personal safety. The Alberta Court of Appeal, in *R. v. Lerke (1986)*, recognized the potential catastrophic results of making an arrest by acknowledging that a situation could "explode into violence leaving the arresting officer dead or injured."[139]

The *Charter* procedures are made to protect the rights of an offender, a concept that must be respected, but the officer making the arrest has the right to protect him- or herself from death or injury at the time of an arrest.

Therefore, the following points must be emphasized about the procedure that will be explained:

1. The most important priority at the time of an arrest is protection against death or injury.
2. The secondary priority is informing the offender about his or her *Charter* rights.
3. The procedures used to comply with the *Charter* do not all have to be done immediately at the time of the arrest. Some reasonable delay may occur.

Everything about which an arrested person must be informed, such as the reason for the arrest or the right to counsel, may be said either at the following locations or throughout the process involving these locations:

• the scene of the arrest, or
• in the police car while en route to the police station, or
• at the police station.

4. Finally, if some procedure is not followed in an optimum way, the investigation is not ruined. The judicial system cannot ignore the potential for harm and violence at the time of the arrest. Police officers cannot be expected to inform an offender

of all the required information at the scene of an arrest. The concept of sec. 24(2) *Charter* and the *Collins* decision made by the Supreme Court of Canada demonstrate the willingness to admit evidence seized after a *Charter* violation has been committed. The Alberta Court of Appeal made a profound statement, in *R. v. Lerke (1986),* by stating

> Judges cannot be blind to the deaths and injuries suffered by police officers on duty as guns and knives become more common. It is difficult to second-guess any police officer who ensures that a person is not armed when he perceives danger as he makes an arrest or escorts a prisoner.[140]

MAKING AN ARREST—PROCEDURES

The systematic procedure used to make an arrest, with or without a warrant, consists of 15 steps including those that will prevent the commission of a *Charter* violation:

1. Identify yourself as a police officer.
2. Tell the accused that he or she is under arrest.
3. Take physical custody of the accused person.
4. Search the accused immediately.
5. Procedure—Simultaneous arrest of young and adult offender.
6. Inform the accused about the reason for the arrest.
7. Produce the warrant.
8. Inform the accused of the right to counsel.
9. Prove the accused understood the right to counsel in its entirety.
10. Read the caution to the accused.
11. Allow the accused reasonable time to decide whether to exercise the right to counsel.
12. Provide a reasonable opportunity for accused to invoke right to counsel.
13. Question the accused after right to counsel is exercised.
14. Procedure—Waiver of right to counsel.
15. Procedure—Accused invokes right to counsel then changes his or her mind.

Step 1

An officer should *identify him- or herself,* as soon as practicable, as being a police officer, especially when not wearing a police uniform. The identification should prove beyond reasonable doubt that the accused knew that a police officer was making the arrest. This proof becomes significant if the accused commits "resist arrest" or "assault police officer," because the accused's knowledge of the officer's occupation is crucial in the prosecution for both offences.

A police uniform may, in most cases, be sufficient circumstantial evidence to prove the officer's occupation, but a uniformed officer should also identify him- or herself as a police officer to remove any possible doubt in the accused person's mind. The identification may be accomplished by verbally stating, "I am a police officer with [name of police service]," and where practicable, produce a badge for viewing.

Identifying oneself as a police officer is not a statutory or case law requirement to make a lawful arrest. Neither the case law definition of arrest nor the *Criminal Code* states specifically that a police officer must inform a person about his or her occupation *before* a lawful arrest can be made. Additionally, proving that arrest was lawful does not depend on whether the arresting officer informed the accused of his or her name and occupation.

In summary, officers frequently encounter situations where arrest of a violent offender must be made immediately. It must be emphasized that the officers are not expected to pause and identify themselves before the arrest. Any failure to identify will not affect the lawfulness of the arrest. It may affect only a charge of "assault police" or "escape lawful custody."

Step 2

No federal statute states that an accused must be told "**You're under arrest.**" Therefore, it is not a statutory requirement. However, the Supreme Court of Canada, in *R. v. Whitfield (1969)*,[141] stated that a person being arrested must be informed that he or she is being arrested. Consequently, saying "You're under arrest" is a case law requirement.

It must be remembered that an arrest or detention may be made without an officer actually telling an accused that he or she is under arrest. The Supreme Court of Canada, in *R. v. Therens (1985)*,[142] stated that a detention occurs when a police officer makes a demand or direction to a person, or when a psychological compulsion exists within a person that his or her freedom has been removed.

Step 3

Taking *physical custody* of an arrested person, such as by holding or touching the person, is a recommended procedure. No statute or case law creates a mandatory requirement that actual physical custody of a person be taken in order to make a proper arrest. A person may be lawfully arrested without taking actual physical custody.

This recommended procedure of taking hold of an arrested person has two advantages:

1. It helps prove that the accused had knowledge that he or she was the person who was intended to be arrested. This becomes especially important when the accused is in a group of people and doubt may exist about who has been verbally told "You are under arrest." Proving the accused's knowledge that he or she is under arrest becomes crucial in cases where the accused commits the offences of "assault with the intent to resist arrest"[143] or "escape custody."[144]
2. It provides a degree of personal safety and prevention of escape, by eliminating total unrestricted movement by the offender. Taking hold of an offender constitutes use of force that is considered to be ordinary force. Regardless of how minimal the force is, all use of force must be justified. Section 25 C.C. justifies this ordinary force by allowing a police officer to use as much force as is necessary when doing anything during the enforcement of law, such as making a lawful arrest.

The Supreme Court of Canada, in *R. v. Whitfield (1969)*,[145] created the following guidelines relevant to the taking of physical custody of an offender:

1. Any physical custody, such as actual seizure, holding, or touching, with the intent to detain, does constitute an arrest.
2. A person who accompanies an officer who makes only "a mere pronouncing of words of arrest"[146] without taking physical custody is under arrest.
3. It is not necessary to touch or hold the person being arrested. After a person has been told he or she is under arrest, the person is "under a legal obligation to submit to the lawful arrest."[147]

The circumstances of the *Whitfield* case demonstrate the offence committed by a person who resists or escapes an arrest when the officer uses words only and does not touch the offender when arresting. An officer stopped the accused, who had been driving a car. The officer knew that the accused was wanted regarding a valid arrest warrant. The officer approached the car, while the accused remained in the driver's seat. The officer told the accused, "I have a warrant for you. Stop the car and shut off the ignition." The officer had no opportunity to touch or hold the accused. The accused accelerated, was pursued, and was apprehended. The accused was charged with escaping lawful custody.

The Supreme Court of Canada ruled that the accused was guilty. The "mere pronouncement of words of arrest" constitute an arrest.

Step 4

Police officers are authorized to *immediately search* a person after the person has been lawfully arrested, and may seize:

- evidence to any offence, including the offence for which the person was arrested, and any unrelated offence, or
- any item that may cause injury to anyone including the arrested person, or
- any item that may help the arrested person escape.[148]

This authority originates from common law and has been confirmed by the Supreme Court of Canada.

The automatic search means that an officer does not have to form reasonable grounds that the arrested person possesses any of the above before searching. This authority has been extended to the surrounding area where the arrest was made. The police may search the entirety of what may reasonably be considered the surrounding area, including the interior of a car or an entire room.[149]

Step 5

In some cases, an adult offender (18 years or older) and a young offender (ages 12–17 years) are arrested together. The *Young Offender's Act* states that *young offenders must be detained separately from adults*. However, an exception exists in sec. 7(4) Y.O.A., which allows a police officer to detain a young offender with an adult in a police vehicle at the time of arrest. For example, an officer may simultaneously arrest a 17- and an 18 year old for having committed the same offence. Both may be detained in the same vehicle for the purpose of transporting to the police station. Afterward, the young offender must be separately detained from the adult, including at the police station jail cells.

Step 6

Informing the accused about the reason for the arrest is a statutory requirement created by sec. 10(a) *Charter* and sec. 29(2)(b) C.C. Section 10(a) *Charter* imposed a duty to *inform an arrested person promptly of the reasons for the arrest*. The Supreme Court of Canada, in *R. v. Evans (1991)*,[150] explained two reasons for this requirement:

1. An arrested person is not obliged to submit to an arrest if he or she does not know the reason for it.
2. An arrested person cannot exercise his or her right to counsel in a meaningful way if the arrested person does not know the full extent of the severity or nature of the reasons for the arrest.

The court created a *general rule* about what constitutes a proper reason for arrest: the substance of what the accused can reasonably understand, not the formal, precise words used, is the governing factor that will determine whether the accused was properly informed of the reasons for the arrest. Additionally, the reasons told to the accused must be reasonable regarding all the circumstances of the case, and must be sufficient to allow the accused an opportunity to make a reasonable decision to decline to submit to the arrest and whether to exercise the right to counsel.

This rule permits officers to give an arrested person general explanations for the arrest instead of stating the precise name of the offence, at the scene of the arrest. However, when the decision has been made to charge an accused with specific offences, those specific offences should be explained to the accused person.

PROCEDURE

The procedure of informing an offender of the reason of the arrest is divided into two categories:

1. at the scene of the arrest and
2. at the police station.

At the Scene of the Arrest

Upon arrival at or near a crime scene where the offender is arrested then or shortly afterward, an officer has two alternatives about how to inform the accused about the reason for the arrest:

a) Explain a general reason that is reasonable considering the circumstances. Examples include

- "punching that person."
- "stealing that (item)."
- "stabbing that person," or
- "shooting at that person."

Although a general reason does not state a specific offence, it provides a reasonable explanation.

b) If the officer quickly analyzes the circumstance at or near the crime scene and accurately recognizes the offence committed, a specific offence may be given as a reason. Examples include

- assault,
- theft under $5000.00,
- impaired driving,
- attempt murder, or
- mischief under $5000.00.

If a specific offence is given as a reason, the officer has the onus to prove that the accused reasonably understood. Therefore, if doubt exists whether the accused reasonably understands, an additional explanation, providing more information, may be required. For example, the name of some offences, such as "mischief," may not be understood by the accused and would require an explanation.

After the accused is informed of the reason, ask the accused if he or she understands and, if necessary, have the accused explain to you what it means. Record the accused's responses in a notebook for reference during court testimony at a trial.

At the Police Station

After the accused has been transported to the police station and a decision about specific charges has been made, inform the accused about each specific offence with which he or she will be charged, as soon as practicable. Failure to properly inform an arrested person of the proper reason for an arrest constitutes a sec. 10(a) *Charter* violation, which may result in the exclusion of evidence obtained after the violation.[151]

Young Offenders—Notice to Parents

If the arrested person is a young offender, the police have an additional mandatory obligation to fulfill regarding the reason for arrest. Section 9(1) Y.O.A. creates a procedure called "notice to parent." Where a young offender is arrested and detained in custody pending a court appearance, a parent of the young offender must be notified of the arrest, the place of detention, and the reason for the arrest. The officer-in-charge at the time the young offender is detained must make the notification, or the officer-in-charge may instruct another officer to perform this procedure. This notice to parent may be given verbally or in writing. The notice must be given as soon as possible after the arrest.

Step 7

If the arrest is made with a warrant, the *arresting officer must have possession of the warrant and produce it when requested to do so.*[152] This is a statutory requirement created by sec. 29(1) C.C. If an arrest with warrant is made, the warrant must be executed properly. Proper execution is defined as having possession of the warrant when arresting the offender and producing it when requested to do so.

Section 29(1) C.C. allows an exception to the rule of having possession. The section states that the officer must have possession where it is feasible to do so. This permits the arrest to be made when the officer inadvertently finds the accused. After the arrest is made in this case, execution of the warrant may be made when the accused is at the police station. Otherwise, if the officer intends to search for and arrest the accused, the officer should have possession of the warrant.

Although this section requires that the warrant be produced to the accused only if the accused requests it, *production should be made in every arrest with warrant* to prevent arguments in court about whether a request was actually made. A copy of the warrant does not have to be given to the accused and, to prevent improper and illegal use of the copy of the warrant, it should not be given.

Step 8

A police officer must *inform the arrested person of the right to counsel,* without delay, upon arrest or detention.[153] This is a statutory requirement created by sec. 10(b) *Charter.* This section creates only the general base component of the right to counsel. Since the enactment of the *Charter* in 1982, additional components have been created by case law decisions. These components compose the entire right to counsel package although only the base component is printed in sec. 10(b) *Charter.*

The right to counsel consists of four distinct components that apply to both adult and young offenders (ages 12–17 years). However, additional rules apply to young offenders. The components are

1. base component,
2. *Brydges* component (legal aid existence and availability),
3. *Bartle* component (toll-free number), and
4. privacy component.

An accused must be informed of the right to counsel upon arrest or detention, which has been defined by the Supreme Court of Canada, in *R. v. Schmautz (1990),*[154] as "at the moment where he or she is arrested or detained."

Adult offenders must be informed of the right to counsel only upon arrest. This means that an adult offender (18 years or older) does not have to be informed of the right to counsel when mere suspicion exists and the offender voluntarily accompanies the officer for any purpose such as questioning. For example, if mere suspicion exists that Eddie (19 years) has committed a robbery, and Eddie consents to be questioned by a police officer, the officer does not have to inform Eddie of the right to counsel because he has not been arrested or detained.

The rule for young offenders differs. A young offender must be informed of the right to counsel at any time during an investigation, including during voluntary accompaniment when no arrest or detention occurs. Essentially, a young offender (ages 12–17 years, inclusive) must be informed of the right to counsel any time an officer has contact with, deals with, or speaks to him or her, including during voluntary accompaniment when only mere suspicion exists.[155]

BASE COMPONENT—ADULT

The right to counsel must be clearly communicated to an arrested person.[156] The base component used to inform an adult offender of the right to counsel is, "It is my duty to inform you that you have the right to retain and instruct counsel without delay. Do you understand?"

The officer has the onus of proving that the accused understood the right. Usually, the question, "Do you understand?" and an affirmative answer of "Yes" by the accused is sufficient to prove knowledge. The offender's verbatim response should be recorded (in a notebook) rather than "the accused understood." If circumstances exist that may suggest that the accused does not understand, then the officer must provide an additional explanation such as, "This means you have the right to call a lawyer of your choice." Record the explanation and the offender's response verbatim. Avoid paraphrasing such as, "I explained it further, and then the accused understood."[157]

BASE COMPONENT—YOUNG OFFENDER

The base component used to inform a young offender of the right to counsel includes the same information used for adults plus the following additional information. In addition to a lawyer, a young offender must be informed of the right to call three other types of people:

1. a parent,
2. any adult relative, and
3. any other appropriate adult chosen by the young offender.[158]

A young offender must be informed of the right to have any number of these four persons present.[159]

All information told to a young offender must be said in language compatible with that particular young person's intelligence.[160] Consequently, an officer may have to inform a young person about the right to counsel in simple language that the young person understands. Afterward, the young person must be asked if he or she understands. If the young person acknowledges by stating, "yes," he or she should be asked to *explain* the right to counsel. The answer must reflect the correct meaning of the right to counsel. If the young person answers incorrectly, inform the young person about the correct explanation and ask him or her again to explain it. Write the entire conversation, verbatim, in a notebook, including the right to counsel and all responses made by the young offender. Court testimony should reflect the recorded verbatim conversation. Do not paraphrase the conversation by simply stating, "I informed the accused of the right to counsel and he or she understood." This phrase will be insufficient during court testimony because it is a conclusion that only the trial judge may make.

This base component represents only the first component and is not the total right-to-counsel information. Case law has added additional requirements, or components. If an officer informs an adult or young offender about only the base component, a sec. 10(b) *Charter* violation will have occurred because the base component by itself is insufficient.

BRYDGES COMPONENT

The Supreme Court of Canada, in *R. v. Brydges (1990)*,[161] added a second mandatory component to the right to counsel. An officer must inform both adult and young offenders about the existence and availability of legal aid, regardless of the accused person's financial status.

Legal aid refers to legal advice and service provided to an accused person who is eligible for it. The service extends during the course of the prosecution and court proceedings.[162] Additionally, temporary, free legal advice is available immediately after an arrest. Therefore, the police are required to inform an accused person of two elements that compose the *Brydges* component:

1. the availability of temporary, free, and immediate legal service, and
2. that the accused may be eligible for permanent legal aid, meaning through the completion of court proceedings.

The specific content of the *Brydges* component is printed on "right to counsel" cards with which police officers are provided. It must be read to all arrested persons, regardless of whether he or she can afford a lawyer. Failure to inform an accused person of the *Brydges* component constitutes a sec. 10(b) *Charter* violation, which may result in the exclusion of evidence that the police obtain after the violation is committed.[163]

BARTLE COMPONENT

The Supreme Court of Canada, in *R. v. Bartle (1994)*,[164] added a third mandatory component to the right to counsel. Police officers must inform both adult and young offenders of a toll-free telephone number regarding duty counsel. This telephone number provides an accused person with a specific method of obtaining temporary, free, and immediate legal advice. This telephone number must be given to all arrested persons, in all cases, whether the accused can afford a lawyer or has a lawyer that he or she uses or calls regularly. In other words, no exceptions exist because it is a mandatory obligation.

Failure to inform an arrested person of the toll-free number constitutes a sec. 10(b) *Charter* violation and may result in the exclusion of evidence obtained by police after the violation occurs.[165] Again, the trial judge considers various factors in determining whether to admit or exclude the evidence.

PRIVACY COMPONENT

The Ontario Court of Appeal, in *R. v. Jackson (1993)*,[166] added both a mandatory and recommended procedure about informing an arrested person about the right to exercise the right to counsel, in private. Whether mandatory or recommended depends on certain circumstances.

Mandatory

A police officer has a mandatory obligation to inform all adult and young offenders of the right to privacy if any of the following conditions exist:

1. The accused says something to, or in the presence of, the officer who informed the accused of the right to counsel, that indicates to the officer that the accused either

   • does not understand that he or she has the right to counsel in private, or
   • is concerned about whether such a right exists.

2. The accused knows that the right to privacy exists but is concerned about whether privacy will be given.
3. The circumstances surrounding the informing of the right to counsel causes the accused to reasonably believe that he or she will have no privacy to exercise that right and must telephone a lawyer in police presence.

An example of circumstances that cause the accused to reasonably believe that no privacy will be given is found in the *Jackson* case. The accused was arrested for "over 80" and informed of his right to counsel upon arrest. A breathalyzer demand was made, and the accused was transported to a police station.

The accused was seated in an interview room; a police officer sat across from the accused, pointed to a phone book and a telephone on a desk, and asked him if he wanted to call a lawyer. The officer made no move to leave, and the accused said "no." During the 30 minutes they remained together in the room, the officer repeated the right to counsel and the accused again refused.

At the trial, the accused testified that he would have called his lawyer but chose not to because he believed he would not have been afforded privacy. The court ruled that a sec. 10(b) *Charter* violation occurred because of the following reasons:

1. These circumstances would sufficiently cause a reasonable person to believe that the right to phone a lawyer had to occur in the officer's presence and that no privacy would be given.
2. These circumstances sufficiently caused the officer to have a reasonable apprehension that the accused believed that no privacy would be given.

Recommended

It is not mandatory for an officer to inform an accused person of the right to privacy if no circumstances exist that would cause the accused to reasonably believe that privacy will not be given. However, the court added a recommended procedure for officers to use in all cases by stating that it is a "simple matter" for police officers to add the words "in privacy" to the right to counsel information content. Additionally, the court stated that "it is desirable that this be done."[167]

Step 9

The Supreme Court of Canada, in *R. v. Evans (1991)*,[168] stated that an accused person cannot be expected to exercise the right to counsel if the accused fails to understand it. Consequently, officers have the onus to clearly communicate the right and *prove that the accused understood it.*[169] In most cases, the question "Do you understand?" with a response of "Yes" infers that the accused understood what was said.[170] It is recommended that this response always be followed with a question such as "What does this mean?" The purpose of this question is to elicit a correct explanation from the accused person that accurately reflects the meaning of the right to counsel and proves that the accused had sufficient intelligence to understand it. A correct explanation should include a reference to the right to call a lawyer. Record the response verbatim. During court testimony, state the question asked and the response made instead of paraphrasing by saying, "the accused understood." Paraphrasing must be avoided during court testimony because it represents a conclusion that only a trial judge may make.

However, if a "positive indication" exists that the accused does not understand the right, the Supreme Court added the following: "The police cannot rely on their mechanical recitation of the right to the accused; they must take steps to facilitate that understanding."[171]

An example of a positive indication is a response made by the accused that indicates no understanding, or doubt about the ability to understand. An accused's limited capacity is another example of a positive indication. In the *Evans* case, the police were aware of the accused's limited mental capacity, and the accused said he did not understand the right to counsel. If the accused positively indicates that the right to counsel is not understood, the right to counsel must be explained in simple language, such as

- it means you can call a lawyer and talk to him or her, or
- you can talk to a free legal aid lawyer right now, or
- this is the free 1-800 telephone number that you can call and talk to a lawyer for free, or
- you can apply to legal aid, and you might receive a free lawyer for the trial if you are eligible.

Record the additional explanation verbatim and the accused's response in a notebook. After receiving the response, ask the accused to explain the right. Record the explanation verbatim. The accused's explanation should accurately reflect the officer's simpler explanation. Whenever the accused's knowledge of an issue requires proof, the best proof is the accused's verbatim response that includes the correct additional explanation learned from the officer's instructions.

Another example of possible indication of failure to understand is an accused's intoxication. A slightly or moderately intoxicated person—meaning a person who is coherent and capable of having a conversation—may be capable of understanding what is told to him or her. However, in these cases, the following procedure may remove doubt about the accused's knowledge:

1. explain the right to counsel in simpler language, regardless if the intoxicated accused says that the right is understood, and
2. ask the accused to explain it, then
3. repeat the procedure after the accused becomes sober.

Young offenders must have all the right-to-counsel information explained to them in language compatible with the specific young person's intelligence. This procedure is a preventative measure to avoid the potential exclusion of evidence, such as confessions or physical evidence obtained afterward.

Step 10

The caution is a warning to the accused that he or she does not have to say anything to the police but that if he or she says anything, it may be used in evidence at the trial. An example of a formal caution is: "Do you wish to say anything in answer to the charge? You are not obliged to say anything unless you wish to do so, but whatever you say may be given in evidence."

The caution is not a statutory requirement. No statute, such as the *Charter* or the *Criminal Code*, creates a mandatory requirement to inform an accused person of the formal caution. Consequently, failure to caution the accused is not a *Charter* violation. The caution is a guideline, or a recommended practice, included in the Judges' Rules as established in England in 1912. The purpose of the caution is to assist officers with the onus of proving that confessions made by accused persons are voluntarily made. Voluntariness of a confession is a prominent factor that must be proven to ensure the admissibility of the confession. Reading the caution to an offender after an arrest does not automatically result in admissibility of a confession. The entire circumstances of, and conversation during, an interrogation determine voluntariness and admissibility of a confession. Therefore, the caution is an advantage that is available to police officers to help prove the voluntariness of a confession.

In summary, failure to caution an accused simply represents the failure to utilize an advantage that facilitates admissibility of a confession.[172] Failure to caution an accused person will not result in automatic exclusion of a confession or any other evidence obtained as the result of interrogation.

Step 11

After the accused is informed of the right to counsel, he or she has two choices or options regarding the right to counsel:

1. invoke the right to counsel for the purpose of exercising it (ask to call and speak to a lawyer).
2. waive the right to counsel (decline the right to call a lawyer).

The police have a duty to provide the accused with a *reasonable time to decide whether to exercise the right to counsel.* An exact number of minutes is not specified regarding the time to decide. Instead, the amount of time must be reasonable—depending on the circumstances of each case.

The British Columbia Court of Appeal, in *R. v. Hollis (1992),*[173] created two rules that are relevant to the accused's decision by stating

1. If the accused understands the right, the decision by the accused is expected to be made quickly. (Again, no specific amount of time that applies in every case was stated.)
2. The accused's decision about calling a lawyer must be the product of free choice. This means that the police cannot persuade or influence the accused in any manner, or use any inducements to force the accused to make a specific decision.

The Supreme Court of Canada, in *R. v. Burlingham (1995),*[174] addressed the issue of police persuasion or influence regarding the accused's decision to call a lawyer. The court ruled that sec. 10(b) *Charter* specifically prohibits the police from "belittling" an accused's lawyer with the "express goal or effect of undermining the accused's confidence in and relationship with defence counsel." This prohibition is a component of sec. 10(b) *Charter.* In the *Burlingham* case, the police denigrated the role of the defence lawyer by making disparaging remarks about the lawyer's loyalty, commitment, availability, and amount of legal fees. Additionally, the police suggested that they were more trustworthy than the accused's lawyer. These comments constituted a section 10(b) *Charter* violation, and significant evidence that was obtained afterward, including a confession, was excluded under section 24(2) *Charter.*

In some cases, the accused makes no decision and gives no response about exercising the right to counsel. When the accused does not say whether he or she wants to invoke or waive the right to counsel, the question arises, "Are the police to assume that the accused has invoked the right to counsel?" The British Columbia Court of Appeal answered that question in the *Hollis* case with the following rule: "If the accused does not state a decision, the police have no obligation to assume or guess that the accused will decide to call a lawyer and may continue the investigation as if the right to counsel has been waived."[175] In summary, the accused may

- ask to call and speak to a lawyer (invoke and exercise the right), or
- decline to call a lawyer (waive the right), or
- make no decision, which means *the right is waived.*

Step 12

Invoking the right to counsel means asking for an opportunity to call and speak to a lawyer. An accused person may invoke the right to counsel at any time while he or she is in police custody, from the time after an arrest is made until the time of release. The accused is not limited or restricted to a time period, e.g., having to invoke the right immediately after being informed of it.

The Supreme Court of Canada, in *R. v. Manninen (1987),*[176] imposed two mandatory obligations upon police officers when the accused asks to invoke the right to counsel:

1. Give the accused person a **reasonable opportunity to exercise the right to counsel**, after the right is invoked.
2. Cease questioning, delay the investigation, and do not attempt to obtain evidence from the accused until he or she has had a reasonable opportunity to call and speak to a lawyer.

The following nine rules and procedures must be followed after the accused invokes the right to counsel by asking to call a lawyer:

RULE 1

Provide the accused with an opportunity to call a lawyer without unnecessary delay.[177] The opportunity is not defined by a specific amount of minutes or hours.

RULE 2

Delay the investigation and do not attempt to elicit evidence from the accused until the accused has exercised the right by actually speaking to a lawyer and receiving legal advice. This rule prohibits the questioning of an accused person between the time the accused asks for the opportunity to call a lawyer (invoked) and the time the accused actually speaks to a lawyer (exercised).

If the police initiate questioning during that time and the accused confesses, a sec. 10(b) *Charter* violation will have occurred and the confession will likely be excluded under sec. 24(2) *Charter*.

RULE 3

How much time constitutes a reasonable opportunity? How long must the police delay their investigation? The Supreme Court of Canada answered these questions in *R. v. Smith (1989)* by ruling that an accused must be *reasonably diligent* in attempting to call a lawyer.[178] This imposes a time limit upon the accused to call a lawyer, but the time limit is not in specific minutes. Instead, it prevents the accused from causing unnecessary delays in an investigation. Without this limit, it would be possible to intentionally hinder an investigation and cause evidence to be destroyed or lost.

Consequently, the police obligation to cease questioning and delay the investigation is cancelled if the accused is not reasonably diligent in exercising the right to counsel. The accused person does not lose the right to counsel, the police simply do not have to delay the investigation unreasonably until the right is exercised.

A variety of specific circumstances may indicate the lack of reasonable diligence. For example, it does not take several hours to call a lawyer. An example of circumstances that indicated a lack of reasonable diligence are found in the *Smith* case.

The accused was arrested at 7:00 p.m. for "robbery." He was informed of his right to counsel at that time but did not invoke the right at that time. He did invoke his right two hours later. The officers gave the accused a telephone book and a telephone. The accused decided not to call his lawyer at that time because the phone book indicated only an office number. The officers suggested that he call the number because possibly an answering service would be available. The accused rejected this suggestion and decided to postpone the phone call until the morning.

One hour after the accused invoked his right, the officers interrogated the accused, who initially declined to answer questions about the robbery until he could speak to his lawyer in the morning. Interrogation continued, and the accused eventually made an "off the record" confession.

The Supreme Court of Canada ruled that the accused *had not been reasonably diligent* in exercising the right to counsel because of the *casual attempts* to call the lawyer. Consequently, the police did not have to delay the investigation and were allowed to continue questioning. No sec. 10(b) *Charter* violation occurred. The confession was admissible. The court summarized this decision by establishing the following rule: When the police offer an opportunity to exercise the right to counsel, *the accused has the onus* of proving that it was impossible to speak with his or her lawyer at that time. This presents an advantage to the police when officers must decide if the accused is not being reasonably diligent. After the accused is given a reasonable opportunity to phone a lawyer, the accused is required to make a reasonable attempt to contact the lawyer, including leaving a message with an answering service. If the accused refuses to leave a message and wants to postpone the phone call until office hours, the investigation may justifiably continue. In order to delay an investigation, the onus is on the accused to prove that no possible method exists to contact a lawyer.

RULE 4

Where should the accused be given the opportunity to call a lawyer? Ensuring personal safety and preventing escape are primary concerns after an arrest is made. It is recommended that the opportunity to call a lawyer be given at the police station, if the accused is transported there justifiably. Permitting the accused to phone in public, or from a residence, poses a risk. Any arrested person is capable of using violence toward the arresting officer and is capable of attempting an escape.

The accused's movement in public, or in a house, should be restricted after an arrest. The accused should be placed in the police car as soon as possible. If an accused makes a phone call before being transported to the police station, he or she may be calling someone other than a lawyer to seek assistance in escaping while en route to the police station. Additionally, too many consequences are possible during the time that an accused takes to call in public, or in a house, because of the accused's ability to move freely. For example, the accused may know of and easily remove a weapon that is stored near the phone. Therefore, giving the accused the opportunity to call a lawyer from the police station minimizes unnecessary risks.

It must be emphasized that the only possible consequence of delaying the opportunity to call a lawyer until arrival at the police station is the *possible exclusion of a confession that the accused may give during the delay while en route to the police station.*

If the circumstances do not justify continued detention and transportation to the police station, the accused may call from the location of the arrest.

RULE 5

Some time will elapse between the time after the right to counsel is invoked and before it is exercised. If the accused initiates conversation during this time, record the accused's remarks verbatim in your notebook. The police cannot initiate conversation or questioning during that time. However, if the accused initiates conversation and confesses or makes incriminating verbal statements, that evidence should likely be admissible.[179]

RULE 6

Do not limit the accused person to only one phone call.[180] Informing an accused that only one phone call will be allowed or limiting the accused to only one phone call constitutes a sec. 10(b) *Charter* violation, according to the Ontario Court of Appeal, in *R. v. Pavel (1989).* A reasonable opportunity to exercise the right to counsel does not limit the accused to any specific number of phone calls. Instead, the accused must be allowed to make reasonable attempts to contact a lawyer. It must be emphasized that a young offender's right to counsel includes the right to contact and speak to parents or other appropriate adults whom the young offender believes may provide assistance or give advice. Consequently, a young offender may require several phone calls to contact a lawyer, parents, or adults for the entire right to counsel to be exercised.

An adult's right to counsel guarantees the right to receive advice from a lawyer only. Section 10(b) *Charter* does not specifically include the right for an adult offender to contact other adults, such as parents or spouses. Consequently, a problem may arise when an offender who is 18 years old, or older, requests to call a parent, spouse, or other adult. The solution is to determine whether such a phone call is reasonably necessary in order to contact a lawyer. Most lawyers have answering services after business hours. Phone books and lists of lawyers' phone numbers are provided to an accused at most police stations. Therefore, the need to call another adult to help contact a lawyer usually would be unnecessary. Unnecessary phone calls to other adults have potential consequences, such as the destruction or loss of evidence. This consequence must be prevented to ensure a successful investigation.

RULE 7

Allow the accused to make phone calls and speak to a lawyer in private.[181] The right to counsel includes in it the right to privacy, according to case law decisions. Accused persons must be allowed to make phone calls and speak to lawyers in private, and do not have to ask for privacy; the right to privacy is automatically allowed. Therefore, officers cannot remain in a room when the accused makes phone calls or while an accused speaks to a lawyer in person, nor can the conversation be monitored or over-heard by any means. Any confessions or incriminating evidence obtained as the result of this privacy violation will likely be excluded.

RULE 8

After the accused person makes a phone call, determine the result of the phone call. The right to counsel is exercised only after the accused has spoken to and received advice from a lawyer. Then the officer is permitted to question the accused. In many cases, particularly after business hours, an accused person must leave a message with an answering service in order to contact a lawyer. A message left by the accused for a lawyer to call the police station *does not constitute* the exercising of the right.

When the accused makes a phone call, an officer will not be in the room and will not be listening to the conversation. Therefore, the officer must determine the result of the phone call in order to begin the questioning of the accused. The officer must obviously rely on the response of the accused. The accused may give the officer one of three responses:

- he or she spoke to a lawyer, or
- a message was left, or
- *no response*—the accused does not say whether a lawyer was spoken to.

If the accused says that he or she spoke to a lawyer, questioning may begin at this stage. If a message was left, the officer cannot initiate questioning while waiting for the lawyer to call. However, if the accused initiates the conversation and makes incriminating statements, record them.

The Nova Scotia Court of Appeal, in *R. v. MacKenzie (1991)*,[182] ruled that an accused's confessions to police while waiting for a lawyer to call after a message was left are admissible if the accused initiates the conversation. Although the accused's conviction was later overturned, the reasons were not related to this circumstance.

The Supreme Court of Canada, in *R. v. Hebert (1990)*,[183] stated that, "in the absence of eliciting behaviour on the part of the police, there is no violation of the accused's right to choose whether or not to speak to the police" if the accused initiates conversation and confesses.

If the accused makes no response and does not tell the officer whether or not a lawyer was spoken to, two questions, which are answered in case law, arise:

1. Does the officer have to ask the accused about the result of the phone call?
2. Does the accused have an onus to tell the officer that a message was left?

The British Columbia Court of Appeal, in *R. v. Ferron (1989)*,[184] ruled that *the police are not obliged* to "ask again and again" if the accused has spoken to a lawyer, after the accused makes phone calls. The Alberta Court of Appeal, in *R. v. Top (1989)*,[185] ruled that the *accused should inform the police* about the results of the phone calls, particularly if a message is left.

Consequently, if the accused makes no response after making a phone call, the officer may assume that the accused exercised the right and may question the accused.

In summary, if an accused person invokes his right to counsel, then exercises it by calling a lawyer and leaving a message, use the following procedure:

1. If the accused does not state that a message was left, question the accused.
2. If the accused states that a message was left

    a) do not initiate conversation with the accused; however,

    b) if the accused initiates conversation, allow him or her to continue.

RULE 9

If the accused is a young offender and he or she speaks to parents or other adults, allow an additional reasonable opportunity to call a lawyer.[186] The Supreme Court of Canada, in *R. v. T.(E.) (1993)*, stated that a parent is not an alternative to a lawyer. Consequently, a young offender who speaks to a parent or adult is entitled the additional right to speak with a lawyer. Do not prevent the right to counsel from being exercised because the young offender has received advice from a parent or adult.

Step 13

Interrogation is a crucial investigative technique that may yield substantial evidence.

ADULT OFFENDER

After an adult accused exercises the right to counsel by speaking to a lawyer, no rule prohibits the police from questioning the adult in the absence of counsel.[187] When a lawyer speaks to an accused, the advice likely will be to remain silent. The right to remain silent is a fundamental principle that is included in sec. 7 *Charter*.

However, the Supreme Court of Canada, in *R. v. Hebert (1990)*,[188] stated that no rule prohibits the police from questioning an accused adult in the absence of a lawyer, after the accused has spoken to the lawyer. The police must allow the accused an opportunity to decide whether to remain silent or not, but if the accused "volunteers information," then no *Charter* violation will have occurred.

Additionally, the police are permitted to persuade the accused to answer questions provided that the "police persuasion" does not "deny the suspect of the right to choose" to remain silent.

In summary, questioning is allowed after an accused adult speaks to a lawyer, if the accused chooses not to remain silent or volunteers information and initiates conversation.

YOUNG OFFENDER

After a young offender exercises the right to counsel, questioning is allowed, but the lawyer or adult whom the young offender consulted with must be present, unless the young offender waives this in writing.[189] Section 56 Y.O.A. creates the following rule: A young offender may be questioned after a lawyer or adult is consulted with, but the young offender decides who will be present during the questioning.

The young offender may have a lawyer, parent, or adult present, if he or she chooses. If the young offender chooses otherwise, the young offender must sign a written waiver. The police do not decide who will be present during a young offender's questioning.

Step 14

Choosing not to invoke the right to counsel means to decline an opportunity to call a lawyer. If an accused person chooses not to invoke the right to counsel after being informed of it, the *right to counsel is then waived*, and the investigation and questioning may continue immediately.[190] A waiver of the right to counsel means that the person relinquishes the sec. 10(b) *Charter* right to retain a lawyer and receive legal advice.

After a valid waiver has been made by an accused person, the police have no other obligations regarding the right to counsel and may question the accused person. The onus is on the prosecution to prove that the accused made a valid waiver of the right to counsel. The Supreme Court of Canada, in *R. v. Prosper (1994)*,[191] stated that the standard of proof required for a valid waiver must be "very high" and that "courts must ensure that the right to counsel is not too easily waived."

The elements that compose a valid waiver and that must be proven by the police are

1. The waiver must be clear and unequivocal. This means it must be unmistakable and not vague. The accused's words must specifically indicate that he or she does not want to call or speak with a lawyer. If any another inference may be made by the reader, reasonable doubt will exist about the waiver's validity.

2. The waiver must be voluntarily made. It must be free from inducements, meaning "direct or indirect compulsions," such as threats or promises that may force an accused to waive the right to counsel.
3. The accused must understand the entire nature of the right to counsel, referring to the meaning of all the components.
4. The accused must understand "what is being given up," which refers to legal advice.[192]

An officer's testimony relating to a waiver must be meticulous and include verbatim (direct quote) conversation that composed the waiver. A simple phrase such as "The accused waived his right to counsel" would be insufficient to prove a clear, unequivocal waiver. Consequently, the verbatim conversation should be recorded, rather than paraphrased in a notebook. A young offender's waiver must be in writing.[193] A verbal waiver is sufficient only regarding an adult offender's waiver.

Failure to prove any of the elements that compose a waiver constitutes a sec. 10(b) *Charter* violation.

WAIVER BY INTOXICATED PERSON

Accused persons at the time of an arrest are often intoxicated, posing a potential problem to the police if the accused waives the right. If an intoxicated accused person waives the right to counsel, the officer must prove that the accused was aware of the consequences of waiving the right.[194]

The Supreme Court of Canada, in *R. v. Clarkson (1986)*, stated that the prosecution has the onus of proving that an intoxicated accused person, who waives the right to counsel, was aware of the consequences of the waiver. Therefore, the officer must prove

1. the elements that compose the waiver, and
2. that the accused had knowledge that

   - legal advice will be given up, and
   - information obtained afterward, such as a confession, may be used as evidence at the trial.

The following procedure may fulfill this onus:

1. Read all the components of the right to counsel.
2. Ask the accused if each component is understood.
3. Record the response verbatim.
4. State additional explanation in ordinary language and record the explanation verbatim.
5. Ask if it is understood and record the response.
6. Ask the accused to explain the right to counsel to you and record it verbatim.
7. Record the waiver verbatim.
8. Explain that the consequences of the waiver are that legal advice will be given up and that evidence obtained may be used at the trial. Record the explanation verbatim.
9. Ask if it is understood. Record the response verbatim.
10. Ask the accused to explain the consequences of the waiver. Record the explanation verbatim.

Various degrees of intoxication exist, ranging from slight to moderate to advanced. Slightly or moderately intoxicated offenders are often coherent and may converse rationally, with an operating mind. Consequently, if the officer believes that the accused has understood all aspects of the waiver, questioning may occur immediately after.

If the intoxication is advanced, causing incoherence that prevents comprehension of the required elements, questioning should be delayed until the accused is sober. Then, the right to counsel procedure should be repeated at that time.

Step 15

If the accused person invokes the right to counsel, then changes his or her mind and waives it, inform the accused that a reasonable opportunity will be given to contact a lawyer.[195] The Supreme Court of Canada, in *R. v. Prosper (1994)*, created a mandatory obligation for police officers where an accused person initially invokes the right to counsel, changes his or her mind, and later waives the right. Under these circumstances, the police must inform the accused of the following:

1. the right to a reasonable opportunity to call a lawyer and
2. the police obligation to "hold off" questioning and their investigation during the reasonable opportunity.

Failure to inform an accused of both elements constitutes a sec. 10(b) *Charter* violation.

COMMENTARY

What impact does the right to counsel procedure have on an investigation? How will a sec. 10(b) *Charter* violation affect a confession from an accused person? Experience provides the best answer to these questions.

I learned that an investigation of a serious offence may be ruined by making a simple yet crucial mistake during the right-to-counsel procedure. I investigated a break, enter, and theft that occurred at a dwelling-house owned by the owner of a business, where $5000 cash and several thousands of dollars in payroll cheques, stored in a canvas bag, were stolen. Reasonable grounds were formed by means of an informant's statement that Eddie (20 years) had confessed to the informant that he had committed the offence.

I arrested Eddie at his house and I informed him of his right to counsel. En route to the police station, Eddie invoked his right to counsel. Eddie phoned his lawyer at the police station. The call concluded at 6:32 p.m. He informed me that he left a message on the lawyer's answering machine, instructing the lawyer to call the police station. Since he had not yet exercised the right to counsel, Eddie and I sat in silence in an interview room for five minutes. No conversation occurred during that time.

At 6:37 p.m., I had waited long enough for the lawyer to return the phone call, and I was concerned about recovering the complainant's stolen money. I decided to initiate a conversation by asking Eddie if he still had possession of the cheques. He made no response. I asked him if he cashed the payroll cheques. Eddie shook his head. "Did you destroy them?" I asked. He immediately confessed that he had thrown the cheques in the canal. Additionally, he confessed that he committed the break and enter, and explained in detail how he committed the offence.

The conversation easily led to a confession. Eddie was extremely cooperative. He made no denials, and made no attempt to lie. Eddie gave a written confession. All this started with a simple question, asking if he still had the cheques. Case closed. I wrote an arrest report, and I prepared to call the complainant to inform him that the investigation was solved.

At 7:05 p.m., Eddie's lawyer phoned the police station. Twenty-eight minutes had passed since Eddie left the message. Eddie talked to him. Too late, I thought. I got the confession that I needed. I did not subpoena the informant, to protect his identity. The confession was the only evidence in the case.

At the trial, I testified about the events and the verbatim conversation. The trial judge ruled that the confession was voluntarily made. However, the judge ruled that a sec. 10(b) *Charter* violation had occurred because I had initiated the conversation before Eddie exercised his right to counsel after he had invoked the right. Determining the admissibility of the confession under sec. 24(2) *Charter* was the next step. The judge excluded the confession, stating that the admission of the evidence would bring the administration of justice into disrepute. In his concluding remarks, the judge commended me on my "honesty and lack of malice" about testifying that I had initiated the conversation.[196]

If the confession had been admitted, the reputation of the criminal justice system would have suffered. That was the reason why the confession was excluded. The complainant was present in court and heard the evidence and the ruling. He was shocked.

What did I learn? Wait until the offender speaks to a lawyer and interrogate afterward. Do offenders confess after speaking to a lawyer? Yes, they do.

Problem-Solving Case Studies

You are a police officer in each case. Each offender is an adult, unless otherwise indicated.

PROBLEM 37

While investigating a "fraud over $5000.00" you obtain an eyewitness statement from Helen and a cheque that both implicate Bill. You arrest Bill after this evidence is obtained. You fail to properly inform Bill of the right to counsel. Afterward, Bill confesses, and you recover the property obtained by the fraud.

a) Will the right-to-counsel *Charter* violation result in exclusion of Helen's eyewitness observation or the cheque as evidence?

_____

_____

_____

b) Will the right-to-counsel *Charter* violation result in automatic exclusion of the confession or the property that had been obtained by fraud?

_____

_____

_____

c) Will the confession likely be admitted or excluded?

_____

_____

_____

PROBLEM 38

You arrive at a bar in response to a disturbance. Upon arrival, you are met by the victim, Doug. He and two other witnesses inform you that they saw Bill assault Doug with a weapon (baseball bat). They can identify Bill. You find Bill inside the bar and decide to arrest him.

a) Explain the procedure you would use to arrest Bill inside the bar and what information you will tell Bill at the scene of the arrest.

_____

_____

_____

_____

_____

_____

_____

_____

_____

_____

_____

_____

_____

_____

_____

_____

_____

_____

b) If Bill makes no decision after you inform him of the right to counsel, about invoking or declining the right, what can you assume? Can you question Bill?

_____

_____

c) If Bill is employed and can afford a lawyer, do you have to inform him of the existence and availability of legal aid?

_____

_____

PROBLEM 39

You are investigating a "theft under $5000.00." You suspect that Greg committed the offence. Greg voluntarily accompanies you to the police station for questioning. Do you have to inform of the right to counsel before questioning him?

_____

_____

PROBLEM 40

While on patrol, you stop Doug. A CPIC message reveals that a valid arrest warrant exists. You arrest him and transport him to the police station. What do you have to do to execute the arrest warrant?

_____

PROBLEM 41

You arrest Wally for one count of "break, enter, and theft" and one count of "robbery." Can you withhold the reasons for the arrest if you believe that telling him will affect your investigations?

PROBLEM 42

You arrest Ellen for "attempt murder." She invokes her right to counsel.

a) How much time must you provide her to exercise her right?

b) Can you limit Ellen to only one phone call?

c) Does Ellen have a right to phone other adults?

d) Ellen makes a phone call. She does not inform you of the result of the call. Can you continue the investigation and question her?

e) If Ellen tells you that she does not want to leave a message with her lawyer and wants to wait until business hours begin, can you continue the investigation and question her?

f) If Ellen initially invokes the right to counsel, then changes her mind, and waives it later, do you have to inform her of any information?

PROBLEM 43

You arrest Greg for "robbery." The arrest is made at his house right now. The offence occurred three days ago.

a) If you fail to "caution" him, will you have committed a *Charter* violation?

b) If you fail to caution him and he later confesses, will the confession be automatically excluded?

_____

_____

_____

c) What is the significance of the failure to caution Greg?

_____

_____

PROBLEM 44

You arrest Walter for sexual assault. You inform him of the right to counsel. He waives the right.

a) What does a waiver mean and represent?

_____

_____

b) Who has the onus to prove that Walter waived his right?

_____

c) How is a waiver proven to be valid?

_____

_____

_____

_____

_____

_____

_____

_____

d) Does the waiver in this case have to be in writing?

_____

e) After the waiver is made, do you have any additional obligations?

_____

_____

PROBLEM 45

You see Claire (16 years) driving a stolen car on King St. right now. You stop her and arrest her.

a) How do you inform Claire of the right to counsel?

_____

_____

_____

_____

b) If Claire invokes her right to counsel, whom may she contact?

_____

_____

_____

c) If Claire waives her right to counsel, how must the waiver be obtained?

_____

_____

d) Upon arrest at the police station, what procedure, created by sec. 9(1) of the Y.O.A., must you follow?

_____

_____

_____

_____

_____

PROBLEM 46

You arrest Rick (18 years) and Laura (17 years) right now at the scene of a break-in. Can you place both in custody together in the back of your police vehicle?

_____

_____

_____

PROBLEM 47

You are investigating a "mischief under $5000.00" complaint. You suspect that Drew (16 years) committed the offence. Drew voluntarily accompanies you for questioning. Do you have to inform him of the right to counsel?

_____

_____

_____

Test Yourself

1. You stop a car on King St. at 11:45 p.m. Ward (32) is the driver. You arrest him for impaired driving. Explain in detail all the steps and procedures, in chronological order, that you would use to make this arrest, including all the measures you would take to prevent the commission of *Charter* violations.

_____

_____

_____

_____

_____

_____

_____

_____

_____

_____

_____

_____

_____

_____

_____

_____

_____

_____

_____

_____

_____

_____

_____

_____

2. You arrest Wally (28) for theft under $5,000 right now. You inform him of his right to counsel. Explain in detail the relevant procedures to follow if he

   a) invokes his right to counsel, or
   b) waives his right to counsel.

_____

_____

Unit 2

Learning Outcomes

In this unit, the student will learn

- general rules of release and detention,
- specific rules and procedures that determine the end of an arrest,
- specific rules and procedures that justify continued detention,
- the types and contents of release/compelling documents,
- the principles of a bail hearing, and
- the procedures used to conduct a bail hearing

CHAPTER

SIX

Release/Detention

Learning Outcomes

The student will be able to

- interpret sec. 498-529 C.C.,
- identify circumstances when an arrested person must be released, and
- identify circumstances that justify continued detention.

INTRODUCTION

After a police officer arrests or detains an adult or young offender, the officer must determine

1. Whether to release the accused or continue detention.
2. The length of time of detention.
3. Whether or not to compel an accused to court.
4. What document to serve to compel a court appearance.

"Release" refers to the termination of arrest, detention, and custody. When an offender is released from custody, he or she has freedom restored. An arrested person cannot be held in custody arbitrarily. Specific rules and procedures found in Part XVI (sections 498–529) of the *Criminal Code* govern the length of detention or custody, and determine when an arrested person must be released. They apply to both adult and young offenders.

"Compelling" an adult or a young offender to court refers to ensuring that the offender appears in court. An offender who is compelled to court is forced to appear in court. Compelling a court appearance requires a decision that is closely related to the decision regarding the release of an offender, but the topics are separate. Compelling a court appearance requires the issuance of a document. In some cases, these documents may also coincide with the release of the offender. Several documents are available for the police to use.

In this unit of the textbook, students will learn how to interpret and apply the laws relating to release and compelling an accused person's court appearance.

RELEASE—GENERAL RULES

Part XVI of the *Criminal Code* lists four factors that determine the release or justified continued detention of an adult or young offender. These factors apply anywhere in Canada because the *Criminal Code* is a federal statute.

1. **r**epetition of the offence (the offender was arrested for) or any other offence,
2. **i**dentity of the arrested person,
3. **c**ourt appearance, and
4. **e**vidence relating to the offence.

RICE is an acronym that may be used informally to help you learn and remember these four factors. Each letter in RICE represents one factor that determines the release or the justified continued detention of an arrested person. RICE is an informal term not used in the *Criminal Code*. These factors are circumstances that must be used to determine whether an arrested adult or young offender must be released or if continued detention and custody of the arrested person is necessary in the public interest.[1]

RICE FULFILLED

This is an informal term that represents the existence of cumulative circumstances that fulfill the requirements of mandatory release. The fulfillment of these four factors does not make continued detention and custody of an arrested person necessary in the public interest. Specifically, RICE fulfilled means that all of the following circumstances exist:

1. no reasonable grounds of repetition of any offence will occur,
2. correct identity of the accused has been established,
3. no reasonable grounds that the accused will fail to appear in court, and
4. evidence regarding the offence (arrested for) has been secured or preserved.

Consequently, the following general rule is established:
When RICE is fulfilled, detention must end, and the arrested person must be released from custody. Continued detention is not justified.

RICE NOT FULFILLED

This is an informal term that refers to circumstances that justify the necessity (in the public interest) of continued detention and custody of an arrested person.

Specifically, it means that at least one of the following circumstances exists:

1. reasonable grounds exist that offence repetition will occur,
2. accused's identity has not been properly established,
3. reasonable grounds exist that the accused will fail to appear in court, and
4. evidence relating to the offence exists and has not been secured or preserved.

The existence of at least one of these circumstances means that the release of an arrested person is not beneficial to the public interest. Continued custody is necessary in the public interest.

Consequently, the following general rule is established:
When RICE is not fulfilled, continued detention is justified, and the accused does not have to be released.

Problem-Solving Case Studies

You are a police officer in each case. Each offender is an adult, unless otherwise indicated.

PROBLEM 48

You arrest Greg for "fraud under $5000.00." Generally, how long can you continue to detain him?

_____

_____

PROBLEM 49

You arrest Helen for "cause a disturbance." Generally, when must this arrest or detention end and when must Helen be released?

_____

_____

DETERMINING RICE FULFILLMENT—PROCEDURE

The *Criminal Code* does not explain the specific type of evidence needed to prove whether RICE is or is not fulfilled. Consequently, investigative techniques must be used to obtain evidence or information relevant to the RICE factors while using the definition of reasonable grounds.

The presence or absence of the following evidence may determine the fulfillment or nonfulfillment of each RICE element.

REPETITION

Examples include

- verbal statements made to the police or any citizen indicating the intent to commit the same offence again or another offence,
- accused's physical or mental condition, including intoxication and hostility,
- past record of criminal convictions, violent acts, psychological disorders, narcotic dependency,
- financial means of support, and

- accused's arrest for recently committed single or multiple offences.

    The absence of this evidence may prove that this RICE element is fulfilled.

IDENTITY

Examples include

- official documents such as birth certificate, driver's licence
- verification by family members or persons familiar with the accused, including officers who are (usually) familiar with many offenders.

Failure or refusal to identify proves RICE is not fulfilled. An accused cannot be released if his or her identity is unknown, because an information and release document requires the accused's name. A refusal to identify does not constitute an offence; the offender cannot be charged with "refusing to identify." Instead, the refusal represents justification to continue detention.

Also, intentional wrong identification constitutes the indictable offence of "obstruct justice" because the accused may evade prosecution while an innocent person is implicated.

COURT APPEARANCE

Examples include

- past record of failure to attend court,
- severity of the offence,
- factors that may bind a person to the community, or motivate an accused to move away from the territorial jurisdiction where he or she was arrested, including, for example, the presence or absence of

    a) fixed address,
    b) employment, means of income,
    c) family, and
    d) ownership of property and assets.

When determining whether an accused will attend court or fail to appear by possibly leaving the area, this question should be asked, "Will the severity of the offence and its consequence be sufficient to cause the accused to leave his or her current status within the community?" The severity of the offence must be analyzed in conjunction with what the accused would be leaving behind.

EVIDENCE

For example:

- loss or destruction of evidence if accused is released

This element does not allow the police to detain a person while attempting to obtain evidence. Sufficient evidence should have existed prior to the arrest to have constituted reasonable grounds. Essentially, the *Criminal Code* is asking, "Will the accused remove or destroy existing evidence if he or she is released?" Therefore, to use this factor to justify continued detention, the officer must reasonably believe that evidence does exist that requires securing and preservation after the accused has been arrested.

In summary, the police have a twofold obligation:

1. If the absence of evidence proves RICE is fulfilled, the accused generally must be released because continued detention is not justified.
2. Conversely, if the presence of evidence proves RICE is not fulfilled, the officer has an obligation to protect the public by not releasing the accused. Continued detention is justified when the public is threatened or at risk by the accused's release.

TO SUMMARIZE

RICE fulfillment is a fluctuating concept, meaning that the status of RICE changes and is not always constant. The RICE elements must be analyzed at each level of release to determine if any changes have occurred.

Problem-Solving Case Studies

You are a police officer in each case. Each offender is an adult, unless otherwise indicated.

PROBLEM 50

You attend at a business premises in response to a shoplifting complaint. Upon arrival, a security guard has custody of Ward, who committed "theft under $5000.00" by stealing a $15.00 cassette tape. Ward is married, has two sons, lives in the same city where the arrest was made, is employed full-time, and has no criminal record. The cassette tape is recovered. The security guard provides an eyewitness written statement. Ward identifies himself correctly by means of a driver's licence with a photograph. Is RICE fulfilled?

_____

_____

_____

_____

PROBLEM 51

You arrest Eddie for "impaired driving"; he is intoxicated. Eddie has no criminal record and lives with his parents in the same city where the arrest is made. He has a full-time job and is a part-time student. Eddie properly identifies himself. Is RICE fulfilled?

_____

_____

_____

PROBLEM 52

You attend at a bar regarding a disturbance. Wally is found intoxicated and is shouting obscenities at Eddie. Wally is hostile and aggressive toward Eddie. You arrest Wally for "cause a disturbance." Is RICE fulfilled?

_____

_____

_____

PROBLEM 53

You arrest Eddie for "theft under $5000.00." Eddie has no means of support and has no fixed address. Is RICE fulfilled?

_____

_____

PROBLEM 54

You arrest a person for "attempt break and enter" at a house. The offender has no identification documents and refuses to identify himself. Is RICE fulfilled?

_____

_____

_____

_____

LEVELS OF RELEASE/DETENTION

The *Criminal Code* essentially creates three levels, or stages, of release where release provisions must be analyzed to determine whether an accused must be released or detained in custody until the next level. Each level includes a general location and person who must consider the release provisions and make a decision.
The following table demonstrates the tri-level concept.

Although the term "level of release" is not used in the *Criminal Code* i.e., the terms Level 1, Level 2, and Level 3 are not *Criminal Code* terms, they are used in this textbook for teaching reasons and to facilitate interpretation of the relevant *Criminal Code* provisions.

TABLE 6.1

LEVELS OF RELEASE/DETENTION

Level	Location	Person
1	• at scene of arrest (before arrival at police station)	• peace officer[2] (refers to arresting officer)
2	• at the police station	• officer-in-charge[3] (refers to a supervisor, such as a staff sergeant), or any peace officer (new amendment that now includes any police officer who is not a supervisor, e.g., a constable
3	• at bail hearing	• justice[4] (refers to a justice of the peace [JP] or a provincial court judge)

RELEASE DOCUMENTS—COMPELLING COURT APPEARANCE

After a person is arrested, the police have two decisions to make:

* whether or not to charge and compel the offender to court, or
* whether to release the offender or continue detention.

DECIDING WHETHER TO CHARGE AND COMPEL A COURT APPEARANCE

Officers may use discretion to decide whether to

1. Charge the offender and compel him or her to court. This method requires two separate procedures:

   a) laying an information, and

    b) compelling the accused to court, which means forcing the accused to attend court and answer to the charge, giving the accused no choice or option.

2. Not charge the offender and use an alternative means other than court to solve the problem. This method is referred to as an unconditional release. It represents a "warning or break" given to the offender. "Unconditional" means that the condition of attending court in answer to a charge will not be imposed on the offender. The success of this method largely depends on the officer's communication skills to solve the problem without a court proceeding.

The prominent factor to consider when deciding which problem-solving method will be used is the *elimination of the worst consequence,* such as a risk or threat to the public (including death, injury, or property damage) that may occur if the offence is repeated in the future.

Test Yourself

1. You attend at a business regarding a shoplifting complaint. Upon arrival, a security guard had custody of Eddie (24), who stole a $30 CD.

Explain in detail everything you will ask him and what information you will determine in order to decide whether to release or detain him.

2. You stop a car on Main St. The driver, Wally (29), is drunk. You arrest him for impaired driving. He identifies himself, lives in the same city where he has been arrested, and is employed as a teacher. He has no criminal record. Explain in detail what additional information you will attempt to elicit, what action you will take relating to custody, and how you will decided whether to detain or release him.

_____

_____

_____

_____

_____

_____

_____

_____

_____

_____

_____

_____

_____

_____

_____

_____

_____

_____

_____

_____

_____

_____

_____

_____

_____

_____

SEVEN

*Release/Compelling
Documents*

Learning Outcomes

The student will be able to

- complete a release document, and
- identify which release document applies in a specific set of circumstances.

DECISION TO COMPEL A COURT APPEARANCE

If a decision is made to charge the offender, two documents are necessary:

1. a sworn information, to formally charge the offender, and
2. a release/compelling document, to force the offender to appear in court.

A sworn information represents the formal charge and is a separate document that accompanies the release/compelling document. The procedure used to charge an offender is explained in Unit Three of this textbook.

A *release/compelling document* is a written order that directs an accused to appear at a specific court location on a specific date and time. The release/compelling document does not formally charge the accused. Numerous types of release/compelling documents exist. They are found in Part XXVIII, sec. 841 *Criminal Code*. The types of documents include

- summons (form 6),
- appearance notice (form 9),
- promise to appear (form 10),
- recognizance—officer-in-charge (form 11),
- recognizance—justice (form 32),
- undertaking—justice (form 12), and
- undertaking—peace officer or officer-in-charge (Form 11.1). This type of undertaking must be used in conjunction with a promise to appear or a recognizance by an officer-in-charge. It is not a compelling document if used alone.

Most release/compelling documents are served to the accused upon release, except a summons, which may be served either after release or in lieu of arresting the offender.

CONTENTS OF A RELEASE/COMPELLING DOCUMENT

All release/compelling documents have the same purpose and have the *same contents*. They must instruct a specific accused person to appear at a specific court location on a scheduled date at a scheduled time.

The following information must appear on all release/compelling documents:

1. name of accused, name of offence, and date, time, and location/address of the court appearance.[5]

A date, time, and location for the accused to appear to be fingerprinted and photographed is optional. The police are permitted to take fingerprints and photographs of an offender after he or she is arrested or charged for an indictable or dual procedure offence. Depending on the availability of officers, offenders may be fingerprinted or photographed before release. If these procedures cannot be completed prior to release, the accused may be compelled to attend at a police station on a specified date and time, for the purpose of fingerprinting and photographs.[6] This information may be included on the release document. Failure to appear in court is a dual procedure offence. Failure to appear for fingerprints and photographs constitutes a different dual procedure offence.[7]

A "recognizance" and "undertaking" may have additional requirements. A recognizance (officer-in-charge) may be accompanied by a money deposit not exceeding $500.00 if the accused lives outside the province or beyond 200 km from the place where the accused was arrested and is in custody.[8] A justice may direct any sum of money as a deposit if the accused lives out of province or beyond 200 km from the place of arrest.

An undertaking (peace officer, officer-in-charge, or justice) and recognizance (justice) may also include conditions. Regardless of whether the undertaking is with or without conditions, it is named an "undertaking" and refers to only one document.[9]

SEQUENCE OF ISSUANCE—SWORN INFORMATION AND RELEASE/COMPELLING DOCUMENT

A sworn information must accompany a release/compelling document to complete the process of compelling an accused to court. The order of issuance is significant. When a justice is not required to release, an officer may release and is permitted to serve some release/compelling documents before an information is laid. This expedites the accused's release because a justice may not always be available when a release is justified.

However, other release/compelling documents, such as those required to be issued by a justice, must be served after an information is laid. The following table explains the order of issuance regarding sworn information and release/compelling documents:

TABLE 7.1

ORDER OF ISSUANCE

INFORMATION laid first	RELEASE document issued
Release document follows	Information laid afterward
• summons	• appearance notice
• undertaking (justice)	• promise to appear
• recognizance (justice)	• recognizance (officer-in-charge)
	• undertaking (peace officer or officer-in-charge; used in conjunction with PTA or recognizance)
These documents are served after an information is laid. They cannot be served before an information is laid.	These documents may be served before an information is laid. Once the documents served, an information must be laid as soon as practicable afterward.[10]

UNCONDITIONAL RELEASE

As explained in the previous section of this text, an officer may choose to "solve the problem" by granting an unconditional release. No document is given to the accused that signifies or explains an unconditional release. The releasing officer simply releases and explains it verbally. An unconditional release is not a binding, formal agreement, and it gives the offender no formal legal assurance that a charge will never be laid. The officer may still charge the offender after an unconditional release. Therefore, an unconditional release does not prohibit a police officer from changing his or her mind and charging the offender.

NOTICE TO PARENT—YOUNG OFFENDERS

Upon release of a young offender, the police have a mandatory obligation to give a notice to parent in writing, which must include the charge(s) and the court date, location, and time.[11]

If the parents' whereabouts are unknown, the notice may be given to an adult relative or, if none is available, to an appropriate adult who is known to the young offender and who is likely to assist him or her. If the young offender is married, the notice may be served to the spouse.[12]

A notice to parent must also be made as soon as possible after the arrest of a young offender. This notice may be made verbally or in writing by the officer-in-charge of the police station or another officer instructed by the officer-in-charge. The first notice must inform the parent of the place of detention and reason(s) for the arrest. This first notice will suffice when a young offender is released unconditionally.[13]

Test Yourself

1. Circle the correct answer relating to when the information has to be laid, corresponding with the release/compelling document.

Document	Information	
Undertaking (Justice)	Before	After
Promise to appear	Before	After
Recognizance (OIC)	Before	After
Appearance notice	Before	After
Summons	Before	After
Undertaking (peace officer/OIC)	Before	After
Recognizance (justice)	Before	After

a) What is the purpose of a release/compelling document?

_____

_____

_____

_____

_____

_____

_____

_____

_____

b) What content must appear on all compelling/release documents?

_____

_____

_____

_____

_____

_____

_____

_____

_____

CHAPTER

EIGHT

Level 1 Release

Learning Outcomes

The student will be able to

- interpret and apply Section 497 of the *Criminal Code.*

INTRODUCTION

The *Criminal Code* explains specific circumstances where the release of an accused person is mandatory at each of the three levels of release. The determining circumstances include RICE fulfillment and the classification of the offence. Each level of release has specific methods of release, including relevant documents that may be issued by the releasing person. Conversely, the justification for continued detention is created by circumstances not included in those that require mandatory release. These release provisions were amended by *Bill C-42*, which became law on April 1, 1995.

PROCEDURES AND RULES

"Level 1" is an informal term that refers to the first stage of release considerations as established in sec. 497 *Criminal Code*. The term Level 1 is not actually used in the *Criminal Code*; it is used to informally distinguish this stage from the other levels that are created by the *Criminal Code*.

Level 1 release refers to the scene of the arrest and applies to the interval between the time of arrest and the time of arrival at the police station. The decision at this level is made by the arresting officer.

MANDATORY RELEASE

The arresting officer must release without a warrant at the scene of the arrest (before arrival at the police station) if

1. RICE is fulfilled, and
2. the offence is either

   • summary conviction, or
   • dual procedure.[14]

Release is mandatory when these circumstances exist, meaning that the officer is not justified in transporting the accused to the police station.

METHODS OF RELEASE

The arresting officer may use any of the following methods of release Level 1 when release is mandatory:

Appearance notice

Issued to the offender at the scene, before an information is laid.[15] The information must be laid as soon as practicable after the issuance of the appearance notice.[16] The accused must sign the appearance notice, to assure his or her appearance in court. Refusal to sign means that RICE is unfulfilled because of the failure to assure the court appearance.

The intention of serving a summons at a later time after release[17]

A summons cannot be served at the time of release because an information must be laid first. The offender is released without a document served to him or her. Afterward, the officer must appear before a justice, lay an information, and have a summons issued. Therefore, the summons is served some time after the actual release.

Unconditionally[18]

Referring to no intention to charge or compel the arrested person to court. No document is served. The unconditional release is simply recorded on the arrest report and in the officer's notebook. The arresting officer, at the scene, cannot serve any other release/compelling documents such as a promise to appear, recognizance, or undertaking.

This *mandatory rule* applies when the entire status of RICE is not known before the arrest is made but is determined at the scene, shortly after the arrest is made. When RICE is fulfilled at the scene regarding summary conviction and dual procedure offences, the officer is not justified in continuing detention by transporting the accused to the police station.

Note: During an investigation, and before an arrest is made, if the officer determines that RICE is fulfilled regarding a summary conviction or dual procedure offence, the arrest cannot be made. Instead, the officer may serve only an appearance notice or a summons to the accused person.[19]

JUSTIFIED CONTINUED CUSTODY

The arresting officer is justified in continuing custody of an accused by bringing the accused to the police station (Level 2), if

- the offence is purely indictable, regardless of RICE fulfillment, or
- the offence is summary conviction or dual procedure and RICE is not fulfilled, or
- the arrest is made with a warrant, regardless if it is endorsed or unendorsed. As explained in Unit One, a justice may endorse an arrest warrant, which authorizes release from the police station (Level 2) only. An endorsed warrant does not authorize release at the scene (Level 1).

Problem-Solving Case Studies

You are a police officer in each case. Each offender is an adult, unless otherwise indicated.

PROBLEM 55

You arrest Eddie at a department store for "theft under $5000.00." You determine that RICE is fulfilled.

a) Do you have to release?

_____

b) Can you serve an appearance notice to Eddie at the scene, before an information is laid?

_____

c) Can you serve a summons to Eddie at the scene, before an information is laid?

_____

d) Can you release Eddie with the intention of serving him with a summons?

_____

_____

_____

e) Can you release Eddie unconditionally?

_____

f) Can you serve Eddie with the following documents at the scene?
  • promise to appear?

_____

_____

  • recognizance?

_____

  • undertaking?

_____

Can you bring Eddie to the police station?

_____

PROBLEM 56

You arrest Eddie for "theft under $5000.00" and release him with the intention of serving him with a summons. After the summons is issued, how can it be served?[20]

_____

_____

_____

_____

_____

_____

_____

PROBLEM 57

You serve a summons to Eddie. How can you prove that the summons was served, if Eddie fails to appear in court?[21]

_____

_____

_____

_____

_____

PROBLEM 58

You arrest Eddie for "trespass by night." RICE is fulfilled.

a) Do you have to release?

_____

b) Can you bring Eddie to the police station?

_____

PROBLEM 59

You arrest Wally for "robbery" on King Street. Can you automatically bring him to the police station?

_____

_____

PROBLEM 60

You arrest Wally for "assault" at a bar. RICE is not fulfilled. Can you bring him to a police station?

_____

PROBLEM 61

You arrest Ward on Niagara St. regarding a warrant for "fraud under $5000.00." The warrant is endorsed by the justice for release.

a) Can you release?

_____

b) Can you automatically bring Ward to the police station?

_____

PROBLEM 62

You arrest June on Parkdale Ave. for "theft under $5000.00." You complete an appearance notice because RICE is fulfilled. June refuses to sign the appearance notice and states that she will not attend court. Can you bring her to the police station?

_____

_____

_____

Test Yourself

1. You arrest Ward (33) in the parking lot of a bar on Barton St. for "cause a disturbance." Explain

   • the release provisions that you have to consider in this case, and
   • how you will decide whether to release or detain.

_____

_____

_____

_____

_____

_____

_____

_____

_____

_____

_____

_____

_____

_____

_____

_____

_____

_____

_____

_____

_____

_____

_____

_____

_____

_____

_____

2. You arrest June (31) for fraud under $5,000.00 that was committed eight days ago when she bought a $2,000 TV with an NSF cheque. Explain

   • the release provisions you have to consider; and
   • how you will decide whether to release or detain.

_____

_____

_____

_____

_____

CHAPTER

NINE

Level 2 Release

Learning Outcomes

The student will be able to

- interpret and apply sec. 494 C.C. (citizen's powers of arrest).

INTRODUCTION

Level 2 release consideration begins with the accused person's arrival at the police station. In 1995, *Bill C-42* created significant changes regarding this level of release. Before April 1, 1995, the officer-in-charge (OIC) was the only officer who could release a person at the police station. The OIC is defined as "the officer for the time being in command of the police force responsible for the lock-up or other place to which an accused is taken after arrest," or "a peace officer designated by the OIC, who is in charge of that place at the time an accused is taken to that place to be detained in custody."[22] Essentially, the OIC is often the staff sergeant or sergeant who is the supervisor of the on-duty shift or platoon of officers. Additionally, before *Bill C-42*, an undertaking could not be used as a release document by the OIC at this level.

Now, any police officer or OIC may release at the police station, and an undertaking may be used as the release document in conjunction with a promise to appear or a recognizance.

PROCEDURES AND RULES

MANDATORY RELEASE—SECTION 498 C.C.

The OIC must release a person who has been taken to the police station if

1. the arrest was made without a warrant, and
2. RICE is fulfilled, and
3. the offence is

   - summary conviction, or
   - dual procedure, or
   - indictable with a maximum penalty of five years or less, and committed in the same province as the arrest.[23]

The OIC has *no discretion* about continuing detention if these conditions exist; release is mandatory. The accused must be released and cannot be detained or brought to a justice for a bail hearing (Level 3).

METHODS OF RELEASE

When an accused person must be released from custody at the police station, the following methods and release/compelling documents may be used:

1. With the intention of serving a summons at a later date after an information is sworn. No document is served at the time of release when this method is used; the accused is verbally informed of the intention to serve a summons later.[24]
2. A promise to appear (PTA).[25] A PTA may be issued to the accused person at the police station, at the time of release. A PTA is served before the accused is actually charged.
3. Recognizance. The OIC may direct the accused to deposit a sum of money up to $500.00 if the accused lives outside the province where he or she is arrested or beyond 200 km from the place of custody.[26]
4. Unconditionally.[27] This means that the accused is released without the condition of attending court being imposed. Essentially, the officer has used his or her discretion and has decided not to charge the offender. No document is served to the accused to signify this form of release; the offender is verbally informed. However, unconditional release does not prevent the police from charging the offender at a later time. The police may decide later to charge the offender and swear an information. In other words, an unconditional release is not a binding agreement or contract that promises the accused immunity from charges.

   The following means of release cannot be used at the police station:

   - appearance notice,
   - summons, when the arrest is made with a warrant. A summons may be issued only instead of a warrant, or

- unconditionally, when the arrest is made with a warrant. If a warrant exists, an information has already been laid. Only the Crown attorney may withdraw an information.

DISCRETIONARY RELEASE—SECTION 499 C.C.

The OIC may release a person who has been taken to the police station if

1. the arrest was made with a warrant, and
2. the offence is summary conviction, dual procedure, or indictable, other than a sec. 469 C.C. offence such as murder, and
3. the warrant has been endorsed by a justice, authorizing the release of the accused.[28]

METHODS OF RELEASE

Release may be made by serving

1. promise to appear,[29] or
2. recognizance.[30]

Additionally, the officer-in-charge may require that the accused enter into an undertaking in which the accused agrees to any or all of the following conditions that the OIC decides to impose, in conjunction with a promise to appear or a recognizance:

1. remain within a specific territorial jurisdiction,
2. notify a peace officer of any change in

   - address, or
   - employment, or
   - occupation

3. abstain from

   - communicating with any witness or any other person named in the undertaking, or
   - going to a place named in the undertaking, except in accordance with conditions specified in the undertaking

4. deposit the accused's passport with the peace officer or other person specified in the undertaking,
5. abstain from possessing a firearm and surrender any firearm in the possession of the person and any authorization, licence or registration certificate, or other document enabling that person to acquire or possess a firearm,
6. report at specified times to a peace officer or other person designated in the undertaking,
7. abstain from the consumption of

   - alcohol or other intoxicating substances, and/or
   - drugs, except in accordance with a medical prescription.[31]

The accused person cannot be forced to agree to any condition imposed but, if the accused fails to agree and fails to sign the undertaking, the accused may be detained to be brought before a justice for a bail hearing.

An undertaking with conditions may be given to an accused only in conjunction with a promise to appear or recognizance. It cannot be issued alone.

"Breach of undertaking," by failing to comply with any condition of this type of undertaking, is a dual procedure offence, under sec. 145(5) C.C.[32]

This undertaking procedure is optional, not mandatory.

DISCRETIONARY RELEASE—SECTIONS 503(2) AND (2.1) C.C.

Any police officer or the OIC may release an accused person who has been taken to a police station if

1. the arrest was made

   - without a warrant, or
   - with a warrant, regardless of whether the warrant is endorsed, and

2. the offence is summary conviction, dual procedure, or indictable, other than a sec. 469 C.C. offence, such as murder.

Sections 503(2) and (2.1) allow any peace officer to release an arrested person by means of a PTA, recognizance, or undertaking with the same conditions listed above.

METHODS OF RELEASE

Any of the following

1. with the intention of serving a summons at a later date, after an information is served (without a warrant only),
2. unconditionally (without a warrant only),
3. promise to appear (with or without warrant), or
4. recognizance (with or without warrant).

An undertaking, with any or all of the same conditions as allowed by sec. 499 C.C., may be given to an accused in conjunction with a promise to appear or recognizance.

Although this provision gives discretion about release, sec. 498 C.C. (mandatory release) must be remembered—if the offence is summary conviction, dual procedure, or indictable with a maximum penalty of five years or less and the arrest is made without a warrant, then release is mandatory if RICE is fulfilled. This new provision actually serves the following purposes:

1. It increases the number of officers who may release. Instead of only the OIC, now any police officer (including the arresting officer) may release from the police station (Level 2).
2. It expands the number of offences for which the accused may be released, including persons arrested for indictable offences with a maximum penalty of over five years, other than sec. 469 C.C. offences, such as murder. Previously, it was mandatory that these offenders be brought before a justice for a bail hearing in order to determine release. The release should occur only if RICE is fulfilled, to protect the public.

Persons arrested for any unendorsed warrant, other than a sec. 469 C.C. offence, may be released instead of being brought before a justice for a bail hearing, if RICE is fulfilled. Essentially, this discretionary provision expedites the release of offenders when RICE is fulfilled, prevents unwarranted, time-consuming bail hearings, and prevents unjustified or unreasonable detention of an accused person. The apparent intent of facilitating the release of an offender who poses no risk to the public (RICE is fulfilled) is to preserve the presumption of innocence of every arrested person.

JUSTIFIED CONTINUED CUSTODY

The OIC is justified in continuing detention of the accused and bringing him or her to a justice for a bail hearing (Level 3) if

1. The offence is indictable with a maximum penalty of over five years and the arrest is made without a warrant, or with an endorsed warrant, regardless of whether RICE is fulfilled.
2. The offence is summary conviction, dual procedure, or indictable with a maximum penalty of five years or less, and

   a) the arrest was made without a warrant, and
   b) RICE is not fulfilled.

3. The arrest was made with an unendorsed warrant, for any type of offence.
4. The offence is a sec. 469 C.C. offence, such as murder.

TABLE 9.1

RELEASE/DETENTION CHARTS, LEVEL 1

Level 1

Accused must be released

- at the scene of arrest
- by the arresting officer

1. If arrested without a warrant for

- summary conviction, or
- dual procedure and RICE is fulfilled

Method

- appearance notice
- summons
- unconditional release

Level 1

Accused must be brought

- to the police station

1. If arrested without a warrant for

- summary conviction, or
- dual procedure and RICE is not fulfilled

2. If arrested without a warrant for

- indictable

3. If arrested with a warrant

RELEASE/DETENTION CHARTS, LEVEL 2

Level 2

Accused **must** be released

- at the police station
- by the OIC or any police officer

If arrested without a warrant for

- summary conviction

Method

- summons
- unconditional release
- promise to appear
- recognizance

Level 2

Accused **may** be released

- at the police station
- by the OIC or any police officer

If arrested

1. without a warrant for any offence except a sec. 469 offence

2. with a warrant (endorsed or unendorsed) for any offence except a sec. 469 offence. and **RICE is fulfilled**

Method

- promise to appear
- recognizance

Level 2

Justified detention

Accused **may** be brought to a JP for a bail hearing

If arrested

1. without a warrant for:

- summary conviction
- dual procedure
- indictable (5 years or less)

and **RICE is not fulfilled**

2. Indictable (over 5 years)

3. with an unendorsed warrant

4. for a sec. 469 C.C. offence

* undertaking may accompany PTA or recognizance

Problem-Solving Case Studies

Each offender is an adult, unless otherwise indicated.

PROBLEM 63

Eddie is arrested for "cause a disturbance" and is taken to the police station. RICE becomes fulfilled two hours later.

a) Does Eddie have to be released?

b) Who may release Eddie?

_____

c) What documents may be used to release Eddie?

_____

_____

_____

_____

_____

d) Can an appearance notice be used to release from the police station?

_____

e) Can Eddie be released unconditionally after he has been taken to the police station?

_____

f) If RICE is fulfilled, can Eddie be detained and brought before a justice for a bail hearing?

_____

_____

PROBLEM 64

Ward is arrested for "theft under $5000.00" and is taken to a police station. RICE becomes fulfilled one hour later.

a) Does Ward have to be released?

_____

b) Can Ward be detained and brought before a justice for a bail hearing?

_____

c) Who may release?

_____

_____

PROBLEM 65

Wally is arrested for "robbery" and is taken to the police station.

a) Can Wally be detained and be brought before a justice for a bail hearing?

_____

_____

b) Is it possible for Wally to be released at the police station by the OIC or any other police officer, before being brought to a justice?

_____

_____

c) Can Wally be released by means of an appearance notice?

_____

d) Can Wally be released by means of a promise to appear?

_____

e) Can Wally be released by means of a recognizance with a $500.00 deposit?

_____

_____

f) Can the OIC or any police officer release Wally by means of an undertaking with conditions, without bringing him before a justice for a bail hearing?

_____

_____

_____

_____

g) Can the OIC or any police officer impose conditions on an undertaking, in conjunction with a promise to appear, prohibiting Wally from communicating with Eddie (a known offender) and prohibiting Wally from attending Eddie's house?

_____

_____

_____

h) Can the OIC or any police officer impose a condition of a curfew, requiring Wally to be inside a specific place between specified hours?

_____

_____

PROBLEM 66

June is arrested with an endorsed warrant for "fraud over $5000.00" and is taken to a police station.

a) Can she be released at the police station, before being taken to a justice for a bail hearing?

_____

_____

_____

b) Can the accused be automatically brought before a justice for a bail hearing?

_____

_____

_____

PROBLEM 67

Ward is arrested with an unendorsed warrant for "break, enter, and theft," and is taken to a police station.

a) Can Ward be released at the police station, before being taken to a justice for a bail hearing?

_____

_____

_____

_____

b) Can Ward be automatically brought before a justice for a bail hearing?

_____

_____

_____

PROBLEM 68

Ward is arrested for "first or second degree murder" and is taken to the police station. Can he be automatically brought before a justice?

_____

PROBLEM 69

Eddie is under arrest at the police station. The OIC prepares to release him on a promise to appear. Eddie refuses to sign it. What can the OIC do?

_____

_____

_____

_____

PROBLEM 70

Wally is under arrest at the police station, for "theft over $5000.00." A patrol officer decides to release him by means of a promise to appear and an undertaking with the condition that Wally not communicate with Eddie (a known offender). Wally refuses to agree to this condition and refuses to sign the undertaking. What can the officer do?

_____

_____

PROBLEM 71

Ward is under arrest at the police station, for "assault." The OIC decides to release Ward with conditions. Is an undertaking with conditions the only document given to the accused?

Test Yourself

1. You respond to an alarm at a business at 2:15 a.m. You find Eddie (18) and Wally (17) inside the building. They forced entry, but had no time to steal anything. Explain

   a) the release provisions that you need to consider, and
   b) how you will decide about release or detention.

_____
_____
_____
_____
_____
_____
_____
_____
_____
_____
_____
_____
_____
_____
_____

2. You arrest Eddie (28) today for assault causing bodily harm that was committed two days ago. The victim, Wally, is still hospitalized. Eddie lives in the same city where the offence occurred, is unemployed, and has two convictions two years ago for assault. Explain

   a) the release provisions you must consider, and
   b) which you will choose.

_____
_____
_____
_____
_____
_____
_____
_____
_____
_____
_____

CHAPTER TEN

Level 3 Bail Hearing

Learning Outcomes

The student will be able to

- interpret and apply sec. 515 of the C.C, and
- apply bail hearing procedures.

INTRODUCTION

Bail hearings are the third and final level of release. The person who is responsible for this level of release and who conducts the bail hearing is a justice, defined in sec. 2 C.C. as a justice of the peace or a provincial court judge. The rules for bail hearings are found in sec. 515 C.C. These rules apply to both adult and young offenders; however, the *Young Offender's Act* (Y.O.A.) imposes additional rules.

The term "bail hearing" is not used in sec. 515 C.C. It is an informal term commonly used within the criminal justice system. The *Criminal Code* lists sec. 515 as *judicial interim release*, which means the release or detention of an accused by a justice during the time interval between the arrest and the trial.

A bail hearing is also called a "show cause hearing." "Show cause" means to show reasons why the accused should be detained or released.

PURPOSE OF A BAIL HEARING

A bail hearing has a single purpose—to determine whether the accused person should be released or detained in custody until the trial. The purpose is not to determine

* guilt or innocence, or
* whether sufficient evidence exists to have a trial.

The accused is permitted to plead guilty at his or her appearance before a justice, which thus removes the obligation to conduct a bail hearing, because no trial will be conducted. The justice will then determine whether the accused will be released or detained in custody until a sentencing date, if sentencing is scheduled for a future date.[33] A guilty plea must not be confused with determining guilt or innocence. If a bail hearing is conducted because the accused does not plead guilty, a justice cannot convict or acquit the accused at the conclusion of the bail hearing. Nor can the justice determine whether sufficient evidence exists to have a trial; this determination is made at a preliminary hearing.

TIME OF APPEARANCE BEFORE A JUSTICE (TIME OF BAIL HEARING)

When the officer-in-charge or any police officer is justified in detaining an accused instead of releasing him or her, sec. 503(1) C.C. creates the following rule that governs when the accused must be taken before a justice for a bail hearing:

1. without unreasonable delay and within 24 hours after the time of arrest, if a justice is available, and
2. if no justice is available within 24 hours of the arrest, as soon as possible.[34]

When the accused is brought before a justice, a bail hearing must be conducted, unless

1. the accused pleads guilty and the justice accepts it,[35] or
2. the accused is charged with a sec. 469 C.C. offence, such as murder.

When a person charged with a sec. 469 offence is brought before a justice, the justice must detain the accused in custody and cannot release.[36] After the justice issues a detention order, the accused must apply for a bail hearing before a judge of the superior court of criminal jurisdiction e.g., in Ontario, a General Division Court Judge.[37]

ADJOURNMENT

After an accused is brought before a justice, the prosecutor or accused may apply for an adjournment to prepare for the bail hearing. The justice may grant an adjournment at any time before the bail hearing starts or during the bail hearing. The adjournment cannot be longer than three clear days, which is calculated by excluding the day of the adjournment.[38] The adjournment may exceed three clear days only if the accused consents. The accused is remanded in custody during the adjournment.[39]

The three-day adjournment is not granted automatically to the prosecution. An application must be made after the accused is brought to the justice. When the prosecution applies for the adjournment, the onus is on the prosecution to prove reasons to justify the need for the three-day adjournment. Examples of reasons are the complexities of the investigation and the amount of time needed to prepare the case for the prosecution.

Two points must be emphasized:

1. The accused must first be brought before the justice within 24 hours or as soon as possible in order to apply for the three-day adjournment.
2. The justice cannot grant an adjournment without an application by either the prosecutor or the accused.

STATUS OF ACCUSED

The accused is presumed innocent during a bail hearing. This fact must be emphasized to understand the nature and degree of evidence required to prove why an accused person should be held in custody until the trial, during the period when the accused is presumed innocent.

Pretrial detention orders are not made when weak evidence exists; the accused has not yet been convicted of the offence. Pretrial jail custody is informally referred to as "dead time," because this type of custody is not a sentence. It is served during a period when the accused is presumed innocent.

LOCATION

Bail hearings may be conducted at the following locations:

1. at a police station or in a JP's office, which serves as a temporary courtroom,
2. in provincial court, usually before a provincial court judge.

PARTICIPANTS

The following people are the participants in a bail hearing:

1. Justice;
2. Prosecutor:[40] The prosecutor may be either

   - a Crown attorney, if held in provincial court, or
   - a police officer, or Crown attorney, if held at a police station. A police officer, usually a detective assigned to the investigation, is the prosecutor at the majority of police station bail hearings.

3. The accused person. An accused person must be in physical attendance at a bail hearing. An exception exists under the following conditions:

   - the accused may appear by any suitable telecommunication device, including a telephone, if

     a) this means of appearance is suitable to the justice (the justice has discretion to allow or reject it), and
     b) both the prosecutor and accused agree to this appearance.

A bail hearing cannot be conducted in the absence of the accused's appearance. An adult offender is permitted to have a lawyer present. A young offender is permitted to have a lawyer, parent, or adult whom the justice considers suitable.[41] If the young offender is not represented by counsel, the justice must inform the young offender of the right to be represented by counsel and must give the young offender a reasonable opportunity to obtain counsel.[42]

FACTORS DETERMINING RELEASE OR CUSTODY

The elements that compose the release provisions (RICE) are essentially the same factors that determine release or custody at a bail hearing, but two different terms are used to describe these elements:

1. primary ground,[43] and
2. secondary ground.[44]

"Primary ground" refers to the necessity of custody to ensure a court appearance.[45] "Secondary ground" refers to the necessity of custody to protect the public, having regard to all the circumstances including a substantial likelihood that the accused will commit a criminal offence or interfere with the administration of justice.[46] If primary ground exists, then reasonable grounds exist that the accused may fail to appear in court. If secondary ground exists, then reasonable grounds exist that the accused may commit a criminal offence and endanger the public.

A justice is justified in making a detention order and holding the accused in custody until the trial, if either primary or secondary ground exists.[47] Primary ground is explored first and if it is proven to exist, a detention order is made. If primary ground is absent, secondary ground is explored. If secondary ground is proven to exist, a detention order is made.[48] If absent, the accused must be released.

In summary, the release and detention rules are

1. If only primary ground exists, a detention order is made.
2. If only secondary ground exists, a detention order is made.
3. If neither exists, the accused must be released.

ONUS

The onus at a bail hearing refers to the burden of proof, or the responsibility of proving the presence or absence of primary and secondary grounds. Generally, the prosecutor has the onus to prove why the accused should be detained in custody.[49] However, exceptions exist in limited circumstances where a reverse onus occurs and the accused has the onus to prove that he or she should be released.[50]

REVERSE ONUS SITUATION

When a reverse onus situation exists, the burden of proof reverses, or shifts to the accused. The accused then has the onus to prove why he or she should be released. In other words, the accused has the burden to prove the absence of primary or secondary grounds in order to be released from custody until the trial date. If the accused fails to do so, he or she will be detained in custody until the trial date.

A reverse onus situation will exist if the accused is charged with

1. An indictable or dual procedure offence while awaiting trial for another indictable or dual procedure offence.[51] This refers to situations where the accused is charged with an indictable or dual procedure offence and released, then commits and is charged with another indictable or dual procedure offence before the trial for the first offence is complete. If either offence is summary conviction, the prosecutor has the onus.
2. An indictable or dual procedure offence and does not live in Canada.[52] If a person lives in another country and commits an indictable or dual procedure offence, the accused automatically has the onus at the bail hearing regardless of whether the accused is awaiting trial. If the offence is summary conviction, the prosecutor has the onus.
3. "Fail to appear" or "breach of undertaking" while awaiting trial for any criminal offence (summary conviction, dual procedure, or indictable).[53]
4. Any of the following *Controlled Drugs and Substances Act* offences:
   - trafficking in substances,
   - possession of substance(s) for the purpose of trafficking,
   - importing substance(s), and
   - exporting substance(s).[54]

A person charged with any of these *Controlled Drugs and Substances Act* offences automatically has the onus at a bail hearing, regardless of whether he or she is awaiting trial for any other offence. However, if a person is charged with "possession of narcotics" only, the prosecutor has the onus.

5. An indictable offence, other than a sec. 469 offence, that is an offence under sec. 467.1 C.C. (participation in a criminal organization) or an offence under any federal statute committed for the benefit of, at the direction of, or in association with

a criminal organization for which the maximum punishment is imprisonment for five years or more.[55]

PROSECUTOR ONUS—PROCEDURE

The following is a step-by-step summary of the bail hearing procedure when the prosecutor has the onus.

Step 1

The police must lay an information before the bail hearing starts. A bail hearing cannot be conducted without an information being sworn first.[56]

Step 2

The accused is brought before a justice within 24 hours after the arrest, without unreasonable delay.

Step 3

The accused is arraigned, meaning that the information is read to the accused. The accused is permitted to plead guilty.

Step 4

If the accused does not plead guilty, the justice asks the prosecutor, "Do you wish to show cause?" This question asks the prosecutor if he or she intends to prove the existence of primary or secondary grounds, meaning if RICE is not fulfilled.

Step 5

If the prosecutor answers "No," the prosecutor concedes that primary and secondary grounds do not exist, and that RICE is fulfilled. In this situation, the accused must be released by means of an undertaking without conditions. The justice has no discretion to impose conditions on the undertaking when the prosecutor chooses not to show cause.[57]

Step 6

If the prosecutor answers "Yes," the prosecutor intends to introduce evidence relating to primary and/or secondary grounds. The bail hearing begins, and the prosecutor presents his or her case first.

Step 7

The prosecutor may introduce evidence by calling witnesses to testify, or calling only the investigating police officer to testify. The latter is the one usually chosen. The investigating officer's testimony amounts to hearsay.

"Hearsay" evidence is admissible at a bail hearing if the evidence is "considered credible or trustworthy."[58] Hearsay evidence is defined as observations that were not perceived by one's own senses; the observations were made by another person. A recipient of hearsay evidence is a person who was informed about observations by a person who actually perceived them with his or her senses. An example of a recipient of hearsay evidence is a police officer who is informed about observations by a witness.

The admissibility of hearsay evidence represents a significant advantage for the prosecutor because the investigating officer alone may present all the evidence by reading facts and witness statements, without calling other witnesses. This does not apply at the trial, where hearsay evidence is generally inadmissible.

If the bail hearing is conducted at the police station, and the investigating officer is the prosecutor, this same officer may also testify for the prosecution. The prosecutor has the option of calling all the witnesses, or having the investigating officer testify and read the witness statements.

All witnesses who are called must be sworn before testifying. Consequently, a witness who intentionally lies or fabricates evidence while testifying under oath at a bail hearing may be charged with perjury.

Step 8

The prosecution may introduce evidence that is restricted generally to primary and secondary grounds, including

- a summary of the incident that shows the circumstances of the offence, to prove a probability of conviction.[59] Although guilt or innocence is not determined at a bail hearing, and the accused is not on trial, the probability of conviction is a relevant factor to primary and secondary grounds.
- accused's criminal record.[60]
- any "fail to appear" or "breach of undertaking" offences that the accused has committed in the past, whether the accused was charged or convicted of these offences,[61]
- any criminal offences that the accused has been charged with and is awaiting trial for, although he or she has not yet been convicted,[62] and
- any topic relevant to primary or secondary ground.

Step 9

The accused person may cross-examine all prosecution witnesses.

Step 10

After the prosecutor concludes his or her case, the accused may introduce evidence to show why he or she should be released. The accused has the option to testify, but no one can compel the accused to testify; this decision belongs exclusively to the accused.

Step 11

All defence witnesses may be cross-examined by the prosecutor, including the accused if he or she chooses to testify. However, the accused cannot be cross-examined about the offence unless the accused testifies about the offence.[63]

Step 12

The justice makes one of the following rulings:

1. If the prosecutor fails to prove that primary or secondary ground exists, the justice must release[64] by means of a

   a) recognizance (form 32)[65]

   - with or without sureties, referring to posting of bond for the accused, or
   - with a deposit of a sum of money directed by the justice, if the accused lives in another province or beyond 200 km from the place of arrest, or
   - with conditions, or

   b) an undertaking (form 12)[66]

   - with, or
   - without conditions.

   The justice may impose any one or more of the following conditions on an undertaking or recognizance:

- report to a police officer at a specific time at a specific police station,
- remain within a specified territorial jurisdiction,
- notify a specified police officer of any change in address, employment, or occupation,
- abstain from communicating with any witness or person specifically named,
- refrain from going to any place specified by the justice,
- deposit his or her passport,
- any other reasonable condition that the justice considers desirable, such as a curfew that compels the accused to be inside a specified place during hours specified by the justice, e.g., 11:00 p.m.–7:00 a.m.[67]

A court date, time, and location are included on the release order. If the accused agrees to all the conditions imposed by the justice, the accused signs the release document. If the bail hearing is conducted at the police station, the officer should witness the signature, initial it, and record these details in a notebook; all of which will be relevant if the accused violates any of the conditions. Each violation of a condition is a separate dual procedure offence under sec. 145(3) C.C. If the accused refuses to agree and sign the undertaking, then the accused will be detained in custody because of the existence of primary or secondary ground.

2. If either primary or secondary ground is proven and the accused is an adult, the justice must order that the accused be detained in custody until the trial. The detention order must include a statement of reasons for making the order.[68] After a detention order is made, the *Criminal Code* allows a bail review to be made. The accused may apply to a judge at any time before the trial for a bail review.[69] Additionally, an automatic mandatory bail review must occur

   • within 30 days, if the offence is summary conviction, or
   • within 90 days, if the offence is indictable.[70]

   A bail review is conducted in the same manner as the bail hearing. The purpose remains the same; if primary or secondary ground still exists, detention continues. If not, the accused is released.[71]

3. If primary or secondary ground exists, and the accused is a young offender, the justice may not detain the young offender in custody if the following conditions exist:

   a) a responsible person is willing and able to take care of and exercise control over the young offender, and
   b) the young offender is willing to be placed in the care of that person, and
   c) both the person taking care of the young offender and the young offender consent in writing.[72]

   If these conditions exist, the justice has discretion to release the young offender, instead of making a detention order, and may impose conditions on the undertaking. If the young offender does not consent, he or she will be detained in custody.

   If the person who takes care of the young offender after his or her release is no longer willing or able to care for or exercise control over the young offender, or if for any other reason it is no longer appropriate that the young offender be in the care of that person, any person may apply to a youth court judge or a justice for

   • an order relieving the person and the young offender of their obligation, and
   • an arrest warrant for the young person.[73]

   After the young person is arrested, he or she must be brought before a youth court judge or justice forthwith for a bail hearing.[74]

REVERSE ONUS—PROCEDURE

The following is a step-by-step summary of the bail hearing procedure when a reverse onus situation occurs.

Step 1

An information must be laid.

Step 2

The accused is brought before a justice and is arraigned.

Step 3

The justice asks the accused, "Do you wish to show cause?" which asks the accused whether he or she intends to introduce evidence that shows reasons why he or she should be released.

Step 4

If the accused responds "No," the accused concedes that primary or secondary grounds exist. The justice must make a detention order and hold the accused in custody.[75]

Step 5

If the accused responds "Yes," the accused introduces evidence first, by his or her testimony or by other witness testimony.

Step 6

The prosecutor may cross-examine all defence witnesses.

Step 7

The prosecutor may then introduce evidence.

Step 8

The defence may cross-examine.

Step 9

The justice makes a ruling, in the same manner as in a prosecutor-onus bail hearing.

YOUNG OFFENDER—NOTICE TO PARENT

Whenever a young person is released from custody and served any compelling document, including a summons, a notice to parent must be given by the police. Section 9(2) Y.O.A. creates a mandatory procedure that obliges the OIC, or any officer instructed by him or her, to give a notice to parent in writing. The written notice to parent must include the charge(s), court date, and court location. The notice must be given as soon as possible after release or after the compelling document is served. Section 9(3) and 9(4) Y.O.A. permits the notice to be given to an adult relative who is likely to help the young offender, if a parent cannot be found. If an adult relative is unavailable, the notice may be given to an appropriate adult who is known to the young offender and who is likely to assist him or her. If the young offender is married, the notice may be given to the spouse instead of a parent.

Problem-Solving Case Studies

You are a police officer in each case. Each offender is an adult, unless otherwise indicated.

PROBLEM 72

Ward is arrested for "attempt murder" and is brought to the police station.

a) Can Ward automatically be brought before a justice for a bail hearing?

_____

b) When does he have to be brought to a justice?

_____

_____

c) If the police require additional time to prepare for the bail hearing, can they bring Ward to a justice three days later instead of within 24 hours?

_____

_____

_____

_____

_____

PROBLEM 73

Ward is arrested for "first degree murder" and is taken to the police station.

a) Where is Ward brought next?

_____

b) Under what circumstances can a bail hearing occur?

_____

c) Who will preside over a bail hearing for first degree murder?

_____

d) Who will have the onus at a bail hearing for first degree murder?

_____

PROBLEM 74

June is arrested for "robbery" and is taken to the police station. She is brought before a justice for a bail hearing. She is not awaiting trial for any other offence. She was convicted three years ago for "assault," and one year ago she was investigated for a "theft under $5000.00" complaint but was not charged.

a) Who will have the onus at this bail hearing?

_____

b) Can this bail hearing be conducted without an information being laid first?

_____

c) Where can this bail hearing be conducted?

_____

d) Can the investigating police officer be the prosecutor?

_____

_____

_____

e) Can the bail hearing be conducted in the absence of any appearance by June?

_____

_____

f) Can June plead guilty?

_____

_____

g) The justice asks the prosecutor, "Do you wish to show cause?" The answer is "No." What will occur?

_____

_____

_____

  • Does the justice have discretion to impose conditions?

_____

h) The prosecutor informs the justice that he or she wishes to show cause. Who presents the case first?

_____

i) Do all the Crown witnesses have to be subpoenaed to this bail hearing?

_____

_____

_____

j) The investigating officer begins testifying. Can the officer
  • read a summary of the office?

_____

  • state the conviction for assault?

_____

  • state June's employment status?

_____

  • state the circumstances of the "theft under $5000.00 complaint?

_____

k) Can June cross-examine the officer?

_____

l) Can June be compelled by either the justice or the prosecutor to testify?

_____

m) If June testifies, can she be asked about the offence?

_____

n) Can the justice convict June after the bail hearing?

_____

o) Can the justice withdraw the information or release June unconditionally (no charge)?

_____

_____

_____

p) If only primary ground is proven, can June be detained in custody?

_____

q) If only secondary ground is proven, can June be detained in custody?

_____

r) If neither primary nor secondary grounds are proven, what must occur?

_____

_____

s) How many conditions can the justice impose?

_____

PROBLEM 75

Eddie was arrested two weeks ago for "break, enter, and theft" and was released on an undertaking without conditions. The trial is scheduled four months later. Today, Eddie is arrested for "theft over $5000.00" and is brought before a justice for a bail hearing. Who will have the onus?

_____

_____

PROBLEM 76

Wally was arrested one month ago for "cause a disturbance" and was released by a promise to appear. The trial is scheduled for five months later. Today, Wally is arrested for "robbery" and is brought before a justice for a bail hearing. Who will have the onus?

_____

_____

PROBLEM 77

George was arrested for "cause a disturbance" 10 days ago and was released on a promise to appear. Today, he is arrested for "fail to appear" in court and is brought before a justice for a bail hearing. Who will have the onus?

_____

_____

PROBLEM 78

Sam is arrested today in Toronto for "fraud over $5000.00." He lives in Buffalo, New York. He is brought before a justice for a bail hearing. Who will have the onus?

_____

_____

_____

PROBLEM 79

Sally is arrested for "impaired driving" in Vancouver. She lives in Toronto. She is brought before a justice for a bail hearing. Who will have the onus?

_____

PROBLEM 80

Walter lives in Vancouver. He is arrested in Vancouver for "trafficking narcotics." This is his first offence. Who will have the onus?

_____

PROBLEM 81

Eleanor is brought before a justice for a bail hearing regarding a charge of "robbery." A reverse onus situation exists. The justice asks, "Do you wish to show cause?"

a) To whom is the question directed?

_____

b) If the answer is "No," what must occur?

_____

Test Yourself

1. You respond to a bank alarm at 2:50 p.m. A robbery occurred five minutes ago. You search the area and lawfully arrest Wally (21). You transport him to the police station. Explain

    a) what information you will determine to conduct a bail hearing, and
    b) the procedures that will be conducted at his bail hearing.

_____

_____

_____

_____

_____

_____

_____

Unit 3

Learning Outcomes

In this unit, the student will learn

- the definition of an information,
- the procedure used to complete and lay an information,
- the procedure used to conduct an *ex parte* hearing,
- the definition of an indictment and how one is drafted,
- the purpose of a preliminary hearing, and
- the possible outcomes of a preliminary hearing.

CHAPTER ELEVEN

An Information

Learning Outcomes

The student will be able to

- interpret and apply sec. 504–508 and 788–789 C.C., and
- understand the procedure to complete an information.

INTRODUCTION

Release/compelling documents do not formally charge a person with an offence. For example, when the police serve an appearance notice or promise to appear to a person, he or she has not been formally charged at that particular time.

The arrest of a person does not represent a formal charge. Arrest refers only to the physical custody of a person. Charging a person formally requires the laying of an information. An "information" is the name of a sworn, written document that formally alleges that a specific adult or young offender has committed a specific offence—of any classification.[1] The following key points are drawn from this definition:

1. An information is the document used to charge either an adult or a young offender.
2. An information is the document used to charge an offender in relation to summary conviction, dual procedure, or indictable offences.
3. The procedure used to lay an information is the same for adult and young offenders, and for any classification of criminal offence.
4. An information charges the person; it does not compel a person to court.
5. A formal allegation must be sworn and in writing.

The term "laying an information" refers to completing the document, bringing it before a justice, and swearing the contents of the document under oath.[2] After the information is laid, a procedure occurs where reasonable grounds must be proven that the person named on the information committed the offence described on the information. Afterward, the justice decides whether or not to sign the information. The accused person is formally charged when the justice signs the information.

The document used as an information is called a Form 2, and is found in sec. 841 C.C. The document is illustrated in that section of the *Criminal Code*. The procedures and rules explaining how to lay an information are found in sections 504–08 and 788–89 of the *Criminal Code*.

PURPOSES OF AN INFORMATION

The four general purposes of an information are

1. to commence proceedings against the accused,
2. to inform the accused about the specific allegation,
3. to indicate that the allegation has been sworn under oath before a justice, and
4. if the offence is summary conviction, to indicate that a formal charge was laid within six months of the offence date.[3]

LAYING AN INFORMATION

The following general rules apply to the process of laying an information.

Rule 1

Anyone may lay an information if he or she can prove reasonable grounds that the person to be charged committed a criminal offence.[4] This means that a police officer or *any citizen can lay an information,* for any classification of offence, if the person can prove reasonable grounds. However, the vast majority of informations are laid by police officers.

The person who lays an information is called the *informant*.[5] This is the legal name of the person who makes the formal allegation, and it must not be confused with the term "confidential informant" from whom the police receive evidence during an investigation. Thus, the police officer who lays the information is referred to as the informant.

Rule 2

Receiving an information means to accept it to review the information for the purpose of determining whether reasonable grounds exist to formally charge the offender.

An information must be laid before a justice, defined as a justice of the peace (JP) or a provincial court judge.[6] The vast majority of informations are laid before a JP. Therefore, a justice is the person who receives, or accepts, the information. A justice has no discretion about receiving an information regarding an indictable or dual procedure offence. The justice *must* receive it.[7] Receiving it does not mean that the offender will automatically be charged.

Regarding summary conviction offences, sec. 788(2) C.C. does not state that a justice must receive an information. It states that a justice *may* receive it, which apparently means that a justice has discretion about whether to receive it or not.

Rule 3

An information is not laid in open court. The location may be anywhere other than open court, usually in a justice's office.

Rule 4

The time limit for laying an information depends on

- the classification of the offence, and
- whether a release/compelling document was served first (before an information is laid).

The first determining factor is the classification of the offence. If the offence is summary conviction, the information must be laid within six months of the offence date. After the six-month time limit expires, an information cannot be laid, and the offender cannot be charged.[8] If the offence is indictable or dual procedure, no time limit exists to lay an information. An information may be laid at any time after the offence occurs.

The second factor is the type of compelling document used. An information must be laid *as soon as practicable* afterward and before the court date specified on the document,[9] if an offender is arrested and then released by means of one of the following

- appearance notice, or
- promise to appear, or
- recognizance (by the officer-in-charge or peace officer), or
- undertaking (by the officer-in-charge or peace officer) in conjunction with a promise to appear or recognizance.

No specific time limit is imposed, but unreasonable delays should be avoided.

If a summons is used to compel an accused's court appearance, an information must be laid first, before the compelling document is served. The classification of offence time limit applies to the laying of an information in this situation.

If an offender is arrested and is detained for a bail hearing, an information must be laid before the bail hearing begins. This means that an information will be laid before a justice releases the accused or before the justice detains the offender in custody until the trial.

CONTENTS OF AN INFORMATION

GENERAL RULES

The "contents" of an information refers to the facts and details that must be written on the information (Form 2) in order for the information to be sufficient, or valid. The following general rules apply to the contents of an information:

Rule 1

The contents must be sufficient enough for the accused to be reasonably informed of the charge, permitting the accused to prepare a full defence and allow for a fair trial.[10]

Rule 2

All the facts-in-issue of the offence must be written on the information, including

- accused's name (identity),
- date of offence,
- location of offence, and
- specific elements that compose the offence.[11]

Rule 3

An information must fully allege at least one count, defined as one charge on an information.[12] For example, a person charged with one assault is charged with one count of "assault." If the accused is charged with three assaults, he or she is charged with three counts of "assault."

Rule 4

Each count must include a statement that alleges one complete offence.[13] The statement must contain all the elements that compose the offence and must give reasonable information about the offence to the accused.[14]

Rule 5

A statement that alleges one count of an offence is informally called a wording. A wording cannot contain irrelevant words or language that is not essential to the offence.[15] Therefore, unnecessary words must be avoided when writing a wording.

A wording cannot be composed of the short-form name of an offence, such as "theft under $5000.00," or "break, enter and theft." It must be composed of a lengthier statement that includes each specific fact-in-issue that is found in the section that creates the offence.[16] A wording that lacks at least one fact-in-issue is insufficient or invalid. The prosecution has the onus of proving all the facts-in-issue written on the information beyond reasonable doubt.

SPECIFIC CONTENTS

The specific contents of an information are described on Form 2, which is the specific document that is used as an information. It is illustrated in sec. 841 C.C. Eight areas must be completed when an information is laid:

1. CANADA
    PROVINCE of [insert territorial division or region]
        2. Information of [informant's name], [occupation], hereinafter called the informant.
        The informant says that he or she believes on reasonable grounds that
            3. [accused's name and address]
            4. on or about the [date] day of [month], 20___,
            5. at the [city], in the [territorial division or region]
            6. wording
                          7. _____
                                (informant's signature)
8. Sworn before me this [date] day
    of [month], 20____
    at [city]

                          _____
                                (JP's signature)
                    A justice of the peace in and for [province]

SPECIFIC CONTENTS—EXPLANATION

Item 1

Territorial jurisdiction or region This refers to the judicial district or region where the offence occurred. These districts are determined by province. For example, Central West Region includes Oakville, Burlington, and Milton, Ontario.

Item 2

Informant's name This refers to the person who lays the information, usually a police officer. The informant's occupation must be included. The person named must have a belief based on reasonable grounds that the accused committed the offence. An information cannot be laid anonymously by withholding or concealing the informant's name.

Item 3

Accused's name and address Before inserting the accused's name and address, determine these facts accurately. Do not write assumptions. Prove the offender's name by relevant documents or by the offender's admission. The accused's date of birth may be mentioned also.

Item 4

Offence date Form 2 has the phrase "on or about" printed on the document, accompanied by spaces to indicate a specific date. This format may be used when evidence exists that the offence actually was committed on a specific date. (The time of the offence does not have to be specified.)However, in some cases, the specific offence date is not known. The evidence may prove only that the offence was committed between two dates. When this evidence exists, the informant is permitted to place a single line through "on or about" and replace that phrase with "between." Two dates must be written afterward.

For example, an offender is arrested for breaking into a house. The owner reports that she left on Friday, March 1st at 5:00 p.m. and returned on Sunday, March 3rd at 9:00 a.m. *The "between" dates should not include possible offence dates.* The "between" dates must be days when the offence could not have occurred. For example, the correct "between" dates for this example: February 28th and March 4th. The offence did not occur on February 28 or March 4. The informant must prove the offence occurred between those dates, which includes March 1 (5:00 p.m.–11:59 a.m.), March 2, and March 3 (12:00 a.m.–9:00 a.m.). If the informant wrote "between March 1st and March 3rd," he or she is alleging that the offence occurred on March 2nd.

No time limit exists regarding time periods that may be used in "between" dates. For example, the Supreme Court of Canada, in *R. v. Colgan (1987),*[17] ruled that a time period of more than six years was suitable.

In *R. v. B.(G.) (1990),*[18] the Supreme Court of Canada established the following rules regarding the offence date component of an information:

- The exact time of offence does not have to be specified.
- The date or dates used must provide reasonable information to the accused about when the offence occurred.
- What constitutes reasonable information will vary from case to case.
- Lengthy time periods are acceptable if no evidence indicates a specific date.
- If evidence does indicate a specific date, then a specific date must be written on the information.
- If evidence introduced at the trial regarding the offence date conflicts with the date or dates written on the information, the accused may be convicted if it "is not an essential element of the offence or crucial to the defence."[19] If it is an essential element or crucial to the defence, then the accused must be acquitted.

Item 5

Location of offence The entries regarding the location of the offence are situated above the wording. Only the city is specified as the location, not the street or address. Where applicable, the street or address is specified in the wording. Do not enter the city name alone; use the term "city of" to precede the name (e.g., at the "city of Calgary"). Next to this entry, specify the judicial district or region. The phrase "in the said region" is sufficient because it refers to the same district or region named at the top of the information.

Item 6

Wording The wording is the most important feature of an information. Short-form names of offences, such as "break, enter, and theft," cannot be used as formal wordings on an information. Actual formal wordings are not found within the *Criminal Code*. The Ministry of the Attorney General for each province prepares wordings that are used by the province's police officers. Publishers of criminal codes have suggested wordings in their publications. A prosecutor should be consulted if doubt exists when drafting the wording.

The following are examples of suggested wordings:

Example 1   Break, enter, and theft (short-form name) sec. 348(1)(b)C.C.:

did break and enter a certain place, TO WIT: [specify place including address] and did commit therein the indictable offence of [specify offence i.e.: THEFT], contrary to sec. 348(1)(b) of the *Criminal Code*.[20]

The facts-in-issue of "break, enter and theft" are

- break,
- enter,
- place, and
- commit an indictable offence therein

The wording (above example) contains all the facts-in-issue. Two of them require additional explanation:

Place Section 348(3) C.C. defines place as

- a dwelling house, or
- a building, or
- a structure, or
- railway vehicle, or
- vessel, or
- aircraft, or
- trailer, or
- a pen or enclosure for fur-bearing animals.

Therefore, one of these must be specified as being the type of place, including the address. The phrase TO WIT means "that being" or "specifically." Examples of how to complete the place specifications are

- **If the place is a house** place, TO WIT: a dwelling-house situated at 10 King St. (Do not include the city after the street. The city is written above the wording.)
- **If the place is a business premises** place, TO WIT: a building (store or factory is also acceptable) situated at 100 Main St. (Do not use the name of the business premise only, such as Fred's Video or City College, because these are not included under the definition of place.)

Commit an indictable offence therein Include the specific indictable offence committed, such as "theft" or "mischief" (it is not necessary to include under or over $5000.00).

Example 2   Theft under $5000.00, sec. 334(b)C.C.:

did steal [specify item] the property of [insert the property owner's name] of a value not exceeding $5000.00, contrary to sec. 344(b) of the *Criminal Code*.[21]

When the description of property is required, specify

- general type, i.e., television set, bicycle, and
- brief specific description to distinguish the item from any other similar item that the complainant owns.

Elaborate descriptions should be avoided since each word used in the description must be proven. Simple descriptions should be used to a degree that reasonably informs the accused of the specific offence.

Example 3   Assault, sec. 266 C.C.:

did commit an assault on [insert victim's name], contrary to sec. 266 of the *Criminal Code*.[22]

Item 7

Informant's signature The informant signs the information, signifying his or her belief that the contents are true. However, this does not signify that the accused is formally charged.

Item 8

Sworn oath The informant swears under oath that the contents are believed to be true. The justice writes the date, month, year, and city where the information is sworn *but the justice does not sign it at this stage.* A hearing then begins where the informant has the onus of proving that reasonable grounds exist. If the justice is satisfied that reasonable grounds exist, the justice signs the information. The accused is formally charged at that time. If the justice concludes that no reasonable grounds exist, the justice will not sign the information and the accused will not be charged.

JOINDER OF COUNTS

An offender often commits multiple offences, requiring that he or she be charged with more than one count. In these situations, the informant has two alternatives about how to charge the offender and how to complete an information:

1. Lay a separate information for each offence. Each document will have one count; or
2. Join counts on one information. This procedure is referred to as joinder of counts.[23]

The following are rules regarding joinder of counts:

Rule 1

Summary conviction offences may be joined only with other summary conviction offences, but not with indictable or dual procedure offences.[24]

Rule 2

Indictable or dual procedure offences may be joined only with other indictable or dual procedure offences, but not with summary conviction offences.[25]

Rule 3

Each count must be distinguished as being separate.[26] This means that each count must have its own individual wording. Conversely, one wording must allege only one count.

Rule 4

Unlimited counts may be joined on one document. If additional pages are required, counts may be typed on blank paper and attached to the original document. Joined counts may be separated by inserting the term "and further" between the counts.

For example:

on or about the **10th** day of January, 1997, in the city of Hamilton,
did [insert wording for count 1],
contrary to section _____ of the *Criminal Code,*
and further,
on or about the **12th** day of **January,** 1997, in the city of Hamilton,
did [insert wording for count 2],
contrary to section _____ of the *Criminal Code.*

Any number of counts may be added in similar fashion. Joining counts saves repetition of the contents that are written on the first page of the information, such as the accused's name, the informant's name, and the judicial district.

JOINDER OF PARTIES

Offences are commonly committed by more than one offender. In situations where multiple offenders commit an offence or offences, the informant has two alternatives about how to charge them and how to lay an information:

1. **Separately** This refers to laying separate informations for each offender. Each separate information charges only one offender. The offenders charged in this manner are known as accomplices. Accomplices who are charged separately may be subpoenaed by the Crown attorney to testify against each other.[27]

2. **Jointly** More than one offender may be named on one single information. This refers to joinder of parties, or charging offenders jointly. Jointly charged offenders are called co-accused persons. The prosecution cannot subpoena a co-accused to testify against other co-accused persons.[28] Consequently, this procedure is restrictive and eliminates the possibility, for the prosecution, of introducing incriminating evidence from one co-accused against other co-accused person(s).

The testimony of one offender against another is valuable evidence. Each accomplice must be considered an eyewitness in relation to the other accomplices' trial. Credible eyewitness observations will provide reasonable grounds during the investigation for various procedures, including arrest, search, and laying an information. Additionally, credible accomplice testimony will convict the other accomplices without any other supporting evidence.

Consequently, the goal in every investigation involving multiple offenders should be to elicit evidence from one or all of the offenders and to ensure their testimony against each other. Even if accomplices remain silent at the time of their arrests, they may change their mind before the trial and decide to implicate and testify against the other offenders shortly before the trial. Charging offenders separately will permit this possibility. Charging offenders jointly will prevent it. Even though charging offenders jointly provides the benefit of reducing the number of documents needed, it eliminates an enormous advantage for the prosecution.

In summary, charging multiple offenders separately is the recommended procedure to leave open the advantage of having accomplices testify against each other.

TWELVE

Ex Parte *Hearing*

Learning Outcomes

The student will be able to

- understand the *ex parte* hearing procedures.

EXPLANATION

An informant writes the contents of the information, brings it before a justice, signs it, and swears under oath that the contents are true. Before the justice can sign it, an *ex parte* hearing must be conducted. "*Ex parte*" means "without the party," referring to the accused. The *ex parte* hearing is mandatory and cannot be waived by the justice.[29] The hearing must be held whether the information is laid before a summons/arrest warrant is issued or after the accused has been arrested and released by means of an appearance notice, promise to appear, or recognizance.[30] In other words, an *ex parte* hearing cannot be waived or avoided simply because the offender was arrested and already released.

PURPOSE

The purpose of an *ex parte* hearing is to prove that reasonable grounds exist to believe that the person named on the information committed the offence described in the wording of the information.

ONUS

The informant has the onus of proving the existence of reasonable grounds.

LOCATION

The hearing is held anywhere other than open court. Usually, it occurs in a justice of the peace's office at a police station.

PARTICIPANTS

The accused person is never present and cannot be present. The participants are the justice, the informant, and, if the justice considers it necessary, witnesses who may give relevant evidence regarding reasonable grounds.[31]

EVIDENCE

Only the informant's side of the story is heard at an *ex parte* hearing. The accused cannot cross-examine or introduce evidence because he or she is not present.
Hearsay evidence is allowed at an *ex parte* hearing. Therefore, the informant may give all the relevant evidence, including witness statements. The police officer who is the informant usually is the only person who gives evidence at an *ex parte* hearing. However, witnesses may be called if the justice considers it desirable or necessary.[32] All witnesses who testify, including the informant, must be sworn under oath before giving evidence through testimony.[33]

EX PARTE HEARING—PROCEDURE

The following steps should be followed whether the accused is an adult or a young offender.

Step 1

The informant, a person who has a belief based on reasonable grounds that a person committed an offence, writes an information on Form 2. The information is completed before bringing it to a justice.

Step 2

The information is brought before a justice, usually a JP, at the JP's office in a police station. The location may be anywhere but open court.

Step 3

The informant signs the information, preferably before the JP. However, the information may be signed before bringing it to the JP. The signature does not represent a formal charge.

Step 4

The informant swears under oath that the contents are true and that he or she believes, on reasonable grounds, that the accused person committed the offence. The accused is not formally charged at this stage.

Step 5

An *ex parte* hearing begins.

Step 6

The informant swears under oath and testifies about the evidence that forms the basis of the informant's belief. Hearsay evidence is allowed. A summary of the offence and witness statements may be read by the informant.

Step 7

If the JP deems it necessary, witnesses may be called to testify under oath at the *ex parte* hearing.

Step 8

At the conclusion of the *ex parte* hearing, the justice takes the following action:

a) If the justice is satisfied that reasonable grounds exist, he or she signs the information, which means that the offender is formally charged at that point.

   - If the accused has not yet been arrested, the justice issues a summons to compel the accused's court appearance or issues an arrest warrant if the officer proves reasonable grounds that the warrant is necessary in the public interest.
   - If the accused has been previously arrested and released by means of an appearance notice, promise to appear, or recognizance, the justice confirms the respective document, which compels the accused to court.

The Crown attorney is not present at the *ex parte* hearing. Despite the absence of the Crown attorney, the following rules are significant:

i) After the justice signs the information, the Crown attorney becomes the owner of the information.
ii) Only the Crown may withdraw the information.
iii) No one can change or alter the information after the justice signs it. For example, if the accused confesses to additional offences after the information is signed, the new charges cannot be added to the signed information. A new information must be laid requiring another ex parte hearing.

b) If the justice is not satisfied that reasonable grounds exist, the justice cannot sign the information and the offender is not charged at this point. Additionally

   - no summons or arrest warrant is issued, or
   - the appearance notice, promise to appear, or recognizance is cancelled.

If this occurs, the informant is not restricted to only one *ex parte* hearing. The informant may lay a new information when additional evidence is obtained, although the first information used during the unsuccessful *ex parte* hearing cannot be reused. The *Criminal Code* does not impose any limits regarding the number of attempts or opportunities to lay an information.

PATH OF AN INFORMATION

After a sworn information is laid and signed by a justice, the information follows a distinct path through the criminal justice system. An information is the formal allegation in some trials, but it is replaced by another document called an "indictment" in other trials.

The path of an information is illustrated using a figure that explains the locations where the information represents the formal allegation and introduces the topics of indictments and preliminary hearings. The topic of indictments must be learned in conjunction with an explanation of preliminary hearings. Both are explained in this unit of the textbook.

Before we look at the path of an information chart, the levels of trials and the accused's election of court level must be learned.

LEVEL OF TRIAL

Any sec. 469 C.C. offence, such as "first degree murder," must be tried in Superior Court with a jury.

The following offences must be tried in provincial court:

- purely summary conviction offences,
- dual procedure offences that the Crown classifies as summary conviction, and
- sec. 553 C.C. offences, including "theft under $5000.00" and other "under $5000.00" offences, regardless of the Crown's decision.

The majority of purely indictable offences and dual procedure offences that the Crown selects as indictable are called "election indictable" offences. The accused has a choice when he or she is charged with an election indictable offence to be tried in

1. Superior Court of criminal jurisdiction with a jury (judge and jury),
2. Superior Court of criminal jurisdiction without a jury (judge alone), or
3. provincial court.

If an accused chooses to be tried in Superior Court with or without a jury, a preliminary hearing must be conducted first, before the trial. All preliminary hearings are conducted in provincial court.

If an accused elects to be tried in provincial court, no preliminary hearing will be conducted before the trial. All trials held in provincial court are tried without a jury.

ACCUSED'S ELECTION

1. Superior Court—judge and jury
2. Superior Court—judge alone

————————————————— preliminary hearing line *
3. Provincial court
   *If accused chooses 1 or 2 "above the line," a preliminary hearing must be held. Conversely, "below the line," (3) means no preliminary hearing.

PATH—GENERAL RULES

A sworn information signed by a justice is used only in proceedings conducted in provincial court, including

- first appearance,
- trials for

  a) summary conviction offences,
  b) sec. 553. C.C. offences,
  c) indictable offences, where the accused elects to have the trial conducted in provincial court

- preliminary hearing.

The path of the original information ends when a preliminary hearing concludes and the information is replaced with an indictment.

FIGURE 12.1   Path of an Information

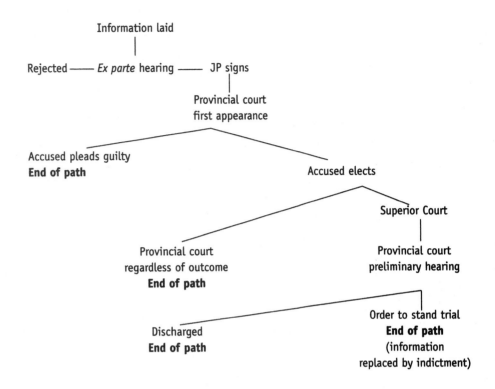

Therefore, an information is not used during trials conducted in **Superior Court** because an indictment, which formally charges the accused, replaces it in these trials (e.g., general division court, in Ontario).[34]

COMMENTARY

An indictment, like an information, is a document that represents a formal allegation or charge against an offender. In essence, except for the form on which they are written, the two are exactly the same. Informations and indictments serve the same purpose and have the same contents. The replacing of an information with an indictment is an example of an unnecessary complexity that exists in Canadian criminal law. The concept of starting court proceedings with one document (an information) and later changing to another document (an indictment) for certain trials is confusing for students to learn primarily because there is no need for two documents and there is no logical purpose for this procedure.

The replacement of an information with an indictment for certain trials is a law that could bear reform and change. The purposes of an information and an indictment are the same, and the purpose of a trial is the same regardless of what level of court tries the offender. It would then seem logical to use one common document throughout the entire court proceeding.

Test Yourself

1. You have reasonable grounds to charge Ward Cleaver (31), 5295 Barton St., Hamilton, with assault for punching Eddie (28) in the face on March 15, 2002 at 1525 King St., Hamilton.

   a) Go to sec. 841 C.C. Find the document that depicts an "information" and complete it; and
   b) explain how the *ex parte* hearing will be conducted.

THIRTEEN

Indictment—
Preliminary Hearing

Learning Outcomes

The student will be able to

*   interpret and apply sec. 535-551 C.C.

INTRODUCTION

The topics of indictments and preliminary hearings are directly related and must be learned together to understand the basic police procedures involved in dealing with them. The concept of an indictment cannot be understood without learning the procedures relating to a preliminary hearing.

Consequently, general rules relating to an indictment will be explained before the purpose and procedures of a preliminary hearing. Finally, the two topics will be connected in a summary.

INDICTMENT

PURPOSE

An indictment is a written document that formally charges an offender.[35] It has the same contents as an information. However, unlike an information, the term "laying" an indictment is not used. Instead, an indictment is *preferred*. The reason for the difference in terminology is that an indictment is not "laid" before a justice like an information is. An indictment is written by a Crown attorney (prosecutor), and becomes valid without it being brought before a justice.

Thus, when a Crown attorney writes and signs an indictment, the procedure is called *preferring an indictment*. In other words, the indictment is issued by a Crown attorney, not a justice.[36] A police officer cannot prefer an indictment, only a Crown attorney may do so. Most important, an indictment cannot be used to initiate proceedings against an accused person.

An indictment replaces an information when a trial is conducted in Superior Court of criminal jurisdiction, most commonly after a preliminary hearing concludes and the accused is ordered to stand trial. An indictment cannot be used for proceedings in provincial court, such as trials and preliminary hearings. An information is the document that is used in all provincial court proceedings.

PRELIMINARY HEARING

PURPOSE

The purpose of a preliminary hearing is to determine whether sufficient evidence exists to conduct a trial. The purpose is not to determine guilt or innocence.[37]

The preliminary hearing also represents "live" disclosure of the prosecution's case to the accused person. The prosecutor's case must be disclosed in writing to the accused; however, the preliminary hearing is an additional opportunity for the accused to analyze the prosecution's evidence.

When is a preliminary hearing required?

A preliminary hearing is required only before a trial scheduled in Superior Court of criminal jurisdiction, with or without a jury.[38] A preliminary hearing is not conducted if the trial is scheduled for provincial court.

An accused person may waive the preliminary hearing, with the consent of the prosecutor.[39] By waiving a preliminary hearing, the accused concedes that sufficient evidence exists to go to trial but is not acknowledging guilt.

Where is a preliminary hearing conducted?

A preliminary hearing is conducted in provincial court. A jury cannot be used in provincial court.[40]

What document is used as the formal allegation during a preliminary hearing?

The information that was initially laid to commence proceedings is the document that is used as the formal allegation against the accused at all preliminary hearings. An indictment is not used during the preliminary hearing.

What are the possible results of a preliminary hearing?

The judge may make one of the following rulings at the conclusion of a preliminary hearing:

1. **Discharge** This refers to a judge's conclusion that insufficient evidence exists. The accused is not ordered to stand trial. However, the accused is not acquitted; he or she is no longer charged. The original information terminates and cannot be used again in the future.[41] After an accused is discharged, new evidence may be obtained and the Crown may prosecute the accused at that time. It is possible to charge the offender in the future by laying a new information, but this requires the personal written consent of the attorney general.[42]
2. **Order the accused to stand trial** This refers to a judge's conclusion that sufficient evidence exists for a trial to be conducted. The prosecutor has proven a prima facie case; however, the accused has not been convicted.[43]

RULES AND PROCEDURES

The provisions that govern preliminary hearings are found in Part XVIII *Criminal Code* (sec. 535–51 C.C.). They create the following rules and procedures.

Rule 1

The prosecutor has the onus to prove that a *prima facie* case exists. This means that all the facts-in-issue are proven and sufficient evidence exists to go to trial. The prosecutor does not have to prove guilt beyond reasonable doubt but that the evidence is sufficient to obtain a conviction at a trial.[44] Proving that sufficient evidence exists requires a lesser standard than beyond reasonable doubt.

Rule 2

The prosecutor has *no obligation to introduce all the evidence* that exists in the Crown's case. The prosecutor has the choice to produce as much or as little evidence as he or she chooses, provided that the evidence is sufficient to convict at a future trial. For example, a prosecutor's case consists of five witnesses and the accused's confession. The prosecutor has the option of introducing all the evidence, or partial evidence such as the confession and one eyewitness only, provided that it will prove a *prima facie* case exists.[45] The judge cannot order the Crown to call witnesses or introduce evidence.[46]

Rule 3

The Crown presents his or her case first. The accused may cross-examine any Crown witness who testifies.[47]

Rule 4

All witnesses must be sworn under oath.[48]

Rule 5

At the conclusion of the Crown's case, the defence has the option of introducing evidence.[49] The choice belongs to the accused. The Crown may cross-examine any defence witness who is called by the defence to testify.

Rule 6

The judge cannot exclude evidence, under sec. 24(2) *Charter*. This exclusionary rule does not apply to preliminary hearings.[50]

Rule 7

After hearing the evidence introduced, the judge discharges the accused or orders the accused to stand trial. If the accused waives the preliminary hearing, the accused will be ordered to stand trial without the hearing being conducted.[51]

Rule 8

After the accused is ordered to stand trial, the information, the evidence introduced at the hearing, and the release document are transferred from provincial court to the Superior Court of criminal jurisdiction where the trial will be held.[52]

The information will not be used at the trial in Superior Court of criminal jurisdiction. Instead, the prosecutor prefers (writes and signs) an indictment to replace the information, meaning that the prosecutor completes the indictment and signs it. Other than the indictment not being sworn before a justice, the indictment is similar to the information.[53]

Direct Indictment

Section 577 C.C. affords the prosecution two significant advantages in expediting a trial. The Crown is permitted to cause an accused to stand trial in Superior Court by

1. preferring an indictment before a preliminary hearing is conducted, essentially bypassing a preliminary hearing, or
2. preferring an indictment after the accused has been discharged at the conclusion of a preliminary hearing, essentially reversing a judge's discharge of an accused.

The prosecutor must obtain the personal written consent of the attorney general or the deputy attorney general in order to prefer an indictment in these situations. This type of indictment, which is not commonly used, is called a direct indictment.[54]

Problem-Solving Case Studies

You are a police officer in each case. Each offender is an adult, unless otherwise indicated.

PROBLEM 82

Wally and Eddie have known each other for several years. Eddie assaulted Wally three days ago. Can Wally lay an information today to charge Eddie?

_____

_____

_____

_____

_____

PROBLEM 83

Ward is a security guard in a department store. He sees Eddie commit "theft under $5000.00." Can Ward lay an information anonymously so that Eddie will not know who charged him?

_____

PROBLEM 84

You form reasonable grounds today that Ward committed "fraud over $5000.00" eight months ago, and you arrest Ward without a warrant today. Ward is subsequently released at the police station by means of a promise to appear.

a) When must you lay an information?

_____

_____

b) Before whom must the information be laid?

_____

_____

c) Where must the information be laid?

_____

_____

d) You complete the information and bring it to a JP. You sign the information. What must occur afterward?

_____

e) After you sign the information and swear under oath, is Ward formally charged?

_____

f) Does an *ex parte* hearing have to be conducted even though you had arrested Ward without a warrant?

_____

g) What is the purpose of the *ex parte* hearing?

_____

_____

h) Can you introduce all the evidence, including reading witness statements, without calling the witnesses?

_____

_____

i) Do you, and any other witnesses, have to be sworn under oath before testifying at the *ex parte* hearing?

_____

j) Will Ward be present at the *ex parte* hearing?

_____

k) What will occur if you fail to prove that reasonable grounds exist?

_____

_____

l) What will occur if you successfully prove that reasonable grounds exist?

_____

m) When is Ward formally charged?

_____

n) Who owns the information after the information is signed by the JP?

_____

o) Could you have preferred an indictment instead of laying an information?

_____

_____

PROBLEM 85

Can an information be laid to charge an offender with either summary conviction, dual procedure, or indictable offences?

_____

_____

PROBLEM 86

You investigate two robberies that occurred during the past seven days and form reasonable grounds that Wally committed both offences. Can one wording allege both counts?

_____

_____

PROBLEM 87

Ward and June live at 1000 E. 200th St., Hamilton, Ontario. They leave their house on Saturday, March 23 at 9:00 a.m. and return on Sunday, March 24 at 9:00 p.m. They discover that a break and enter occurred during their absence. A 26-inch colour TV, valued at $700.00, was stolen. You form reasonable grounds on March 27 that Eddie committed the offence.

a) Should the offence date allege "between March 23rd and March 24th?"

_____

b) What should the alleged offence date be?

_____

_____

c) Does the address have to be included in the location portion that precedes the wording?

_____

d) Is the following a valid wording: "did commit a break, enter and theft?"

_____

_____

e) What wording should be used?

_____

_____

_____

f) After this information is signed by a JP, you question Eddie about other offences. Eddie confesses that he committed another break and enter at another house on the same street. Can another count be added to the signed information?

_____

_____

PROBLEM 88

Wally and Eddie commit three robberies, on April 5th, 6th, and 7th, respectively.

a) Can all three counts of robbery be joined on one information?

_____

_____

b) Can Wally and Eddie be joined on the same information?

_____

c) If Wally and Eddie are joined on the same information, can the prosecutor subpoena them to testify against each other?

_____

_____

_____

d) How should they be charged if the prosecution wishes to subpoena Wally and Eddie to testify against each other?

_____

_____

_____

PROBLEM 89

You arrest Ward for "attempt murder." June is the victim.

_____

a) How are proceedings commenced?

_____

b) Can the *ex parte* hearing be waived by the justice?

_____

c) The JP signs the information. Ward later appears in court. If Ward elects to have the trial in provincial court, will a preliminary hearing be conducted?

_____

_____

d) If Ward elects a trial in Superior Court of criminal jurisdiction (e.g., general division, Ontario), judge and jury, or judge alone, will a preliminary hearing be conducted?

_____

e) Where will the preliminary hearing be conducted?

_____

f) Will the information be used at the preliminary hearing?

_____

g) What is the purpose of the preliminary hearing?

_____

h) Who has the onus?

_____

i) Does the prosecutor have to introduce all the evidence at the preliminary hearing?

_____

_____

j) Can Ward be found guilty or not guilty at the conclusion of the preliminary hearing?

_____

k) If Ward is discharged, can an information be laid in the future when additional evidence is obtained?

_____

l) If Ward is discharged, can the prosecutor prefer an indictment?

_____

m) If Ward is ordered to stand trial, what happens to the information?

_____

_____

n) How is an indictment preferred?

_____

o) Could the preliminary hearing have been bypassed?

_____

_____

_____

Unit 4

Search and Seizure

Learning Outcomes

In this unit, the student will learn

- to interpret the authority to identify conditions and circumstances that permit lawful search and seizure,
- to analyze the circumstances of a case or problem,
- to recognize whether authority exists to lawfully search for and seize evidence, and
- to obtain and execute various search warrants.

INTRODUCTION

Police officers do not have authority to arbitrarily search persons or places, or to seize physical evidence. Instead, an officer must be authorized by a specific law that allows search and seizure under specific circumstances.

Search and seizure authorities may be defined as specific laws that explain circumstances and conditions that permit a police officer to lawfully search a person or a place, and to seize physical evidence. These authorities establish rules and procedures that govern search and seizure. However, they are not listed in any rulebook or statute; instead, they are found in various sources of law including the *Criminal Code*, CDSA, *Charter*, case law, and common law.

Applying search and seizure authorities is a crucial problem-solving skill used during an investigation.

FOURTEEN

Learning Outcomes

The student will be able to

- define terms relevant to search and seizure authorities.

INTRODUCTION

The following definitions are relevant to the subject of search and seizure.

Search is defined as looking for things, including spoken words, to be used as evidence of an offence.[1]

Seizure is defined as the taking of a thing from a person, by a public authority, without that person's consent.[2]

A search may be authorized in relation to persons and places.

Person includes

- clothes worn by the person,
- items on the person's body,
- items inside the clothes,
- items held by the person, **and**
- bodily substances, including blood and hair.

Place, in relation to searches, is not defined in the *Criminal Code.* The definition of place, found in sec. 348 (3) C.C., relates to break and enter offences only. Place, in relation to searches, includes

1. dwelling-house, defined as an entire, or any part of a, building or structure that is kept or occupied as a permanent residence, including

   - any building that is connected to the house by a doorway or covered and enclosed passageway, e.g., an attached garage is a dwelling-house
   - a unit designed to be mobile and to be used as a permanent or temporary residence, and is being used as a residence[3]

2. perimeter of a dwelling-house.[4]
3. building, referring to a structure that is not used as a permanent residence, including

   - business premise,
   - office, or
   - school.

4. receptacles, referring to a structure that is used to contain property, such as sheds and lockers, and
5. vehicles, referring to cars, trucks, and other motor vehicles that are not designed to be used as a temporary or permanent residence and are not being used as a residence, whether being operated or parked and unoccupied.[5]

UNLAWFUL/UNREASONABLE SEARCH OR SEIZURE

An unlawful search or seizure is one that is conducted without any lawful authority to do so. This type of search or seizure has three possible consequences:

1. *Criminal liability* If intentional, it may constitute a criminal offence such as "assault," "theft," or "mischief."
2. *Civil liability* If intentional or unintentional, a civil suit may result.
3. *Charter violation* If intentional or unintentional, a *Charter* violation will occur, and the evidence seized may be excluded from the trial.

FIFTEEN

Charter *Violations*

Learning Outcomes

The student will be able to

- interpret Section 8 of the *Charter*, and
- interpret Section 24 (2) of the *Charter*.

SECTION 8 *CHARTER*

Section 8 *Charter* has the most profound effect on a police officer's authority to search for and seize evidence. The section is composed of one sentence, which simply states, "everyone has the right to be secure against unreasonable search or seizure." Although seemingly simple, it has an extensively broad meaning and interpretation, requiring significant case law analysis to determine guidelines.

Section 8 *Charter* does not specifically define what constitutes a reasonable search or seizure. It does not establish or list any specific search or seizure authorities that the police may use. Instead, it limits the police powers of search and seizure to those circumstances and conditions that are found in various sources of law.[6]

The Supreme Court of Canada has identified a specific purpose of section 8 *Charter:* to secure and protect a citizen's right to a reasonable expectation of privacy against unjustified governmental intrusions by state agents, which include the police.[7] The court emphasized that this guarantee protects only a reasonable expectation of privacy. The circumstances that constitute reasonable expectation of privacy vary. Determining factors include the methods that the police use to conduct a search or seizure in a specific situation.

To prevent unjustified police violations of a person's reasonable expectation of privacy before it occurs, the Supreme Court of Canada, in *Hunter v. Southam Inc. (1984),*[8] established the following general principles relating to search and seizure:

1. Prior judicial authorization is required for the police to search or seize, unless exigent circumstances exist. Prior judicial authorization means a valid search warrant.
2. The person who may grant the authorization must be a judicial officer, meaning a justice of the peace or a provincial court judge.
3. The judicial officer must assess and evaluate a written application stating the evidence that composes the reasons for wanting to search. The assessment must be done in an entirely neutral, impartial, and unbiased manner.
4. The evidence described in the reasons for applying for the authorization, or warrant, must satisfy the judicial officer that reasonable grounds exist of the following:

   a) an offence has been committed, and
   b) the items intended to be searched for will be evidence that proves the offence has been committed, and
   c) the items are in the place to be searched. The judicial officer must be satisfied by a belief that must be based on a strong reason to believe, stated under oath. A belief that evidence may be found is insufficient to justify a search, because it suggests only a possibility of finding evidence. A possibility constitutes a suspicion, and searches cannot be based on suspicion.

5. If exigent circumstances exist, the police may search without prior judicial authorization. No warrant is needed. Exigent circumstances means an urgency exists where there is no time to obtain a warrant. Specific conditions that constitute exigent circumstances are found in various sources of law, which will be explained in this unit of the textbook.
6. If a search is conducted without prior judicial authorization, the same standards of belief apply as with a warrant. Reasonable grounds must be proven that

   a) an offence was committed, and
   b) the item to be searched for will prove the offence, and
   c) the item is in the place or on the person, and
   d) no time existed to obtain a warrant, and
   e) law authorized the search in that situation.

In summary, an unreasonable search constitutes a section 8 *Charter* violation. General examples of an unreasonable search, and a sec. 8 *Charter* violation, are when a police search or seizure

- violates a person's reasonable expectation of privacy, or

- is conducted without prior judicial authorization (warrant), no exigent circumstances, and without the authorization of a specific law that allows the search without a warrant, or
- is conducted with prior judicial authorization, but this authorization does not comply with the principles of properly obtaining a search warrant.

CONSEQUENCE OF A SECTION 8 *CHARTER* VIOLATION

Evidence obtained as the result of a sec. 8 *Charter* violation may be excluded from the trial; however, it is not automatically inadmissible or excluded at the trial. This represents a significant advantage for the police because evidence that is obtained as the result of an unreasonable or unauthorized search and seizure may be admissible at a trial despite the commission of a sec. 8 *Charter* violation.

Section 24(2) *Charter* governs the admissibility of evidence that is obtained as the result of a *Charter* violation. A trial judge uses this section to determine whether to allow the evidence or to exclude it.

SECTION 24 (2) *CHARTER*

A judge is responsible for determining whether evidence should be admissible or excluded (inadmissible) at a trial. He or she uses rules of evidence to make this determination. Section 24(2) *Charter* is an *exclusionary rule* that governs the admissibility of unreasonably obtained evidence resulting from a sec. 8 *Charter* violation.

The admissibility of evidence must be determined during a trial, not before the trial. Section 24(2) *Charter* becomes applicable during a trial only after it has been proven that a section 8 *Charter* violation has been committed in relation to a search or seizure. The general rule created by sec. 24(2) *Charter* is, "evidence obtained in a manner that violates a *Charter* right must be excluded if the admission of the evidence would bring the administration of justice into disrepute."

Three elements compose sec. 24(2) *Charter*:

1. A *Charter* violation, such as an unreasonable search or seizure, must be proven to have occurred.
2. The *Charter* violation must be proven to have occurred before the evidence was obtained or during the course of obtaining the evidence.
3. The judge must decide whether the evidence will be admissible or excluded. The determining factor will be whether the admission or the exclusion of the evidence would bring the administration of justice into disrepute.[9]

Accordingly, the trial judge has discretion whether to exclude or admit evidence obtained resulting from a *Charter* violation. Despite the commission of any *Charter* violation committed by the police, the judge does not have a mandatory obligation to exclude evidence.

The reputation of the administration of justice is the prominent factor that a judge considers when deciding whether to admit or exclude evidence under sec. 24(2) *Charter*. However, the *Charter* does not provide guidelines for judges regarding this decision. Instead, the Supreme Court of Canada, in *R. v. Collins (1987)*,[10] created general policies and guidelines regarding how to decide the admissibility of evidence under sec. 24(2) *Charter*.

"Disrepute" was defined as a concept that involves some element of long-term community views and values. Accordingly, the court established the "reasonable person test," which involves the perception and opinion of an average Canadian person within a reasonable Canadian community. Therefore, a trial judge must answer the following question when using discretion to admit or exclude evidence, "Would the reputation of the administration of justice suffer in the opinion of a reasonable Canadian person, if the evidence was admitted at a trial despite the fact that the evidence was obtained as the result of a *Charter* violation?" In other words, the judge should ask him- or herself, "What would the average Canadian citizen think of the justice system if I admit unreasonably obtained evidence?"

The Supreme Court listed the following factors that must be considered when answering that question:

1. The type of evidence obtained.
2. The type of *Charter* violation.
3. The severity of the *Charter* violation.
4. Whether the *Charter* violation was deliberate, or inadvertent, or committed in good faith.
5. Whether the *Charter* violation occurred because of urgency or necessity.
6. Whether other investigative methods were available to obtain that evidence.
7. Whether the evidence would have been obtained without the violation.
8. The severity of the offence.
9. Whether the evidence was essential to prove the charge.[11]

If the fairness of the trial is in some way affected by the admission of the evidence, exclusion of the evidence should result.

CLASSIFICATION OF EVIDENCE

The Supreme Court created additional specific rules governing admissibility under sec. 24(2) *Charter,* based upon two classifications that the court divided evidence into:

1. **Self-incriminating evidence** That which originates or emerges from the accused person, such as confessions, blood, breath, or hair samples.
2. **Physical evidence** That which does not originate or emerge from the accused, including items such as weapons, narcotics, and stolen property.

Two rules were developed from these classifications:

1. Evidence emerging from the accused that was obtained after a *Charter* violation occurred *should usually be excluded* because this type of evidence did not exist before the violation occurred, and it is self-incriminating in nature. However, the exclusion of the evidence is not mandatory.
2. Physical items, not emerging from an accused, obtained after a *Charter* violation *usually should be admitted* because this type of physical evidence existed before the *Charter* violation occurred. This represents a profound advantage for a police officer because physical items seized will usually not be excluded after the *Charter* violation is committed. However, the admission of this type of evidence is not mandatory, and the evidence may be excluded.[12]

R. V. STILLMAN (1997)[13]

The *Collins* decision has been regarded as the first to provide landmark guidelines relating to the admissibility of evidence. In 1997, the Supreme Court of Canada, in *R. v. Stillman (1997)*, added significant factors affecting admissibility of evidence.

The interpretation of the *Stillman* decision begins by dividing the *Collins* guidelines into three groups or factors that affect the reputation of the administration of justice:

1. trial fairness,
2. seriousness of the *Charter* violation, and
3. the possibility that the administration of justice could be brought into disrepute by excluding evidence that was obtained after a *Charter* violation occurred.

The *Collins* guidelines remain the basic principles that trial judges use to determine admissibility of evidence under sec. 24(2) *Charter.*

The *Stillman* case adds other principles relating specifically to group 1 (trial fairness) guidelines of the *Collins* case. The *Stillman* principles are intended to eliminate confusion about

a) what constitutes "real" evidence, and
b) the circumstances under which the exclusion or admission of real evidence would render a trial unfair.

Essentially, the *Stillman* principles determine whether a trial is unfair or fair relating to the admissibility of evidence. They do not determine the second and third group of *Collins* factors and do not replace the *Collins* principles. Trial fairness for an accused person is a cornerstone of Canadian democracy. The primary objective and the purpose of trial fairness is to prevent an accused person from being compelled, forced, or conscripted to provide evidence, in the form of statements or bodily samples, for the benefit of the state, while having *Charter* rights infringed. The general rule of trial fairness is, "if an accused is compelled *as a result of a Charter violation* to participate in the creation or discovery of self-incriminating evidence in the form of confessions, statements, or the provision of bodily samples, the admission of that evidence would *generally* tend to render a trial unfair."

Exclusion of the evidence is not automatic because exceptions to the rule exist, but the exceptions are rare. A three-step analysis, or test, was created by the Supreme Court of Canada to determine trial fairness. A summary of the test or analysis is as follows:

Step 1

Classify the evidence as *conscriptive* or *nonconscriptive.*

- Classification is based on the manner in which the evidence was obtained.
- If the evidence is classified as nonconscriptive, its admission will not render a trial unfair. The trial fairness test is complete at this point, and the judge will then revert to the *Collins* guidelines and determine the second and third group of *Collins* admissibility factors, being the severity of the *Charter* violation and the effect of exclusion on the reputation of the administration of justice.
- If the evidence is classified as conscriptive, the judge continues to the next step of this trial fairness test.

Step 2

If the evidence is classified as conscriptive, the Crown has the onus to prove, on a balance of probabilities, that the evidence would have been discovered by alternative nonconscriptive means.

- If the Crown fails to prove this, then the admission of the evidence will render the trial to be unfair. A *general* rule is then created. The judge will generally exclude the evidence at this point without considering the second and third groups of Collins factors i.e., the judge will not have to consider the severity of the *Charter* violation or the effect of exclusion on the reputation of the administration of justice. Essentially, once a trial has been ruled to be unfair, exclusion of evidence must occur because an unfair trial would bring the administration of justice into disrepute. This is the prominent rule created by *Stillman*. After a trial is ruled unfair, the *Collins* test is also complete, and exclusion of evidence generally will occur under sec. 24(2) *Charter*.
- However, if the Crown successfully proves that the conscriptive evidence would have been discovered by alternative nonconscriptive means, then the judge proceeds to step 3 (below) of the trial fairness test.

Step 3

If evidence is classified as conscriptive, and the Crown successfully proves on a balance of probabilities that the evidence would have been discovered by alternative nonconscriptive means, then the admission of the evidence will generally not render a trial unfair.

- The evidence is not automatically admissible at this point.
- The judge then reverts back to the *Collins* test and determines admissibility after considering the second and third group of *Collins* factors. In other words, the admissibility of the evidence is dependent on the severity of the *Charter* violation and the effect of exclusion on the reputation of the administration of justice.

CLASSIFICATION OF EVIDENCE

After it has been proven that a *Charter* violation has occurred, the trial judge must classify the evidence as conscriptive or nonconscriptive.

Conscriptive evidence is defined as evidence with which an accused is compelled to incriminate him- or herself, by means of a statement, the use of the body, or the production of bodily samples, at the request of the state. The most common types of conscriptive evidence are

- confession made by an accused following a *Charter* violation such as the right to counsel, and
- the compelled taking and use of bodily substances, e.g., blood, which lead to self-incrimination.

The following general rules were created:

1. Compelled confessions or statements obtained as a result of a *Charter* violation generally tend to render a trial unfair.
2. Police actions that intrude upon an individual's body in more than minimal fashion, without consent or an authority that permits the intrusion, constitute a sec. 7 *Charter* violation in a manner that generally renders a trial unfair.

Nonconscriptive evidence is defined as evidence that the accused was not compelled to participate in the creation or discovery of. This type of evidence existed independent of the *Charter* violation in a form usable by the state. The admission of nonconscriptive evidence generally does not render a trial unfair.

Real evidence is a term referring to a physical item or any *tangible* item that exists as an independent entity. Blood and hair samples are often categorized as real evidence. A misconception has existed that real evidence is always admissible.

The key element that distinguishes conscriptive evidence from nonconscriptive evidence is *not* whether the evidence is "real." Instead, the distinguishing element is whether the accused was compelled to make a statement or provide the evidence in violation of the *Charter*. Consequently, "real" evidence can be classified as conscriptive evidence. This means that the status of an item as being "real" evidence is irrelevant to the determination of admissibility under sec. 24(2) *Charter*. In summary, nonconscriptive evidence refers to evidence found without the participation of the accused, e.g., a murder weapon found at a crime scene.

Derivative evidence is related to conscriptive evidence; it is a subset of conscriptive evidence and frequently described as conscripted "real" evidence. Derivative evidence is defined as "an item of real evidence that is discovered as the result of conscripted evidence" (usually a statement) after a *Charter* violation has occurred. Essentially, it is "real" evidence that is derived from conscriptive evidence. The sequence leading to derivative evidence is

1. a *Charter* violation occurs first,
2. the accused is conscripted against him- or herself, and then
3. an item of real evidence is discovered afterward.

Essentially, the unlawfully conscripted evidence is the cause of the discovery of the real evidence. The derivative evidence should not be considered "real evidence," which rarely renders a trial unfair. Instead, derivative evidence is considered conscriptive or self-incriminating evidence discovered as the result of an accused's being conscripted to provide that evidence, following a *Charter* violation.

In summary, the admission of derivative evidence will generally render a trial unfair. An example is found in *R. v. Black (1989)*.[14] In this case, the accused was arrested for murder; the police committed a sec. 10(b) *Charter* violation. Afterward, the accused made an inculpatory statement. The accused was then taken to her apartment by the police. She produced a knife from a kitchen drawer and gave it to the police. She told the officers that it was the murder weapon. The statement was conscriptive evidence. The knife was derivative evidence because it was obtained as a direct result of the conscripted statement.

After evidence, including derivative evidence, is classified as conscriptive, the judge then proceeds to the next step of the test to determine whether the admission of the evidence would render the trial unfair. As stated previously, the general rule is that conscripted evidence *tends* to render a trial unfair. This means that it is possible for conscriptive and derivative evidence to be admissible.

The general rule regarding the admissibility of conscriptive evidence is as follows. The admission of conscriptive evidence will not render the trial unfair where the evidence would have been discovered in the absence of the conscripted evidence. This general rule is called the "discoverability principle." Two principles determine whether conscriptive or derivative evidence will be admissible or excluded, according to the "discoverability principle":

• existence or absence of an independent source of evidence, and
• whether the discovery of the evidence was inevitable.

An "independent" source of evidence refers to an alternative nonconscriptive means by which the police could have obtained the evidence that had been classified as conscriptive. Therefore, when the Crown proves on a balance of probabilities that an independent source, or alternative nonconscriptive means, exists and the police would have discovered it, then the admission of the conscriptive evidence would not render a trial unfair. An example exists in *R. v. Colarusso (1994)*, which is explained in Chapter 15 of this text. In this case, a medical-purposes blood sample was seized by the police without a warrant. The sample was given to the police by a coroner, who obtained it from a lab technician. The police could have obtained a warrant to seize the sample, which would have represented an independent source, or nonconscriptive means of obtaining the evidence. The admission of the warrantless, seized evidence would not render the trial unfair. "Inevitable discovery" refers to a reasonable likelihood that the police *would have discovered* the conscripted or derivative evidence. An example is found in *R. v. Black (1989)*.[15] In this case, the accused's sec. 10(b) *Charter* right to counsel was violated. After the *Charter* violation occurred, police questioning resulted in an inculpatory statement made by the accused. The accused was taken to her apartment by the police where she led officers to a knife—the murder weapon. The court excluded the statement because its admission would render the trial unfair. The statement was conscriptive evidence. The knife was derivative evidence. The court then applied the "discoverability principle." It ruled that the police undoubtedly would have searched the accused's apartment, which represented the crime scene. The police would have discovered the knife without the accused's assistance. Consequently, the knife's discovery was inevitable, and its admission would not render the trial unfair.

An example of evidence that *would not have been discovered* in the absence of conscripted evidence is found in *R. v. Burlingham (1995)*.[16] In this case, the police arrested the accused for murder. They then committed a *Charter* violation. Afterward, the accused made a statement that was ruled to be conscriptive. The murder weapon (a gun) was discovered at the bottom of a frozen river as the result of the accused's conscriptive statement. It was ruled that the investigation would never have led the police to discover the gun without the accused's statement. The weapon's discovery was not inevitable, and the admission of the gun would render the trial unfair.

In summary, the following are the key points of the *Stillman* principles:

• The *Collins* case creates factors that determine admissibility of evidence under sec. 24(2) *Charter*.
• The *Collins* factors are divided into three groups; the first group is trial fairness.
• The *Stillman* principles relate only to the determination of trial fairness.
• The *Stillman* and *Collins* principles apply only after a *Charter* violation has occurred.
• Trial fairness is then determined in stages.
• First, the evidence obtained after a *Charter* violation must be classified as conscriptive or nonconscriptive.
• Conscriptive evidence is self-incriminating evidence such as a compelled statement or seizure of bodily substances.
• Conscriptive evidence may lead to the seizure of derivative evidence.
• Conscriptive evidence tends to render a trial unfair.
• After evidence is classified as conscriptive, a second stage is required to determine whether the evidence would have been discovered in the absence of the *Charter* violation.

- Discoverability is proven by
  - an independent source, or
  - inevitability of discovery.

- The probability of discovery means that the admission of conscriptive evidence would not render a trial unfair; the court must then determine the second and third groups of *Collins* factors to decide admissibility.
- The absence of probability of discovery negates the need to consider the remaining *Collins* factors; the evidence will be excluded under sec. 24(2) *Charter*.
- Nonconscriptive evidence generally will not render a trial unfair; the court then considers the remaining *Collins* factors to determine admissibility.

For the purpose of offering preventative measures against exclusion of evidence, the remainder of Unit Four will examine what circumstances will result in the admissibility of breath and blood samples or their exclusion under sec. 24(2) *Charter*.

SUMMARY

Section 24(2) *Charter* prevents automatic exclusion of all evidence that is seized after the commission of a *Charter* violation. It provides a common-sense, rational approach to determining the admissibility of evidence that a police officer seizes, after the accused's *Charter* rights are violated. The process includes considering the opinion of a reasonable Canadian citizen, representing a logical means of administering justice. Theoretically, sec. 24(2) *Charter* is a concept that is intended to preserve the fairness and integrity of the Canadian judicial system, and ensure that its reputation does not diminish in the perception of Canadian citizens. When properly applied, sec. 24(2) *Charter* not only ensures that evidence will be admitted in trials of serious offences if the police acted on good faith but also prevents the police from searching people and places by intentional, unlawful means without any accountability.

Problem-Solving Case Study

You are a police officer in this case. The offender is an adult.

PROBLEM 90

You arrest and charge Ward for "attempted murder." You search Ward's car and find a knife that was used in the offence. Afterward, Ward confesses to you that he committed the offence.

a) Can the admissibility of the knife be determined before the trial?

_____

_____

b) If a sec. 8 *Charter* violation is proven to have occurred after the knife was lawfully seized, does sec. 24(2) *Charter* apply to determine its admissibility?

_____

c) It is proven that you committed a sec. 8 *Charter* violation before the knife was seized and before the confession was obtained. Will the knife automatically be excluded under sec. 24(2) *Charter*?

_____

_____

d) Will the knife likely be admitted or excluded?

_____

_____

_____

e) Will the confession automatically be excluded?

_____

_____

_____

f) Will the confession likely be admitted or excluded?

_____

_____

_____

_____

_____

_____

_____

_____

_____

_____

_____

_____

_____

_____

_____

_____

_____

_____

_____

_____

SIXTEEN

Learning Outcomes

The student will be able to

- obtain lawful "consent" to search for and seize evidence, and
- execute a consent search.

INTRODUCTION

Consent is a valuable effective investigative technique that facilitates many police procedures, including interrogation, search, and seizure of evidence. Obtaining valid consent significantly expands the circumstances regarding where a police officer may conduct a search and seizure.

1. Consent removes the obstruction of having to obtain a search warrant prior to the search, and
2. It removes the restrictions that accompany the warrantless search provisions found in various sources of law. These provisions require a belief, based on reasonable grounds, that a number of circumstances exist, prior to conducting the search.

Obtaining *consent* to search during an investigation has significant advantages for the police officer:

1. Persons and any type of place, including a house, may be searched by consent.
2. Consent may be obtained even if only mere suspicion exists. A belief based on reasonable grounds does not have to be formed before consent is obtained.
3. Consent may be obtained to search for any type of item (e.g., stolen property, weapons, narcotics).
4. The time required to obtain a search warrant, usually about one hour, is eliminated. This minimizes the possibility of losing evidence.

The police must follow certain procedures and rules to obtain valid consent. The Crown and the police have the onus to prove that valid consent was obtained before the search began and before the items were seized. Despite the prevalent use of consent, no Canadian statute provides laws or guidelines that instruct a police officer about the procedures that must be used to obtain valid consent. For this reason, case law will be interpreted in this section to create a procedure that may be used to obtain valid consent.

CONSENT AUTHORITY

Remarkably, there is no Canadian legislation or statute that specifically authorizes a warrantless search by consent, i.e., none that creates guidelines and procedures to follow for the purpose of obtaining valid consent.

Consent searches are authorized at common law.[17] The following statement is the common law doctrine that authorizes consent searches: "One who has invited or assented to an act being done towards him cannot, when he suffers it, complain of it as wrong."[18]

The *theory of consent search* is based on the premise that the search does not constitute an "actionable intrusion." According to this theory, a person who consents to a police search waives the right to invoke legal protection against any intrusion that may result because of the search. The giving of consent has been considered to be a "private transaction between individuals." Consequently, consent searches are lawful regardless of whether the police had reasonable grounds to search by means of any other alternative authority.[19]

Although common law authorizes and recognizes consent searches, *common law does not create specific procedures and rules for the police to follow.*

In addition to common law authority, consent searches have been authorized by case law decisions. Two prominent case law decisions create distinct rules and procedures relevant to consent searches. Both decisions will be interpreted in this section.

DEFINITION

No Canadian statute defines consent. Valid consent is defined in case law as a "voluntary and informed decision to permit the intrusion of the investigative process upon his constitutionally protected rights."[20] The key elements of this definition are

1. Consent is an informed decision. The person making the decision must be informed of sufficient facts and must have adequate knowledge of exactly what has been decided.
2. The decision must be voluntarily made. No person is obliged to give consent to the police to permit a warrantless search. Every person has the choice to give or refuse consent.

SECTION 8 *CHARTER* WAIVER

Valid consent to search or seize constitutes a waiver of the sec. 8 *Charter* right. Waiving a *Charter* right means to surrender it or give it up. If the consent given is valid, the search or seizure will be reasonable and no sec. 8 *Charter* violation will have occurred. The seized item will be admissible.

Conversely, if valid consent is not obtained and the police search for or seize evidence, a sec. 8 *Charter* violation will have occurred. Exclusion of evidence obtained by means of invalid consent may occur, but *the evidence will not be automatically inadmissible.* If a physical item is seized as the result of a search and seizure resulting from invalid consent, the item should usually be admissible according to the Supreme Court of Canada guideline established in the *Collins case.*

OBTAIN CONSENT—PROCEDURE

Neither the *Criminal Code* nor the *Charter* creates guidelines or procedures for obtaining valid consent. Two case law decisions establish procedures that guide the obtaining of valid consent:

R. v. Wills (1992) Ontario Court of Appeal[21]
R. v. Borden (1994) Supreme Court of Canada[22]

ONTARIO COURT OF APPEAL GUIDELINES

The *Wills* case is a prominent case in that it creates seven elements that compose valid consent. Each element must be proven by the prosecution. The following is a list of the elements that the court created. The court did not recommend specific procedures to prove the elements. Following each element is a suggested procedure that may be used to prove each one, for optimum results:

1. Consent must be expressed or implied

The content of the accused's consent must be unequivocal. This means that the accused's words must clearly and unmistakably state that he or she is giving consent. No ambiguity may exist about what the accused said in relation to consent. If what the accused says is vague, no valid consent will exist.

Consent from an adult offender may be obtained verbally or in writing. Consent in writing refers to a written consent form, or statement signed by the consenting person. Written consent has the advantage of helping to prove the validity of the consent that was given. Verbal consent refers to conversation that is not written or signed in a statement form. Instead, it is recorded verbatim by the officer in a notebook.

Consent from a young offender should be obtained in writing. Written consent is a statement written either on a statement document or in an officer's notebook. The content should include the seven elements that compose valid consent, and it should be written in the first person of the consenting person e.g., "I, Robert Johnson, consent …" The consenting person then signs the statement.

Procedure Record *verbatim* all conversation with the accused. This refers to direct, word-for-word quotes including all questions, comments, and responses. When testifying in court, state the conversation verbatim. Do not paraphrase the accused's words when recording them or during testimony. Paraphrasing refers to condensing or summarizing the accused's verbatim response into a general statement such as "the accused consented." This is a conclusion that the judge must make. A paraphrase is vague and does not prove unmistakable consent.

Obtain written consent from a young offender by drafting a consent statement in your notebook or on a statement form. Obtain the young offender's signature. This procedure may be used for adults, but verbal consent from adults is also sufficient.

2. Consent must be voluntary

Voluntary means free from coercion, oppression, inducements, or any other external conduct that prevents the accused from choosing whether or not to give consent. Inducements are defined as threats or promises. The accused must be aware of what he or she is doing and cannot be influenced by any threats or promises. *Voluntariness is proven by the absence of inducements* made by the police when obtaining consent. Again, recording and testifying about verbatim conversation is essential to prove the absence of inducements.

Procedure Inform the accused that he or she has no obligation to consent and that the decision to consent is exclusively his or hers. Avoid using any words that constitute or imply

- threats of violence, or of being arrested or charged if consent is denied, or
- favourable promises, such as in relation to arrest, charge, and release.

Include an emphasis that "the choice is yours." Ask the accused if this is understood and record the response to prove the accused's knowledge that the decision belongs exclusively to him or her.

Record the entire conversation verbatim. Avoid paraphrasing, such as "the accused voluntarily consented" or "I did not threaten or make promises to the accused" during testimony.

3. The accused must be aware of the specific act to be conducted

The accused must have specific knowledge of what procedure the officer intends to complete. The exact nature of the search and seizure cannot be withheld from the accused.

Procedure Inform the accused

- that a search and/or seizure is being requested, and
- what the target of the search is (e.g., person or specific place), and
- the specific evidence that is being sought, if it is known, and
- the type of offence that is being investigated.

Providing the accused with as much information as possible not only ensures that the consent will be valid but also may convince the accused to cooperate and surrender the property voluntarily before a search is conducted.

4. The accused must be aware of the potential consequences of giving consent

The accused must have knowledge of what may result after the search and seizure is complete. Consequences of a search or seizure are prosecution and/or admissibility of the evidence seized.

Procedure Inform the accused

- that charges may be laid,
- of the specific offence, if it is known, and
- that the evidence may be used at a trial.

5. The accused must have knowledge that consent may be refused

No law exists in Canada that compels or obliges a person to consent to a search or seizure. Additionally, refusal to consent is not an offence. A person cannot be charged or arrested for refusing to consent. The accused must know that he or she has a choice to allow the search or refuse to consent.

Procedure Inform the accused, "You don't have to consent. You may refuse to give consent. The choice is yours. If you refuse, you cannot be charged for refusing."

6. The accused must have knowledge that consent may be revoked at any time after consent is initially given

After a person consents to a search, the consent is not irrevocable. The person may stop the search at any time by removing consent. The accused must be informed about this fact, and the prosecution will be required to prove the accused's knowledge of this fact.

Procedure   Inform the accused, "If you consent to this search, you can revoke consent at any time you choose and stop the search."

7. If the accused gives consent, he or she did not then revoke consent at any time during the search

The prosecution has the onus to prove that the accused said or did nothing during the search that directly indicated or indirectly implied an intent to terminate the search. This element is proven by the absence of any statement or conduct made between the time that consent was given and the time that any seizure was made.

Procedure   This cannot be proven by simply paraphrasing, "the accused did not revoke consent at any time during the search." This is a conclusion reserved for the judge. Instead, record all conversation verbatim, between the time consent was given and the time the seizure was made. Note the time periods when the accused was silent. Record the location and conduct of the accused during the search.

When testifying, state the entire conversation, periods of silence, and all relevant observations. The absence of any statement made by the accused that indicates the removal of consent will prove this element.

SUPREME COURT OF CANADA GUIDELINES

The circumstances in *R. v. Borden (1994)*[23] provide examples of invalid consent and how sec. 24(2) *Charter* is applied to determine the admissibility of the evidence that originated from the accused (e.g., blood samples).

Situation   The police arrested an adult accused for one count of sexual assault; he was suspected of committing a second count of sexual assault. The police sought blood samples from the accused regarding the second count of sexual assault for the purpose of DNA comparison. The accused signed a written consent form that simply indicated that he consented to the taking of a blood sample "for the purpose relating to their investigations." The accused was not informed that the blood sample was taken specifically for the second count of sexual assault. After the blood sample was obtained, a positive comparison was made, and the accused was charged with the second count of sexual assault. Was the consent valid?

No. Although the use of the plural "investigations" was deliberate, the consent form did not specify that the blood sample was to be used specifically for the second count. The second investigation exceeded the exploratory stage. The police were obliged to inform the accused that the blood sample was intended to be used in a different investigation from the one for which the accused was detained. The accused was uninformed of the main purpose of the blood sample. The taking of blood was a seizure, and the consent was invalid, constituting a sec. 8 *Charter* violation. The Supreme Court of Canada ruled that the admission of the blood sample would bring the administration of justice into disrepute. Consequently, the blood sample was excluded under sec. 24(2) *Charter*.[24]

In the *Borden* case, the Supreme Court considered the *Wills* ruling made by the Ontario Court of Appeal, and listed similar elements that compose valid consent:

1. The accused must have the volition to decide whether or not to consent. The decision must be voluntarily made.
2. The accused must be informed of sufficient available information by the police.
3. The accused must know that he or she is not required to consent.
4. The accused must understand the specific investigation in which the police intend to use the product of the seizure.
5. If the police arrest or detain an accused for one offence and ask for consent to seize evidence to use in the investigation of an unrelated offence, the accused must be informed of this fact.
6. The police do not have to ensure that the accused has a detailed comprehension of every possible outcome of giving consent. The accused must understand generally the consequences of giving consent by knowing that the item seized by consent will be used for another specific investigation.

7. If the police arrest or detain an accused for one offence and are in only the exploratory stage of another unrelated offence, the police have no obligation to inform the accused that evidence he gives by consent, regarding the offence for which he is arrested, may be used in the investigation of another offence. If the investigation is beyond the exploratory stage and the police suspect the accused in the other offence, the police must inform the accused that the evidence seized will also be used in the other investigation.

R. v. Clements (1996)[25] is a Supreme Court of Canada case that provides an excellent example of circumstances that constitute valid consent, and a general rule regarding the admissibility of a physical item seized by means of invalid consent, under sec. 24(2) *Charter*.

CASE LAW

R. V. CLEMENTS (1996)

Issue   Consent

Offence   "robbery"

Circumstances   Four robberies occurred at stores in one community. The offender wore a Halloween mask and carried a revolver during each offence. Witnesses gave only general descriptions of the offender, the gun, and the mask.

While on patrol some time after the last robbery, two officers received a radio transmission informing them about a Crime Stoppers tip. Two persons, a male and a female, had tried to sell cocaine in a nearby city. A description of the suspect's car and licence plate number was broadcast. Shortly afterward, the officers saw the car and followed it for three miles to a gas station. The officers stopped the car and conducted an investigation that consisted of two separate searches of the suspect's car. The driver was male and the passenger was female.

The officers believed that the information received did not constitute reasonable grounds that narcotics were in the car, preventing a lawful search of the car without a warrant. Both occupants of the car were escorted to the cruiser and were seated inside. One officer asked to search the car. The driver complied with the request.

A search began, resulting in the seizure of a loaded and cocked handgun, found under the driver's seat. After the search ended, the officers arrested both occupants for the possession of a restricted weapon. They were informed of their right to counsel. They invoked the right and exercised it after they arrived at the police station.

After consulting with a lawyer, the driver signed a written consent permitting a second search of the car. As a result, a Halloween mask was seized from behind the dashboard. The driver was subsequently charged with four counts of robbery.

Trial   The evidence relating to consent was composed of

1. the officer's statement, "If you let me have a quick look in your car, I can solve this here, or right now,"

2. the accused's lack of protest after the officer's request, and

3. the accused's awareness that giving consent was not compulsory, proven during his testimony, when he testified that he "knew they had no right to search my car."

The officer who requested the first search testified that he could not remember informing the accused about what they were investigating or that he could have refused to give consent. However, the accused's testimony proved that he had knowledge about the drug investigation, having learned this by means of some communication between the officers.

The defence brought a motion to exclude the gun and the mask because of sec. 8 (unreasonable search), sec. 9 (arbitrary detention), and sec. 10(b) (right to counsel) *Charter* violations.

The trial judge ruled that

• A sec. 9 *Charter* violation occurred. The occupants were detained; they did not enter the cruiser by consent.

continued

- A sec. 10(b) *Charter* violation occurred. The occupants were entitled to be informed of their right to counsel upon detention. Instead, they were informed a few minutes later, after the first search concluded.

- Both *Charter* violations lasted only two or three minutes.

- Reasonable grounds did not exist to search the car for narcotics without a warrant.

- The search and seizure did not constitute a sec. 8 *Charter* violation because valid consent was obtained before both searches.

The gun and the mask were not excluded under sec. 24(2) *Charter*. The accused was convicted, and he appealed to the Ontario Court of Appeal.

Appeal   The appeal was dismissed by a 2–1 decision. The following rulings were made:

- The consent regarding the first search was valid because it was voluntary and informed. The accused knew the officers were searching for drugs, and he could have refused to give consent.

- The accused's identity was proven by the similarities of the gun, mask, and accused's height, weight, and hair, with the general descriptions given by the witnesses.

- The content of the Crime Stoppers tip, in this case, did not constitute reasonable grounds to search without a warrant.

- If valid consent had not been obtained in this case, which would have resulted in a sec. 8 *Charter* violation, the gun would not have been excluded under sec. 24(2) *Charter* because

  a   the crime was serious, and

  b   the officers acted in good faith, without displaying oppressive conduct, and

  c   the loaded, cocked gun represented danger to the police and public, and

  d   the gun was physical evidence that existed before any potential *Charter* violation.

The admission of the gun would be "realistic" and would not diminish the public's respect for the justice system if the consent had been invalid. Sec. 9 and 10(b) *Charter* violations occurred prior to the second search and the seizure of the mask. However, the mask was not excluded under sec. 24 (2) *Charter* because its admission would not bring the administration of justice into disrepute. The obtaining of formal, written consent was a significant factor that contributed to this decision. The accused appealed his conviction to the Supreme Court of Canada.

Supreme Court of Canada Appeal   The accused's appeal was dismissed. The court ruled that valid consent had been obtained and that no sec. 8 *Charter* violation occurred because "the appellant testified that he knew the police had no right to search the car. It is apparent that he gave his consent freely and voluntarily."

SUMMARY

The *Clements* case represents the *profound advantage police have* regarding consent searches during the investigation of a serious offence and the admissibility of physical items including weapons. The summary of principles created in *Clements* include

1. The prominent elements to prove consent are the accused's knowledge that

    - the police have no legal authority to compel consent, and

    - consent may be denied by the accused (consent from an adult may be obtained verbally).

2. Valid consent may be obtained with less than the optimum procedures. The officer's conversation with the accused, in relation to consent, was relatively brief. The information conveyed to the accused was minimal in comparison to the extensive guidelines created in the *Wills* and *Borden* cases.

continued

3. The accused's statements during the investigation and during court testimony are crucial evidence to prove knowledge. The accused cannot be compelled by the prosecution to testify. If the decision is to testify, he or she may be cross-examined by the Crown attorney. The accused's testimony may be used to prove that he or she knew that no legal obligation exists to consent and that consent may be denied.

4. Weapons and physical evidence seized in relation to serious offences will likely be admissible even if valid consent is not obtained.

COMMENTARY

Principle 4 (above) may represent one of the most significant investigative advantages for police officers because it does not impose unreasonable obligations upon police officers in dangerous situations.

The court has effectively demonstrated what the *priorities* are in cases involving serious offences and weapons. The importance of admitting a weapon at a trial outweighs the deficiency of the consent that was obtained to search. The court is not simply accepting or advocating mediocrity from the police. Instead, the court acknowledged the reality that investigations often involve dangerous situations where time is of the essence for the investigating officer. If the time restriction causes the consent to be invalid, the court will not penalize the prosecution by excluding evidence. This principle is a logical, rational method of ensuring that justice is administered properly.

Therefore, police officers must be cognizant that invalid consent is not always detrimental to an investigation, if the error was committed in good faith. The absence of reasonable grounds when a suspected, armed offender is stopped should not deter or delay an attempt to search by consent. If mere suspicion exists, police officers should either obtain additional evidence quickly by means of visual observations or by questioning the suspect, or search by consent. It is important to use effective communication skills to obtain consent quickly and not delay the search with unnecessary or meaningless conversation.

Effective communication skills are learned through experience and practice. If the information conveyed to the suspect is not sufficient to constitute valid consent due to the urgency and the time restrictions caused by the potential risk created by the presence of weapons, the prosecution of the offender will not usually be adversely affected.

Finally, if weapons seized by invalid consent are excluded at a trial under sec. 24(2) *Charter*, the investigation is not a failure. The seizure of the weapon ensured that the officer would not be harmed or killed at the time of the investigation. That had a higher priority than exclusion of evidence at a trial.

THIRD-PARTY CONSENT (MULTIPLE OCCUPIERS)

Who may give lawful consent to search a place? If a consent search is conducted in relation to a place, the police must prove that the person who consented had lawful authority to do so. This becomes significant when more than one person occupies, lives in, or uses a place that the police intend to search by consent. Third-party consent refers to consent given by one person to search a place that he or she does not own. Additionally, it also refers to situations where a person consents to the search of a place and another person's property is seized.

The following general principles and rules were established by the Supreme Court of Canada, in *R. v. Edwards (1996)*,[26] relating to third-party consent searches where multiple persons occupy one place:

1. The legality of a search by consent of a third party depends on whether the accused had a reasonable expectation of privacy.
2. A reasonable expectation of privacy is determined on the total circumstances of each individual case. The factors that are considered, but not strictly restricted to, include

- presence of the accused at the time of the search,
- possession or control of the property or place searched,
- ownership of the property or place,
- historical use of the property or place,
- the ability to regulate access of people into the place, including the right to admit or exclude others from the place,
- the existence of a subjective expectation of privacy. Subjective refers to a belief that exists in the accused's mind, not external circumstances, and
- the objective reasonableness of the expectation. Objective refers to actual external circumstances, not the accused's belief.

If the accused establishes that a reasonable expectation of privacy existed, then the judge must decide whether the search was conducted in a reasonable manner. Additionally, the court ruled that an occupant of a place who is a guest or visitor has *no expectation of privacy*. A visitor, in the *Edwards* case, was defined as a person who

- did not contribute to the rent or household expenses,
- kept a few personal belongings in the owner's apartment,
- had a key to the apartment, and
- lacked the authority to regulate access of people into the owner's apartment.[27]

Essentially, these principles may be interpreted and summarized as follows:

1. Persons who have a reasonable expectation of privacy in a place are owners, and lawful occupiers. These persons have authority to give consent to the police to search the place. Additionally, these persons may refuse to give consent and may revoke consent at any time after it is given. However, an owner's authority will supersede a lawful occupier's authority.
2. A lawful occupier refers to a person who

   a) has possession or control of the place or property, and
   b) has the ability to regulate access of persons into that place, including the right to allow other people to enter, or prohibit entry, or remove others from the place. If an owner or lawful occupier gives consent to the police to search a place, the police may search for and seize evidence that is possessed by a guest or visitor.

3. Guests and visitors have no reasonable expectation of privacy in a place because they do not have control of the place and have no right to allow people to enter, or to prohibit or remove people from that place.
4. A person who is not authorized by the owner to regulate access of people into the place, such as a guest or visitor, does not have lawful authority to give consent to the police to search a place.

OBTAIN THIRD-PARTY CONSENT—PROCEDURE

The following is a list of procedures and rules that may be used to obtain consent to search places that multiple people are occupying, living in, or using:

1. Determine who the owner of the place is and if he or she is present. If present, obtain consent from that owner, who has the most lawful authority to give consent.
2. If the owner is absent, and other occupiers are present, ask the occupiers

   - who has possession or control of the place, and
   - who has the right to regulate access of people into the place.

   Obtain consent from a person who qualifies as a lawful occupier based on the answers to these questions.

3. Do not obtain consent from a guest or visitor, or any other person who does not control the place or the entry or removal of people from the place. In other words, do not obtain consent to search the place from a person who cannot regulate access of persons into the place.
4. If consent is obtained from the owner or lawful occupier, search all areas and seize any evidence, including any that is in the possession of a guest or visitor.

5. If the owner or lawful occupier who gives consent is an adult, he or she does not have to be informed of the right to counsel prior to the search because he or she is not detained.

6. If the person who gives consent is a young person, aged 12–17 inclusive, inform the person of the right to counsel prior to the search.

OWNER (MANAGEMENT)—TEMPORARY OCCUPIERS

Some places where the police may need to search are owned or managed by one person and temporarily occupied by another person who has rented, leased, or been given a place to use. Examples include

*   apartments owned by landlords and rented by tenants,
*   hotel rooms rented to guests,
*   offices owned by employers and given to employees, and
*   lockers owned by schools and leased or given to students.

The question relevant to an investigation is, "Does the owner or management of a place have authority to give the police consent to enter and search the place that is

CASE LAW

R. V. EDWARDS (1996)

Issue   Third-party consent

Offence   "possession of narcotics for the purpose of trafficking"

Circumstances   The police conducted surveillance of the accused (adult) after receiving information that he was trafficking narcotics out of his car, and that the narcotics were either on his person, at his residence, or at his girlfriend's apartment. His girlfriend was an 18-year-old Grade 11 student who lived alone.

On the arrest day, the police saw the accused drive his girlfriend from a residence to her apartment. The accused entered the apartment and remained there briefly. Afterward, the accused left alone, drove away, and was stopped by the police, who knew he was a suspended driver. Driving under suspension is an arrestable offence under the *Highway Traffic Act of Ontario*. As the police stopped and approached the car, they saw the accused talking on a cellular phone and swallow an object about one-half the size of a golf ball that had been wrapped in cellophane. The accused kept the car doors locked until he had swallowed the object. The police then arrested him for drive under suspension, towed his car, and transported him to the police station.

The police suspected that crack cocaine was in the girlfriend's apartment, but they considered the belief to be insufficient to obtain a search warrant. Two officers attended at the apartment and interviewed the girlfriend.

The significant part of the interview was the statements made by the officers to the girlfriend for the purpose of obtaining consent to search the apartment. Some of what the officers said were "lies and others were half-truths." Specifically, the officers informed her of four things:

1. Her boyfriend had informed the police that narcotics were in the apartment.

2. If she refused or failed to cooperate, a police officer would remain in her apartment until a search warrant was obtained.

3. Obtaining a search warrant would be an inconvenience for the officers because of the paperwork that was involved.

4. One of the officers would be going on vacation the following day. The girlfriend and the accused would not be charged, regardless of what the police found in the apartment.

The girlfriend was never informed of her right to refuse to consent to police entry and search. Conflicting evidence existed about whether these statements were made before or after the officers were admitted into the apartment.

continued

After the police entered, the girlfriend directed the officers to a living room couch. Six bags of crack cocaine, valued between $11 000 and $23 000, were found beneath a pillow. The narcotics were seized, and the officers left. They returned 20 minutes later and arrested the woman on the instructions of a superior officer, after consultation with a Crown attorney. The police still did not inform her of the right to counsel.

During questioning, the accused's girlfriend gave a statement implicating the accused as having placed the narcotics under the cushion on the couch. The accused and the girlfriend were charged jointly with possession of narcotics for the purpose of trafficking. The charge against the girlfriend was later withdrawn on the trial date.

On the evening of the arrest, the police attended at the vehicle compound where the accused's car was stored. Without a warrant, they seized the accused's cellular phone and pager, and intercepted calls for several hours from people ordering small amounts of crack cocaine.

Trial At the trial, the accused denied being the owner of the narcotics. The accused was convicted. His appeal to the Ontario Court of Appeal was dismissed. The accused then appealed to the Supreme Court of Canada.

Supreme Court of Canada Appeal The only issue at appeal was, "Did the accused have the right to challenge the admission of evidence obtained as a result of a search of a third party's place?" The manner in which the police obtained consent was not an issue.

The Supreme Court dismissed the accused's appeal. The following reasons and rulings were made:

- The accused had no expectation of privacy because he contributed nothing to the rent or household expenses, and had no authority to regulate access of people into the apartment. "He was no more than a privileged guest."

- The accused could not contest the admissibility of the evidence under sec. 24(2) *Charter*, because no personal right of the accused's was affected by police conduct.

- The court found it unnecessary to consider whether the accused's girlfriend actually gave valid consent to search the apartment.

COMMENTARY

Investigations are successful despite less than optimum procedures being used to obtain consent. The procedures used by the police were not in accordance with guidelines created by other case law decisions. However, this issue was not involved in the appeal or the ruling. This case illustrates the necessity to carefully read case law decisions. The decision would be confusing if only a summary of the circumstances were read.

This case demonstrates the value and advantages of using consent during investigations when the object of the search is a physical item. Consent is especially valuable when only mere suspicion exists. It is equally effective when reasonable grounds to obtain a search warrant exist. The procedures that comply with the *Borden* and *Wills* guidelines should obviously be used whenever possible to obtain consent, but less than optimum procedures will not always result in the exclusion of evidence. Finally, if consent is refused, two other alternatives exist:

1. search warrant, and

2. search without warrant provisions.

The conditions of these methods of search will be examined in Chapter 18.

temporarily occupied by another person who has rented, leased, or been given use of the place?"

Generally, the owner or management cannot give the police consent to enter and search the place if the temporary occupier has been given the authority to regulate access of persons in that place. If the temporary occupier has that authority, then he or she has a reasonable expectation of privacy and will likely be considered to be the *lawful occupier* of that place.

Two examples that the police commonly confront apply to

1. landlord and tenant, and
2. hotel management and guests.

Although a landlord owns a building where tenants live, a landlord cannot regulate access of persons into a tenant's apartment. Only a tenant may grant or refuse consent to enter an apartment, not the landlord. Consequently, a landlord has no authority to give valid consent to the police to enter and search a tenant's apartment.[28]

Guests who rent hotel rooms have a reasonable expectation of privacy while they are temporarily occupying a hotel room. Accordingly, hotel management has no authority to give consent to the police to enter and search a guest's room. This rule was created by the Ontario Court of Appeal, in *R. v. Mercer (1992)*,[29] which provides an excellent explanation of consent searches relating to hotel rooms. Additionally, this case provides another example of how sec. 24(2) *Charter* is applied to searches and seizures resulting from invalid consent.

CASE LAW

R. V. MERCER (1992)

Issues

1. Can hotel management search a guest's room without a warrant and without the guest's consent?

2. Does a hotel guest have a reasonable expectation of privacy in a hotel room?

3. Can hotel management give consent to the police to search a guest's room?

4. Will evidence seized from a guest's hotel room be admissible under sec. 24(2) *Charter*, after a warrantless search?

Offence   "possession of narcotics for the purpose of trafficking"

Circumstances   Two co-accused persons rented a suite in a hotel. The rooms were registered in their names although payment was guaranteed by a brother of one of the co-accused persons. The suite consisted of a living and dining area, a bedroom, a hallway, and closet that stored tables and chairs that were intended to be used for the purpose of converting the living area into a boardroom. The closet was accessible only to the guests having a key to the room.

During the accused persons' stay at the hotel, a maid attended at the room and found a "Do Not Disturb" sign on the door. The maid consulted with the manager who instructed her to knock and then enter the room. The maid subsequently entered the room in the absence of the accused persons and without their consent. The maid noticed that a pillow was missing. She searched for it and found it in the storage closet. She then searched inside the pillowcase and found a quantity of money. She immediately notified the hotel manager, who attended at the room and also searched the pillowcase. The manager noticed the money and a brown, waxy brick or block. The manager decided to call the police. She suspected illegal activity had occurred in the room, and reported what she found in the closet, but she did not mention the word "drug" when she reported this suspicion.

Two officers arrived at the hotel and entered the room by invitation of the manager. They searched the pillowcase, found a block of cannabis resin, and $6900 in cash. The evidence was returned to the closet. The officers left to obtain a search warrant. Other officers secured the room during the period of time required to obtain the search warrant. The accused persons arrived at the room before the search warrant could be obtained. Both were arrested immediately.

continued

Trial   The accused persons were convicted. The following conclusions were made:

- Neither of the police officers had reasonable grounds to believe that narcotics were in the room prior to their entry.

- The hotel manager did not have reasonable grounds to believe that narcotics were in the room.

- The belief of the police and the manager was based on mere suspicion.

- The officers believed that they had authority to enter the room and search it by the manager's consent because of the manager's invitation.

Appeal   The co-accused persons appealed their convictions to the Ontario Court of Appeal. The appeal was dismissed, and the convictions were upheld. The court gave the following reasons:

- Hotel guests have a reasonable expectation of privacy in hotel rooms that they have rented. A guest's knowledge that cleaning staff will enter the room daily does not remove their reasonable expectation of privacy. A hotel room can be considered an "office away from the office" where private papers and confidential business documents are protected from "uninvited viewers."

- Hotel management cannot give consent to the police to search a guest's hotel room without a warrant.

- A warrantless search of a hotel room with a "Do Not Disturb" sign on the door, in the guest's absence, based on mere suspicion of criminal activities constitutes an impermissible intrusion on a reasonable expectation of privacy, and a sec. 8 *Charter* violation.

- *However, the narcotics were not excluded from the trial.* They were admissible under sec. 24(2) *Charter* because the administration of justice would not be brought into disrepute by the admission of the narcotics. The reasons for this conclusion were

  - Although the police mistakenly believed that they could enter the room at the manager's consent, they "did not have the benefit of Canadian case law clearly stating otherwise."

  - The police acted in an investigation where the circumstances have "little statutory or judicial guidance."

  - The police made a reasonable mistake, in good faith.

  - The search was not initiated by the police but occurred in response to the hotel manager's request.

SUMMARY

This case raises several significant key points. The court acknowledged the absence of statutory laws that govern warrantless searches of hotel rooms, without the consent of the guests. Secondly, this case establishes two rules:

1. Hotel guests reasonably may expect privacy and are protected from warrantless searches of their personal property and documents.

2. Hotel management cannot give consent to the police to search guests' rooms without a warrant.

However, the court displayed tolerance for reasonable mistakes made by the police in good faith, and showed reluctance to exclude seized evidence as a result of reasonable mistakes. This translates to an advantage for law enforcement personnel. The dismissal of the accused's appeal shows that offenders may be convicted in cases where mistakes are made and where statutory law does not create clear procedures or guidelines.

Problem-Solving Case Studies

You are a police officer in each case. Each offender is an adult, unless otherwise indicated.

PROBLEM 91

While on patrol, you receive a radio transmission that a blue car has left the scene of a break and enter at a business premises. The description of a stolen TV and a calculator are also broadcast. You see a car of a similar description, and you stop it. Eddie is the driver and Wally is a passenger. Both are 18 years old. The car is owned by Eddie's father. You have only mere suspicion that they were involved in the offence.

a) Is the car a "place" for the purpose of a search?

_____

_____

_____

_____

_____

b) Can you obtain consent to search the car if only mere suspicion exists?

_____

_____

c) Do you have to obtain consent from both persons in order to search the car?

_____

_____

_____

d) Do you have to tell Eddie that you wish to search the car specifically for the stolen TV and calculator?

_____

_____

_____

e) Do you have to tell Eddie that he may refuse to consent?

_____

_____

_____

f) Do you have to tell Eddie that he may revoke consent after he initially gives consent?

_____

_____

g) If Eddie refuses to consent, can you tell him that a refusal is incriminating evidence that makes him look guilty, and can be used against him?

_____

_____

_____

h) If Eddie refuses to consent, can he be arrested or charged for refusing?

_____

i) If Eddie consents to a search of the car, can you automatically search both persons?

_____

_____

_____

j) After you obtain consent, you search the interior. You ask Eddie to open the trunk. He refuses. Can you forcibly open the trunk?

_____

_____

_____

_____

_____

k) If you do not obtain valid consent, or obtain it improperly, and search the car and seize the stolen property, will the seized evidence automatically be inadmissible in court?

_____

_____

_____

_____

_____

l) Do you have to obtain consent in writing, on a specific consent form, in this case?

_____

_____

_____

_____

_____

PROBLEM 92

You are investigating a "theft under $5000.00" complaint. After an initial investigation, you develop mere suspicion that George committed the offence and that he may have the stolen property in his apartment. You attend at the apartment complex. George is not home. Walter, the landlord of the apartment, is present. Can you obtain consent from the landlord to search George's apartment? [30, 31]

_____

_____

_____

PROBLEM 93

You respond to a residence regarding a loud party. Upon arrival, you find numerous people inside the house. Several are loud and appear impaired. You suspect that drugs may be in the house. You learn that Ward and June are the owners. Both are absent. Their son Wally (19) is present with a number of his friends. Eddie (19) lives next door and is present inside Wally's house. You speak to Eddie, who appears cooperative. Can you obtain consent from him to search the house for drugs?

_____

_____

_____

_____

_____

_____

_____

_____

_____

_____

_____

_____

Test Yourself

1. You are dispatched to a loud party at 5110 Forman St., Toronto. Upon arrival at 11:15 p.m., you see numerous teenagers inside the house. You approach the door and hear a loud party. No other observations are made. No adults can be seen. You are suspicious that drugs or other illegal property may be on the premises. Explain exactly how you will obtain consent to search the house.

_____

_____

_____

_____

_____

_____

_____

_____

_____

_____

_____

_____

_____

_____

_____

_____

2. You stop a suspicious car that is driving slowly on Forman St., Toronto, at 3:20 a.m. You stop the car. Eddie (22) is the driver. Wally (21) is the passenger. CPIC checks for both are negative. You are suspicious about what may be in the car. Explain exactly how you will obtain consent to search the car.

_____

_____

_____

_____

_____

_____

_____

_____

_____

_____

_____

_____

_____

_____

SEVENTEEN

Learning Outcomes

The student will be able to

- understand the procedures used to obtain the following search warrants:
  - sec. 487 C. C.,
  - general warrant,
  - telewarrant,
  - tracking warrant,
  - telephone number records warrant,
  - DNA analysis warrant,
  - impression warrant, and
  - drugs and substances warrant.

INTRODUCTION

A search warrant is a written document that represents judicial authorization for peace officers to enter and search a specific place for specific items, and to seize those items that are evidence to the offence, if they are found.

"Judicial authorization" refers to authority given by a justice, defined as a provincial court judge or justice of the peace (JP), who must be unbiased and neutral. The police *apply* for the warrant and a justice decides whether or not to grant it. Search warrants are generally directed at places, not persons. However, recent *Criminal Code* amendments established a warrant to obtain bodily substances for forensic DNA analysis.

The objective of a search warrant is to search for specific evidence that will prove an offence has been committed. Search warrants are not automatically granted based simply on a request by the police; an application must precede the search warrant. The contents of the application must convince the justice that reasonable grounds exist to believe that the specific items are in the place intended to be searched. These requirements prevent the police from conducting "fishing expeditions," a phrase used to describe searches based on mere suspicion.

TYPES OF SEARCH WARRANTS

Search warrants are found in the *Criminal Code* (C.C.) and *Controlled Drugs and Substances Act* (C.D.S.A.). Recent *Criminal Code* amendments have added other types of search warrants to the existing list. The types of search warrants that will be studied are

- sec. 487 C.C. (ordinary search warrant),
- sec. 487.01 C.C. (general warrant—use of device, including video surveillance),
- sec. 487.1 C.C. (telewarrant),
- sec. 492.1 C.C. (tracking warrant—tracking device),
- sec. 492.2 C.C. (telephone number recorder),
- sec. 487.04 C.C. (bodily substances for forensic DNA analysis),
- sec. 487.091 (impression warrant), and
- sec. 11 C.D.S.A. (drugs and substances).

SECTION 487 C.C. SEARCH WARRANT

This is the most common type of search warrant. It is referred to as a sec. 487 C.C. search warrant or simply as a *Criminal Code* search warrant. This type of warrant is used to search any type of place for physical items that constitute evidence that proves an offence. It is the most basic search warrant used during investigations. The following general rules apply to this warrant:

Rule 1

A sec. 487 C.C. search warrant authorizes the search of a

- building, or
- receptacle, or
- place (as defined in Chapter 14 of this textbook).

Therefore, when the police intend to search a place for evidence, a sec. 487 C.C. search warrant (prior judicial authorization) must be obtained unless a lawful authority exists to search without a warrant.

Rule 2

This search warrant authorizes the seizure of anything

- on or in respect of which any criminal offence under any federal statute has been, or is suspected of having been committed, or

- that there are reasonable grounds to believe will afford evidence to the commission of any classification of criminal offence, or
- that will reveal the whereabouts of a person who is believed to have committed any classification of criminal offence, or
- that there are reasonable grounds to believe is intended to be used for the purpose of committing any criminal offence, against the person for which a person may be arrested without a warrant, or
- that is "offence-related property." This term is defined in section 2 C.C. as any property, within or outside Canada,

  a) by means or in respect of which a criminal organization offence is committed,
  b) that is used in any manner in connection with the commission of a criminal organization offence, or
  c) that is intended for use for the purpose of committing a criminal organization offence, but does not include real property, other than real property built or significantly modified for the purpose of facilitating the commission of a criminal organization offence.

Essentially, the warrant authorizes the search for and seizure of tangible, physical items that are evidence that proves the commission of any classification of offences under any federal statute.

Rule 3

A sec. 487 C.C. search warrant cannot be obtained or used to search

- a person, or
- a place to find a person.

The warrant authorizes only the search of a physical item that will prove the whereabouts of the person who is believed to have committed the offence.

Police officers are authorized by Supreme Court of Canada decisions to enter and search a place (including a dwelling-house) without a warrant, to arrest a person if reasonable grounds exist that the person is inside the place and lawful authority exists to arrest the person.

Rule 4

The warrant may be issued to a peace officer or a person named therein. Consequently, police officers or citizens who are specifically named on the warrant are authorized to execute the warrant. A citizen may assist the police in the execution of a search warrant provided that a police officer controls and is accountable for the search.[32]

Rule 5

Section 487 (2.1) permits the search of computer systems for data and authorizes the following procedures by a person authorized by the warrant to search for data:

- Any computer system at the building or place may be used or caused to be used to search any data contained in or available to the computer system.
- Any data may be reproduced or caused to be reproduced in the form of a printout or other intelligible output.
- The printout or other output may be seized for examination or copying.
- Any copying equipment at the place may be used or caused to be used to make copies of the data.

Section 487 (2.2) imposed a mandatory obligation on the person who is in possession or control of the place being searched. After the warrant is presented to that person, he or she must allow

- any computer system to be used to search for data,
- a hard copy of the data to be obtained and seized by the police,
- copying equipment at the place to be used by the police to make copies of the data.

Rule 6

An application under oath must always be made to a justice before a sec. 487 C.C. search warrant may be issued. The application is called an "Information to Obtain a Search Warrant." The "Information to Obtain" must satisfy a justice that specifically listed items are in a specific place and must explain the reasonable grounds for this belief.

Rule 7

After the search warrant is executed and the named items are seized, the police must make a "return." A return is made by bringing the seized items, or a written report, to a justice as soon as practicable after the seizure is made.

APPLYING FOR THE WARRANT—INFORMATION TO OBTAIN

The issuance of a *Criminal Code* search warrant is not automatic. It must be preceded by an application that is named an "Information to Obtain a Search Warrant." This document is called Form 1. It is illustrated in Part XXVIII sec. 841 *Criminal Code*. Refer to that section to see an example of the actual search warrant.

The general contents of an Information to Obtain a Search Warrant must include

- the *place* intended to be searched,
- the *offence* that the evidence to be searched for will prove,
- description of the *items* to be searched for,
- *reasonable grounds* for belief that the items are in the place, and
- the *applicant's name and signature.*

All of the above contents must be sufficiently proven to a justice. If one area is deficient, the application will be rejected. The general contents must be explained and described with a great degree of specificity, by adhering to the following:

PLACE TO BE SEARCHED

Only *one* place may be named on one information to obtain. The address must be precise, leaving no doubt about the place intended to be searched. For example, if the place is an apartment, the unit number must be specified. The owner's name is desirable to help prove the credibility of the application, but the owner's name is not a mandatory requirement. It is possible for the search warrant to be authorized by stating the address only without the owner's name because the warrant is directed toward the place, not the person. If the place is vaguely described, causing doubt about what premises are intended to be searched, the justice will reject the Information to Obtain and deny authorization to search.[33]

OFFENCE COMMITTED

A specific offence must be named to show what the evidence that is intended to be searched for will prove. Short-form names of offences, such as "break, enter, and theft," will usually not suffice and should be avoided. A formal wording, similar to that used on an information, is usually required, including the date and location of the place.

However, case law decisions indicate that an imprecise wording will not affect the validity of the warrant. The wording on an Information to Obtain does not require the same precision as a wording on an information or indictment. It has been accepted that the police are in only the investigation stage when an Information to Obtain is drafted, which justifies some lack of specificity in the wording.[34]

ITEMS TO BE SEARCHED FOR

The Information to Obtain must list specific items that the police intend to search for. A statement such as "any evidence that will prove the offence" is insufficient, and the warrant will not be issued. The following rules serve as guidelines to describe items sufficiently:

Rule 1

A connection must exist between the item and the offence. The item must serve as evidence to prove the offence named on the Information to Obtain.[35]

Rule 2

Broad terms cannot be used to describe items. "Broad terms" refers to a general description, one that will prevent the searching officers from recognizing and identifying an item, if it is found.[36]

Rule 3

The description should have sufficient specificity to allow the searching officers the ability to positively recognize and identify the items.[37]

Rule 4

Model and serial numbers should be included if they are known.[38] If this information is unknown, unique features should be included. These include features such as damage, wear, tear, or markings. Unique features allow identification and recognition of items. General descriptions, such as size and colour, are not usually sufficient to positively identify an item.

Rule 5

A reasonable latitude in descriptions is permitted where the nature of the item prevents precision or specificity. However, proper discretion must be used to determine whether an item found is the same item described. If the description causes doubt regarding recognition and identification, the item must not be seized.[39]

Procedure

The space provided on the Information to Obtain is usually insufficient to list and describe all the items properly. Therefore, a separate blank page should be used and attached to the information to obtain. The page is entitled "appendix A." On the space provided on the information to obtain, write "refer to appendix A."

List each item separately. Each item's description should include

- general description: type of item, make, model, colour, and
- specific description: serial number or any unique feature such as damage or marks that will allow positive recognition and identification.

Examples of items that may be searched for include

- *stolen property*, e.g., television sets, stereos, videocassette recorders,
- *weapons* used to commit an offence,
- *documents*, e.g., written plans to commit a robbery,
- *clothing*, e.g., ski masks used as disguises worn during offences, and
- *fingerprints*, e.g., a victim's fingerprints to prove presence at a crime scene.

REASONABLE GROUNDS FOR BELIEF

This represents the most important part of the Information to Obtain. This belief must be written in a lengthy summary, which requires separate pages attached to the Information to Obtain. The space provided will undoubtedly be insufficient. Write "refer to appendix B" on the space provided and entitle the written supplementary "appendix B."

The objective of the written belief is to convince the justice that the *items listed are in the specific place named, right now*. The amount of evidence used to explain the belief must constitute reasonable grounds.

The following circumstances are examples of evidence that may constitute reasonable grounds:

1. One credible eyewitness who

- saw the item in the place, or
- was told by the offender that the item is in the place.

2. Circumstantial evidence that exceeds mere suspicion.

    The following examples are circumstances that constitute mere suspicion—referring to an insufficient belief—and will result in a rejection of the application:

- the item may be in the place, or
- the item may be in one of several places, or
- the item may be evidence to prove the offense.[40]

CONFIDENTIAL INFORMANT

The reasonable grounds for belief are often based on the report and observations of a confidential informant, referring to a witness whom the police choose not to identify. Protecting an informant's identity, by referring to him or her as an anonymous informant, is permitted.[41] The Supreme Court of Canada has ruled that a common law authority exists that prohibits the disclosure of informants by police officers. Additionally, a person cannot be compelled to state whether he or she is or has been a police informant. The need to protect an informant's identity is based on public interest, and the "essential effectiveness of the criminal law."[42]

    Determining whether a confidential informant's report constitutes reasonable grounds is based on the following rules:

Rule 1

The informant's report must be based on more than mere rumour or gossip.[43] A simple conclusory statement made by an informant to a police officer does not constitute reasonable grounds.[44] A conclusory statement may be defined as a general conclusion or opinion made without explaining the basis for the conclusion or opinion. An example: "an anonymous informant reports that the suspect has two stolen television sets in his house."

Rule 2

The informant must explain the basis of his or her information, such as a conversation with the accused, or eyewitness observation.[45] The basis must explain specifically how the informant learned that the item(s) are in the place.

Rule 3

The informant should be able to identify the participant(s) of the offence.[46]

Rule 4

The informant must be credible and reliable. This may be proven by explaining past dealings with the informant where he or she has been accurate, or by witnesses who have seen the informant and the accused together.[47]

Rule 5

The informant's report should be supported by some police investigation.[48] It is not necessary for the police to confirm each detail if the sequence of events reported by the informant sufficiently indicates an "anticipated pattern" that eliminates the possibility of coincidence. However, if the informant's credibility cannot be evaluated or if he or she reports fewer details, the level of verification requires a higher standard.[49]

STRUCTURE OF WRITTEN GROUNDS

The structure of the written reasonable grounds for belief should be as follows:

Step 1

Summarize the facts of the offence to prove that it actually occurred.

Step 2

Describe the place to be searched by stating the specific address, if it is a building. Include the owner's name, if it is known. If the place is a motor vehicle, include a precise description, the owner's name, and the location of the vehicle.

Step 3

Introduce the informant, state the date and time that the information was received, and the person who received the information (recipient).

If you decide to have the informant remain confidential, do not identify or name the informant. Refer to the informant as an anonymous informant. Do not describe characteristics or explain circumstances that would permit a person to accurately guess or determine the informant's identity. The Information to Obtain may become a public document before the trial and may be discussed during a trial. An appropriate introduction in this case would simply be, "As the result of an interview on [date/time] information was received by [recipient] from a person who will remain anonymous." If no need exists to protect the informant's identity, name him or her.

Decision to Maintain Confidentiality

If the informant's identity is protected, proving credibility will require providing additional facts in the written grounds. Some suspicion of doubt may naturally exist simply because the information and existence of an anonymous person may easily be fabricated. Naming the informant often removes doubt and the possibility of fabrication.

Although naming the informant may have a greater degree of credibility, maintaining the confidentiality of an informant is usually the decision that is made. Informants represent valuable long-term investigative benefits in law enforcement, and arguably may be the most important factor in an investigator's career. Case law decisions have recognized the need to maintain informants' anonymity. Consequently, the following general principles may guide the decision to protect or divulge an informant's identity:

a) *Divulge* an informant's identity if

- no threat exists regarding the person's safety, or
- he or she has never provided information in the past, or
- no intention exists to use the person in the future as an informant, or
- the person will be subpoenaed by the police to testify in court.

b) *Protect* an informant's identity if

- the person's safety will be jeopardized by divulging his or her identity, or
- he or she has provided information in the past, or
- the intention exists to receive information from the person in the future, or
- no intention exists to subpoena the person to testify in court.

If the informant's identity is not divulged, explain the *accuracy and results* of past dealings and information received from that person. Caution should be used to not specify detail that will permit the informant's identity to be determined. A balance must be attained that will convince the justice about the informant's credibility and reliability, while protecting his or her identity. Often, a simple summary of the *number of times* that the informant has been used in the past combined with the resulting accuracy should suffice. *The absence of any past deceit or fabrication by the informant should be included.* If the informant has never lied in the past, state that fact at the conclusion of the explanation of the informant's past performance with the police.

Step 4

Precisely explain the informant's observations. Avoid *simple conclusory statements* made by the informant. Do not paraphrase an informant's observations. To increase precision and provide a basis for the informant's observations, include the following:

a) Time and the place where the observations were made. Whether the informant saw an item in a place or was told relevant information by the accused, the informant should be capable of remembering where and when this occurred. If not, the information should be doubted and fabrication should be suspected.

b) Description of items seen. The informant should provide general and unique features when describing an item.

c) Location of items. Explain exactly where the item was seen in the place to be searched. Avoid general terms such as "inside the house."

d) Describe the surroundings. Describe the interior of the place and other items surrounding the evidence. This will help corroborate the informant's presence at that place.

e) Verbatim conversation with the accused. If the accused has told the informant the location of evidence, or any other significant incriminating statements, the accused's direct quotes should be used. Avoid paraphrasing. Again, include the time and place where the conversation occurred.

f) Names of other persons present during the observation or conversation. Caution must be used with this fact. It may cause someone to determine the identity of the informant. Name other persons present only if these people are commonly in the accused's company. Avoid including this fact if the people were not frequent visitors.

g) Degree of familiarity between informant and accused. This includes

- duration of time that the informant has known the accused ,
- the frequency of the informant's visits with the accused, and
- the accused's other relevant activities known by the informant.

Step 5

Explain the results of any other investigative methods that corroborate the informant, such as surveillance or another person's observations or knowledge that supports any aspect of the information received from the informant.

Step 6

Give information about the accused's

- criminal record,
- past participation in offences where no charge was laid, or
- any other relevant information known about his or her past, learned from prior investigations.

Step 7

Summarize the connection between the item(s) intended to be searched for and the offence committed. Although the connection may seem obvious, write a summary that explains how the item will be evidence in relation to the offence, and what exactly it will prove.

Step 8

If applicable, include reasonable grounds explaining the need to execute the warrant at night. Section 488 C.C. states that a sec. 487 C.C. search warrant must be executed by day unless reasonable grounds exist for authorization to execute it at night. "Day" is defined in sec. 2 C.C. as between 6:00 a.m. and 9:00 p.m. Conversely, "night" is between 9:00 p.m. and 6:00 a.m.

Step 9

If applicable, state reasons to apply for an order prohibiting public access to the information to obtain (refer to "public access" in this section).

Step 10

If applicable, include a statement proving the need for a telewarrant (refer to "telewarrant" in this section).

Special Circumstances—Informant

What circumstances will compel a police officer to disclose a confidential informant during court testimony? The need to protect an informant's identity has been recognized in several Supreme Court of Canada decisions. The only exception to the nondisclosure rule, where the identity of the informant must be disclosed, is when the accused's innocence is at stake. This requires evidence that the informant lied to the police, or was mistaken. In informal terms, there must be proof that the accused was framed by the informant. Additionally, evidence must exist that the officer who applied for the search warrant knew or ought to have known that the informant was mistaken or lied.[50]

Without evidence that the accused's innocence is at stake, the police do not have to disclose the informant's identity in the Information to Obtain, or during court testimony. Additionally, cross-examination questions (from the defence) that will produce answers that might disclose the informant's identity do not have to be answered during testimony.[51] The Crown attorney has the privilege to prevent the answering of these questions.

In cases where items are found and seized as the result of an informant's observations, the innocence at stake exception will not apply, and the informant's identity may be protected.[52]

NAME OF APPLICANT

A space is provided at the top of the Information to Obtain for the name of the applicant, which must be provided. The applicant, formally known as the informant, cannot remain anonymous. Usually the informant is the police officer investigating the offence. (This term must not be confused with the confidential informant who is the source of the information given to the police.)

APPLICANT'S SIGNATURE

The information to obtain must be signed by the informant. The signature must be made before the Information to Obtain is presented to the justice. *It is improper to present an unsigned Information to Obtain to a justice.*[53]

The officer may sign it at any time before meeting with the justice but as a matter of protocol the officer should sign it in the presence of the justice, prior to presenting it to the justice.

The significance of the officer's signature must be emphasized. The signature, combined with a subsequent oath, signifies that the officer believes that the contents of the Information to Obtain are true and not intentionally fabricated.

APPLYING FOR THE WARRANT—PROCEDURE

The following is a step-by-step procedure that is used to apply for a search warrant.

Step 1

The applying officer, known formally as the informant, completes the Information to Obtain before bringing it to the justice. No assistance may be given by the justice in the preparation of the Information to Obtain. The officer must complete the contents of the Information to Obtain without any suggestions or recommendations by the justice. Any assistance given by the justice in the preparation of the contents of the information to obtain constitutes a serious sec. 8 *Charter* violation, which may result in the exclusion of evidence seized.[54]

Step 2

The officer must sign the Information to Obtain any time before presenting it to the justice. An unsigned Information to Obtain cannot be presented to a JP. As a matter of protocol, sign the Information to Obtain in the presence of the JP, prior to presenting it.

Step 3

The Information to Obtain is brought and presented to a justice, usually a JP, anywhere other than in open court. Commonly, the location is a JP's office in a police station. A JP is not usually a full-time justice. Therefore, the Information to Obtain may have to be brought to another place for convenience, such as the JP's residence. Presenting the Information to Obtain means that the document is signed and ready for examination by the JP to determine whether a search warrant will be authorized. Do not ask the JP to review the contents of an unsigned Information to Obtain for deficiencies, for the purpose of correcting any errors before the formal presentation is made. The JP must be neutral, an unbiased evaluator, and cannot participate in the officer's investigation by correcting an unsigned Information to Obtain.[55]

Step 4

The JP will ask the officer to swear the signed Information to Obtain, under oath. The officer is swearing under oath that he or she believes that the contents are true. The officer is essentially swearing that nothing in the contents is fabricated. Intentionally fabricated information (lies), sworn under oath, constitute perjury. However, if the officer believes an informant, based on a reasonable grounds belief, and the evidence is not found, the officer will suffer no consequences.

Step 5

The JP analyzes the contents of the sworn Information to Obtain for the purpose of evaluating and determining whether reasonable grounds exist to believe that the items are in the place, right now. No verbal evidence should be given by the officer. The only evidence that the JP can evaluate must be written on the sworn Information to Obtain, in accordance with sec. 487 C.C. In summary, no verbal communication should occur between the officer and the JP during the JP's analysis and evaluation. Commonly, the JP asks the officer to leave and conducts the analysis in private. The officer should leave, whether asked or not, to prevent verbal, unsworn evidence being communicated and contributing to the JP's evaluation. No other persons, such as witnesses, are required to be present.

Step 6

The JP makes one of the following two decisions:

- If reasonable grounds *do not exist* in the JP's opinion, the application will be rejected, authorization to search will be denied, and the search warrant will not be issued. The Information to Obtain is kept by the JP. A rejection does not prohibit additional applications in the future. The police may reapply for a search warrant if additional information is obtained. The JP may inform the officer about the specific area of deficiency that the JP has identified. The deficiency may be corrected by the officer, and the JP may then evaluate the corrected version on another application.[56] However, the original Information to Obtain cannot be used to reapply; a new one must be drafted for each new application.

  If a JP rejects an Information to Obtain, the officer cannot bring the same Information to Obtain to another JP to seek a second opinion. It is improper to make repeated attempts to other JPs with the same Information to Obtain after a denial was made by the original JP.[57]

- If the JP is satisfied that reasonable grounds do exist, a search warrant will be issued. The JP keeps the Information to Obtain, and it becomes court property. The JP completes the sec. 487 C.C. search warrant on Form 5.[58] The officer does not complete the search warrant and does not keep the original Information to Obtain.

FORM 5—CONTENTS

A sec. 487 C.C. search warrant is set out on Form 5, found in Part XXVIII C.C. The following is a list of contents that must appear on the search warrant:

1. the names of the province and territorial division,
2. the phrase "to the peace officers in the said (territorial division)" is preprinted on Form 5. This means that warrant is directed to all peace officers in that territorial division. Any number of officers are authorized to participate in the search. Each officer's name does not have to be written on the warrant,
3. the name of the applying officer who acted as the informant must be written on the warrant. This officer may or may not participate in the search but should be present during the search,
4. any citizen whom the JP authorizes to assist the officers during the search must be named individually,
5. a list of items to be searched for must be named on the warrant or on a separate, attached page entitled, "appendix A,"
6. a description of the offence must be written; the formal wording and section number should be used,
7. the type of place, e.g. dwelling-house,
8. the address of the place,
9. the date or dates when the search may occur must be specified. Generally, only one date will be authorized but multiple days may be possible if authorized,
10. the hours when the search may be conducted must be stated. A sec. 487 C.C. search warrant must be executed by day,[59] between 6:00 a.m. and 9:00 p.m.[60] A search during night hours is possible if the JP authorizes it. The authorized time of search is expressed by writing "between [time] to [time],"
11. the date of issuance and city where issued, and
12. signature of the justice.

TELEWARRANT: SECTION 487.1 C.C.

A telewarrant is a warrant obtained by telephone or other means of telecommunications. Telecommunications is defined in sec. 35(1) *Interpretation Act* as any

- transmission,
- emission or reception of signs,
- signal,
- writing, or
- images or sounds or intelligence of any nature by wire, radio, visual, or other electromagnetic system.

Section 326 C.C. has the same definition of telecommunication, but it applies only to sections 326 and 327 C.C.

A peace officer may apply for a telewarrant if a belief is proven that

- an indictable or dual procedure offence has been committed, and
- it would be impracticable to appear personally before a justice to apply for a warrant

Proving impracticability is difficult in most urban areas. A telewarrant cannot be obtained for convenience or because of urgency. The key element to prove is that the officer cannot practicably appear personally before a justice for a reason such as proximity.

Until 1997, a telewarrant could be obtained only for a sec. 487 C.C. search warrant and a sec. 256 warrant to obtain blood. Recent amendments now permit telewarrants to be obtained for the following warrants:

- sec. 487 C.C. search warrant,
- sec. 256 C.C. warrant to obtain blood,
- general warrant,[61]
- forensic DNA analysis warrant,[62]
- impression warrant,[63]
- warrants to enter a dwelling-house,[64] and
- *Controlled Drugs and Substances Act* search warrant.

Only two warrants cannot be obtained by telewarrant:

- tracking warrant, and
- number recorder warrant.

OBTAIN A TELEWARRANT—PROCEDURE

The following procedure applies to telewarrants:

Step 1

Submit an Information to Obtain under oath by telephone or other telecommunications to a justice designated by the chief judge of that jurisdiction for issuing telewarrants.

Step 2

The justice records the Information to Obtain verbatim. The contents of the Information to Obtain are the same as for a conventional sec. 487 C.C. search warrant, but one significant addition must be included. A statement must be submitted of the circumstances that make it impracticable for the peace officer to appear personally before a justice.

Step 3

The justice may issue a search warrant on Form 5.1. if he or she is satisfied the reasonable grounds exist.

The important question is, "What document will the police officer have in his or her possession when executing the warrant?" The answer depends on the device used to communicate between the officer and the justice. Two devices are possible:

1. If the communication is made by telephone or other means of telecommunication that *does not produce a writing*, obviously the justice cannot send the warrant to the officer. Under these circumstances the following procedure is used to enable the officer to possess a search warrant document.

   a) The justice must complete and sign a search warrant by using Form 5.1. The time, date, and place of issuance must be included. It must be emphasized that the justice cannot transmit this warrant to the officer.
   b) Afterward, the officer also completes a warrant using Form 5.1 on the direction of the justice. This means that during the communication the justice will instruct the officer about what contents to write on the officer's copy of the search warrant. Essentially, the justice dictates the contents and the officer records it verbatim.

2. If the warrant is issued by a telecommunication that produces a writing, the justice completes Form 5.1 and transmits a facsimile to the officer. The officer must obtain a second facsimile of the warrant afterward for records.

SPECIAL CIRCUMSTANCES

- If the warrant is executed at an occupied premises, the officer must give a facsimile of the warrant to any person present and in control of the place, before entering or as soon as practicable after entry.
- If the warrant is executed in an unoccupied place, the officer must affix a facsimile of the warrant in a prominent place inside the place where the warrant will likely be seen.
- After the warrant is executed, the officer must file a written report, the Information to Obtain, and the warrant with the clerk of the court within seven days. The report must include the time and date of execution, and a list of all items seized.[65]

EXECUTION OF THE SEARCH WARRANT

Execution refers to carrying out the search warrant by conducting the entry and search of the place. The following rules apply to the procedure of executing a sec. 487 C.C. search warrant:

Rule 1: Who may search?

A sec. 487 C.C. search warrant is directed to all peace officers in the territorial division that is named on the warrant. Consequently, any number of officers may participate in the search. The participating officers do not have to be individually named on the search warrant.

The officer who is named on the warrant as the informant does not have to be present during the search but should be a participant because he or she will likely have more knowledge about the investigation and the items to be searched for. It is also important that one officer, usually the named officer, control and supervise the search.

Rule 2: When must the search be conducted?

The warrant must be executed on the date, or dates, and between the hours specifically written on the warrant by the JP. The hours will be between 6:00 a.m. and 9:00 p.m. (day) only, unless the JP authorized specific night hours (9:00 p.m.–6:00 a.m.) on the warrant.

Commonly, only one day is named on the search warrant, making it valid only for that specific day. The justice has discretion to extend the warrant to include more than one day. The reasonable grounds, on the Information to Obtain, must specify reasons for requiring more than one day.

Rule 3: Can force be used to enter the place?

No specific *Criminal Code* provision directly explains use of force (procedure or guidelines) relating to a sec. 487 C.C. search warrant. Sec. 25 C.C. provides general authority to use as much force as is necessary when a police officer is justified in doing what he or she is authorized to do. However, a specific procedure is not explained.

Sec. 8 *Charter* is the highest governing provision regarding use of force, and it requires that the search be reasonable. However, the *Charter* does not explain precisely whether force may be used to enter a place with respect to reasonableness.

Specific guidelines and procedures are found in common law and case law. A common law rule prohibits automatic, unlimited use of force to enter a place to execute a sec. 487 C.C. search warrant. The reason that unannounced entry or use of force is generally prohibited is because unexpected entry into a place such as a house may provoke violence. To prevent violent reactions, a proper announcement before entry is generally required.

The Supreme Court of Canada defined a proper announcement as being composed of three notices:

- notice of presence, by knocking or ringing the doorbell, and
- notice of authority, by identifying oneself as a law enforcement officer, and
- notice of purpose, by stating a lawful reason for entry, e.g., search warrant.[66]

Before entering a place to execute a search warrant, officers must give the three notices and *request entry*. If the request is granted, there will obviously be no justification for use of force. If the entry is denied, officers may then enter, and force may be used if necessary.

Admission may be denied in two ways. A verbal denial is clear and unmistakable. Entry may then be made, and force may be used if necessary. However, admission may be denied by no response, which poses the problem of how long officers should have to wait to enter and use force if necessary. The Supreme Court of Canada stated that officers "minimally" should request admission and have it denied. No other guideline was given. The court did not impose any obligation to wait for any specified time. Consequently, sec. 8 *Charter* will be the governing factor. Officers must act reasonably when no response is made to a request for admission. If persons are in the place, hesitation to enter may be a risk to personal safety. Entry should be made as soon as possible without delay because the announcement combined with no response may reasonably suggest that violence may occur or that evidence inside the place may be destroyed. In other words, officers become targets for violence in this situation.

Commonly, some evidence will exist to determine whether persons are inside, such as parked cars, sounds from inside, observations through a window, or information received from a witness or informant. If no evidence exists that clearly indicates that persons are in the place, officers have minimal means of positively determining that no occupants are in the place. Merely assuming that no one is inside may be dangerous. A search warrant does not specify that the place must have occupants within to execute it. Additionally, the Supreme Court of Canada stated only that admission be requested and denied. The court did not add an obligation to determine positively that persons are inside. Therefore, entry should be made after the least hesitation possible after the request is made.

An exception exists to this proper announcement rule. Entry may be made with the use of force, if necessary, and without a proper announcement if exigent circumstances exist. Exigent, or urgent, circumstances exist when an officer believes that

- a real threat of violent behaviour, directed at the police or anyone else, exists, or
- evidence may be lost or destroyed.[67]

When force is used to enter, with or without an announcement, the police have the onus to prove that reasonable grounds existed that exigent circumstances were present *and* that the belief existed at the time that force was used. At the trial, the Crown and police must introduce reasons to justify the use of force, by means of sworn verbal testimony. The testimony must include the facts that provide a basis or foundation for the belief that exigent circumstances existed. For example, the testimony must prove a reasonable belief that weapons were inside the place at the time officers arrived to execute the warrant. The belief does not have to be proven beyond reasonable doubt.

Failure to give evidence that sufficiently explains the reasons or basis for using force to enter constitutes a serious sec. 8 *Charter* violation, according to the Supreme Court of Canada. The court recommended that judges be reluctant to admit evidence that was obtained as the result of unjustified, excessive force. Therefore, such evidence will usually be excluded.[68]

Rule 4: Do occupants have to be present at the time of the search?

(i.e., can the warrant be executed at an unoccupied place?) The occupants of a place may not always be at the home or other premises when the police arrive to execute the search warrant. The *Criminal Code* does not directly address the situation. The search warrant does not state that it may be executed only when the occupants are present. Specific procedures and guidelines are found in case law.

If officers positively determine that no occupants are inside, the next guideline must be followed. When no occupants are inside the place, the execution of a search warrant depends on the presence or absence of exigent circumstances. If exigent circumstances exist, entry and search of the place will be reasonable. The following factors compose exigent circumstances:

- no knowledge of when the occupants will return, and
- certainty of the items being in the place, and
- a reasonable belief that the items would be lost or destroyed before the next attempt to execute the search warrant.[69]

If no exigent circumstances exist, the search warrant cannot be executed. A search conducted in the absence of exigent circumstances will be considered unreasonable. Factors that may indicate the *absence* of exigent circumstances are

- more than one date named (as authorized dates of search) on the warrant, or
- temporary absence of the occupants, or
- sufficient time existing to conduct surveillance on the place until the occupants return.[70]

Rule 5: Production of the search warrant

The officer who executes the warrant has two obligations. The officer must

- have possession of the search warrant, if feasible, and
- produce it when requested to do so by an occupant.

It is recommended that the officer hold the warrant while the occupant reads it, to prevent destruction of the warrant. The request may be made by any occupant. The officer should produce it to the owner or person having control of the place, regardless of whether a request is made. Allowing the occupant to read the warrant may encourage the occupant to relinquish all the items named on the warrant.

No requirement exists to give a copy of the warrant, and a copy should not be given. This will prevent the use of the copy by the occupant for unlawful purposes such as personating a police officer and stealing property.[71]

Rule 6: Arrest or detention of occupants

The search warrant itself does not authorize the arrest or detention of any occupant. Officers must comply with the arrest-without-warrant provisions found in sec. 495 C.C. Consequently, an arrest may be made if any criminal offence is found being committed or there exists reasonable grounds that an occupant has committed or is about to commit a dual procedure or indictable offence. Examples of situations that may occur during the search are

- intentional obstruction or interference of officers conducting the search ("obstruct police"). Movement by occupants that does not intentionally interfere or obstruct the search does not constitute obstruct police, and is therefore allowed,
- possession of weapons, stolen property, or narcotics, including possession of any of these items while attempting to destroy or conceal them, and
- reasonable grounds that an arrest warrant exists for any of the occupants.

The Supreme Court of Canada has permitted officers to control occupants during a search, primarily during narcotic searches by confining them to a specific area, when circumstances exist requiring the preservation of evidence.[72] Additionally, officers may detain persons to prevent the commission of dual procedure or indictable offences if reasonable grounds exist that an occupant(s) is about to commit one of these types of offences.[73]

Obstruct police is an example of a dual procedure offence that may be prevented. For example, an occupant informs officers that they will not be permitted to search and he or she will interfere with the officers if they try to search.

It must be emphasized that no arrests may be made automatically, without justification. If an occupant wants to leave the premises, and no lawful justification exists to detain or arrest the person, he or she must be allowed to leave. A person leaving may be arrested only if lawful arrest authority exists under sec. 495 C.C. e.g., if in possession of an item obtained by crime, a narcotic, or a weapon, or attempting to conceal or destroy evidence named on the warrant to obstruct the search.

Rule 7: Search of occupants

The search warrant itself does not authorize the search of persons found inside. In order to search a person, justification must exist. The authorities that justify such a search will be explained later in this chapter, including

- search after a lawful arrest or
- reasonable grounds that the occupant(s) has possession of a weapon or firearm[74] or narcotics.[75]

Otherwise, in the absence of any authorization, the search of a person may be conducted only by consent of the person.

Rule 8: Areas that may be searched

A search warrant does not restrict a search to partial areas of a place. The warrant authorizes a search of an entire place. However, sec. 8 *Charter* requires that the areas searched must be reasonable. Consequently, the size of the listed items, specifically the smallest item, will determine the areas of search. For example, if jewellery is the smallest item, the areas of reasonable search broaden. If a television set is the smallest item, certain areas, such as desk drawers, cannot reasonably be searched. A house garage may be searched if the garage is attached to a dwelling-house and the warrant is directed to the house. Detached garages, sheds, and motor vehicles on the property are separate places. Authority to search these places requires them to be named on the warrant by the JP; otherwise a separate warrant is necessary.

Rule 9: Seizure of items not listed

During the execution of a search warrant, other evidence, not listed, that is related or is not related to the offence named on the search warrant, may be found. Any item not listed on the warrant may be seized if reasonable grounds exist that the item was obtained by or has been used in the commission of any offence, including offences unrelated to the offence named on the warrant.[76]

Rule 10: Time limit/expiry of warrant

Five time limits exist that govern the expiry of search warrant. The search warrant expires and the search must discontinue at any of the following times or circumstances:

- at 9:00 p.m., if the authorization is for day only,
- if authorized for night and the time, such as midnight, is stated on the warrant,
- when all the items have been found, regardless of the actual time of seizure and how much time remains before the expiry time stated on the warrant,
- the search of the place concludes and nothing is found. If the search was thorough, continued search may be unreasonable, and
- the police stop the search and leave the property, regardless of whether the search was thorough or complete.

If officers remain on the premises after the expiry of the warrant, without consent or any other authority, they will be considered trespassers.[77]

"RETURN" OF SEIZED ITEMS

If items are seized as the result of a search warrant being executed, the officer must comply with the combined requirements of sections 487(1)(e) and 489.1 C.C. The requirements form a procedure that is formally called a "report by peace officer." It is informally called a "return" to a justice. A return may be defined as a notification, or report, to a justice that explains what was seized and determines the disposition of the item by ordering detention of the item or releasing it to the lawful owner.

Section 487(1)(e) C.C. states that the search warrant authorizes the seizure of the item and the return of the item to a justice, in accordance with sec. 489.1 C.C. In other words, this provision gives the authority for the police to keep custody of the seized item to return it to a justice.

Section 489.1 C.C. creates the procedural guidelines relating to the manner in which the return must be made. Two alternative procedures exist under sec. 489.1 C.C. Choosing the appropriate method depends on whether the seized item is needed for an investigation or trial.

If it is needed, the item must be lawfully detained. If the item is not needed, it must be returned to its owner.

Detaining a Seized Item

The concept of a return to a justice when a seized item requires detaining for an investigation or trial has two elements. First, a justice authorizes the search for and seizure of the item. Consequently, the justice must be notified of the results and the item must be "returned" to the justice. Secondly, only a justice has the authority to allow the police to keep the item until the trial, without returning it to the owner.

When must the return be made?

No specific time limit is imposed. The return must be made as soon as practicable after the item is seized, meaning that no unjustified delay may occur.

How is a return made?

A return may be made by using either of the following two methods:

1. Bring the actual seized items before a justice.
2. Complete a document named a "Report to a Justice" and bring the document, instead of the actual items, before a justice.[78] The "Report to a Justice" is Form 5.2 in Part XXVIII. The contents of this document include

- seizing officer's name,
- type of search warrant executed, e.g., sec. 487 C.C.
- address of place searched,
- list of and description of items seized,
- date and time of seizure, and
- officer's signature.

The seizing officer has discretion to use either method. No particular reasons determine which return method is used, other than the convenience afforded by the "Report to a Justice" document.

A return may be made to either the justice who issued the search warrant or any other justice in the same territorial division.[79] After the return is made, a decision is required about whether to detain the item or release it to the lawful owner. If *charges are laid* shortly after the search, the JP must immediately order detention of the items, without a hearing, until the trial.[80]

If *charges are not laid* after the search because a lengthier investigation is required, the property may be detained for three months unless the justice authorizes extended detention, having regard to the nature of the investigation.[81] If the *three months*, or *extended detention time expires*, and no charges have been laid because the investigation is continuing, extended detention may be authorized after a hearing.[82] If no charges will be laid, the seized items must be returned to the lawful owner.[83]

When the seizing officer is satisfied that there is no dispute as to who is the lawful owner of the item, and the item is not needed for any investigation or trial, the officer must return the seized item to the lawful owner. A receipt must be obtained from the owner. Afterward, the officer must report the return to a justice.[84]

PHOTOGRAPHS

Where charges are laid, rules of evidence generally require the production of the original item at the trial unless it is impracticable to do so. Photographs of the items, instead of the actual item, are not permitted in every case; however, they may be taken and introduced in court instead of the actual item if the offence is

- theft under or over $5000.00,
- robbery,
- break, enter with intent, or commit an indictable offence,
- false pretences under or over $5000.00, or
- fraud under or over $5000.00.

Using a photograph allows the item to be released to the lawful owner instead of having it kept in police custody for several months until the trial.[85] The photographs will be admissible under two conditions:

1. The photographer is a peace officer or one who took the direction of a peace officer, and completes a certificate stating that he or she took the photograph and that the photograph is a true photograph.[86]
2. The accused is given reasonable notice before the trial.[87]

NO ITEMS FOUND

If the search warrant is executed and no items are seized, the officer signs the back of the search warrant and writes the date of execution. The search warrant is then returned to the JP.

SEARCH WARRANT NOT EXECUTED

In some cases, circumstances will arise after the issuance of a search warrant that may prevent execution before the expiry time. When no execution occurs, the search warrant cannot be executed after the expiry time and must be returned to the JP. If the reasonable grounds still exist, a new application must be made to obtain another search warrant.

PUBLIC ACCESS

The confidentiality of the content of an Information to Obtain is often necessary to protect the identity of an anonymous informant, ongoing investigations, and intelligence-gathering techniques that will be used in future investigations. Consequently, the issue of public access to the Information to Obtain is critical to the protection of investigations.

In 1997, sec 487.3 C.C. was enacted to serve as a procedure that results in the denial of public access to an Information to Obtain. Before this provision is explained, a Supreme Court of Canada decision, in *MacIntyre v. Nova Scotia (A.G.)(1982)*, will be examined. The *MacIntyre* case is the predecessor to sec. 487.3 C.C. and is useful in interpreting the new provisions.

The *MacIntyre* decision created two rules that served as guidelines to public access to an Information to Obtain:

1. Public access was denied after a search warrant was executed and no seizure was made.
2. Public access was allowed after warrant was executed and items were seized. Access was allowed to any member of the public. The only exception was if the course of justice would have been obstructed by having the public read it.[88]

Sec. 487.3 C.C. allows a judge or justice to make an order prohibiting the public access to and the disclosure of any information relating to the warrant or authorization. The discretion to make the prohibition order is contingent upon an application being made at the time of issuing any warrant authorized by the *Criminal Code* or any other federal statute, or at any time after the warrant is issued. The application must prove grounds for requiring the prohibition order. The grounds are

- the ends of justice would be subverted by the disclosure for one of the reasons in sec. 487.3(2) C.C. or the information might be used for an improper purpose; and
- the ground that justified the prohibition outweighs in importance the access to the information.

Any one of the following reasons proves that the ends of justice would be subverted by the disclosure if the disclosure would

- compromise the identity of a confidential informant,
- compromise the nature and extent of an ongoing investigation,
- endanger a person engaged in particular intelligence-gathering techniques and thereby prejudice future investigations in which similar techniques would be used, or
- prejudice the interests of an innocent person.

Section 487.3(2) C.C. states that "any other sufficient reason" justifies a prohibition order. After a prohibition order is made, all documents relating to the application shall be placed in a packet and sealed by the justice immediately on determination of the application. The sealed packet must be kept in the custody of the court in a place where the public has no access.

Section 487.3(4) C.C. provides that an application to terminate the prohibition order may be made in order to gain public access. The subsection does not impose restrictions on any person who wishes to apply for termination of the order. Consequently, any member of the public, including the accused, may be the applicant.

The following is a summary of the procedural rules relating to a prohibition order of public access to an Information to Obtain:

A prohibition order cannot automatically be made; an application must precede the order. Making the application begins the process of determining whether the order will be made or not. After an application is made, the justice has discretion about granting or denying it. A justice cannot make an order without an application being made.

When does the application have to be made?

The application may be made
- at the time the warrant is issued, or
- at any time after the warrant is issued.

Who may make the application?

The section does not directly specify who may apply, but it does not restrict any person either. The lack of limitation infers that any person may apply. Usually, the applicant will be the officer who completes the Information to Obtain.

How does the application have to be made?

The section does not specify the manner in which the application must be made. It does not state whether the application must be in writing, what document must be used, or whether the application must be under oath. In sec. 487(1) C.C., specific reference is made to the manner of applying for a search warrant by use of the phrase "by information on oath." This phrase is not used in sec. 487.3 C.C. The absence of specific procedures suggests that verbal unsworn evidence may suffice as an application. Additionally, it would appear that the grounds for the application may be included on the Information to Obtain.

What has to be proven in the application?

The application must prove that disclosure of the Information to Obtain will result in any one of these four consequences:

1. the identity of a confidential informant will be divulged, or
2. the investigation is ongoing and the nature and extent of it will be jeopardized, or
3. a person who is using intelligence-gathering techniques during the investigation will be endangered and future investigations will be prejudiced, or
4. an innocent person's interest will be prejudiced.

Additionally, "any sufficient reason" may be specified on the application. However, this phrase obviously lacks precise guidelines about what is "sufficient."

What occurs if an order is made?

The justice seals all relevant documents in a packet and stores the packet in a place that is inaccessible to the public.

DRUG SEARCH WARRANTS

Two search warrants are available during a drug investigation:

1. Section 11 *Controlled Drugs and Substances Act* (C.D.S.A.)
2. Sec. 487 C.C.

Both types of warrants authorize police officers to search places for drugs; therefore, the relevant procedures need to be compared. Comparison will assist in the decision regarding which warrant to use. The C.D.S.A. is a federal statute that was enacted in 1997, and replaces two statutes, the *Narcotics Control Act* (N.C.A.) and the *Food and Drugs Act* (F.D.A).

The C.D.S.A. is legislation that regulates substances formerly called narcotics and drugs, now called "controlled substances." The basic design of the C.D.S.A. is similar to the N.C.A. and the F.D.A.

Section 11 C.D.S.A. creates a search warrant relating to controlled substances. The following are general rules that apply to this warrant. The included case law decisions were made before the C.D.S.A. was enacted, but are still considered useful regarding procedural guidelines.

RELEVANT DEFINITIONS AND TERMS

- controlled substances—a substance included in Schedule I, II, III, IV, or V,
- precursor—a substance included in Schedule VI,
- Schedule I substances—include cocaine and heroin
- Schedule II substances—include cannabis (marijuana) and its derivatives,
- Schedule III substances—include LSD, amphetamine,

- Schedule IV substances—include barbiturates, anabolic steroids,
- Schedule V substances—include pyrovalerone, and
- Schedule VI substances—include ephedrine, lysergic acid.

Rule 1

A C.D.S.A. warrant authorizes the search of any place, including a dwelling-house and any building that is not a dwelling-house.[89] This contrasts with the N.C.A. search warrant, which could be used only for dwelling-houses. Additionally, a sec. 487 C.C. search warrant authorizes the search of any place.

Rule 2

An application must be made to obtain a C.D.S.A. search warrant. The document is called an Information to Obtain a C.D.S.A. search warrant.

Rule 3

An Information to Obtain a C.D.S.A. search warrant must include the same contents as required for an Information to Obtain a sec. 487 C.C. search warrant: place, offence, items, reasonable grounds. The same degree of sufficiency is required to describe the content as with an Information to Obtain a sec. 487 C.C. search warrant.

Rule 4

The C.D.S.A. search warrant authorizes the search for and seizure of the following:

- a controlled substance or precursor relating to a C.D.S.A. offence,
- anything in which a controlled substance or precursor is contained or concealed,
- offence-related property, or
- anything that will afford evidence relating to a C.D.S.A. offence.

The Information to Obtain must specify the items that are believed to be in the place. The use of the words "controlled substance" or "precursor" is insufficient. Instead, the name or type of substance must be named. Other items that may be included in the application that will afford evidence relating to C.D.S.A. offences include weight scales and packages. The items must correspond with the reasonable grounds for belief.

A specific quantity of a substance should accompany the type of substance to comply with the reasonableness requirement of sec. 8 *Charter.*

A specific quantity defines the extent of the search and adds credibility to the reasonable grounds for belief. Additionally, it imposes a reasonable limit to the search. If a greater quantity is found, it "may be seized."[90]

Rule 5

Anonymous informants may be used to prove the reasonable grounds for belief. The Supreme Court of Canada, in *R. v. Scott (1990)*,[91] recognized the need to protect the identity of informants in drug-related investigations to ensure their assistance and facilitate the relationship of trust between them and the police. The sufficiency of an informant's observations is determined by the same rules relating to an Information to Obtain a sec. 487 C.C. search warrant. For example, a simple conclusory statement, meaning one without an explanation that forms the basis for the informant's report, is insufficient. The basis of the informant's report must be explained. The informant's credibility and reliability must be proven by past dealings or by supporting investigation.

Rule 6

The justice cannot assist the officer in the preparation of the Information to Obtain and must act as a neutral evaluator.

Rule 7

The Information to Obtain is presented to the justice in the same manner as an Information to Obtain a sec. 487 C.C. search warrant. The officer signs, preferably in the presence of the justice, and swears under oath that the belief is true. The justice analyzes and evaluates the Information to Obtain, and decides whether the grounds for belief are sufficient. If the application is rejected, no warrant is issued, and the document is kept by the justice. The officer may re-apply when additional evidence is uncovered. If the grounds are sufficient, the justice issues the search warrant and keeps the Information to Obtain, which becomes property of the court.

Rule 8

The C.D.S.A. search warrant must be directed to at least one officer. This means that at least one officer must be named on a C.D.S.A. search warrant[92] to act as the specific officer who will be responsible for the control and conduct of the search. The Supreme Court of Canada created the following rules relating to the named officer provision:

1. More than one officer may be named but not an entire drug unit. Listing an entire drug unit may render the naming requirement ineffective.
2. Naming two officers is acceptable.
3. The named officer(s) must
   a) participate in the search, and
   b) closely control and supervise the search.
4. Any number of unnamed officers may participate in the search and seize narcotics, but the seizures must be taken into the possession of a named officer, who controls and supervises the search.
5. Failure to name any officer at all constitutes a sec. 8 *Charter* violation.[93]

Rule 9

A C.D.S.A. search warrant may be executed at any time, meaning by day or night. Night searches do not require special authorization by a justice, as is required for a sec. 487 C.C. search warrant. However, as a matter of practice, justices commonly type the hours of search on the warrant. For example, the hours typed on the warrant may include from the time the warrant was issued (e.g., 2:00 p.m.) until 11:59 p.m., which will then include the night hours (after 9:00 p.m.) of the authorized day of the search. It is possible for the justice to authorize the warrant for more than one day. The reasonable grounds must include justification for requiring the authorization of more than one day.

Rule 10

Section 12 C.D.S.A. authorizes the officer who executes the C.D.S.A. warrant to "enlist such assistance as the officer deems necessary." This would authorize, for example, bringing a number of officers to assist in the execution of the warrant if the officer can prove the justification for it, as well as the use of as much force as is necessary in the circumstances.

This provision does not contain a requirement that any announcement must be made prior to entry. Despite this nonrequirement, sec. 8 *Charter* requires that all searches be reasonable. Consequently, force cannot be automatically used in all cases.

The Supreme Court of Canada established rules relating to the sec. 12 C.D.S.A. authorization of use of force in two cases: *R. v. Genest (1989)*[94] and *R. v. Gimson (1991)*.[95] Entry without prior announcement is justified when reasonable grounds exist that evidence may be destroyed or actual danger is present. For example, a reliable informant's report that narcotics are being sold in a dwelling-house and that the front door might be barricaded creates the inference that the occupant wishes to have time to destroy evidence. The use of force under sec. 12 C.D.S.A. is justified under those circumstances. However, the court did not address the issue of whether a blanket authority exists to enter without a prior announcement when executing a drug search warrant.

The fact that narcotics may be easily disposed of often necessitates an unannounced entry. A common practice used by officers is to enter unannounced and make an announcement shortly after entry.

The sec. 12(b) C.D.S.A. use of force authority is not limited only to entry. It extends to "exercising any of the power" that is authorized in sec. 11 C.D.S.A. This would include using force to break open items inside the place to conduct the search. This general use of force authority replaces a provision that was included in the N.C.A. that authorized specific use of force to break open doors, floors, containers, walls, ceilings, plumbing fixtures, and "any other thing." Section 12 C.D.S.A. authorizes the same use of force if it is proved to be reasonably necessary.

Rule 11

Although the C.D.S.A. does not require that occupants of a dwelling-house be present when the search warrant is executed, the sec. 8 *Charter* requirement of reasonableness does not permit automatic entry by force into a house when the occupants are absent.

Two cases provide rules and guidelines regarding the execution of an C.D.S.A. search warrant when the occupants are not home. In *R. v. Grenier (1991)*,[96] the Quebec Court of Appeal ruled that the execution of a search warrant and use of force to enter were justified when the occupants were not home because the police knew that 17 marijuana plants were in the house, they had no knowledge about when the occupants would return, and had no way of knowing if the narcotics would still be there if the execution of the search warrant was delayed until the occupants returned. However, the search must be delayed in cases where no urgency exists.

In *R. v. McGregor (1985)*,[97] the Manitoba Court of Queen's Bench stated that forced entry and search of an unoccupied house is not justified if the house can be kept under surveillance while attempts are made to locate an occupant of the house.

Therefore, the determining factor is the existence or absence of exigent circumstances, referring to urgency. Entry and search of an unoccupied house is justified when reasonable grounds exist that the evidence will be destroyed or lost if the search is delayed until the occupants return.

Rule 12

The officer who executes the search warrant must have possession of the warrant and must produce it when requested by any occupant to do so.[98]

Rule 13

The C.D.S.A. search warrant does not authorize the arrest of the occupants. Arrests must be authorized by sec. 495 C.C.

Rule 14

The C.D.S.A. warrant authorizes the search of occupants found in the place but not automatically. The authority to search occupants is contingent upon proving reasonable grounds to believe that the occupant has any of the substances or items named on the warrant "on their person."[99] If this belief is absent, search of occupants may be conducted by consent only.

Rule 15

In addition to named substances and items, the officer may seize the following evidence that is not named on the warrant:

* any controlled substance, precursor, container with those substances in it, and any item that is evidence to any C.D.S.A. offence,[100] and
* any unrelated item that is evidence to any offence, under any statute.[101]

Rule 16

An C.D.S.A. search warrant expires

- at 11:59 p.m., or any other time specified, on the authorized day stated on the warrant, or
- when all the named items have been found, or
- when the house is thoroughly searched and nothing is found, or
- when the officers leave the dwelling-house.

Rule 17

A "return" to a justice must be made after items are seized. Section 13(1) C.D.S.A. states that the "return" provisions under sec. 489.1 and 490 C.C. apply to anything seized by means of a C.D.S.A. warrant. The "return" procedure is the same as explained under the sec. 487 C.C. search warrant part of this textbook. Additionally, when a police officer seizes a controlled substance, by means of a warrant, the officer must cause a copy of Form 5.2, "Report to a Justice," to be sent to the Ministry of Health. The report must identify the place searched, the controlled substance, and the location where it is detained.[102]

The following table summarizes the differences regarding the two types of search warrants.

TABLE 17.1

TYPES OF SEARCH WARRANTS

C.D.S.A. Search Warrant		Sec. 487 C.C. Search Warrant
Any place.	PLACE	Any place.
Directed to one officer who will closely supervise the search. Two are acceptable, but not an entire drug unit.	DIRECTED TO	Directed to all peace officers in the territorial jurisdiction.
Same as above.	NAMES OF OFFICERS	Name of the applying officer who acted as the informant must be written.
Mandatory that the officer to whom the warrant is directed participate. Optional the number of additional	PARTICIPATING OFFICERS	No mandatory requirements that the applying officer attend, but he or she should.
Day or night.	TIME OF EXECUTION	Day only. Justice may authorize night search if the grounds justify it.
Sec. 12 C.D.S.A. specifically authorizes the use of as much force as is necessary, but force must be reasonable. Case law proper announcement rule applies.	USE OF FORCE	No specific provision regarding type of force used; force must be reasonable according to case law requirements, i.e., proper announcement, and sec. 25–28 C.C.
Mandatory requirement.	RETURN	Mandatory requirement.

ELECTRONIC SURVEILLANCE

Electronic surveillance may significantly contribute to the success of an investigation by helping the investigator obtain information or evidence to prove the commission of an offence.

Several types of electronic surveillance exist, including

- video recording,
- tracking device, and
- number recorders.

Electronic surveillance constitutes a search and seizure. Unreasonable electronic surveillance constitutes a sec. 8 *Charter* violation when it is committed by a state agent.

A series of Supreme Court of Canada decisions have had significant impact on the laws relevant to electronic surveillance. In response to these decisions, new search warrants have been added to the *Criminal Code* that authorize various forms of electronic surveillance.

GENERAL WARRANT—SECTION 487.01 C.C.

This is a new warrant that was added to the *Criminal Code* in 1993. It is referred to as a "general" warrant, but this term is misleading because it implies that it authorizes the seizure of a variety of items. This warrant does not permit the search for and seizure of general items; a sec. 487 C.C. authorizes the general search of places for items.

The sec. 487.01 C.C. general warrant was enacted in response to a Supreme Court of Canada decision made in *R. v. Wong (1993)*.[103] The court made the following rulings:

1. Video surveillance of activity constitutes a search.
2. Video surveillance of places where persons have a reasonable expectation of privacy cannot be conducted without a warrant. (An example of a place where a person has a reasonable expectation of privacy is a motel room.)
3. Video surveillance in those places, conducted without a warrant, is unreasonable and constitutes a sec. 8 *Charter* violation.

Consequently, the sec. 487.01 C.C. search warrant was enacted. A sec. 487.01 "general" warrant is not used to search for and seize items. Instead, it is intended to be used by *peace officers only* to obtain *information* concerning the commission of any offence under any federal statute. Information may be obtained by

- any device, or
- investigative technique or procedure, or
- doing anything that would otherwise be an unreasonable search or seizure.

Specific devices and investigative techniques that may be authorized are surveillance by means of a television camera or other similar electronic device.[104] Video surveillance of an activity in a public place does not require a warrant if the person being observed does not have a reasonable expectation of privacy.

Consequently, a general warrant is primarily associated with *video surveillance,* but it includes the obtaining of *information by means of observations* made with or without electronic devices.

Examples of observations made without an electronic device are

1. The entry of the perimeter of a dwelling-house, looking inside the house for information of an offence such as possession of narcotics for the purpose of trafficking. The perimeter of a house is a place. The visual observations made of the interior of the place constitute a search.
2. Making photocopies of the outside of envelopes and packages of mailable material while the material is in a post office.[105]

A sec. 487.01 C.C. general warrant may be used to authorize these investigative techniques in order to obtain *information by observation* that is relevant to the offence being investigated. A general warrant may also be considered to be an investigative means of obtaining information by observations to help *form reasonable grounds to obtain a sec. 487 C.C. warrant to search a place for items.*

If the police apply specifically for the use of an electronic device to make observations, the procedure used to obtain a general warrant must be the same as that used to intercept private communications, which is described in Part VI *Criminal Code,* sections 183–96. For example, if the application includes a request to conduct video surveillance, the offence must be one as defined in sec. 183 C.C., such as "conspiracy," "counselling," or attempt to commit one of the listed offences.[106]

OBTAIN AND EXECUTE A GENERAL WARRANT—PROCEDURE

The following procedure applies to a general warrant.

Step 1

An application must first be made by completing an Information to Obtain. The section does not specify a document that must be used. Therefore, Form 1 (as illustrated in sec. 841 C.C.) may be varied to suit the case.

Step 2

The applicant, referred to as the informant, must be a peace officer. A citizen cannot apply for or obtain this warrant.

Step 3

The Information to Obtain must include written reasonable grounds to believe

- that a criminal offence under any federal statute has been or will be committed. The offence may be in contravention of the *Criminal Code* or the *Controlled Drugs and Substances Act,* and
- that *information* concerning the offence will be obtained. The type of information is not specified, but it must be information that can be learned by observation. It cannot be an item.

Step 4

The Information to Obtain must specify the technique, procedure, device, or "doing of the thing" that will obtain the information. If a television camera or similar electronic device is requested, the specific type of device must be named.

Step 5

The Information to Obtain must explain that no other provision in any statute authorizes the type of procedure that is requested. For example, other provisions in the *Criminal Code* authorize warrants to search for items, track the location of persons or items, and seize bodily substances for DNA analysis. However, no statute authorizes the making of observations with or without electronic means.

Step 6

The informant must sign the Information to Obtain and bring it to a provincial court judge or a judge of a superior court of criminal jurisdiction. *It cannot be brought to a justice of the peace.*

Step 7

The judge may deny or issue the warrant. If the warrant is issued, Form 5 may be varied to suit the case. Section 487.01 C.C. does not specify the type of document that must be used as the warrant.

The judge must specify on the warrant precise *terms* and *conditions* that the judge considers advisable to ensure a reasonable search or seizure.[107] This means that there is no mandatory time limit that must be imposed regarding the length of time the police may use video surveillance or the procedure specified. Additionally, the conditions will likely include the method used to install the device to justify any entry into a place.

TRACKING WARRANT—SECTION 492.1 C.C.

A tracking warrant is a relatively new warrant that any citizen or peace officer may obtain. A *tracking device* is defined as any device that may help ascertain the location of any thing or person, by electronic or other means, when the device is installed in or on any thing.[108]

The installation of a tracking device for surveillance purposes constitutes a search. The Supreme Court of Canada, in *R. v. Wise (1992)*,[109] ruled that the installation of a tracking device without a warrant constitutes a sec. 8 *Charter* violation. The warrantless installation of a tracking device constitutes an unreasonable search because it violates a person's reasonable expectation of privacy.

Section 492.1 C.C. creates the authority for a citizen or peace officer to apply for and obtain a warrant that authorizes

- the installation, maintenance, and removal of a tracking device, in or on any thing, including a thing carried, used, or worn by any person, and
- the monitoring of the installed tracking device.

This new warrant was enacted in 1993 in response to the *Wise* decision. Its purpose is to obtain information that is relevant to an offence, including the whereabouts of a person. This section does not restrict the type of place where entry may be made to install the tracking device. The warrant authorizes entry into any place including a dwelling-house.

An Information to Obtain must be completed to apply for a tracking warrant. If the application is accepted, a tracking warrant is issued and is valid for a maximum period of 60 days.[110]

OBTAIN AND EXECUTE A TRACKING WARRANT—PROCEDURE

The following procedure applies to a tracking warrant.

Step 1

An Information to Obtain must be completed. The applicant may be a citizen or a peace officer.

Step 2

Section 492.1 C.C. does not specify what form must be used to apply. Form 1 (Information to Obtain, illustrated in sec. 841 C.C.) may be adapted for use in applying for a tracking warrant.

Step 3

The Information to Obtain must include a written belief that reasonable grounds exist to suspect that

- any offence under a Canadian federal statute has been/will be committed, and
- *relevant information* regarding the commission of that offence, including the whereabouts of any person, can be obtained through the use of a tracking device.

The key points of this rule are

- The belief does not have to be as convincing as the one required to obtain a sec. 487 C.C. search warrant because the applicant needs to prove only that a suspicion exists reasonably.
- A tracking warrant may be used during investigations of offences under the *Criminal Code, Controlled Drugs and Substances Act,* or any other federal statute.
- There are no restrictions about the type of information that can be acquired for the investigation. The reason for using the tracking warrant may be to obtain any relevant information, including the location of any person.

Step 4

The Information to Obtain must specify the item, and the location of the item, where the tracking device is intended to be installed in or on.

The key points of this rule are

- Section 492.1 C.C. uses the singular form of "a tracking device," signifying that the installation of only one tracking device may be applied for on one Information to Obtain. If more than one tracking device is required for investigative purposes, a separate Information to Obtain must be completed for each individual tracking device.

- Only one item may be named where the tracking device is intended to be installed, because the section states the singular form of "thing." No restriction is placed on the type of "thing" where the device may be installed. The only requirement is that the "thing" be capable of having a tracking device installed in it or on it. The item may include clothes or any "thing" carried, used, or worn by a person.
- The location of the item must be specified. This is required to authorize the *entry of the place* where the item is situated, in order to install it.

Step 5

The Information to Obtain must be signed by the applicant and brought to a justice (JP or provincial court judge). The applicant must swear the information under oath.

Step 6

The JP evaluates the Information to Obtain and determines whether a reasonable suspicion exists that relevant information can be obtained through the use of a tracking device regarding an offence that has been or will be committed.

The application may be rejected, causing the JP to deny the warrant. If it is denied, other applications may be made when additional evidence is obtained to justify the need for the warrant.

If the justice is satisfied that the suspicion exists, the justice may issue a warrant. Sec. 492.1 C.C. does not specify a form on which a tracking warrant must be issued. Consequently, Form 5 (a sec. 487 C.C. search warrant, illustrated in sec. 841 C.C.) may be adapted to suit the case.

The justice must specify a time period on the warrant, not exceeding 60 days. The warrant is valid during the mentioned time period, allowing the tracking warrant to be *maintained* and *monitored*.

Step 7

After the authorized time period expires, the original warrant authorizes the removal of the tracking device and entry into a place to accomplish this. A justice may issue further warrants after the original warrant expires.[111] The original warrant cannot simply be extended. Instead, if additional time is required, an Information to Obtain must be submitted to the justice for each subsequent request for a further warrant.

NUMBER RECORDER WARRANT—SECTION 492.2 C.C.

A number recorder warrant is a relatively new warrant that any citizen or peace officer may obtain. A "number recorder" is defined as any device that can be used to *record or identify*

1. the telephone number, or
2. the location of the telephone from which a telephone call originates or at which it is received or is intended to be received.[112]

The recorder is also called a DNR, referring to a dial or digital number recorder. The device is attached to a telephone number. The DNR is commonly used on the suspect's telephone to monitor his or her outgoing calls. It is activated when the telephone is taken "off the hook." The monitored telephone emits electronic impulses that are recorded on a computer printout tape. The tape discloses the telephone number dialled when an outgoing call is made. The DNR does not record

- whether the receiving telephone was answered, or
- the conversation.[113]

DNR signals are not private communications.

Consequently, the authorization to intercept private communications, as permitted by sec. 184 C.C., does not apply to DNR signals and does not have to be obtained to use DNR.

If an incoming call is made to the monitored phone, the DNR records only that the phone is "off the hook" and the length of time that it is "off the hook."[114]

Phone companies possess tracing devices that are installed on complainant's telephones, with the consent of the complainant. Trace devices are investigative means of determining a suspect in order to use a DNR. For example, if a person is receiving obscene phone calls and the caller's identity is unknown, trace devices are installed on the complainant's telephone with the complainant's consent. The trace device can determine the source of the call by identifying the address and the name of the person to whom the phone circuit is registered. Afterward, a DNR may be used to monitor the outgoing phone calls made by the suspect.[115]

The recording or identifying of a telephone number by means of a DNR constitutes a search.[116] Bell Canada may conduct this type of search without a warrant if it is conducted without direction from the police. Bell Canada is not a state agent if it conducts a DNR search without the police initiating the search.[117]

However, any DNR search initiated or requested by the police requires a warrant, called a number recorder warrant, which is provided for in sec. 492.2 C.C. The sec. 492.2 C.C. warrant also authorizes the seizure of any telephone records of calls that originated from a telephone, or were received or intended to be received at a telephone.

OBTAIN AND EXECUTE A NUMBER RECORDER WARRANT—PROCEDURE

The following procedure applies to a number recorder warrant.

Step 1

An application must be completed on an Information to Obtain. Section 492.2 C.C. does not specify a document that must be used to apply. Therefore, Form 1 (as illustrated in sec. 841 C.C.) may be adapted for use as the application for this type of warrant.

Step 2

A citizen or peace officer may be the applicant, (the "informant").

Step 3

The Information to Obtain must include a written explanation of evidence that causes a belief based on reasonable grounds to *suspect*

- that any criminal offence under any federal statute has been or will be committed, and
- information that would assist in the investigation of that offence could be obtained through the use of a DNR.[118]

Step 4

The Information to Obtain must also include

- the suspect's name, address, and telephone number, or
- the address of a place (e.g., Bell Canada) where any person or body lawfully possesses records of telephone calls originated from, or received, or intended to be received.

Step 5

The Information to Obtain must be brought to a justice and must be signed by the informant. The informant must swear the Information to Obtain under oath.

Step 6

The justice evaluates the Information to Obtain and denies or issues a warrant.

If the warrant is issued, the justice may use Form 5 and adapt it to suit the case. Sec. 492.2 C.C. does not specify a form that must be used as the warrant.

The justice must specify a time period on the warrant, not exceeding 60 days, for which the warrant will be valid.[119]

Step 7

The warrant authorizes the installation, maintenance, and removal of the DNR, and the monitoring of the DNR during the time period specified on the warrant. After the time period expires, the justice may issue further warrants, if further applications are made to justify the new warrants. The original warrant cannot simply be extended without new applications.[120]

FORENSIC DNA ANALYSIS—SECTION 487.04 WARRANT

This new search warrant came into force in July 1995. It authorizes the seizure of certain bodily substances, in restricted circumstances, for the purpose of forensic DNA analysis.

This warrant represents a significant, advantageous investigative procedure for the police. Prior to this warrant, no specific authority existed to seize bodily substances for forensic DNA analysis. Police had relied on indirect authorities, such as consent and search of a person after an arrest. Some of these seizures, in certain cases, were ruled to be sec. 8 *Charter* violations and were excluded under sec. 24(2) *Charter*.

DNA is defined as deoxyribonucleic acid.[121] "Forensic DNA analysis" is defined as analysis of the bodily substance obtained in execution of a warrant, and the comparison of the result of that analysis with the results of the analysis of the DNA of the bodily substance found at the crime scene, on or within the victim's body, or on or within the body of any person or thing associated with the commission of the offence.[122]

Forensic DNA analysis warrants may be obtained only in relation to designated offences, which include

- murder
- manslaughter
- robbery
- break, enter with intent
- break, enter and commit
- arson (all types)
- mischief causing danger to life
- sexual offences
- assault causing bodily harm
- assault with a weapon
- aggravated assault
- unlawfully causing bodily harm
- piratical acts
- kidnapping
- hostage taking
- hijacking
- criminal negligence causing bodily harm
- criminal negligence causing death

OBTAIN AND EXECUTE A SECTION 487.04 WARRANT—PROCEDURE

The following procedure applies to a sec. 487.04 warrant.

Step 1

An application must be made by completing an Information to Obtain. A peace officer must be the informant. The contents of the Information to Obtain must include reasonable grounds to believe that

- a designated offence has been committed,
- a bodily substance has been found

  - at the place where the offence was committed,
  - on or within the victim's body,
  - on anything worn or carried by the victim at the time when the offence was committed,

- on or within the body of any person or thing, or
- at any place associated with the commission of the offence.

- a person was a party to the offence, and
- forensic DNA analysis of a bodily substance from the person will provide evidence about whether the bodily substance was from that person.[123]

Step 2

The Information to Obtain must be sworn before a provincial court judge only. A justice of the peace cannot issue this warrant. The judge may issue the warrant if he or she is satisfied that the required reasonable grounds exist and that it is in the best interests of the administration of justice to issue the warrant.[124] The determining factors are

- the nature and circumstances of the designated offence, and
- whether there is a peace officer who is able, by virtue of training or experience, to obtain a bodily substance by means of a specified investigative procedure, or
- whether there is another person who has training or experience to obtain the bodily substance by means of a specific investigative procedure, under the direction of a peace officer.[125]

If the warrant is issued, it authorizes a peace officer to obtain, or cause another person to obtain under his or her direction, a bodily substance from the person mentioned in the warrant. The bodily substances that may be seized are restricted to hair, saliva, and blood. The procedures to obtain the bodily substances are restricted to the following:

hair   the plucking of individual hairs from the person, including the root sheath,
saliva   the taking of buccal swabs by swabbing the lips, tongue, and inside the cheeks of the mouth to collect epithelial cells
blood   the taking of blood by pricking the skin surface with a sterile lancet.[126]

Only one of these substances may be seized. The warrant must include any terms and conditions that the judge considers advisable to ensure that the seizure is reasonable.[127]

Step 3

Before a forensic DNA analysis warrant is executed, a peace officer has a mandatory obligation to inform the person of the following:

- the contents of the warrant,
- the nature of the investigative procedure that will be used,
- the purpose of obtaining the bodily substance,
- the possibility that the results of forensic DNA analysis may be used as evidence at a trial, and
- the peace officer and anyone under his or her direction has authority to use as much force as is necessary for the purpose of executing the warrant.

Young Offender

A young offender has the right to a reasonable opportunity to consult with and have present at the time the warrant is executed any of the following persons:

- lawyer,
- parent,
- adult relative, or
- any appropriate adult chosen by the young offender.[128]

Step 4

The executing officer has the authority to

- detain the person for a reasonable period, and
- require the person to accompany him or her to execute the warrant.[129]

Right to Counsel

Although this section does not create a mandatory obligation to inform an adult offender of the right to counsel before the warrant is executed, adults should be informed of the right to counsel because the person will have been detained during the execution of the warrant. Sec. 10(b) *Charter* imposes a mandatory obligation for the police to inform any person who has been detained.

Both adult and young offenders may waive the right to counsel. A young offender's waiver must be

- recorded on audiotape, or
- recorded on videotape, or
- recorded in writing and containing a statement signed by the young offender that he or she has been informed of the right.[130] These requirements do not apply to adult offenders. However, recording an adult's waiver in this manner will help prove the credibility of the waiver. Otherwise, the waiver should be recorded verbatim in a notebook.

Step 5

After the bodily substance is seized, it may be analyzed for DNA only in relation to the investigation of the designated offence stated in the warrant. It cannot be used in the investigation of any other offence. The use of a bodily substance, or the DNA analysis results, in any other investigation other than for the designated offence constitutes a summary conviction offence.

Step 6

The bodily substance must be destroyed

- forthwith after the results show the person was not the offender; or
- one year after the person is acquitted at the trial or discharged after a preliminary hearing.[131]

However, a provincial court judge may order that the bodily substance and the DNA analysis result not be destroyed if reasonable grounds exist that they may be required in the investigation or prosecution of that person for another designated offence.[132]

IMPRESSION WARRANT—SECTION 487.091 C.C.

An "impression" includes a

- handprint,
- fingerprint,
- footprint,
- foot impression,
- teeth impression, or
- other print or impression of the body.

Prior to 1997, no warrant existed that allowed the police to obtain these types of impressions from a person. The *Identification of Criminals Act* allows the police to take fingerprints from a person after the person has been arrested or charged with an indictable offence. Otherwise, impressions could be obtained only by consent.

Section 487.091 C.C. was enacted in 1997, creating a warrant to obtain impressions from a person. This provision apparently is in response to *R. v. Stillman (1997)*, where it was ruled that taking dental impressions from an offender, without a warrant, as part of a search incident to an arrest, constituted a sec. 7 and sec. 8 *Charter* violation.

An Information to Obtain must first be presented, under oath, to a justice. Reasonable grounds must be proven that

- a criminal offence has been committed,
- information concerning the offence will be obtained by the print or impressions, and

- the issuance of the warrant is in the best interests of the administration of justice.

After the justice is satisfied that the reasonable grounds exist, a warrant may be issued authorizing a peace officer to do anything, or cause anything to be done under the direction of a peace officer, to obtain an impression from the person named in the warrant.

The warrant must contain terms and conditions that the justice considers advisable to ensure that the search and seizure is reasonable in the circumstances.

Problem-Solving Case Studies

You are a police officer in each case. Each offender is an adult, unless otherwise indicated.

PROBLEM 94

You are investigating a "theft under $5000.00" offence that occurred at a business premises in a shopping mall 10 minutes ago. You receive information to form reasonable grounds that the stolen property is in a car owned by Eddie. The car is parked on King St., in front of Eddie's house.

a) Can a sec. 487 C.C. search warrant be obtained to search a car for stolen property?

_____

_____

b) What other authority may be used to search Eddie's car for the stolen property?

_____

PROBLEM 95

You are investigating a summary conviction offence, and you form reasonable grounds that an item that is evidence to the offence is currently in Ward's office. Can a sec. 487 C.C. search warrant be obtained in relation to this classification of offence?

_____

_____

PROBLEM 96

You form reasonable grounds that Wally committed a robbery yesterday.

a) Today, you form reasonable grounds that a letter written by Wally is in Eddie's house. The letter states Wally's new address. Can a sec. 487 C.C. search warrant be obtained to search the house for the letter?

_____

_____

_____

b) Today, you form reasonable grounds that Wally is currently in a house situated at 10 King St. Can a sec. 487 C.C. search warrant be obtained to enter the house and search for Wally?

_____

_____

PROBLEM 97

You are investigating a robbery, and you form reasonable grounds that a mask and clothing worn by Ralph, the offender, are currently in Ralph's house.

a) Can you enter and search the house without first obtaining a sec. 487 C.C. search warrant and without consent if you suspect that the evidence will be destroyed before you arrive with the warrant?

_____

_____

b) Can you obtain a sec. 487 search warrant without first applying by completing an Information to Obtain?

_____

_____

PROBLEM 98

You are investigating a "theft over $5000.00" offence. You receive information that the stolen items may be in either Mary's office, Betty's house, or Gloria's car.

a) Can you apply on one Information to Obtain to search all three places?

_____

_____

b) Will you be able to obtain three search warrants to search all three places, under these circumstances?

_____

_____

_____

_____

PROBLEM 99

You are investigating a murder. You determine that John is a suspect and that he is temporarily living at Gord's house. Can you apply for a search warrant and write "any evidence relating to the murder" as the items on the Information to Obtain?

_____

_____

_____

_____

PROBLEM 100

Marg reports the following to you at 10:00 p.m. today: She was in Jeanette's house 30 minutes ago. Jeanette's brother Reg and his friend Dave were present. Reg showed Dave a 20-inch colour TV set that was operating in the living room and told him that he stole it last night when he committed a break and enter at The Store. Reg asked Dave and Marg if either wanted to buy it. Both declined. Reg left a few minutes later. Marg has known Reg for 15 years, and she has given you accurate confidential information in the past. She is associated with many known criminals. You begin writing an Information to Obtain.

a) Can you list the item to be searched for as a "20-inch colour TV"?

_____

_____

_____

_____

b) Do you have to name an offence for which the TV will be evidence?

_____

_____

_____

_____

c) What should be the first part of the written reasonable grounds for belief?

_____

_____

d) If you do not know that Jeanette is the owner of the house, will the warrant be automatically rejected?

_____

_____

_____

_____

e) Can you protect Marg's identity on your written grounds for belief?

_____

_____

_____

_____

_____

_____

f) Will the following statement in appendix B constitute reasonable grounds for belief: "Information has been received from an anonymous informant that a stolen TV is inside Wally's house"?

_____

_____

_____

_____

_____

_____

_____

_____

_____

_____

g) Will Marg's information likely constitute reasonable grounds?

_____

_____

_____

h) To what should the last part of the written grounds refer?

_____

i) Can you get advice from the JP about what to include in the contents of your written grounds?

_____

_____

j) Where do you have to meet the JP to present the Information to Obtain?

_____

k) Can you give the JP an unsigned Information to Obtain for an opinion about accuracy and sufficiency?

_____

_____

l) You sign the Information to Obtain and swear the contents under oath. What will occur next?

_____

_____

_____

m) The JP decides that reasonable grounds exist and will issue the search warrant. Who keeps the original Information to Obtain?

_____

n) Which officers must be named on the search warrant?

_____

_____

_____

o) Can this warrant be executed at night?

_____

_____

p) You attend at Jeanette's house to execute the warrant. How many officers can participate in the search?

_____

q) Can you enter the house forcibly without any announcement?

_____

r) You receive no answer and believe no one is home. Can you execute the warrant?

_____

_____

_____

_____

s) If Reg is home and answers the door, what do you have to inform him of or give to him?

_____

t) Four other people are inside the house. Does the search warrant authorize the arrest and search of the occupants?

_____

u) If Reg immediately gives you the TV, the only item listed, can you continue searching the house?

_____

_____

v) You complete the search, and the TV is not found. You and all the officers leave the premises. You phone Marg, who tells you that Reg called her and said that he saw the police arrive and he hid the TV in the attic before the police entered. Can you return and search the house on the authority of the original warrant?

_____

_____

w) Could you have gone to Reg's house and arrested him for "break, enter and theft" without first applying for the search warrant?

_____

_____

PROBLEM 101

You receive confidential information from Theodore that Eddie has one pound of cocaine in a garage station that Eddie owns. What type of search warrant should you obtain?

_____

_____

_____

PROBLEM 102

You receive information from Eddie that one pound of marijuana is in June's house.

a) What type of search warrant should you obtain?

_____

b) You apply for a C.D.S.A. search warrant. Do the rules regarding the Information to Obtain differ from applying for a sec. 487 C.C. search warrant?

_____

c) The JP authorizes a search warrant. What officers must be named on this?

_____

_____

_____

d) Does the named officer have to participate in the search?

_____

e) How many officers may participate in the search?

_____

_____

f) Can a C.D.S.A. search warrant be automatically executed at night?

_____

EIGHTEEN

*Search and Seizure
without Warrant or
Consent*

Learning Outcomes

The student will be able to

- interpret and apply the common law "search incident to arrest",

- interpret and apply the plain-view doctrine,

- interpret and apply firearm and weapon searches without a warrant and without consent,

- define terms relevant to firearms and weapons,

- explain the procedure to obtain a firearms and weapons search warrant,

- explain the procedure to make a "return,"

- interpret and apply warrantless search authorities under the C.D.S.A,

- interpret and apply sec 487.11 C.C. (warrantless search for ordinary evidence), and

- prevent *Charter* violations relevant to warrantless searches.

INTRODUCTION

A "search without warrant" or consent refers to the limited authority a police officer has to search

1. a place, without judicial authorization or consent of the owner or occupier, or
2. a person, without consent. (A warrant cannot be obtained to search a person for physical evidence.)

When a search without warrant is made, the police officer, not a justice, makes the decision to search. However, police officers cannot arbitrarily or automatically search places or persons without a warrant or consent. Authority must exist in some source of law that permits the police to do so. An unauthorized search without a warrant or consent constitutes a sec. 8 *Charter* violation, which may result in exclusion of the seized evidence from the trial, under sec. 24(2) *Charter*. Additionally, it may expose the officer to criminal or civil liability depending on the circumstances and the intent of the officer.

Police officers have limited authority to search without a warrant or consent. These authorities are not found in one specific statute. Instead, they are found in various sources of law, including common law, case law, the *Criminal Code,* and the *Controlled Drugs and Substances Act.*

This section will examine the most common authorities that allow police officers to search places and persons without a warrant or consent. The authorities include

1. search of person after arrest (search incident to arrest),
2. plain-view doctrine,
3. sec. 489 C.C,
4. firearms and weapons (sections 117.02 and 117.04(2) C.C.),
5. drugs (sec. 11(7) C.C.),
6. warrantless entry to preserve evidence while awaiting search warrant, and
7. sec. 487.11 C.C.—evidence to any offence.

SEARCH AFTER AN ARREST

Police officers are authorized to immediately search a person after the person has been lawfully arrested and may seize

1. Evidence relating to any offence, including the offence for which the accused was arrested and any other unrelated offence. The evidence may be any item in the accused's possession or any clothing that is evidence to prove an offence. If clothing is seized as evidence, police stations have suitable apparel for accused persons to wear while in police custody.
2. Items capable of causing injury to any person, including the accused. In addition to weapons, any clothing, jewellery, or other items in pockets may be seized from the accused before he or she enters a police jail cell in order to prevent injury or suicide. Belts, shoelaces, jewellery, and lighters should always be seized and kept in a property locker while the accused is in a police jail cell. The accused is usually allowed to wear his or her own clothing. Clothing should be seized only when some evidence indicates or suggests that the accused is suicidal. All efforts must be made to prevent a suicide while an accused is in police custody.
3. Any item that can facilitate escape.[133]

The only item that cannot be seized without consent is money that is not evidence and is lawfully owned by the accused.[134] Usually, an officer asks the accused for consent for the money to be kept in a police property locker for safekeeping while the accused is in the police cells. Consent is commonly given.

Items seized that are evidence to any offence may be kept until court proceedings conclude. Items seized that are not evidence or are illegal, but taken to prevent injury or escape, must be returned to the accused at the time of release from custody.

An arrested person may be *automatically* and immediately searched after the arrest is made. This means that the arresting officer *does not have to prove* that reasonable grounds existed to believe that the accused possessed any of the items that may be seized, before a search may be made.[135] The only requirement necessary to prove is that lawful authority existed to arrest.

The Supreme Court of Canada stated that the *exercise of this authority*, meaning the actual extent of the search, is not unlimited. The court explained this rule as follows:

1. This search authority does not impose a duty upon the police. Officers do have discretion not to search an arrested person when the officer is satisfied that a search of the person is not necessary.
2. The purpose of the search must be to search for weapons and evidence. The search cannot be used to "intimidate, ridicule, or pressure" the arrested person to obtain a confession.
3. The search cannot be conducted in an "abusive fashion," which is defined as unjustified physical or psychological constraint.[136]

The authority to search after an arrest is not found in any Canadian statute. It is a common law authority, originating in English cases in 1853. Canadian courts recognized this common law authority in 1895. The Supreme Court of Canada, in *Cloutier v. Langlois (1990)*, supported the lawfulness of the search of an arrested person. This common law authority is formally called a "search incident of arrest."

COMMENTARY

It is difficult to imagine how a police officer can be positively satisfied beyond all doubt that an arrested person is unarmed without searching the person. Any arrest poses a potential risk to the arresting officer.

Any officer who has routinely arrested persons has learned through experience that no arrested person may be assumed to be unarmed or incapable of using violence.

DELAY BETWEEN ARREST AND SEARCH

The common law search-incident-to-arrest authority does not specify how much time may elapse between the arrest and the search. During some investigations, a delay may occur. The Supreme Court of Canada, in *R. v. Caslake (1998)*,[137] made significant rulings about this issue. Additionally, the *Caslake* decision is relevant to the questions of

1. whether the common law search authority extends to vehicles, and
2. the validity of an "inventory search" of a car conducted six hours after the arrest.

IMMEDIATE SURROUNDINGS

In addition to searching the arrested person, this authority permits an officer to search the immediate surroundings of the place where the accused was arrested. No warrant or consent is required.[138] The specific dimensions of "immediate surroundings" of a place has not been defined by the Supreme Court. The size of the area searched is governed by the requirement of reasonableness under sec. 8 *Charter*. Appeal courts in Ontario and British Columbia have ruled that immediate surroundings include the following areas, when the accused is arrested in a vehicle:

- the interior of a vehicle (Ontario C.A. & B.C.C.A.),[139]
- the trunk of a vehicle (B.C.C.A.),[140] and
- the inside of a vehicle door, after the police remove a door panel (B.C.C.A.)[141]

Other case law decisions have established the following guidelines regarding the immediate surroundings of places other than vehicles:

1. In *R. v. Lim (1990)*,[142] the Ontario H.C.J. stated, "The scene of an arrest may yield valuable evidence which will assist the police in their investigation and in determining what should be done with the arrested person. This common sense proposition lies at the root of the common law rationale for searches as an incident of arrest."[143]

The court added that warrantless searches after an arrest justify prompt and effective seizure of evidence relevant to the accused's guilt or innocence. Finally, a sig-

CASE LAW

R. V. CASLAKE (1998)

Issues

1. Does the common law search-incident-to-arrest authority apply to vehicles?

2. Is an "inventory search" of a car conducted six hours after the arrest reasonable as part of a search incident to an arrest?

Offences "possession of marijuana for the purpose of trafficking" and "possession of cocaine"

Circumstances A Natural Resources officer saw a car parked by the side of a highway and stopped to investigate. The officer saw the accused standing in tall grass, about 40 feet from the roadway. The officer questioned the accused, who stated that he was relieving himself. They returned to their respective vehicles, and the accused drove away.

   The officer then returned to the area where the accused had been standing. A garbage bag containing about nine pounds of marijuana wrapped in cellophane was found and seized. The officer returned to his vehicle, contacted the RCMP, pursued the accused, stopped him, and arrested him.

   An RCMP officer arrived at the scene and took custody of the accused, transporting him to an RCMP detachment. The accused's vehicle was towed to a garage. Approximately six hours after the arrest, the RCMP officer went to the garage, unlocked the accused's vehicle, and searched it without a warrant and without consent. According to the officer's testimony, the search was conducted pursuant to RCMP policy requiring that inventory be taken of a vehicle's condition and contents seized during an investigation. The officer testified that this was the sole reason for the search. The search resulted in the seizure of two packages containing 0.25 g of cocaine each, and $1400.00 in a case.

Trial The accused was convicted. His appeals were based on the grounds that the search violated sec. 8 *Charter* and that the evidence should be excluded under sec. 24(2) *Charter*. The accused argued that the six-hour delay between the arrest and the search was excessive to make the search "incident" to the arrest. Appeals to the Manitoba Court of the Queen's Bench and to the Manitoba Court of Appeal were both dismissed because no substantial wrong or miscarriage of justice had occurred.

Supreme Court of Canada The Supreme Court of Canada dismissed the accused's appeal. The court was unanimous in deciding to admit the seized evidence.

   However, the reasons given by the majority differed from the minority. The majority ruled that a sec. 8 *Charter* violation occurred but admitted the evidence under sec. 24(2) *Charter*. The minority ruled that no *Charter* violation had occurred.

Majority Reasons The three main purposes of a search incident to an arrest are

•   ensuring the safety of the police and the public,

•   preventing destruction of evidence, and

•   discovering evidence that can be used at the accused's trial.

   A search conducted after an arrest must be "truly incidental" to the arrest, meaning that the police must be attempting to achieve a valid purpose relating to the arrest.

   Ordinarily, the accused has the onus to prove the commission of a *Charter* violation except in cases involving a warrantless search, which are unreasonable unless the Crown proves otherwise. Consequently, the Crown has the onus to prove that a warrantless search is reasonable. In order to be reasonable, a search must be authorized by a statute or common law. If a search is not authorized by law, a theft or trespass may have occurred.

   There are three ways that the Crown may fail to prove that a search was authorized by law:

1. No statute or common law actually authorized the search.

2. The search was authorized by law but was not executed in accordance with the procedures stipulated by that law.

continued

3. The search exceeded the scope of the search authority, relating to factors including the place, items seized, and time of the search.

The Crown relied on the common law search-incident-to-arrest authority to prove reasonableness. No readily ascertainable limits exist relating to the scope of this search authority because it is a common law power. Consequently, the courts are responsible for establishing procedural boundaries that may limit the authority.

The scope of the search incident to arrest authority extends to both persons and places, including vehicles. The Supreme Court of Canada, in this decision, stated that this power to search may be used to search automobiles if it constitutes the accused's immediate surroundings because no "heightened expectation of privacy" exists to prohibit the search. However, some limits are imposed relating to vehicle searches incident to arrest. The reasonableness of a vehicle search incident to arrest will depend on certain factors including

- the basis for the search,

- the location of the vehicle in relation to the place of the accused's arrest, and

- other relevant circumstances, such as "temporal" factors, referring to the time that the search was conducted after the arrest.

No specific amount of time exists that may be used as a procedural guideline to determine when a search of a vehicle is "incidental" to an arrest. Time limits do exist and are derived from the same principles that are used to determine whether a search of a vehicle incident to arrest is reasonable. A substantial delay between arrest and vehicle search will not automatically make the search unreasonable. A reasonable explanation may justify a substantial delay.

In this case, the six-hour delay itself was not the problem. Instead, the officer's reasons for searching, to conduct an "inventory search," caused the search to fall outside the scope of the common law authority. An inventory search does not serve a "valid objective in pursuit of the ends of criminal justice." The inventory search in this case constituted a sec. 8 *Charter* violation.

Despite the commission of this *Charter* violation, the evidence was admitted under sec. 24(2) *Charter* because the trial was fair, the *Charter* violation was not serious, and the exclusion of evidence would have had a "detrimental impact" on the administration of justice.

The Supreme Court of Canada minority ruled that no sec. 8 *Charter* violation occurred for the following reasons:

1. a search incident to arrest extends to an accused's automobile as part of the accused's immediate surroundings, and

2. the inventory search was justified because its purpose was related to the lawful arrest and impounding of the vehicle, and was "incidental" to the arrest.

In summary, the following rules apply to the common law search-incident-to-arrest authority:

1. No specific time exists that determines the interval between arrest and search.

2. A substantial delay between arrest and search will not automatically make the search unreasonable. A reasonable delay may be a substantial delay. In this case, the six-hour delay itself was not the problem.

3. The common law search authority extends to both persons and places, including vehicles.

4. The reasonableness of a vehicle search depends on

   - the basis for the search,

   - the location of the vehicle in relation to the arrest, and

   - other relevant circumstances, such as the time interval.

nificant advantageous guideline was created to determine whether a sec. 8 *Charter* violation occurs when immediate surroundings are searched. The court stated that the purpose of sec. 8 *Charter* is to protect individual privacy expectations from unwarranted searches. However, a lawful arrest reduces the arrested person's expectation of privacy. Although this guideline does not define a specific area, it infers that officers are given a wide latitude of search authority, relating to immediate surroundings.

2. In *R. v. Smellie (1994)*,[144] the British Columbia Court of Appeal ruled that the immediate surroundings includes the entirety of what may reasonably be considered the surroundings. This inference suggests that if the accused is arrested inside a place, the entire room where the accused is arrested may be searched without a warrant. It does not infer that the entire house or premises may be searched.

ARREST OUTSIDE A HOUSE

In some cases, an arrest of a person is made outside a house, but in close proximity to it. The question arises whether the house may be searched without a warrant as a search incident to an arrest.

In *R. v. Golub (1997)*,[145] an accused person was arrested outside his house, about 4.5 m (14 feet) from the door. The police reasonably believed that a firearm was in the house and suspected that someone else may have been in the house. Officers entered without a warrant, searched the entire house for other persons, and seized a loaded rifle. In that case, the Ontario Court of Appeal ruled that the search was a justified search incident to an arrest.

The court created the following procedural guidelines about warrantless entry and search of a house when an arrest is made in close proximity, outside the house:

1. A search is justified when "exceptional circumstances" exist.
2. "Exceptional circumstances" are defined as situations "where the law enforcement interest is so compelling that it overrides the individual's right to privacy within the home."
3. The risk of physical harm to persons at an arrest scene constitutes exceptional circumstances that justify a warrantless entry and search of the house.

Note: Refer to Chapter 2 for the complete circumstances of *R. v. Golub*, which illustrates an example of a justified warrantless search of a dwelling-house when the accused is arrested outside, in close proximity.

In summary, the common law search-after-arrest authority provides the advantages of permitting automatic searches of persons and partial places without a warrant. The primary purpose of this authority is self-protection. An immediate search should be conducted after any arrest, regardless of how minor the offence may be, to prevent any possibility of harm being done to the arresting officer.

The Alberta Court of Appeal, in *R. v. Lerke (1986)*, agreed with this opinion by stating that

> the reluctance of Canadian courts to invalidate searches after arrest is understandable. Judges cannot be blind to the deaths and injuries suffered by police officers on duty as guns and knives become more common. Situations which appear quite innocent, with no hostile demonstration by the person being arrested, can explode into violence leaving the arresting officer dead or injured. It is difficult to second-guess any police officer who ensures that a person is not armed when he perceives danger as he makes an arrest or escorts a prisoner.[146]

SEARCH INCIDENT TO DETENTION (ARTICULABLE CAUSE)

In Chapter 2, the articulable cause authority to detain a suspect for investigative purposes was explained. This common law authority allows the police to temporarily detain a suspect when only mere suspicion exists that the person has committed a criminal act. The "articulable cause authority to detain" explanation included the case law interpretation of the common law authority and the circumstances of specific investigations. Refer to pages 35–39 for details.

The second issue regarding articulable cause, after detention, is whether the police have the authority to conduct a search without a warrant or consent during the detention. The following is a summary of the authorities that originate from case law interpretation.

1. A common law authority to search during the detention does exist. The police are authorized to conduct searches during investigative detentions that are based on articulable cause.
2. The formal name for this search authority is "search incident to detention."
3. The scope or extent of the search is determined by "reasonable necessity." This is a general principle that tries to answer questions about who, what, where, and how much the police can search. Can the police search a person? Places? The answer is that the police may search whatever is proven to be reasonably necessary. To determine reasonable necessity, a trial judge will analyze the interference that the search caused on a person's liberty and the importance that the interference served for public purpose. To explain this principle, the B.C.C.A. stated the following rules that serve as valuable procedural guidelines:

   - The police are not obliged to risk bodily harm when they are lawfully trying to determine whether a person currently is or is about to be engaged in a crime.
   - The police have authority to search for weapons as an incident to detention, if the police have a justifiable belief that the person stopped is carrying a weapon.
   - The seriousness of the circumstances that lead to a stop will govern the decision whether to search at all and the scope of the search that is undertaken. The scope of the search must be related to the circumstances that justified the search. The following two examples are given by the B.C.C.A. to explain how these principles apply:

     - questioning an elderly shopper about a suspected shoplifting would not ordinarily need a search for weapons
     - questioning a suspect after a bank robbery might require a search of the detained person and his or her immediate surroundings.

4. The reference by the B.C.C.A. to "immediate surroundings" means that the police may search both the detained person and the place where he or she is found, including a car. The extent of where or how much an officer may search depends on the reasonable necessity, which is dictated by the circumstances.
5. The detained person's personal property may be searched for weapons if the circumstances justify a reasonable necessity. The case law decisions explained in Chapter 2 show examples of circumstances that justified a search of property, such as gym bag and waist pack, for weapons.

   In summary, a comparison may be drawn between two search authorities:

- search incident to arrest, and
- search incident to detention.

   They share the following features:

- both are common law authorities,
- they authorize the search of persons and immediate surroundings, and
- both are conditional. They apply only after a person has lawfully been **arrested** under a sec. 495 C.C. authority or detained by justifiable articulable cause.

   The major difference is the target or reason for the search. If the search follows a formal arrest, weapons and evidence may be seized. If the search follows an articulable cause detention, the search is directed toward weapons only. If other evidence is found, it may be seized. The other items' admissibility will depend on whether the circumstances prove that it was reasonably necessary to search for weapons.

   The procedure for a search incident to an arrest is far more structured and clear than when a detention has occurred. The "articulable cause" detention and search procedures lack the specificity of its counterpart. Yet both are valuable investigative procedures that are also crucial for officer safety.

COMMENTARY

Any experienced police officer will likely acknowledge that any arrested or detained person is capable of possessing a weapon and using it. Personal safety should always be the priority during either type of search. Logically, the primary reason for searching should always be to find weapons. Evidence relating to an offence should be the secondary issue.

PLAIN-VIEW DOCTRINE AND SECTION 489(2) C.C.—SEIZURE WITHOUT WARRANT

Section 489(2) C.C. is a new "seizure without warrant" authority that was apparently enacted in response to a case law seizure authority called the "plain-view doctrine." The concept of the two seizure-without-warrant authorities are similar, but section 489(2) has a certain vagueness in comparison to the plain-view doctrine, which will be interpreted and explained. Essentially, the combined effect of these two authorities represents a significant advantage for police officers during investigations because it permits the warrantless seizure of inadvertently found evidence relating to any offence.

Section 489(2) C.C. authorizes peace officers "lawfully present in a place pursuant to a warrant or otherwise in the execution of duties may, without a warrant, seize anything that the officer believes on reasonable grounds

- has been obtained, or
- has been used, or
- will afford evidence in respect of,

an offence against the *Criminal Code* or any act of Parliament."

To interpret this authority, the case law "plain-view doctrine" that preceded sec. 489(2) C.C. will be explained first because it defines relevant terms related to sec. 489(2) C.C.

PLAIN-VIEW DOCTRINE

The plain-view doctrine is a search-without-warrant authority found in case law. The plain-view rule authorizes the following seizure: "A peace officer who is lawfully on any premises, whether pursuant to a warrant or otherwise, is permitted to seize any evidence, which is in plain view and which is inadvertently found."[147]

"Lawfully on any premises" includes being in a place because of any of the following authorities:

1. a search warrant (any type),
2. consent, including by invitation to enter to take any type of report,
3. entry and search without warrant when authorized by a statute or case law, and
4. entry without a warrant pursuant to a provincial statute such as the *Landlord and Tenant Act of Ontario*. For example, this statute permits the landlord to enter an apartment when an emergency exists and he or she may bring a police officer to act as a witness.[148]

"Any premises" includes a dwelling-house or any other building. "Plain view" means inadvertently found. "Inadvertent" means unexpectedly finding evidence, without having prior knowledge that the item was in the place and without physically searching the place to find the item.

The type of evidence that may be seized under the plain-view doctrine is any item that proves the commission of any offence, including offences unrelated from the one being investigated while lawfully on the premises.

The plain-view doctrine has been drawn from American law and has been recognized and applied in Canada, in the following cases:

- *R. v. Shea (1982)* (Ontario H.C.J.),
- *R. v. Longtin (1983)* (Ontario C.A.),
- *R. v. Nielsen (1988)* (Sask. C.A.),
- *R. v. Belliveau (1986)* (N.B. C.A.), and
- *R. v. Grenier (1991)* (Quebec C.A.).[149]

SECTION 489(2) C.C. INTERPRETATION

The interpretation of the sec. 489(2) C.C. provisions and the comparison to the plain-view doctrine are as follows:

1. **any peace officer**—defined in section 2 C.C., the authority does not include citizens,
2. **lawfully present in a place pursuant to a warrant or otherwise**
   a) "a place"—this authority does not restrict the application of it to any type of place. Consequently, it can be used to seize evidence from any place, including

   - dwelling-house,
   - business premise,
   - office,
   - school, and
   - vehicle.

   b) "lawfully present"—pursuant to a warrant or otherwise means that the police can use this authority to seize evidence if they are on the premises because of any of the following reasons:

   - search warrant—any type, including sec. 487 C.C., general warrant, sec. 529 C.C. warrant to enter house, and C.D.S.A. search warrant,
   - consent—including an invitation to enter a place to interview a complainant regarding any offence, and
   - warrantless entry and search authorized by any federal or provincial statute.

3. **seize anything that is evidence**—While in the place, an officer may seize any item without a warrant if the officer can prove reasonable grounds that the item will afford evidence to any criminal offence. This includes items that have been obtained by or used in the commission of any criminal offence including the *Criminal Code* and *Controlled Drugs and Substances Act*. The item does not have to be evidence related to the offence being investigated; it may be evidence to an unrelated offence. The type of item may be wide-ranging, including stolen property, weapons, drugs, and clothing. The officer must believe beyond mere suspicion that the item was obtained or used in an offence.

   The belief can be based on the officer's positive identification, a witness's recognition, the suspect's admission, or simply the nature of the item such as drugs or unlawful firearm.

4. **discovery of the item**—Section 489(2) C.C. does not authorize a search of a place or person for evidence. The question that arises is, "how does the item have to be discovered in order for the warrantless seizure to be lawful?" The answer is not clearly stated in sec. 489(2) C.C. No reference is made to the terms "plain view" or "inadvertent," which would have facilitated the interpretation. However, the absence of a discernible authority to search suggests that the plain-view doctrine will be used to define and interpret the manner in which discovery of items may be made. Therefore, a seizure under sec. 489(2) C.C. may be made only if the item is in "plain view" or "inadvertent." Inadvertent discovery means the unexpected finding of evidence, without having prior knowledge that the item was in the place.
   An inadvertent discovery may be made in any of the following methods:

   a) A police officer responds to a complaint at a place such as a house. After being invited to enter, the officer sees evidence of any criminal offence, in plain view. The officer is lawfully on the premises by consent. The discovery of the item was inadvertent because no prior knowledge existed that the item was in the place and no physical search was conducted to find the item. The officer may seize the item under sec. 489(2) C.C. without having to obtain a warrant.
   b) A police officer is lawfully searching a place either with or without a warrant. During the search for the intended items, the officer finds other items not named on the warrant or unrelated to the investigation that are evidence to an offence. The items may be seized. A return to a justice must be made after an item is seized, under this authority, according to the procedures described in sec. 489(2) C.C.

PROCEDURE

The admissibility of items seized without a warrant under sec. 489(2) C.C. depends on the following proof:

- the person who made the seizure was a peace officer,
- the officer was lawfully in the place (specify the method),
- an item was found that was evidence relating to a criminal offence,
- reasonable grounds existed that caused the belief that the item was evidence to a criminal offence,
- the discovery was inadvertent—it was in plain view and no prior knowledge existed that the item was in the place, and
- a return was made to a justice either in writing or by bringing the actual item to a justice.

FIREARMS AND WEAPON SEARCHES

In December 1998, new firearms legislation was enacted that amended the *Criminal Code*. The new legislation controls the acquisition, possession, and use of firearms. Changes have been made to certain offences and definitions. However, both the previous and new legislation have similar search-without-warrant authorities. The primary difference is the new terms that classify and define firearms and weapons. The warrantless search authorities are now found in sec. 117.04 C.C.

RELEVANT DEFINITIONS AND TERMS

Weapon (Sec. 2 C.C.)

Anything used, designed to be used, or intended for use

- in causing death or injury to any person, or
- for the purpose of threatening or intimidating any person, and includes a firearm.

Firearm (Sec. 2 C.C.)

A barrelled weapon from which any shot, bullet, or other projectile can be discharged and that is capable of causing serious bodily harm or death to a person and includes any frame or receiver of such a barrelled weapon and anything that can be adopted for use as a firearm.

Imitation Firearm (Sec. 84 C.C.)

Anything that imitates a firearm, including a replica firearm.

Prohibited Weapon (Sec. 84 C.C.)

A knife that has a blade that opens automatically by gravity or centrifugal force or by hand pressure applied to a button, spring, or other device in or attached to the handle of the knife, or any weapon, other than a firearm, that is prescribed to be a prohibited weapon. A regulation lists items that are prescribed as prohibited weapons and includes the weapons listed in the former prohibition orders from No. 1 to No. 8. Examples are

- tear gas, mace,
- *nunchakus,*
- *shuriken,*
- finger ring with one or more blades capable of being projected from the surface,
- constant companion,
- knife-comb,
- spiked wristband, and
- brass knuckles.

Prohibited Firearm (Sec. 84 C.C.)

1. a handgun that

    a) has a barrel equal to or less than 105 mm (6 inches) in length, or
    b) is designed or adopted to discharge a 25 or 32 calibre cartridge

2. a sawed-off shotgun less than 660 mm (26 inches) in length or has a barrel length less than 457 mm (18 inches),
3. an automatic firearm, and
4. a firearm prescribed by regulation, e.g., Taser Public Defender.

Prohibited Device (Sec. 84 C.C.)

Includes

1. a handgun barrel that is equal to or less than 105 mm (6 inches),
2. a silencer,
3. a replica firearm,
4. any component, or part of a weapon, or accessory for use with a weapon that is prescribed by a regulation to be a prohibited device, including an electrical or mechanical device that is designed or adapted to operate the trigger mechanism of a semi-automatic firearm for the purpose of causing the firearm to discharge cartridges in rapid succession.

Ammunition (Sec. 84 C.C.)

A cartridge containing a projectile designed to be discharged from a firearm and includes a caseless cartridge and shot shell.

Prohibited Ammunition (Sec. 84 C.C.)

Means ammunition, or a projectile of any kind, that is prescribed to be prohibited ammunition.

Restricted Firearm (Sec. 84 C.C.)

Means

- a handgun that is not a prohibited firearm
- a semi-automatic handgun with a barrel less than 470 mm
- a firearm that can be reduced to a length of less than 660 mm by folding
- a firearm prescribed by regulation to be a restricted weapon including an M16 rifle.

Restricted Weapon (Sec. 84 C.C.)

Any weapon, other than a firearm, that is prescribed by a regulation.

AUTHORIZATION

Document that allows an individual or business to carry out a particular activity related to firearms or other regulated items.

Four types of authorizations exist including authorization to

- carry,
- transport,
- import, and
- export.[150]

LICENCE

Document that allows an individual or business to

- keep,
- acquire, or

- carry out an activity
- relating to firearms or other regulated items.

Various types of licences exist:

1. Business licence: allows a business to carry out specific activities relating to certain classes of firearms or regulated items.
2. Possession and acquisition licence: allows adults to acquire and possess firearms within a specific class.
3. Non-resident 60-day possession licence: allows non-resident adults to borrow non-restricted firearms while in Canada during a specified 60-day period.
4. Cross-bow acquisition licence: allows acquisition of cross-bows by individuals.
5. Registration certificate: A machine-readable plastic card required to register all classes of firearms. Previously needed for restricted weapons only.[151]

FIREARM AND WEAPON SEARCH AUTHORITIES

The *Criminal Code* has three search authorities that are specifically related to firearms and weapons:

1. Search Warrant for Public Safety Reasons—sec. 117.04(1) C.C.
2. Warrantless Search for Evidence of an Offence—sec. 117.02(1) C.C.
3. Warrantless Search for Public Safety Reasons—sec. 117.04(2) C.C.

Although this section deals with warrantless searches, the search warrant for weapons and firearms is included to provide the best interpretation for warrantless searches.

SEARCH WARRANT—PUBLIC SAFETY

As previously explained, a sec. 487 C.C. search warrant may be obtained to search for and seize any evidence relating to a criminal offence. Consequently, when weapons or firearms are evidence that proves the commission of a criminal offence, a sec. 487 C.C. search warrant is used and authorizes the search of a place for weapons or firearms. However, some investigations may reveal that no offence has been committed relating to weapons and firearms, but a person's possession of those items may represent a risk to public safety.

The following examples illustrate the contrast:

Example 1 An accused robbed a bank using a handgun. He conceals the handgun in his house. The handgun is evidence relating to the robbery. A conventional sec. 487 C.C. search warrant authorizes the search of the house and seizure of the gun.

Example 2 An investigation reveals that a person has threatened to harm others or to kill himself. He possesses weapons or firearms in his house.

The weapons are not evidence directly related to the threatening behaviour. Attempted, or threaten to commit, suicide is not a *Criminal Code* offence. In this example, either no offence has been committed, or an unrelated act has occurred where the weapons and firearms are not evidence. A conventional sec. 487 C.C. search warrant will not authorize the search for or seizure in these circumstances. Another authority is needed that is compatible with those circumstances.

Section 117.04(1) C.C. provides alternative authority to obtain a search warrant relating to weapons, which includes firearms, specifically for public safety reasons. A peace officer may apply for this search warrant by completing an information to obtain. Reasonable grounds must be proven to believe that it is not desirable in the interests of the safety of the person, or of any other person, for the person to possess any

- weapons (includes firearms),
- prohibited device,
- ammunition,
- prohibited ammunition, or
- explosive substance.

The reasonable grounds for belief must include the specific circumstances of the person's conduct, a description of the relevant items, and the place where the items are being possessed.

The section does not restrict the application or the warrant to any specific type of place. Therefore, the place may be a dwelling-house, any other building, or a vehicle. A specific place must be applied for to ensure the reasonableness of the search. The application will be denied if the application requests a search of multiple places on the basis that weapons may be in those places.

The significant element of the reasonable grounds for belief is that the applying officer does not have to prove that an offence was committed.

The weapons do not have to constitute evidence relating to any offence. Instead, it must be reasonably proven that possession of the weapons poses a risk to public safety, including the possession of the weapon. Essentially, the reasonable grounds must include the following facts:

- weapons are in a place,
- the person has possession of the weapons, and
- the possession of the weapons is unsafe for any person.

Essentially, the belief should create a preventative measure.

After the information to obtain is completed, it is brought to a justice. The same procedures apply as explained previously. If reasonable grounds are proven, the justice may issue a warrant. As stated, the section does not restrict the type of place to be searched. The warrant authorizes the seizure of any weapons or devices that may pose a risk to public safety, if they remain in the person's possession. Additionally, the search warrant authorizes the seizure of the following documents relating to the item:

- authorization,
- licence, or
- registration certificate.

This means that the police may seize the weapon and the document that allows possession of the item.

After the justice is satisfied that reasonable grounds exist, the question arises about what document will serve as the warrant. The section does not refer to a type of search warrant that must be used. Consequently, one must refer to sec. 487 C.C., which states that it may be used for the purposes of the *Criminal Code* or any federal statute. Additionally, sec. 487(3) C.C. states that the Form 5 search warrant may be "varied to suit the case." The combination of these provisions allows the Form 5 search warrant to be used with alterations to the content of the document by deleting reference to the commission of the offence. In summary, a sec. 487 C.C. search warrant, in a varied form, may be used as a search warrant for weapons for public safety reasons.

WARRANTLESS SEARCH FOR EVIDENCE (SEC. 117.02[1] C.C.)

In certain circumstances, the police are allowed to search a person, vehicle, and place other than a dwelling-house for firearms and regulated items, without a warrant or consent. This authority may be used during investigations where firearms represent evidence to an offence. The warrantless search authority is not automatic.

The following conditions must exist before a warrantless search is conducted:

1. A peace officer must form a belief based on reasonable grounds. (A citizen cannot use this search authority.)
2. Reasonable grounds must exist to believe

    - a weapon,
    - an imitation firearm,
    - a prohibited device,
    - any ammunition or prohibited ammunition, or
    - explosive substance,

was used in the commission of an offence; or an offence is being or has been committed involving a

- firearm,
- imitation firearm,
- crossbow,
- prohibited weapon,
- restricted weapon,
- prohibited device,
- ammunition or prohibited ammunition, or
- explosive substance.

3. These weapons, firearms, or regulated items are likely to be found

- on a person,
- in a vehicle, or
- in any place other than a dwelling-house.

4. The conditions for obtaining a search warrant exist.
5. Exigent circumstances exist.

"Exigent circumstances" means that no time exists to obtain a warrant because of danger to any persons, or that loss or destruction of evidence is imminent. Obtaining a search warrant often takes about one hour. Conducting a warrantless search for firearms and weapons as evidence requires proof of a reasonable belief that someone may be killed or injured, or that the evidence would be lost or destroyed during the time required to obtain a search warrant. The circumstances that constitute these reasonable grounds have been previously explained.

Although this search authority does not extend to dwelling-houses, section 487.11 C.C. provides a broad warrantless search authority that includes dwelling-houses. Section 487.11 C.C. may be used as authority to search a house for firearms or weapons without a warrant because it allows a warrantless search for any evidence to an offence when exigent circumstances exist. This authority will be interpreted and explained later in this part of the book.

If exigent circumstances are not present, a house or any other place may be searched either by consent or by a sec. 487 C.C. search warrant. Finally, the sec. 117.02(1) C.C. warrantless search authority does not apply to circumstances where an offence is about to occur. Although this situation is not included, it will rarely be a hindrance. Most firearm or weapons situations fall under the category of "currently being committed" because of the variety of possession-related offences. For example, the dual procedure offence of "possession of a weapon dangerous to the public peace" may justify the use of a warrantless search authority. This offence does not require proof that the weapon had been used unlawfully. An example of this situation is as follows:

Example   An officer receives reasonable grounds from a witness who saw a suspect put a baseball bat in his car and heard the suspect state the intention to commit an assault. If the officer stops the suspect before the assault is committed, the officer has reasonable grounds that the suspect is "currently committing" the offence of possession of a weapon dangerous to the public peace. Exigent circumstances exist. Reasonable grounds exist that the weapon is in the vehicle. Although the assault was about to occur, the vehicle may be searched without a warrant. Additionally, the officer may arrest the suspect because reasonable grounds existed that he committed a dual procedure offence. The vehicle may be searched under the common law search-incident-to-an-arrest authority.

After a warrantless seizure of a firearm or weapon is made, the seizing officer must make a return to a justice using the same procedures as a return made after a seizure by warrant.

WARRANTLESS SEARCH FOR PUBLIC SAFETY REASONS (SEC. 117.04(2))

This provision allows the police to execute the same procedures as described in the sec. 117.04(1) C.C. search warrant authority for public safety reasons, but without a warrant and without consent. The condition that allows a warrantless search for public safety reasons is "by reason of a possible danger to the safety of that person or any other person," which makes the obtaining of a warrant impracticable.

This warrantless search authority consists of the following significant elements:

1. The place that may be searched includes a
   - dwelling-house,
   - building, or
   - vehicle.

2. The item searched for does not represent evidence to an offence. Instead, the reason for searching is a reasonable belief that "it is not desirable, in the interests of the safety of the person or any other person" for the person to possess weapons, firearms, or regulated items.

3. An immediate danger to any person must be present. It must be proven that no time existed to obtain a warrant for public safety reasons.

The justification for a warrantless search would be that any person reasonably would have been injured or killed if the police took the time to obtain a warrant to prevent a person from possessing weapons, firearms, or regulated items. An example includes domestic disputes where weapons or firearms are in the house and intoxicated participants are escalating hostilities. Although no offence may have been committed, the circumstances justify the belief that the possession of weapons or firearms under these circumstances represents a danger to public safety and that the danger is immediate. The combined public risk and the urgency justifies a warrantless search for the purpose of preventing harm, despite the fact that no criminal offence has occurred.

The specific procedure, including the conditions to prove, are as follows:

1. A peace officer only, not a citizen, may form the belief.
2. Reasonable grounds must be proven that any weapon (including a firearm) or regulated item is in a specific place, including a dwelling-house.
3. Reasonable grounds must be proven that a person's possession of those items represents a public safety risk. The officer does not have to prove that a criminal offence has been or is being committed.
4. A possible danger to any person exists. The word "possible" infers that the standard of belief does not have to be a positive threat to life, but, instead, a reasonable possibility that any person may be hurt or killed as a result of the possession of weapons.
5. Any weapon, firearm, or regulated item may be seized. Additionally, any documents related to the weapon may be seized, including any
   - authorization,
   - licence, or
   - registration certificate.

If the documents are not seized at the time of the weapons seizure, the documents are revoked.[152]

RETURN TO A JUSTICE

After a seizure of weapons, firearms, or regulated items is made by any of the three authorities, either with or without a warrant, a return to a justice is mandatory.

If a warrantless seizure is made of weapons or firearms that are evidence to an offence, a return must be made according to the previously explained procedures under sec. 490 C.C.[153] The return may be made either in writing or by bringing the item to a justice. If the weapons are evidence, they must be lawfully detained for court.

If weapons or regulated items are seized for public safety reasons, either with or without a warrant, a return is mandatory despite the fact that the items will not be evidence for an offence and no detention for court is required because no charge will be laid. Section 117.04(3) C.C. explains the return procedures:

1. In the case of a seizure by warrant, the actual seized items or documents must be brought forthwith to the justice who issued the warrant. A return in writing cannot be made. The return cannot be made to a justice who did not issue the warrant. "Forthwith" is defined in case law as meaning immediately, without any unjustifiable delay. Additionally, the date of execution must be shown to the justice.

2. In the case of a warrantless search, the actual items or documents must be brought to a justice who "might have" issued a warrant, meaning a justice who has jurisdiction. The seizing officer must prove the reasonable grounds that formed the basis of the warrantless search. The reasonable ground must be written on the "Report to a Justice."

DISPOSITION—WEAPONS SEIZED FOR PUBLIC SAFETY REASONS

When the police seize a weapon, firearm, or regulated item for public safety reasons, under sections 117.04(1) and (2) C.C., with or without a warrant, the seized items cannot be detained for court because no offence will have been committed. Consequently, no charge will be laid and no trial will occur. The items must be dealt with in a different manner. Section 117.05(1) C.C. explains the procedures:

1. The items must be returned to the lawful owner unless a police officer makes an application for a "disposition hearing." The police cannot dispose of the seized items without a hearing.

2. The process for a disposition hearing begins with an application by a police officer. The police have a 30-day time limit, from the day of the seizure, to make the application. The police have discretion to make the application.

3. If the application is not made, no disposition hearing will occur, and the seized items must be returned to the lawful owner.

4. If an application is made by a police officer within the 30-day time limit, a justice must conduct a disposition hearing. The justice has no discretion about conducting it upon receiving the application; the hearing becomes mandatory.

5. After the application is received, the justice schedules a date for the disposition hearing. The hearing is not a trial; the purpose of the hearing is to determine whether the weapons or firearms will be disposed of or returned to the owner.

6. The justice directs that "notice of the hearing be given to such person or in such a manner" as the justice may specify. This means that the justice creates the list of persons who will be subpoenaed to the hearing, including the person from whom the items were seized. Again, this person is not charged with an offence. The hearing will determine only whether he or she will regain possession of the items.

7. At the hearing, the justice may proceed *"ex parte,"* meaning that the hearing may be conducted in the absence of the person from whom the items were seized in the same circumstances in which a summary conviction court may proceed with a trial in the absence of a defendant. Sec. 803(2) C.C. explains that a summary conviction trial may be conducted in the absence of the defendant if he or she has been notified of the time and place of the trial, and consent of the attorney general is obtained.

8. At the hearing, the justice shall hear all relevant evidence, including evidence relating to the value of the seized items. Relevant evidence means evidence relating to whether it is desirable in the public interest for the person to possess the seized items.

9. At the conclusion of the hearing, the justice makes one of two conclusions:

   a) It is not desirable (in the public interest) for the person to possess weapons or regulated items. This finding means that a public risk exists by the person's possession of the seized items. If this finding is made, the justice shall order the following disposition:

      • anything seized be forfeited to Her Majesty or be otherwise disposed of. The justice orders fair and reasonable disposal of any seized item, including destruction or sale of the item; and

      • prohibition of possessing any weapon or regulating items during any period not exceeding five years, if "the justice is satisfied that the circumstances warrant such an action." The prohibition is contingent upon the evidence convincing the justice that the prohibition is necessary. If prohibition is not ordered, the justice must include reasons in the record.

   b) Public safety is not at risk. This finding means that the person's possession of the seized items is not undesirable in the public interest. The items will be returned to the person if this finding is made. The justice must include reasons in the record for making this finding. The attorney general may appeal this finding to the Superior Court.

An example of circumstances that constitute a public safety risk and exigent circumstances that justified a warrantless search is found in *R. v. Golub (1997)*.[154] This case is explained in Chapter 2.

SEIZURE FOR FAILURE TO PRODUCE AUTHORIZATION

Section 117.03(1) C.C. allows the police to demand a person produce an authorization or licence to lawfully possess a firearm and a registration certificate for a firearm, if the officer finds the person in possession of a firearm. The same demand may be made a person found possessing a prohibited weapon, restricted weapon, prohibited device, or any prohibited ammunition.

The demand to produce these documents may be made in any place where the person is found possessing the item. Therefore, a demand may be made in a dwelling-house, any building, or vehicle. The condition for making the demand is that the officer found the person having possession of the item.

For example, if a police officer is lawfully on any premises such as by invitation in a dwelling-house and sees firearms stored in the house, the officer may demand that the possessor produce the proper documents for inspection. The definition of possession under sec. 4(3) C.C. applies to, meaning that possession includes

- actual possession, by having on his or her person; or
- constructive possession, by having it in any place, not on his person, whether or not he owns or occupies the place and has control or access to the item for his use or benefit; and
- joint possession, where two or more persons may possess one item.

If the possessor of the firearm fails to produce the documents after a demand by a police officer, the officer has authority to seize the firearm or regulated item. The officer cannot search for the item because the section does not authorize a search of any nature. The officer may seize only the firearm or regulated item that he or she finds in the possession of a person. The only exception to the seizure is if the possessor who fails to produce the documents, "is under the direct and immediate supervision of another person who may lawfully possess it."

How much time must be given to a person to produce the documents after the demand? The answer is found by the phrase "fails, on demand, to produce." The production of the documents must be immediately made upon demand. The section does not stipulate that the officer give the person any specific amount of time to produce. For example, an officer finds a person having possession of a firearm or regulated item in a car or public place and demands production of documents. If the person fails to produce the documents and states he has them at home, the officer may seize the firearms immediately, when the failure is made. No requirement exists to give the person time to produce the documents after retrieving them from his home.

After the seizure is made, the person from whom the item was seized may produce the documents "within 14 days" to claim the seized item.

If production is made within 14 days, the seized item must be returned "forthwith," meaning immediately and without unjustified delay.[155]

If production of the documents is not made within 14 days, the police have an additional mandatory obligation. A peace officer must take the seized item to a provincial court judge forthwith. This means that the return

- cannot be made to a justice of the peace, and
- must be made immediately after 13 days expire from the time of the seizure.[156]

After the return is made, the provincial court judge may, "after affording the person from whom it was seized or its owner, if known, an opportunity to establish that the person is lawfully entitled to possess it, declare it to be forfeited to Her Majesty, to be disposed of or otherwise dealt with as the attorney general directs." This means that the judge can order forfeiture of the seized item, but a hearing must be held to allow the person an opportunity to prove that he or she has lawful authority to possess it.

PROCEDURE

1. Enter premises lawfully, where applicable. In some cases, this authority will be used inside a place. The officer must lawfully be on the premises by means of a search warrant, without a warrant, or by invitation or consent. Otherwise, this step is not an issue when, for example, an officer is on a street while stopping a car or on a sidewalk with a pedestrian; the officer is not on a premises.
2. Find a person having possession of a firearm or regulated item. Possession includes actual possession, constructive possession, or joint possession. The remainder of the procedure cannot be followed if the person is not seen having possession of the item.
3. Make a demand to the possessor of the firearm to produce relevant documents including

   - authorization,
   - licence, or
   - registration certificate.

4. If the possessor fails to produce the documents, seize the item.
5. Retain custody of the seized item for 14 days. If the person produces the documents within 14 days of the seizure, return the seized item forthwith to that person.
6. If no documents are produced within 14 days, take the seized item forthwith to a provincial court judge.

DRUGS AND SUBSTANCES

Police officers have authority to search for drugs without a warrant and without consent, under sec. 11(7) *Controlled Drugs and Substances Act.* This provision has simplified a more complex authority that had previously existed under the repealed *Narcotics Control Act,* combined with a case law decision made by the Supreme Court of Canada in *R. v. Grant (1993).*[157]

The *Controlled Drugs and Substances Act* (C.D.S.A.) has not only simplified the interpretation of the warrantless search authority but also extended the authority to include a dwelling-house. The *Narcotics Control Act* permitted a warrantless search only of places other than a dwelling-house. Section 11(7) C.D.S.A. states that "a peace officer may exercise any of the powers described in subsection (1), (5), or (6) without a warrant if the conditions for obtaining a warrant exist but by reason of exigent circumstances it would be impracticable to obtain one."

Essentially, the police may search any place, including a dwelling-house, if reasonable grounds exist to believe that a controlled substance or anything that is evidence relating to a C.D.S.A. offence is in that place and exigent circumstances exist that there is no time to obtain a search warrant.

Exigent circumstances require evidence to prove a belief, based on reasonable grounds, exists that there is an imminent danger of the loss, removal, destruction, or disappearance of the drugs, if the search is delayed to obtain a search warrant.

The determining factor relating to exigent circumstances is the potential movement of the drugs from the place they are in during the time required to obtain a search warrant. Approximately one hour is required to complete the procedure needed to obtain a search warrant. Factors to consider when forming reasonable grounds relating to the movement and loss of drugs include

- the type of place: for example, a vehicle. A stronger reason to believe that the drugs will move if a search warrant is obtained exists when it is believed that the drugs are in a vehicle,
- the quantity of drugs,
- the activity conducted by the suspect, e.g., selling or personal use,
- observations made by witnesses, including informants. The significant element is the suspect's intention that was conveyed to the witness relating to the use of the drugs, and

- observations made by the police officer, including excessive customer traffic at the place combined with other circumstances learned during the investigation.

The Supreme Court of Canada, in *R. v. Grant (1993)*,[158] created guidelines that are useful to interpret this authority. Places may be categorized as

1. fixed or stationary, or
2. moving or mobile.

Fixed or stationary places include

- dwelling-house,
- store,
- business premise,
- locker,
- office,
- bar,
- school,
- garage (attached or detached),
- perimeter of a house,[159] and
- garden.[160]

Moving or mobile places include

- motor vehicle,
- water vessel, and
- aircraft.[161]

The following rules are relevant to the determination of drug movement and exigent circumstances:

1. Reasonable grounds that narcotics are in a motor vehicle, water vessel, aircraft, or other "fast-moving" place will often constitute exigent circumstances, but not in every case.
2. No blanket authority exists to automatically search conveyances without a warrant, simply because the place is capable of moving.[162] It is possible for drugs to be in a conveyance with circumstances indicating that the drugs will not move or be lost during the time it takes to obtain a search warrant. An example is drugs in a parked vehicle combined with evidence that the drugs will continue to be stored there while the search is delayed until a warrant is obtained.
3. Conversely, a search warrant is not automatically required to search fixed or stationary places such as a dwelling-house, business, office, or school. Although the place is fixed or stationary, evidence may exist that the drugs will move or be lost if the search is delayed until a search warrant is obtained. A warrantless search of any fixed or stationary place, including a dwelling-house, is justified if it is impracticable to obtain a search warrant due to exigent circumstances.

In summary, the type of place is only one factor that determines the existence or absence of exigent circumstances, but it is not the exclusive element to consider. The exigent circumstances belief must be directed to the drugs, not the place.

The Supreme Court of Canada, in the *Grant* case, also ruled about the status of the "perimeter of a house" as a place. The relevance of this issue is illustrated in the following simple example:

A police officer may develop mere suspicion that drugs are in a house. The officer enters the perimeter of the house and walks to a window. He looks inside to make observations intended to facilitate reasonable grounds formulation that the drugs are in that house. Entering the perimeter and looking in the window constitutes a search. The issue is whether the perimeter is a "place," thus impacting the method of entering it.

The Supreme Court of Canada ruled that the perimeter of a house is a place. Consequently all search and seizure authorities apply. Forming reasonable grounds is the prerequisite. A search warrant is required to enter unless exigent circumstances exist. Otherwise, entering the perimeter to conduct a search without a warrant, based on mere suspicion only, is not authorized.

SEARCH OF PERSON DURING A WARRANTLESS SEARCH FOR DRUGS

During a warrantless search for drugs, persons will likely be found in the place, whether the place is a house, vehicle, or bar. The question arises about whether the persons found in the place during a warrantless search may be searched without consent. The combination of sections 11(7) and (5) C.D.S.A. authorizes the search of a person found in the place, if reasonable grounds exist to believe that the person has any controlled substance on his or her person. The following are the significant elements regarding this authority. A Supreme Court of Canada decision, in *R. v. Debot (1989),*[163] is relevant to these guidelines:

1. An automatic search of all persons found in the place is prohibited.
2. Before searching a person, the officer must have a reasonable belief that the person has actual possession of the substance.
3. Reasonable belief requires only proof of a "reasonable probability" that the person has actual possession of a substance.

   The reasonable belief of possession may be formed by

   * an informant or witness's observations, or
   * an officer's observations, or
   * circumstances, such as the person's close proximity to the specific area where the drugs are believed to be concealed.

   This authority applies when the reasonable grounds are directed to a place. In some cases, the reasonable grounds are directed to a specific person. For example, a witness may inform police that he saw a specific person place cocaine in his pocket. Possession of that substance is a dual procedure offence. The procedure used is to arrest the person first and search the person afterward, using the search-incident-to-arrest authority. Additionally, the immediate surroundings may be searched.

   One exception exists. Possession of under 30 grams (1 ounce) of marijuana is now a summary conviction offence. A lawful arrest may be made only if a police officer finds the possession being committed. If an officer is informed by a witness that a person possesses under 30 grams (1 ounce) of marijuana, a search may be conducted by consent, or an arrest may be made if the person admits having possession. If the reasonable grounds causes a belief of possession of over 30 grams (1 ounce) of marijuana, an arrest may be made because that offence is dual procedure.

Use of Force

Sec. 12 C.D.S.A. authorizes the use of as much force as is necessary in the circumstances. Excessive force may result in criminal and civil liability.

Other Items

Sec. 11(8) C.D.S.A. authorizes the seizure of anything that the police believe on reasonable grounds to be evidence that has been obtained by or used in the commission of any offence. Consequently, unrelated evidence may be seized if it is found during a lawful warrantless search.

Return of Seized Items

Sec. 13 C.D.S.A. creates a mandatory obligation to make a return to a justice using the procedure described in sections 489.1 and 490 C.C. Additionally, a report must be sent to the Minister of Health using the same procedure previously described under the C.D.S.A. search warrant section.

Procedure—Warrantless Search

1. Form reasonable grounds that a controlled substance or anything that will be evidence to any C.D.S.A. offence is in a specific place, including a dwelling-house. A belief based on mere suspicion is insufficient to justify a search.
2. Form reasonable grounds that exigent circumstances exist, making it impracticable to obtain a search warrant.

3. If reasonable grounds exist that a person found in the place has possession of a controlled substance, the person may be searched without consent. All persons cannot automatically be searched. If the reasonable belief does exist, the person may be searched without being arrested first.

4. Any controlled substance or any evidence to a C.D.S.A. offence that is found may be seized.[164]

5. Any other item that is believed on reasonable grounds to be evidence to any offence may be seized if it is found during the search.

6. If any seizure is made, a return must be made in accordance to the procedures described in sections 489.1 and 490 C.C.

7. If the reasonable grounds is directed to a specific person

   • arrest the person,
   • search the person after, and
   • search the immediate surroundings of the place.

ODOUR OF DRUGS

A controversial topic that creates a common problem is whether the odour of drugs in a car constitutes reasonable grounds. No statute or Supreme Court of Canada case law directly answers this issue. Useful guidelines are found in *R. v. Polashek (1999)*,[165] a recent decision made by the Ontario Court of Appeal that provides the most direct explanation. This decision includes rulings related to a number of other police procedures. A complete explanation is found in the case study at the end of the chapter; the following is a summary of the decision relating to the odour of drugs:

• The court agreed in part with the accused's argument that the presence of an odour of drugs alone did not constitute reasonable grounds that the accused was committing an offence.

• However, the court stated that they would "not go so far as was urged by the appellant that the presence of the smell of marijuana can never provide the requisite reasonable and probable grounds for an arrest."

• The court did not make a definite procedure. Essentially, an odour of marijuana alone will usually not constitute reasonable grounds, but in some circumstances it will. The following explanation helps distinguish which circumstances do and do not form reasonable grounds:

   – "The sense of smell is highly subjective. It gives the police unreviewable discretion."
   – Smells are transitory, leave no trace, and are incapable of objective verification.
   – Some officers can convince the trial judge that they have acquired sufficient expertise through experience or training, and that their opinion—that the odour of marijuana shows present possession—is reliable.

• In this case, the officer used the odour of marijuana as one factor combined with others to successfully form reasonable grounds. The other factors that the officer used to form reasonable grounds were

   – the accused's response to the officer's statement that he smelled marijuana. The accused looked to his right and over both shoulders and said, "No, you don't."
   – the geographical area. The place was a fairly small area where drug use was prevalent.
   – the officer's experience. He had made 40 to 50 marijuana seizures in previous cases in the same area.
   – the time, 1:00 a.m.

• The court ruled that the smell of marijuana, combined with the other factors, did constitute reasonable grounds, but recognized that it was a "close case" because the officer did not see smoke or any object in plain view that supported present possession of marijuana.

In summary, the circumstances under which the smell of marijuana is detected will determine whether reasonable grounds actually exist. The smell alone may be sufficient to form reasonable grounds if the officer can justify the opinion with expertise based on experience or training. Otherwise, other factors must be combined with the smell of marijuana to form reasonable grounds.

WARRANTLESS ENTRY TO PRESERVE EVIDENCE WHILE AWAITING WARRANT

During the time required to obtain a warrant to search for narcotics, the police are often concerned about the possible destruction or loss of the narcotics. An effective procedure would be to enter the house without the warrant for the purpose of preserving the evidence by preventing the occupants from destroying the narcotics during the time that the warrant is being obtained. The C.D.S.A. and the *Criminal Code* contain no authority for a warrantless entry to preserve and protect the narcotics while awaiting the arrival of the search warrant.

However, the Supreme Court of Canada, in *R. v. Silveira (1995)*,[166] addressed this issue and created a guideline that permits this procedure, but only in urgent circumstances. The court stated that warrantless entry into a house to preserve evidence while awaiting the arrival of a drug search warrant is justified if exigent circumstances exist. "Exigent circumstances" have been defined as a situation of emergency or importance that may make it impossible to enter by means of the search warrant at that time. Factors that may constitute exigent circumstances include

1. nature of the offence,
2. the arrest of an accused in close proximity to the house to be searched, and
3. reasonable grounds to believe that a warrantless entry is necessary to prevent destruction or removal of evidence while awaiting the issuance and arrival of the search warrant.

No blanket authority exists that automatically allows the police to use this procedure. Exigent circumstances will be judged on a case-by-case basis. The court emphasized that this procedure will be justified in rare cases.

The circumstances of the Silveira case illustrate an example of justified warrantless entry to preserve evidence.

WARRANTLESS SEARCH FOR ORDINARY EVIDENCE—SEC. 487.11 C.C.

Before 1998, no blanket authority existed that allowed the police to search a place without a warrant for ordinary evidence relating to a criminal offence. For example, if the police formed reasonable grounds that stolen property, such as televisions and stereos, was in a place, a sec. 487 C.C. search warrant or consent were the only two alternatives available to the police. The *Criminal Code* did not include an authority to search a place for any ordinary evidence, without a warrant and without consent. In other words, there was no exception regarding a sec. 487 C.C. search warrant, relating to ordinary evidence of an offence.

Section 487.11 C.C. is a warrantless search authority that permits the police to exercise the same authority as a sec. 487 C.C. search warrant in exigent circumstances to search any place, including a dwelling-house. This new amendment may be the most significant investigative procedure that has been added to the *Criminal Code*. It is a wide-ranging search authority that will likely prove to become the most advantageous authority available to the police. This amendment was made partly in response to *R. v. Silveira (1995)*.

Sec. 487.11 C.C. authorizes a peace officer to conduct the same searches as allowed by a sec. 487 C.C. warrant and a sec. 492.1 C.C. tracking warrant if the conditions exist to obtain either warrant, but by reason of exigent circumstances, it would be impracticable to obtain the warrant. After items are seized, a return to a justice is mandatory.

CASE LAW

R. V. SILVEIRA (1995)

Issue   Preservation of evidence while awaiting search warrant.

Offence   "trafficking narcotics"

Circumstances   During a one-week investigation, an undercover police officer made three separate purchases of cocaine from the accused person's accomplice. Each purchase was made in similar fashion; the officer met the accused's accomplice at a community centre where the officer gave advance payment. The accomplice left, met the accused, and they travelled to the accused's house. They entered the house and returned to the officer, giving a quantity of cocaine to the officer.

After the third purchase, police arrested the accused in close proximity to his house. Before being transported to the police station, the accused was questioned, and he confessed that narcotics and money were inside his house. This confession added to existing evidence that would have constituted reasonable grounds to obtain a search warrant.

The accused was transported to the police station. The arresting officer intended to complete an Information to Obtain a search warrant but feared that the narcotics would be destroyed during the time required to obtain the warrant. Six officers were sent to the accused's house to preserve the narcotics until the search warrant arrived.

The officers attended at the house and announced their presence by knocking. When the door was opened, they entered without a warrant and with guns drawn. The accused's family members were present. The officers informed them that they had no search warrant but one was being obtained. Police confined the occupants to the interior of the house. The officers searched for weapons only, for their safety, but did not search for narcotics. The officers remained there and detained the occupants for one hour and 15 minutes. During the wait for the search, the accused's brother arrived. He had knowledge that the accused had been arrested.

The officer who obtained the warrant failed to disclose in the Information to Obtain that the officers were present to preserve evidence. The search warrant was issued and was executed. A quantity of cocaine and money was seized. The accused was charged with trafficking narcotics.

The Supreme Court of Canada upheld the accused's conviction and made the following rulings:

- The warrantless entry was a search unauthorized by law and it constituted a sec. 8 Charter violation.

- However, the narcotics were not excluded under sec. 24(2) *Charter* and were admitted as evidence.

- Drug sales are serious crimes. The severity of the offence, combined with easy destruction or removal of the drugs, arguably should always permit police to enter without a warrant, to preserve evidence, but no statutory law currently authorizes it.

- No search for narcotics occurred during the preservation of evidence. The entry was predicated on good faith. The intention to preserve evidence rather than to search for it diminished the severity of the *Charter* violation.

- The nature of the offence combined with the arrest in close proximity to the house constituted exigent circumstances.

- The failure to disclose police presence at the accused's house, on the information to obtain, did not mislead the justice who issued the search warrant.

- The warrantless search for weapons was justified to protect the officers.

  The momentary display of firearms was justified.

PROCEDURE—ORDINARY EVIDENCE

To conduct a warrantless search for ordinary evidence to a criminal offence, the following procedures apply:

1. Form reasonable grounds that an item is in a building, receptacle, or place. This includes a dwelling-house, business premise, school, locker, or vehicle.
2. Form reasonable grounds that the item

   - is relevant to any criminal offence under any federal statute that has been or suspected to have been committed, or
   - is reasonably believed to afford evidence with respect to the commission of an offence, or
   - will reveal the whereabouts of a person who is believed to have committed any criminal offence under any federal statute, or
   - is reasonably believed to be intended to be used for the purpose of committing any offence against a person, for which the offender may be arrested without a warrant, or
   - is offence-related property.

3. Form reasonable grounds that exigent circumstances exist that would make it impracticable to obtain a sec. 487 C.C. search warrant.

A specific definition of exigent circumstances is not given in sec. 487.11 C.C. A definition is found in sec. 529.3(2) C.C., but it applies only to sec. 529.3(1) C.C. The most useful definition relevant to sec. 487.11 C.C. is found in *R. v. Silveira (1995)*. The Supreme Court of Canada defined exigent circumstances as

> a situation of emergency or importance which may make it impossible to enter a place by means of a search warrant, at that time, and reasonable grounds to believe that a warrantless entry is necessary to prevent destruction or removal of evidence while awaiting the issuance and arrival of a search warrant.

No blanket authority or circumstance automatically constitutes exigent circumstances; it will be judged on a case-by-case basis. The Supreme Court of Canada has emphasized that a warrantless search, especially of a dwelling-house, will be justified in rare cases.

A general situation where this authority may be justified is stopping a vehicle in which evidence, such as stolen property, is believed to be present. Reasonable grounds may be proven by a witness's observations, a police officer's observations, or circumstantial evidence such as a combination of proximity to a crime scene and a similar description given by a witness. Searching a vehicle, which has been stopped as a result of reasonable grounds, without a warrant, will often be justified because of the obvious likelihood that the evidence will be lost if the officer tries to obtain a search warrant.

Countless types of items represent evidence of an offence that offenders wish to destroy as soon as possible after the commission of an offence.

An example is clothing or disguises worn during the commission of the offence, e.g., robbery. Eyewitness evidence that an offender possesses this evidence and intends to destroy it or remove it may be received from a variety of sources, including accomplices and informants.

4. If items are seized, a return to a justice must be made in accordance with sec. 489.1 C.C.

In summary, the sec. 487.11 C.C. warrantless search authority cannot be used liberally or for convenience sake, especially in relation to a dwelling-house. If sufficient time exists to obtain a search warrant, a sec. 487 C.C. search warrant must be obtained.

PROCEDURE—TRACKING DEVICE

To conduct a warrantless installation of a tracking device, the following procedure applies:

1. Form reasonable grounds to suspect that a criminal offence has been or will be committed.
2. Form reasonable grounds that relevant information regarding the offence or the whereabouts of any person can be obtained through the use of a tracking device.
3. Form reasonable grounds that exigent circumstances make it impracticable to obtain a tracking warrant.
4. Install and maintain the tracking device, without a warrant, in or on anything including a thing carried, used, or worn by any person.

WARRANTLESS FORCIBLE ENTRY INTO HOUSE TO PROTECT LIFE

The police have a common law duty to protect life and property, prevent crime, and preserve the peace. This duty is incorporated in provincial statutes that regulate and govern policing, such as the *Police Services Act of Ontario.*

The Supreme Court of Canada, in *R. v. Godoy (1999)*,[167] created an authority that allows the police to forcibly enter a house without a warrant in response to a disconnected 911 call for the purpose of searching the house for an injured person. Additionally, the Supreme Court of Canada stated that police may disregard the person who answers the door and informs the police that there is no problem inside. Entry into the house to search for injured persons is justified despite the refusal of the person who answers the door.

The complete circumstances and ruling of *R. v. Godoy (1999)* is found in "911 Radio Broadcasts/Protecting Life" in Chapter 4 of this text. The following is a summary:

Patrol officers received a radio broadcast stating "911 unknown problem" at a house. Upon arrival, a man answered the door and told officers that there was "no problem" inside. He tried to shut the door on the officers. The officers entered and heard a woman crying. They searched the house and found the man's wife, who reported that her husband had assaulted her. The Supreme Court of Canada ruled that the disconnected 911 call constituted sufficient reasonable grounds to enter the house forcibly, without a warrant, to search for injured persons. The entry was justified by common law authority to protect life.

Procedure

Upon arrival at a house after receiving a radio broadcast stating, "911 unknown problem," the following procedures apply:

1. If an announcement is made by knocking on the door and no answer is received, forcible warrantless entry is justified.
2. If an announcement is made and a person answers the door reporting there is no problem inside, a warrantless entry into the house is justified.
3. If the person who answers the door refuses entry and closes the door, forcible warrantless entry is justified.
4. The Supreme Court of Canada stated that a disconnected 911 call constitutes reasonable grounds that "the caller is in some distress and requires immediate assistance."[168] This constitutes exigent circumstances, which would justify forcible warrantless entry without making an announcement.
5. After entry, the search of the interior is justified only to find injured persons.
6. After an injured person is found, a verbal statement that he or she has been assaulted constitutes reasonable grounds to make an arrest.

"EXPECTATION OF PRIVACY—VEHICLE"

You are a uniform police officer on patrol. You stop a car for speeding. The car has New York State plates. Three occupants are in the car.

The driver has no documentation and tells you that the car is owned by a friend. Three open garbage bags, full of new clothes with price tags attached, are on the back seat. One occupant informs you that they own the clothes. Another tells you that they were in the car when they borrowed it. CPIC reveals that the car has not been reported stolen and a valid arrest warrant exists for the driver regarding unpaid fines. You suspect that the clothes have been stolen. Can you search the trunk without a warrant? Can you seize the clothes?

The new search authority under sec. 487.11 C.C. would not apply because there are no reasonable grounds to believe that stolen property was in the car. Only mere suspicion exists.

The answer begins with an analysis of sec. 8 *Charter* and a person's reasonable expectation of privacy, and an application of those principles as found in *R. v. Belnavis (1997)*.[169]

The Supreme Court of Canada has stated that the purpose of sec. 8 *Charter* is to protect a citizen's right to a reasonable expectation of privacy against unreasonable searches by the police. However, this guarantee protects only a reasonable expectation of privacy. The circumstances that constitute "reasonable" will vary in every case. In *R. v. Edwards (1996)*, the Supreme Court of Canada created the following relevant guidelines:

1. Sec. 8 *Charter* is a personal right that protects people, not places.
2. The right to challenge the legality of a search depends on the accused person's establishing that his or her personal right to privacy has been violated.
3. Sec. 8 *Charter* issues require two separate inquiries:
   a) Did the accused have a reasonable expectation of privacy in the place that was searched?
   b) If the expectation existed, was the search conducted reasonably?

CASE LAW

R. V. BELNAVIS (1997)

Issues

1. What expectation of privacy can a driver and passenger have in a car, relating to a search for stolen property?

2. What are the consequences of a police search of a car for stolen property that violates whatever right to privacy may exist?

Offence "possession of stolen property"

Circumstances A police officer stopped a car, with New York plates, for speeding. Three female occupants were in the car. The driver failed to produce any documents but identified herself verbally. She accompanied the officer to the cruiser as requested. One passenger followed.

The officer intended to write a speeding ticket and suspected that the car may have been stolen. The driver stated that the car was owned by a friend.

The officer returned to the car to search the glove box for an ownership. He then asked the passenger in the back seat to identify herself. At that time, he saw three open garbage bags full of new clothes with price tags attached. The passenger stated that each occupant owned one bag. The officer searched the trunk and found five additional bags full of clothing. After returning to the cruiser, he questioned the driver. She contradicted the previous explanation by stating that the bags were in the car when she borrowed it.

A CPIC check revealed that the car had not been reported stolen. A valid arrest warrant existed for the driver for unpaid traffic fines. The driver was arrested. Afterward, the officer learned that the driver's boyfriend owned the car and had lent it to her.

The clothes were seized. After an investigation, all three women were charged with possession of stolen property.

Trial The accused persons were acquitted. The trial judge ruled that reasonable grounds did not exist to conduct the search or to believe that the clothes had been stolen.

Ontario Court of Appeal The Crown appealed. The court allowed the appeal, quashed the acquittal, and ordered new trials.

Supreme Court of Canada An appeal by the accused persons was dismissed. The issues of this appeal were

- What expectation of privacy can a passenger and driver have in a car?

- What are the consequences of a search of the car, without a warrant, which violates whatever right to privacy may exist?

continued

> The court ruled that the passenger had no expectation of privacy in relation to the car or the property seized. She was not the owner. No evidence existed that she had any control over the car, or had used it before, or had any relationship with the owner that created special access or privilege regarding the car.
>
> The driver did have a privacy right relating to the car. The search constituted a sec. 8 *Charter* violation. However, the seized property obtained after the violation was not excluded under sec. 24(2) *Charter* because the admission of the evidence would not bring the administration of justice into disrepute. The following rulings were made:
>
> * Reasonable grounds existed to search the car.
>
> * The officer had "every right" to search for an ownership, and to open the back door of the car and look inside for safety reasons.
>
> * The garbage bags were in plain view.
>
> The property was not conscriptive evidence.
>
> Therefore, trial fairness was not an issue. The driver did not own the car. No evidence indicated historical use of the car. Consequently, her right to privacy was greatly reduced.
>
> The *Charter* violation was minimal. Society's interest in the prosecution outweighed the *Charter* violation. The quantity of stolen property indicated that more than petty theft had been committed.

A reasonable expectation of privacy is determined by evaluating the totality of the circumstances. The factors to be considered may include, but are not restricted to, the following:

* presence at the time of the search,
* possession, ownership, and historical use of the place,
* ability to regulate access, including the right to admit or exclude persons,
* the existence of a subjective expectation of privacy, and
* the objective reasonableness of the expectation.

If an accused person does establish a reasonable expectation of privacy, a second inquiry will determine whether the search was conducted in a reasonable manner.

The Supreme Court of Canada applied these principles in *R. v. Belnavis (1997)*.

RIGHT TO COUNSEL—PERSON BEING SEARCHED

Two *Charter* questions arise regarding the search of a person: Do the police have a mandatory obligation to

1. inform the person of the right to counsel before being searched?
2. delay the search and give the person a reasonable opportunity to call a lawyer?

The majority of the Supreme Court of Canada answered both questions in *R. v. Debot (1989)*.[170] Regarding question 1, the following procedures must be followed:

Step 1

If the accused is arrested and then searched as an incident to the arrest, the officer must inform the accused of the right to counsel upon arrest, without delay.

Step 2

If the accused is not arrested but is searched under a lawful authority described in this section, the search constitutes a detention, and the person must be informed of the right to counsel upon detention, without delay.

Therefore, the person must be informed of the right to counsel without delay, as soon as he or she is arrested or detained and before the search is conducted. Exceptions to this rule are

CASE LAW

R. V. POLASHEK (1999)

This 1999 case law decision, made by the Ontario Court of Appeal, provides valuable procedural guidelines relating to numerous police procedures that commonly apply during routine investigations.

Issues

1. Circumstances that constitute reasonable grounds to conduct a warrantless search of a car for drugs.

2. Whether the odour of marijuana alone constitutes reasonable grounds.

3. Search of a person incident to an arrest.

4. Warrantless search of the trunk of a car as part of a search incident to an arrest.

5. When to inform an arrested person of the right to counsel.

6. Whether a warrantless search has to be delayed if the person invokes the right to counsel.

7. Admissibility of physical evidence seized after the commission of a sec. 10(b) *Charter* violation.

8. Admissibility of a confession obtained after the commission of a sec. 10(b) *Charter* violation.

Offence   "possession for the purpose of trafficking"

Circumstances   At 1:00 a.m., a police officer lawfully stopped a car, driven by the accused, for a *Highway Traffic Act* violation. The officer had a 20- to 30-second conversation with the accused while the accused sat in his car. During this conversation, the officer detected a "strong odour" of marijuana emanating from inside the vehicle. The officer saw no smoke and could not determine whether the odour was of burnt or unburnt marijuana. The officer told the accused that he smelled marijuana. The accused responded by looking to his right and over both shoulders, and said, "No, you don't."
The officer formed reasonable grounds that the accused had possession of marijuana, based on the following factors:

- the odour,
- the accused's response,
- the time of night, and
- the area, where drug use was common.

The officer asked the accused to leave the car and conducted a cursory search of the accused. The officer found cannabis resin in the accused's pocket. The officer arrested the accused for possession of marijuana and continued the search of his person. The officer found over $4000.00 in cash in his pockets. The accused was handcuffed and seated in the cruiser.
Officers then searched the interior and the trunk of the car. An ownership, found in the glove compartment, showed that another person owned the car. Wrapped bags of marijuana, a scale, rolling papers, and a small amount of LSD were seized from the trunk. The accused was arrested again, for possession for the purpose of trafficking. After this arrest, the officer informed the accused of the right to counsel for the first time. Thirteen minutes had elapsed after the initial arrest. The accused stated he understood and wished to reserve his right to speak to a lawyer until later. The officer questioned the accused, who responded with an inculpatory statement by saying, "What can I say? You caught me; I'm busted."

Trial   The accused was convicted. The trial judge ruled that

- Reasonable grounds existed to arrest.
- The search of the trunk was incident to the arrest.
- No sec. 10(b) *Charter* violation occurred.
- The Crown proved the case without the accused's statement (the accused did not testify at the *voir dire*).

continued

Ontario Court of Appeal   The court made the following decisions:

- The court agreed with the accused, in part, that the odour of marijuana alone does not usually constitute reasonable grounds to arrest for possession because the sense of smell is:

    – highly subjective,
    – leaves no trace, and
    – is an unreviewable opinion.

- However, the court also stated that it "would not go so far [to say] that the presence of the smell of marijuana can never provide the requisite reasonable and probable grounds for an arrest."

- The circumstances will determine whether the smell of marijuana alone forms reasonable grounds. One determining factor is whether the officer can prove that he or she has sufficient expertise, based on experience or training, to justify an opinion of present possession.

- In this case, the odour alone would not have been sufficient to form reasonable grounds.

- Reasonable grounds did exist in this case because the officer did not base his belief solely on the odour. He combined other factors, including the accused's response, the location, the time of day, and the experience of making 40 to 50 marijuana seizures in that area. Additionally, forming reasonable grounds to make an arrest is not as "exacting" as forming it for a search warrant. A lower standard applies.

- The court recognized that this was a "close case" because no smoke or any other object was seen in the car to support the present possession of marijuana.

- The search of the trunk was lawful. It fell within the common-law authority as a search incident to an arrest. The reasons were as follows:

    – The accused was arrested shortly after being removed from the car.

    – The search of his person revealed a quantity of cannabis resin and a large amount of money.

    – The area was known to the officer for drug trafficking.

    – There was a "reasonable prospect" that more drugs would be found in the car.

- The police were not required to delay the search incident to the arrest until the accused spoke to a lawyer.

- The 13-minute delay to inform the accused did constitute a sec. 10(b) *Charter* violation. The Supreme Court of Canada has ruled that the right to counsel must be informed immediately after detention.

- The items found in the trunk were nonconscriptive evidence. Their admission would not affect trial fairness. Therefore, these items were not excluded.

- The inculpatory statement was conscriptive evidence. Its admission would render the trial unfair. The accused did not testify at the *voir dire* during the trial. The trial judge did not have to determine trial fairness. Consequently, the court allowed the appeal, quashed the conviction, and ordered a new trial to resolve whether the admission of the statement would affect trial fairness.

The court made a final significant comment relating to police education. During the trial, the officer was asked what he was taught about when to read an arrested person the right to counsel. The officer testified that, "We're not really taught at any particular point in time, it's just done subsequent to the arrest." The court responded to this by saying, "This suggests a serious systemic failure within the police community, given that the decision in *Debot* was released over six years prior to the arrest in this case."

- in situations where force must be used to subdue the person, or
- for legitimate self-protection, such as searching for weapons.

Regarding question 2, the police do not have to delay the search and do not have to provide the person with an opportunity to call a lawyer before the search.

It must be noted that Supreme Court Justice Sopinka disagreed with the obligation for police to inform a person of the right to counsel before searching the person, stating that no purpose is served by informing the person of the right to counsel if the person will not be provided with an opportunity to call a lawyer before the search is conducted.

Test Yourself

1. June (31) phones the police dispatch and reports the following: Ward (35), her boyfriend, phoned her 15 minutes ago from an unknown number and unknown place. He told her that he was driving to her house with a gun to kill her. She describes his car and plate number. This information is broadcast to you, you see the car on Yonge St., one km (.75 mile) from June's house, and stop it. Ward is the driver. Explain what you can do and the authorities that will determine your investigative procedures.

2. You are dispatched to a domestic at a house situated at 4000 Main St. Upon arrival, you are met by June (34) outside the house. She reports the following: She lives at this house with her husband Ward (30) and two sons ages 9 and 6. Ward arrived home 30 minutes ago. He was drunk. He yelled at her and became increasingly agitated. No assault or threats occurred. Both sons were downstairs in the rec room. June feared for her safety and ran outside to phone the police from a neighbour's house. She believes the two children are still inside with Ward. Ward has three hunting shotguns downstairs in a storage room. There is ammunition in that room. She does not know if they are loaded. Explain what procedures are available to you. Choose your course of action, and explain your justification legally for your actions.

Appendix A

SOLVE IT!

This section includes case studies that uniform patrol officers commonly investigate. You are a uniform patrol officer in each case. The circumstances reflect all the information known in the case. The amount of information varies in each case.

- Analyze the circumstances of each case carefully.
- Each case represents a problem.
- Solve the problem by identifying the procedures that are available and those that are not available.
- Search the entire book for answers to questions, including
  - Can you arrest?
  - Can you charge anyone?
  - Do you have to release or detain?
  - If an arrest can lawfully be made, what steps would you follow to prevent *Charter* violations?
  - Write a thorough explanation for each case study, discussing laws that authorize actions or prevent certain procedures.

CASE 1

12:17 a.m.
- You are on patrol on Main St. in a business district.
- A man is walking on the sidewalk, travelling in the same direction as you.
- You are aware that three break and enters have occurred in this area during the past seven days.
- This man looks at you as you drive past him. You do not recognize him.
- He abruptly stops and runs on the sidewalk in the opposite direction.
- You pursue him; after 30 seconds, he stops as you approach him.

_____

_____

_____

_____

_____

_____

_____

_____

_____

_____

_____

_____

_____

_____

_____

_____

_____

_____

_____

_____

_____

_____

CASE 2

11:23 p.m.
You receive a radio broadcast regarding a "male person, about 25 years, long brown hair, walking on King St. toward Main St. He left Joe's Bar a few minutes ago. A handgun was seen in his jacket pocket. The complaint is anonymous." No other information was received. You search the area.

11:29 p.m.
You see a male person, similar description walking on King St., one block south of Main St. He is alone. He appears sober. He is acting and walking normally.

_____

_____

_____

_____

_____

_____

_____

_____

_____

_____

_____

_____

_____

_____

_____

_____

_____

_____

_____

_____

CASE 3

2:07 a.m.

- While on patrol on Barton St. you see a blue car driving away from the parking lot of a body shop.
- The body shop is closed.
- The car accelerates as it leaves the parking lot.
- There are two people in the front.
- You activate your roof lights, and the car stops two blocks from that premises.
- You approach the driver's door. You recognize the driver, Eddie (27), as a person you arrested for the theft over $5,000.00 two years ago.
- The male passenger is unknown to you.
- Both are sober.
- You ask both for identification and they comply.
- You have a clear view in the back seat.
- You see a number of tools scattered on the back seat.

_____

_____

_____

_____

_____

_____

_____

_____

_____

_____

_____

_____

_____

_____

_____

_____

_____

_____

_____

_____

_____

_____

CASE 4

10:14 p.m.
- You see a red car fail to stop for a red light on Yonge St.
- You activate the roof lights and the car stops.
- Four males are in the car, ages between 21 and 35.
- The driver is sober.
- You detect a strong odour of marijuana emitting from inside the car.

_____

_____

_____

_____

_____

_____

_____

_____

_____

_____

_____

_____

_____

_____

_____
_____
_____
_____

CASE 5

9:47 p.m.
You receive a radio transmission of a disconnected 911 call from a house at 5000 Wellington St.

9:52 p.m.
- Upon your arrival, you knock on the front door.
- A man answers it. He calmly informs you that there is no problem and that you are probably mistaken.
- You see and hear nothing else.

_____
_____
_____
_____
_____
_____
_____
_____
_____
_____
_____
_____
_____
_____
_____
_____
_____
_____
_____
_____

_____

_____

_____

_____

CASE 6

8:45 p.m.
You receive a radio broadcast of a break and enter in progress at a house situated at 6000 Walker Rd.

8:49 p.m.

- June (22) meets you outside the house and reports the following:
    - Her sister (19) and her three-year-old son are visiting her. They are both inside the house.
    - June rents the house.
    - June's ex-boyfriend forced open the front door about five minutes ago.
    - June ran out of the house and thought that her sister and the child followed but they didn't.
    - June is uncertain if her boyfriend Ward (25) is armed.
- You hear a woman and child both screaming.
- Ward's car is parked across the street.

_____

_____

_____

_____

_____

_____

_____

_____

_____

_____

_____

_____

_____

_____

_____

_____

_____

USE OF DISCRETION

> The human faculties of perception, judgment, discriminative feeling, mental activity, and even moral preference are exercised only in making a *choice.* He who does anything because it is the custom makes no choice. He gains no practice either in discerning or in desiring what is best. The mental and moral, like the muscular, powers are improved only in being used.

—John Stuart Mill

INTRODUCTION

Shortly after I was hired as a police officer, I was at the front desk of the police station with the staff sergeant in charge of the uniform platoon. As he read a report, he lamented the decision made by an officer to charge a person with numerous offences that arose from one minor incident. "This guy would charge his own mother," the staff sergeant moaned. "You have to use *discretion.* You can't charge everybody. It's *common sense.* Policing is all about common sense. You'll never get anywhere unless you use common sense. Don't forget that!" I didn't.

The same advice was conveyed to me repeatedly. Discretion and common sense became synonymous. They sound like simple, self-explanatory terms. But, as you learn early in your police career, the use of effective discretion and common sense isn't easy. The use of discretion, like any other skill, has to be learned and developed through experience.

There are two ways of explaining what discretion means and how to use it properly. The first involves a review of philosophical, scholarly literature and the accompanying theoretical concepts. The second is a practical method, explained in ordinary language that is relevant and immediately applicable to daily police work. We'll use a combination of both methods to try to unravel and demystify the concepts of discretion and common sense.

DEFINITIONS

Discretion is defined as the choice, freedom, or authority to act according to one's judgment. In relation to policing, discretion specifically refers to the authority to choose or decide whether or not to avert and/or charge an offender. Common sense is a way of thinking combined with intuition. It specifically refers to logical thinking and strong intuitiveness that permit rational conclusions, judgments or opinions to emerge from the accurate analysis of a set of circumstances.

AUTHORITIES

Police officers are authorized to use discretion by a number of sources including common law, case law, and statutes such as the *Criminal Code,* the *Young Offenders Act,* and provincial police services acts. The words "shall" or "may" are used in procedural provisions of various statues, and are directly relevant to discretion. The use of "shall" imposes a mandatory obligation to do or omit to do something. No discretion can be used when the word "shall" directs police officers. The word "may" authorizes discretion; it allows the police to decide or choose from a number of alternatives. "May" gives the police a choice; "shall" removes a choice.

SIGNIFICANCE

How important is use of discretion? For a police officer, it will be one of many overwhelming responsibilities. First, there is the issue of social injustice. Crime victims, the criminal justice system, and society in general have certain expectations about the police. They expect the police to solve problems; protection is probably their highest expectation. The public will judge the police as a whole based on the collective decisions made by officers.

Secondly, you will be judged individually within a police organization by the nature of your discretionary decisions. Opinions will be made about your logic, intelligence, fortitude, and maturity. *Your decisions will shape the extent of your actual competence; the opinions of your peers and supervisors will shape your perceived competence.* Essentially, your reputation will be at stake.

Thirdly, how you use discretion reveals who you are and how you think. The way you use discretion will be a manifestation of personal characteristics and traits, including the following:

- It shows your values, ideologies, core beliefs, and how you view the world in general.
- It reveals the extent of your experience—where you have been, where you are now, and how far you have to go.
- It demonstrates your attitudes and perception of what policing is and represents—how you view the purpose, objectives, and goals of law enforcement.
- It illustrates your opinions about crime victims, offenders, and how you perceive problems that you will have to solve in relation to both.
- It exposes the extent of your maturity. We usually give maturity a narrow view and definition. We judge maturity superficially—well-mannered, quiet, non-disruptive. These are preferred behaviours by those who create the rules of a specific environment or situation, but maturity has a deeper meaning. It involves a process of personal growth, where a person moves from a low level toward a higher level of various dimensions including autonomy, objectivity, enlightenment, altruism, focus on principles, depth of one's concerns, rationality, and originality.

The discretionary decisions you make show your position on the maturation scale.

INFLUENCING FACTORS

Myriad factors will influence how you use discretion:

1. Perceived severity of the offence—Some crimes have an obvious severity. Murders and violent crimes will be perceived as being severe by everyone. Other crimes are not generically perceived. One person may view a theft as being a minor offence whereas another indivdual may attach greater severity to the same set of circumstances. The way that you will perceive the wide range of offences that you will investigate will be one the most prominent influences on your decision-making

process. Offenders are less likely to receive leniency or "breaks" for offences that are perceived with greater severity.

2. Your worldview—Worldview refers to how you perceive the world, the people in it, your place in it, and the relationship between your place and the place of others. Each individual had his or her own unique worldview. One's worldview is not static; it fluctuates through evolution and development. Worldview is shaped by a number of external sources—parents, teachers, coaches, peers, employees, adversaries, your needs, goals, successes, and failures. How you view offenders, victims, and a wide array of social settings will influence your discretion.

3. Worst possible consequence—The ultimate purpose of using discretion is to *solve* a current problem and *prevent* future problems. The extent to which your mind can predict the worst possible consequence that could happen after your decision is made will influence how you use discretion. A prediction that an offender poses a future risk or may repeat the crime will engender a decision that may differ than if you believe that you have solved the problem and corrected the offender's behaviour.

4. Offender's attitude and history—Every time you decide whether or not to change someone, you will instinctively consider his or her current attitude and behaviour combined with his or her past record. It is human nature, and somewhat logical, to be more lenient with a sincerely remorseful and cooperative offender.

5. Personal ambition—The potential upward mobility in a police organization causes some novice police officers to be excessively concerned with promotions and transfers into specialty units. The amount and nature of charges are often perceived as a measurement of competence. The desire to impress peers and supervisors will be a factor in the decisions you will make.

6. Personal attitude—Our attitude toward people and life in general are not static—they fluctuate. Some of us have a broader range of attitude changes, and the frequency of them. Your attitude during an investigation will be dependent on a number of elements. Your moods may change frequently. Your positive and negative energy will be influenced by events in your professional life and personal life. Frustration, which may emerge from various sources, may be a factor in the types of decisions made.

These variables are only a few that influence use of discretion. Anything that involves cognitive function to form conclusions and make choices in a complex process involves the *interaction* of people and events situationally.

COGNITIVE TRANSITION

Before learning how to use discretion properly, we need to examine how the thought process evolves and develops during a police career. The reason for this analysis is the direct relevance between how thinking occurs and use of discretion during different *stages* of a police career. A caveat must precede it; human conduct cannot be accurately predicted. Any discussion about rules of human behaviour, in relation to certain situations, is strictly based on theoretical concepts. The following cognitive profiles are speculative and conjecture. They are not based on scientific fact. But this hypothesis is premised on informal qualitative research.

This first stage of a police career is the novice stage. It is analogous to the childhood stage of an individual's actual life. A novice stage is characterized by certain dimensions that represent the low end of the maturation scale. The second stage is the veteran stage and represents the high end of the maturation scale.

NOVICE CHARACTERISTICS

Dependence:

Rookies strongly rely on the guidance, advice, and experience of others. Their lack of experience prevents complete autonomous thought.

Subjectivity:

This refers to positioning oneself at the centre of the environment and activities in it. Subjectivity compels novices to focus on the novelty of their new career. It creates a "narrow picture" of policing, preventing a vision of the "big picture."

Low enlightenment:

Enlightenment refers to mastery of vocational knowledge and skills and how to apply them to accurately solve problems. Novices obviously lack this vocational mastery.

Simple task capability:

Rookies have the capability to perform simple tasks only. Complex tasks are beyond their realm.

Narrow interests:

The excitement of being hired as a police officer may prevent the expansion of interests, which represents a significant step toward mature thinking. Anything, including a police career, that causes an individual's field of interests to become "fixated within a given circle or to recede to smaller circles" interferes with cognitive maturation. Developing new interests promotes health.

Absence of altruism:

An altruistic person has fully developed the awareness and magnitude of other person's predicaments, and the capacity to care about and correct them. Early in a police career, the tendency is to focus on "self," particularly how to seek self-gratification through police experiences.

Superficial concerns:

Veteran officers gain perspective on what deeply matters, both present and future. The awareness of deep concerns develops only with experience. Rookies generally are superficially concerned, seeing the surface only in incidents and events.

Conformity:

Novices imitate others. They conform easily to the thoughts and behaviours of others. Very few are capable of being original in the early stage of a career.

Impulsiveness:

This refers to reactions that are not based fully on logic or on an analysis of the totality of the circumstances. It is a reaction to little or no information, or an excessive response that is incompatible with the nature of an event. Impulsiveness is the product of lacking deep self-understanding and self-control.

The novice stage may be marked with overwhelming confusion combined with peculiar pleasure in charging as many people as possible, especially by issuing excessive traffic tickets for relatively trivial offences. There is a prevalent erroneous belief that peak police performance is quantifiable. Thus, number of tickets and charges may wrongly become a measurement of total competence.

An unusual sense of self-gratification may accompany the wearing of a uniform that blurs judgment, logic, and reasoning. If the reason is immaturity, experience and personal growth will correct it. If the reason is the filling of some psychological void, the novice will not correct the harmful behaviour; no measures will correct it because he or she is in the wrong occupation

How long does the novice stage last? There is no specific line that a young officer crosses into the domain of a self-actualized veteran. The novice and veteran stages are joined by a transitional period. Many variables determine the success or failure of the transition. The most prominent variables that influence a successful transition from novice to a fully self-actualized veteran are

- **Mentorship:** A teacher or trainer is simply a person who conveys information. A *mentor* is a coach who is deeply concerned with the development and success of his or her *protégé*. A mentor is not necessarily a friend, supervisor, or guardian. A mentor is committed to building the protégé's strengths and eradicating weaknesses. The wisdom of a mentor is priceless; it has the most profound influence on a novice in any field, any endeavour. Since imitation is a basic human behaviour, the choice of who will be a novice's training or coach officer is the most important decision that will affect a novice.
- **Experience:** Following verbal instruction, observing a task and then doing it *repeatedly* engenders vocational mastery. Uniform officers are dispatched to a number of calls. A novice should attend as many calls as possible; volunteer to take calls; attend as a backup to observe; initiate his or her own investigations; maximize proactive and reactive responses; internalize strategies and actions that succeed; and remember those that failed. This will strengthen a novice's intuitive sense. Investigate as many simple investigations as possible before expecting to investigate complex investigations.
- **Study:** Life-long learning is vital for any type of success. Formal and informal study should become habits, an integral part of a police career. Continuing education in both related and unrelated courses is vital.
- An experienced veteran obviously thinks differently than a novice. A veteran will use discretion by considering many more factors than a novice will. Veterans perceive policing differently; they will view as a *problem-solving* endeavour because they have grown to the maturation dimensions.

PHILOSOPHY

The objective of ethical discretion is attaining fairness and equality. There are four philosophical principles that govern ethical discretionary decisions:

1. The basic principles of comparative justice is that "like cases" are to be treated alike and "different cases" should be treated differently.
2. Injustice is done when individuals who are alike in every relevant respect (not in absolutely every respect) are treated differently, or when individuals who are different in some relevant respect are treated alike.
3. Treat alike (equally) those who are the same (equal) in relevant respects; treat unalike (unequally) those who care unalike (unequal) in relevant respects.
4. Enforcement of the law is unjust when it is irregular, random, or discriminatory, that is, when it is administered unequally among those to whom it applies.

Every investigation has its own degree of uniqueness. No two cases have precisely the same circumstances. Yet, some cases share common features. The four philosophical prinicples create a *purpose* for discretion—to achieve consistency and equality. Similar cases should produce the same outcome. If two cases are alike, then the offences should be treated the same—either both are charged or both are waived. Charging only one but not the other results in the inconsistency and inequality that disrupts the balance of social justice.

Conversely, if cases differ, then the same outcomes should not occur. The difference could be in severity of the incident or the offenders' current status or past histories.

Irregular and random law enforcement can be eliminated by following a *systematic* approach. A *system* is simply a set of procedures and criteria that *solves problems* justifiably. In other words, a system affords the decision-maker the basis by which the reasons are explained for choosing a solution or course of action. A system can ensure that performance is replicated, thereby ensuring consistency.

SYSTEM

The essence of policing is *problem-solving*. All offences represent problems from which a wide range of questions arise—what is the extent of the current or future risk to life? Will the offender repeat the offence? Can a resolution occur without court intervention?

Discretion to charge an offender or warn him is the central focus of problem-solving. A system is needed to make discretionary decisions. The system is predicated on two fundamental principles:

1. A problem can be solved by the police officer without court, or, the responsibility to solve it may be transferred to the criminal justice system.
2. Eliminate the worst possible consequence. The ultimate goal of policing is to prevent crime and protect people. The worse consequence of a problem is death or injury. All other consequences, such as potential theft of or damage to property, are secondary to risk to people.

Deciding whether a problem can be solved with or without court intervention depends on the extent to which an officer can *influence* an offender, combined with the severity of the crime. Both solutions, with or without court, are forms of *influence*. Both methods strive to influence the offender to terminate problem behaviours. The success of warnings or "breaks" depends on the extent of an officer's verbal communication efficiency. The danger of warnings, however, is the fact that human behaviour cannot always be accurately predicted. Therefore, a solution without a charge will never satisfy an officer beyond *all* doubt that the problem is solved and all risks have been eliminated. Instead, a *reasonable* belief that a problem has been solved represents an ethical way to use discretion. Court, then, is the other method of solving problems when the severity is beyond the officer's realm of influence.

The *system* that facilitates reasonable and consistent use of discretion is as follows:

Step 1

Gather *all* available information. The totality of the circumstances is vital to make a meaningful decision. Partial information may lead to blind decision-making.

Step 2

Define the problem. Analyze the totality of the circumstances and accurately determine

1. whether a criminal offence has occurred.
2. if a criminal offence occurred, which one(s) was committed.

Step 3

Identify the worst possible consequences of the problem. After the identification of the offender(s) has been made, the circumstances of the offence and the offender's tendencies must be determined and analyzed. An opinion must be formed about the severity of the offence, whether the offender will repeat it, and what is the worst incident that will occur if the problem is not solved.

Step 4

Identify the alternative solutions. There are two alternatives—change the offender and let the criminal justice system solve the problem or solve the problem by influencing the offender with verbal communications or by means of other social agencies that will correct the root of the offender's problem.

Step 5

Choose the best solution. Select the solution that will eliminate the worst possible consequence. The commission of major crimes usually requires charges and court proceedings. The absence of charges and court is an alternative when the offence has less severity and there reasonably is no risk to life or property, either currently or in the future. Experience will be relied on to determine those circumstances when solutions without court are successful. Experience will facilitate accurate comparisons of similar and different cases that have been solved in the past. The rule to follow is

1. If the worst possible consequence cannot be eliminated without court, charge the offender.

2. If no charges are laid, justify and prove that this solution eliminated the worst possible consequence. Essentially, if no court proceedings will occur, prove that no risk to life or property exists after the solution is implemented.

In summary,

- You have the onus to ensure that no one gets hurt or killed.
- Victims are your first priority. You work for them. Use investigative skills to evaluate their credibility. If they are being truthful about the commission of an offence, nothing supercedes your responsibility to them.
- Not all situations require the laying of charges. Court proceedings are not needed to solve every problem.

ASSIGNMENTS—APPLYING DISCRETIONARY PRINCIPLES

Analyze the following circumstances, make a decision, and justify it by explaining the reasons for your decisions by applying the principles and the system learned in this chapter.

CASE 1

You are on patrol at 1:45 a.m. You see a car swerving on King St. You stop the car. Ward (40) is the driver. He is impaired. He has no criminal record. He has a professional job. He lives 5 km (3 miles) from this location. He is cooperative. What would you do if

- he tells you his wife is at home and will pick him up if you call her, or
- his wife is in the front seat. She is sober and offers to drive home, or
- Ward is alone. You are either related to or acquainted with him.

_____

_____

_____

_____

_____

_____

_____

_____

_____

_____

_____

_____

_____

_____

_____

_____

_____

CASE 2

During a tour of duty you investigate two shoplifting incidents at two different locations, two hours apart. For the first incident, Wally (17) stole a $30 CD. He is belligerent to you, displaying an unpleasant attitude. He has no criminal record.

In the second incident, June (35) stole $30 of cosmetics. She is very upset and extremely remorseful. She has no criminal record. Both businesses don't care whether you charge them or not. They leave the decision to you. The property is recovered in both cases.

What would you do?

_____

_____

_____

_____

_____

_____

_____

_____

_____

_____

_____

_____

_____

_____

_____

_____

_____

_____

_____

_____

_____

_____

_____

_____

_____

_____

_____

Appendix C

USE OF FORCE

Being intentionally murdered is an occupational hazard of policing. If you want to be a police officer, you have to understand that offenders may become violent. Some people who are arrested try to assault police officers; others try to kill police officers. These facts are, unfortunately, inescapable. Policing is the only occupation that I know of where workers have the expectation of being murdered or assaulted.

These violent attitudes and conduct toward members of a profession are a sad social commentary. I recently was a guest on a radio talk show that examined a cluster of incidents where police officers had been shot at and killed. Causes and solutions were explored. A citizen called the show and stated his belief that the recent rash of police officer murders was causing an "overreaction," and that a police officer's job is "not really dangerous, not as dangerous as a construction worker." Although these absurd notions are certainly not the consensus opinion, they demonstrate the acceptance of violence toward police.

If you are serious about being a police officer, you must consider the fact that officers are murdered and are targets of violence. The police profession goes far beyond filling psychological or emotional individual needs and voids that may be satisfied by merely wearing a police uniform. The severity of the nature of policing exceeds all the self-gratification of telling people that you are a police officer. The job has to be taken much more seriously than that. Besides being killed or assaulted, police may be charged with and/or convicted of a *Criminal Code* offence for using "excessive force."

Some college students believe that the "use of force" laws can be condensed as follows, "Use as much force as is necessary." Wrong! This summary is not only a misrepresentation of the "use of force" laws, it is a dangerous belief. You cannot ignore key phrases and words that compose the entirety of the "use of force" laws.

The federal "use of force laws" are found in sections 25–43 of the *Criminal Code*. They are included in this appendix for academic value and the students' benefit. Every student is encouraged to read each section repeatedly and carefully. These provisions are only *general* guidelines; they do not include specific, situational, step-by-step procedures. Additionally, there are countless case law decisions that add to the *Criminal Code* provisions. They are not included in this text because of their number and the fact that they exceed the scope of this appendix and the book.

The *interpretation* of these provisions and how they are *applied*, situationally, is taught by experts at recognized police colleges and police service training branches. However, a few additional notes are added to help you understand the concept of "use of force" laws:

- Read the definition of assault in section 265 C.C. You will notice that intentional "force" without consent constitutes an assault, which is a criminal offence that carries jail time as a potential sentence. Any type of ordinary force constitutes the *actus reus* of assault offences.
- Throughout sections 25–43 C.C. the word "justified" is prevalent. Justified is important for two reasons:
  - It creates *accountability*. If you use force as a police officer, you must specify the reasons why this act was decided upon.
  - It creates *protection*. If the correct legal reasons existed prior to the use of force, the act that would otherwise have been an assault is a justified act; this means that the *mens rea* in sec. 265 C.C. is negated, and the person who used force is *protected* from criminal responsibility; the person who used force will not be charged, convicted, or sent to prison.
- Read section 26 C.C. carefully. Every person, police or citizen, who uses *"excessive force"* is *"criminally responsible."* This means there is no blanket protection given to people who use force. In other words, as much force as an individual *wants* to use in all situations will not be protected. The use of force provisions explain a set of guidelines that apply to *general* categories of violent situations. A person cannot simply use as much force as he or she feels like or wants to; there are limitations and restrictions imposed. If these are exceeded, you may be charged, convicted, and sent to prison for the commission of a criminal offence; civil responsibility is another consequence.

    Let's summarize the enormity of policing for those who want to be police officers:

- The possibility of having to use force to save your life, or the life of others, is real.
- When you learn defensive tactics at police college or through your police services, commit yourself to excellence. Take it seriously and train hard.
- Get in the best physical shape possible. Commit yourself to physical fitness *excellence*. Strive for *peak performance* physically.
- Finally, you must remember that policing has a "catch 22" side—force (that may *kill you*) could be used against you, and if you use too much force against someone else, you could go to jail.

SECTIONS 25–43 OF THE *CRIMINAL CODE*

Protection of Persons Administering and Enforcing the Law 25(1) Protection of persons acting under authority

25. (1) Every one who is required or authorized by law to do anything
in the administration or enforcement of the law
(a) as a private person,
(b) as a peace officer or public officer,
(c) in aid of a peace officer or public officer, or
(d) by virtue of his office,
is, if he acts on reasonable grounds, justified in doing what he is
required or authorized to do and in using as much force as is
necessary for that purpose.

25(2) Idem

(2) Where a person is required or authorized by law to execute a
process or to carry out a sentence, that person or any person who
assists him is, if that person acts in good faith, justified in
executing the process or in carrying out the sentence notwithstanding
that the process or sentence is defective or that it was issued or
imposed without jurisdiction or in excess of jurisdiction.

25(3) When Not Protected

(3) Subject to subsections (4) and (5), a person is not justified for
the purposes of subsection (1) in using force that is intended or is

likely to cause death or grievous bodily harm unless the person
believes on reasonable grounds that it is necessary for the self-preservation of the person or the preservation of any one under
that person's protection from death or grievous bodily harm.

25(4) When Protected

(4) A peace officer, and every person lawfully assisting the peace officer, is justified in using force that is intended or is likely to cause death or grievous bodily harm to a person to be arrested, if
(a) the peace officer is proceeding lawfully to arrest, with or without warrant, the person to be arrested;
(b) the offence for which the person is to be arrested is one for which that person may be arrested without warrant;
(c) the person to be arrested takes flight to avoid arrest;
(d) the peace officer or other person using the force believes on reasonable grounds that the force is necessary for the purpose of protecting the peace officer, the person lawfully assisting the peace officer or any other person from imminent or future death or grievous bodily harm; and
(e) the flight cannot be prevented by reasonable means in a less violent manner.

25(5) Power in case of escape from penitentiary

(5) A peace officer is justified in using force that is intended or is likely to cause death or grievous bodily harm against an inmate who is escaping from a penitentiary within the meaning of subsection 2(1) of the *Corrections and Conditional Release Act*, if
(a) the peace officer believes on reasonable grounds that any of the inmates of the penitentiary poses a threat of death or grievous bodily harm to the peace officer or any other person; and
(b) the escape cannot be prevented by reasonable means in a less violent manner.
R.S., 1985, c. C-46, s. 25; 1994, c. 12, s. 1.

26 Excessive Force

26. Every one who is authorized by law to use force is criminally responsible for any excess thereof according to the nature and quality of the act that constitutes the excess.
R.S., c. C-34, s. 26.

27 Use of Force to Prevent Commission of Offence

27. Every one is justified in using as much force as is reasonably necessary
(a) to prevent the commission of an offence
(i) for which, if it were committed, the person who committed it might be arrested without warrant, and
(ii) that would be likely to cause immediate and serious injury to the person or property of anyone; or
(b) to prevent anything being done that, on reasonable grounds, he believes would, if it were done, be an offence mentioned in paragraph (a).
R.S., c. C-34, s. 27.

28(1) Arrest of Wrong Person

28. (1) Where a person who is authorized to execute a warrant to arrest believes, in good faith and on reasonable grounds, that the person whom he arrests is the person named in the warrant, he is

protected from criminal responsibility in respect thereof to the same extent as if that person were the person named in the warrant.

28(2) Person Assisting

(2) Where a person is authorized to execute a warrant to arrest,
(a) every one who, being called on to assist him, believes that the person in whose arrest he is called on to assist is the person named in the warrant, and
(b) every keeper of a prison who is required to receive and detain a person who he believes has been arrested under the warrant,
is protected from criminal responsibility in respect thereof to the same extent as if that person were the person named in the warrant.
R.S., c. C-34, s. 28.

29(1) Duty of Person Arresting

29. (1) It is the duty of every one who executes a process or warrant to have it with him, where it is feasible to do so, and to produce it when requested to do so.

29(2) Notice

(2) It is the duty of every one who arrests a person, whether with or without a warrant, to give notice to that person, where it is feasible to do so, of
(a) the process or warrant under which he makes the arrest; or
(b) the reason for the arrest.

29(3) Failure to Comply

(3) Failure to comply with subsection (1) or (2) does not of itself deprive a person who executes a process or warrant, or a person who makes an arrest, or those who assist them, of protection from criminal responsibility.
R.S., c. C-34, s. 29.

30 Preventing Breach of Peace

30. Every one who witnesses a breach of the peace is justified in interfering to prevent the continuance or renewal thereof and may detain any person who commits or is about to join in or to renew the breach of the peace, for the purpose of giving him into the custody of a peace officer, if he uses no more force than is reasonably necessary to prevent the continuance or renewal of the breach of the peace or than is reasonably proportioned to the danger to be apprehended from the continuance or renewal of the breach of the peace.
R.S., c. C-34, s. 30.

31(1) Arrest for Breach of Peace

31. (1) Every peace officer who witnesses a breach of the peace and every one who lawfully assists the peace officer is justified in arresting any person whom he finds committing the breach of the peace or who, on reasonable grounds, he believes is about to join in or renew the breach of the peace.

31(2) Giving Person in Charge

(2) Every peace officer is justified in receiving into custody any person who is given into his charge as having been a party to a breach of the peace by one who has, or who on reasonable grounds the peace officer believes has, witnessed the breach of the peace.
R.S., c. C-34, s. 31.

SUPPRESSION OF RIOTS

32(1) Use of Force to Suppress Riot

32. (1) Every peace officer is justified in using or in ordering the use of as much force as the peace officer believes, in good faith and on reasonable grounds,
(a) is necessary to suppress a riot; and
(b) is not excessive, having regard to the danger to be apprehended from the continuance of the riot.

32(2) Person Bound by Military Law

(2) Every one who is bound by military law to obey the command of his superior officer is justified in obeying any command given by his superior officer for the suppression of a riot unless the order is manifestly unlawful.

32(3) Obeying Order of Peace Officer

(3) Every one is justified in obeying an order of a peace officer to use force to suppress a riot if
(a) he acts in good faith; and
(b) the order is not manifestly unlawful.

32(4) Apprehension of Serious Mischief

(4) Every one who, in good faith and on reasonable grounds, believes that serious mischief will result from a riot before it is possible to secure the attendance of a peace officer is justified in using as much force as he believes in good faith and on reasonable grounds,
(a) is necessary to suppress the riot; and
(b) is not excessive, having regard to the danger to be apprehended from the continuance of the riot.

32(5) QUESTION OF LAW

(5) For the purposes of this section, the question whether an order is manifestly unlawful or not is a question of law.
R.S., c. C-34, s. 32.

33(1) DUTY OF OFFICERS IF RIOTERS DO NOT DISPERSE

33. (1) Where the proclamation referred to in section 67 has been made or an offence against paragraph 68(a) or (b) has been committed, it is the duty of a peace officer and of a person who is lawfully required by him to assist, to disperse or to arrest persons who do not comply with the proclamation.

33(2) PROTECTION OF OFFICERS

(2) No civil or criminal proceedings lie against a peace officer or a person who is lawfully required by a peace officer to assist him in respect of any death or injury that by reason of resistance is caused as a result of the performance by the peace officer or that person of a duty that is imposed by subsection (1).

33(3) Section Not Restrictive

(3) Nothing in this section limits or affects any powers, duties or functions that are conferred or imposed by this Act with respect to the suppression of riots.
R.S., c. C-34, s. 33.

SELF-INDUCED INTOXICATION

33.1(1) When defence not available

33.1 (1) It is not a defence to an offence referred to in subsection (3) that the accused, by reason of self-induced intoxication, lacked the general intent or the voluntariness required to commit the offence, where the accused departed markedly from the standard of care as described in subsection (2).

33.1(2) Criminal Fault by Reason of Intoxication

(2) For the purposes of this section, a person departs markedly from the standard of reasonable care generally recognized in Canadian society and is thereby criminally at fault where the person, while in a state of self-induced intoxication that renders the person unaware of, or incapable of consciously controlling, their behaviour, voluntarily or involuntarily interferes or threatens to interfere with the bodily integrity of another person.

33.1(3) APPLICATION

(3) This section applies in respect of an offence under this Act or any other Act of Parliament that includes as an element an assault or any other interference or threat of interference by a person with the bodily integrity of another person.
1995, c. 32, s. 1.

DEFENCE OF PERSON

34(1) Self-Defence against Unprovoked Assault

34. (1) Every one who is unlawfully assaulted without having provoked the assault is justified in repelling force by force if the force he uses is not intended to cause death or grievous bodily harm and is no more than is necessary to enable him to defend himself.

34(2) EXTENT OF JUSTIFICATION

(2) Every one who is unlawfully assaulted and who causes death or grievous bodily harm in repelling the assault is justified if
(a) he causes it under reasonable apprehension of death or grievous bodily harm from the violence with which the assault was originally made or with which the assailant pursues his purposes; and
(b) he believes, on reasonable grounds, that he cannot otherwise preserve himself from death or grievous bodily harm.
R.S., 1985, c. C-46, s. 34; 1992, c. 1, s. 60(F).

35 Self-Defence in Case of Aggression

35. Every one who has without justification assaulted another but did not commence the assault with intent to cause death or grievous bodily harm, or has without justification provoked an assault on himself by another, may justify the use of force subsequent to the assault if
(a) he uses the force
(i) under reasonable apprehension of death or grievous bodily harm from the violence of the person whom he has assaulted or provoked, and
(ii) in the belief, on reasonable grounds, that it is necessary in order to preserve himself from death or grievous bodily harm;
(b) he did not, at any time before the necessity of preserving himself from death or grievous bodily harm arose, endeavour to cause death or grievous bodily harm; and

(c) he declined further conflict and quitted or retreated from it as far as it was feasible to do so before the necessity of preserving himself from death or grievous bodily harm arose.
R.S., c. C-34, s. 35.

36 Provocation

36. Provocation includes, for the purposes of sections 34 and 35, provocation by blows, words or gestures.
R.S., c. C-34, s. 36.

37(1) Preventing Assault

37. (1) Every one is justified in using force to defend himself or any one under his protection from assault, if he uses no more force than is necessary to prevent the assault or the repetition of it.

37(2) Extent of Justification

(2) Nothing in this section shall be deemed to justify the wilful infliction of any hurt or mischief that is excessive, having regard to the nature of the assault that the force used was intended to prevent.
R.S., c. C-34, s. 37.

DEFENCE OF PROPERTY

38(1) Defence of Personal Property

38. (1) Every one who is in peaceable possession of personal property, and every one lawfully assisting him, is justified
(a) in preventing a trespasser from taking it, or
(b) in taking it from a trespasser who has taken it,
if he does not strike or cause bodily harm to the trespasser.

38(2) Assault by Trespasser

(2) Where a person who is in peaceable possession of personal property lays hands on it, a trespasser who persists in attempting to keep it or take it from him or from any one lawfully assisting him shall be deemed to commit an assault without justification or provocation.
R.S., c. C-34, s. 38.

39(1) Defence with Claim of Right

39. (1) Every one who is in peaceable possession of personal property under a claim of right, and every one acting under his authority, is protected from criminal responsibility for defending that possession, even against a person entitled by law to possession of it, if he uses no more force than is necessary.

39(2) Defence without Claim of Right

(2) Every one who is in peaceable possession of personal property, but does not claim it as of right or does not act under the authority of a person who claims it as of right, is not justified or protected from criminal responsibility for defending his possession against a person who is entitled by law to possession of it.
R.S., c. C-34, s. 39.

40 Defence of Dwelling

40. Every one who is in peaceable possession of a dwelling-house, and every one lawfully assisting him or acting under his authority, is

justified in using as much force as is necessary to prevent any person from forcibly breaking into or forcibly entering the dwelling-house without lawful authority.
R.S., c. C-34, s. 40.

41(1) Defence of House or Real Property

41. (1) Every one who is in peaceable possession of a dwelling-house or real property, and every one lawfully assisting him or acting under his authority, is justified in using force to prevent any person from trespassing on the dwelling-house or real property, or to remove a trespasser therefrom, if he uses no more force than is necessary.

41(2) Assault by Trespasser

(2) A trespasser who resists an attempt by a person who is in peaceable possession of a dwelling-house or real property, or a person lawfully assisting him or acting under his authority to prevent his entry or to remove him, shall be deemed to commit an assault without justification or provocation.
R.S., c. C-34, s. 41.

42(1) Assertion of Right to House or Real Property

42. (1) Every one is justified in peaceably entering a dwelling-house or real property by day to take possession of it if he, or a person under whose authority he acts, is lawfully entitled to possession of it.

42(2) Assault in Case of Lawful Entry

(2) Where a person
(a) not having peaceable possession of a dwelling-house or real property under a claim of right, or
(b) not acting under the authority of a person who has peaceable possession of a dwelling-house or real property under a claim of right,
assaults a person who is lawfully entitled to possession of it and who is entering it peaceably by day to take possession of it, for the purpose of preventing him from entering, the assault shall be deemed to be without justification or provocation.

42(3) Trespasser Provoking Assault

(3) Where a person
(a) having peaceable possession of a dwelling-house or real property under a claim of right, or
(b) acting under the authority of a person who has peaceable possession of a dwelling-house or real property under a claim of right,
assaults any person who is lawfully entitled to possession of it and who is entering it peaceably by day to take possession of it, for the purpose of preventing him from entering, the assault shall be deemed to be provoked by the person who is entering.
R.S., c. C-34, s. 42.

PROTECTION OF PERSONS IN AUTHORITY

43 Correction of Child by Force

43. Every schoolteacher, parent or person standing in the place of a parent is justified in using force by way of correction toward a pupil or child, as the case may be, who is under his care, if the force does not exceed what is reasonable under the circumstances.
R.S., c. C-34, s. 43.

PROBLEM-SOLVING CASE STUDIES SOLUTIONS

PROBLEM 1

Yes. You saw a summary conviction offence occur. You may arrest because you found the offence being committed.

PROBLEM 2

Yes. You saw a dual procedure offence occur.

PROBLEM 3

Yes. You saw an indictable offence ("theft over $5000.00") occur, and pursued the offender until apprehension, without losing sight of the offender.

PROBLEM 4

Yes. "Assault" is a dual procedure offence that is treated as indictable for the purposes of arrest. June is an eyewitness, constituting reasonable grounds. No time limit exists to arrest for an indictable offence.

PROBLEM 5

Yes. "Robbery" is an indictable offence. A confession constitutes reasonable grounds. A six-month time limit is not imposed for indictable offences.

PROBLEM 6

Yes. Stealing the car constitutes "theft over $5000.00," which is an indictable offence. Although you saw the offence but lost sight of the offender, you are an eyewitness, which constitutes reasonable grounds. A police officer's authorities for arrest without warrant apply to young offenders.

PROBLEM 7

Yes. "Break, enter and theft" into a house is an indictable offence. A confession to a citizen constitutes reasonable grounds. Wally's report to you is hearsay evidence. Hearsay evidence may be used by you to form reasonable grounds. No time limit exists.

PROBLEM 8

No. "Indecent act" is a summary conviction offence. Although June's eyewitness report constitutes reasonable grounds, you did not see the offence occur. Police officers must find committing to arrest without warrant for summary conviction offences. No lawful authority allows a police officer to arrest without warrant on reasonable grounds for a summary conviction offence. However, it must be emphasized that you may charge Eddie by swearing an information anytime up to six months after the offence date. A summons will then be issued and served to Eddie.

PROBLEM 9

No. "Obscene phone calls" are summary conviction offences. A confession constitutes reasonable grounds. No lawful authority exists for a police officer to arrest on reasonable grounds for summary conviction offences. However, you may charge Eddie at any time until six months after the offence date.

PROBLEM 10

No. No lawful authority exists to arrest if only mere suspicion exists, or for the purpose of questioning in order to form reasonable grounds by means of a confession. In the absence of reasonable grounds, you may question Eddie if valid consent is obtained from him. "Attempted murder" is an indictable offence. You must find committing or have reasonable grounds to arrest without a warrant.

PROBLEM 11

Yes. "Impaired driving" is a dual procedure offence. Reasonable grounds exist that this person is about to commit this offence. You may arrest without a warrant to prevent the offence.

PROBLEM 12

Yes. "Assault" is a dual procedure offence. Reasonable grounds exist that the assault is about to occur. The officer may arrest without a warrant to prevent the assault.

PROBLEM 13

Officers commonly receive information like this about offences that may be committed in the future. The verbal statement made by Eddie to Wally in this case constitutes reasonable grounds. However, the absence of a specific definition for "about to commit" causes a problem; the exact moment that constitutes "about to commit" is not specified in the *Criminal Code*. Yet, if you wait for Eddie to commit the offence, knowing that it may occur, victims could suffer harm and you may then be criticized for not preventing the offence.

PROBLEM 14

Yes. "Wanted" constitutes reasonable grounds that the warrant actually exists. The warrant was signed and issued in Toronto. Therefore, the warrant is valid in St. Catharines and anywhere in Ontario.

PROBLEM 15

Yes. "Wanted" constitutes reasonable grounds that the warrant actually exists. The warrant was signed and issued in Calgary and is valid in Edmonton and anywhere in Alberta.

PROBLEM 16

Yes. Although "trespass by night" is a summary conviction offence, the warrant is valid anywhere in Alberta and the officer has reasonable grounds that it does exist.

PROBLEM 17

Yes. Although the warrant is not valid in Halifax, the existence of the warrant constitutes reasonable grounds that June has committed a dual procedure offence, which is classified temporarily as indictable. A procedure then must be followed to make the "out-of-province" warrant valid in Halifax. This procedure will be explained under "arrest with warrant" in Chapter 3 of this text.

PROBLEM 18

No. "Indecent act" is a summary conviction offence. The warrant is not valid in Regina. No authority exists to arrest on reasonable grounds for a summary conviction offence.

PROBLEM 19

Although reasonable grounds exist that Eddie has committed a dual procedure offence, an arrest is not necessary in the public interest, as outlined above. Therefore, you may charge him by laying an information and compelling him to court by means of a summons or an appearance notice, despite being unable to arrest him.

PROBLEM 20

In this case, the lawful authority exists to arrest without a warrant because there are reasonable grounds that a dual procedure offence has been committed. You must determine whether the arrest is necessary in the public interest.

PROBLEM 21

You may arrest Ward without a warrant for "breach of the peace." You cannot charge Ward for "cause a disturbance" because the incident occurred in a dwelling-house.
Note: Ward cannot be charged for being drunk in a dwelling-house. The charge of "public intoxication" is a provincial offence found in liquor laws and can occur only in public places.

PROBLEM 22

Yes. "Theft under $5000.00" is a dual procedure offence. Ward saw the offence occur and pursued Eddie continuously until apprehension, constituting "find committing."

PROBLEM 23

Yes. "Assault" is a dual procedure offence and Wally found Eddie committing.

PROBLEM 24

No. Ward found Eddie committing a summary conviction offence, "cause a disturbance," on public property. Ward is a nonowner; the offence did not happen in relation to his property.

PROBLEM 25

Yes. "Cause a disturbance" is a summary conviction offence. Ward is a person authorized by the owner. Ward found Eddie committing the summary conviction offence on or in relation to the owner's property. "Cause a disturbance" may occur anywhere except in a dwelling-house.

PROBLEM 26

Yes. "Impaired driving" is a dual procedure offence. Wally has found Eddie committing.

PROBLEM 27

Yes. "Mischief under $5000.00" is a dual procedure offence. Ward has found Eddie committing. Additionally, Ward is the owner of the property. The criminal offence occurred in relation to his property.

PROBLEM 28

Yes. "Trespass by night" is a summary conviction offence. June is the owner of the property. She found a criminal offence being committed, by Eddie, on her property.

PROBLEM 29

No. "Theft over $5000.00" is an indictable offence. A confession constitutes reasonable grounds. June did not find Eddie committing the offence. No citizen may arrest on reasonable grounds.

PROBLEM 30

a) No. Breaking the window is classified as "mischief under $5000.00," a dual procedure offence. Clarence's report constitutes reasonable grounds. June did not find the offence being committed. No citizen may arrest on reasonable grounds.

b) No. Clarence lost sight of Eddie after the offence ended. Clarence's facial recognition of Eddie after the offence, and loss of sight, constitute reasonable grounds. No citizen may arrest on reasonable grounds.

c) Yes. A police officer may arrest without a warrant on reasonable grounds regarding a dual procedure offence.

PROBLEM 31

No. "Robbery" is an indictable offence. Ward did not find the offence being committed. The news broadcast represented reasonable grounds.

PROBLEM 32

No. June has no authority to arrest on reasonable grounds that a person is about to commit an indictable offence. The police should be notified and the reasonable grounds transferred to an officer.

PROBLEM 33

a) Yes. "Aggravated assault" is an indictable offence. Reasonable grounds exist to arrest without a warrant. In other words, you may arrest without obtaining judicial authorization.

b) Yes. An arrest warrant in the first instance may be obtained for any criminal offence.

c) No. The offender must first be charged before the warrant may be issued.

d) You must prove the evidence that constitutes reasonable grounds that Eddie committed aggravated assault.

e) No. If nothing else is proven, the justice will issue a summons to compel Eddie to court.

f) It must be proven that the offender's arrest is necessary in the public interest. The circumstances of this offence may be sufficient. You may also introduce any violence or threats made by the offender in the past.

g) No. You must present only the information to the justice. No other document is required. The justice decides whether to issue a summons or an arrest warrant.

PROBLEM 34

a) No. "Indecent act" is a summary conviction offence. You cannot arrest on reasonable grounds for a summary conviction offence.

b) Yes. You may swear an information before the six-month time limit and prove that an arrest warrant is necessary in the public interest.

PROBLEM 35

No. "Indecent act" is a summary conviction offence. "Wanted" constitutes reasonable grounds; however, the warrant is not valid in Winnipeg.

PROBLEM 36

a) Yes. "Trespass by night" is a summary conviction offence. The warrant is valid in Calgary.
b) No. The warrant usually is valid in the entire province where it is issued. The Edmonton officer may execute the warrant, without an endorsement, take custody of Wally, return him to Edmonton and bring him before a justice within 24 hours or as soon as practicable.

PROBLEM 37

a) No. A sec. 10(b) *Charter* violation does not affect evidence obtained before the violation occurred. Sec. 24(2) *Charter* may result in exclusion of evidence obtained after a *Charter* violation occurred.
b) No. They may be excluded under sec. 24(2) *Charter* if the admission of the evidence would bring the administration of justice into disrepute. They may be excluded or admitted.
c) The confession will usually be excluded. According to *R. v. Collins*, physical items obtained after a *Charter* violation should usually be admitted.

PROBLEM 38

a) Identify yourself to ensure Bill knows you are a police officer.
   - Tell Bill he is under arrest for "assault with a weapon" or that he is under arrest and use any general description that includes hitting Doug with a bat. Either reason is sufficient.
   - Take physical custody of Bill to prevent unrestricted movement.
   - Search Bill immediately to protect yourself and others. Seize
     – any evidence for any offence, or
     – any items that may injure anyone including Bill, or
     – any items that may help Bill escape.
   - Inform Bill of the right to counsel as soon as practicable. This could be done while seated in the police vehicle. Read the following to Bill:
     – the base right-to-counsel component, and
     – the existence and availability of legal aid, and
     – the toll-free telephone number for duty counsel, and
     – the right to talk to a lawyer in private.
   - Ask Bill if he understands each component. Record his response. If he does not understand any component, explain it in simpler language. Then ask Bill if he understands and ask him to explain what it means. Record the response verbatim.
   - Caution Bill by reading, "Do you wish to say anything in answer to the charge? You are not obliged to say anything unless you wish to do so, but whatever you say may be used in evidence. Do you understand?" Record Bill's response verbatim. Record any other comments and conversation that occur.
   - Record Bill's decision regarding exercising the right. You may facilitate the decision by simply asking, "Do you want to call a lawyer?" If Bill informs you that he wants to call a lawyer, record the decision. Provide a reasonable opportunity for Bill to call a lawyer at the police station, not in the bar. Do not question him while en route to the police station. If Bill initiates conversation, record the entire conversation verbatim.
     - If Bill declines to call a lawyer, record the waiver verbatim. This waiver does not have to be formally obtained in writing or signed by Bill. After the waiver, you may question Bill about the offence.
b) You do not have to assume that Bill will decide to call a lawyer. You may assume he has waived the right. You may continue the investigation.
c) Yes. The *Brydges* component is a mandatory component that is required regardless of the accused's financial status.

PROBLEM 39

No. Greg, an adult, must be informed of the right to counsel only upon arrest or detention. Greg is not under arrest in this case. If he confesses, then arrest him and inform him of the right to counsel.

PROBLEM 40

Obtain possession of the warrant and produce it to Doug by letting him read it.

PROBLEM 41

No. Informing Wally about the reasons for the arrest is a mandatory requirement created by sec. 10(a) *Charter*. He must be told about the specific charges as soon as possible so that he may exercise the right to counsel in a meaningful way.

PROBLEM 42

a) No specific time exists. A reasonable opportunity must be provided but Ellen must be reasonably diligent.
b) No. A reasonable opportunity does not limit Ellen to only one phone call.
c) No. Ellen, an adult, must be provided only with a reasonable opportunity to call a lawyer.
d) Yes. Ellen has the onus to inform you about the result of the call, particularly if a message was left for a lawyer. You have no obligation to ask if she has spoken to a lawyer. You may continue the investigation and question Ellen.
e) Yes. Ellen has not been reasonably diligent in attempting to call a lawyer and is causing unnecessary delays in the investigation. You may question her.
f) Yes. You have a mandatory obligation to inform Ellen that she has the right to a reasonable opportunity to call a lawyer, and you have an obligation to "hold off" questioning and the investigation during the reasonable opportunity.

PROBLEM 43

a) No. The caution is not a mandatory requirement nor is it a procedure created by the *Charter*. It is a recommended guideline established by the Judges' Rules.
b) No. Failure to caution will not automatically exclude a confession or any other evidence obtained afterward. The confession will be admissible if it is proven to have been voluntarily made.
c) A failure to caution Greg represents a failure to utilize an advantage that you have to help prove the voluntariness of his confession.

PROBLEM 44

a) It means that Walter has declined to call a lawyer and it represents a forfeiture or surrender of his sec. 10(b) *Charter* right to counsel.
b) The Crown (prosecution).
c) You testify about the verbatim response made by Walter. Avoid simply stating that "the accused waived his right to counsel." Additionally, the Crown must prove that
    – the waiver was clear and unmistakable, and
    – the waiver was voluntarily made, and
    – the accused understood the meaning of each component, and
    – what was being given up.
d) No. Walter, an adult, may waive his right verbally or in writing.
e) No.

PROBLEM 45

a) You must inform Claire, a young offender, of the same four components as you would with an adult, but you must also inform her of the right to call parents, adult relatives, or any appropriate adult, and to have any of these persons present. Informing Claire of the right must be in language compatible with her intelligence.

b) Claire may contact any or all of the people from whom she has the right to seek advice, including a lawyer, parents, or any adult. She cannot be restricted to only contacting a lawyer.
c) A waiver made by Claire, a young offender, must be in writing and signed by her.
d) You must make the first notice to parent. The notice may be made verbally or in writing. It must be made as soon as possible after the arrest. The parent must be informed of the reason for the arrest and place of detention. Additionally, Claire must be detained in jail cells that are separate from adult jail cells.

PROBLEM 46

Yes. The Y.O.A. permits you to place Laura, a young offender, in custody in the police vehicle with Rick at the time of the arrest. They must be detained separately at the police station.

PROBLEM 47

Yes. Drew must be informed of the right to counsel at any time that you speak to him during the investigation, including before questioning, when Drew is not under arrest.

PROBLEM 48

Greg may be detained in custody as long as at least one of the four release factors (RICE) is not fulfilled. This will justify the necessity of continued custody.

PROBLEM 49

Custody is no longer justified when all four release factors (RICE) become fulfilled. Helen must be released when RICE is fulfilled.

PROBLEM 50

Yes. There is no evidence that indicates that Ward will fail to appear in court because he has interests that bind him to the community and the offence is relatively minor. No evidence exists that Ward will repeat this or any other offence. All the evidence has been secured and proper identification has been obtained.

PROBLEM 51

No. Eddie is intoxicated. His condition creates a reasonable belief that he may repeat the offence if he is released at the scene. However, RICE is a fluctuating concept, and it will be fulfilled after Eddie becomes sober.

PROBLEM 52

No. Wally's condition and conduct create a reasonable belief that he may repeat the disturbance or assault Eddie if he is released. However, RICE may become fulfilled after Wally becomes sober and calm.

PROBLEM 53

No. The lack of a fixed address creates a reasonable belief that Eddie may fail to appear in court because he has nothing to bind him to the community and could easily move. Additionally, the absence of financial support combined with the circumstances of this offence creates a reasonable belief that he may repeat this offence.

PROBLEM 54

No. RICE will remain unfulfilled until the offender properly identifies himself. Continued detention is justified during the period of time that the offender's identity remains unknown. "Refusing to identify" is not a criminal offence. The offender cannot be charged for refusing to identify.

PROBLEM 55

a) Yes. "Theft under $5000.00" is a dual procedure offence and RICE is fulfilled. Release is mandatory.
b) Yes.
c) No. An information must be laid first.
d) Yes. You may release Eddie without a document at the time of release. Afterward, you may appear before a justice, swear an information, have a summons issued, and serve a summons at a later date.
e) Yes. You have discretion to release Eddie with no intention of charging him or compelling him to court.
f) No; No; No.
g) No. RICE is fulfilled.

PROBLEM 56

A summons may be served only by a peace officer in one of two ways:
1. Personally—serving it to the person to whom the summons is directed. Personal service may be made anywhere.
2. Substitutionally—if the accused person cannot be conveniently found, a summons may be served only at the accused's house to a person who lives there who is 16 years old or older.

PROBLEM 57

Two methods exist to prove that a summons was served.
1. Sworn affidavit of service—the serving officer may complete the back of the summons, which is called an "affidavit of service." The officer then appears before a justice and swears under oath that the summons was served.
2. Verbal testimony in court—if the accused fails to appear in court, the serving officer may testify under oath about the service of the summons.

PROBLEM 58

a) Yes. The offence is summary conviction. RICE is fulfilled. Release is mandatory.
b) No. RICE is fulfilled.

PROBLEM 59

Yes. The offence is indictable. Release is not mandatory regardless of whether RICE is fulfilled.

PROBLEM 60

Yes. The offence is dual procedure, and RICE is not fulfilled.

PROBLEM 61

a) No. The endorsement authorizes release at the police station (Level 2) only.
b) Yes. The endorsement does not authorize release at the scene of the arrest (Level 1).

PROBLEM 62

Yes. A signature represents a promise or assurance that the accused will attend court. Refusal to sign creates doubt about the court appearance. You may bring her to the police station because RICE is no longer fulfilled.

PROBLEM 63

a) Yes. The offence is summary conviction, and RICE is fulfilled. Release is mandatory.
b) Either the OIC or any police officer because of a combined effect of sec. 498 and sec. 503 C.C.

c) The following documents may be used:
  - a summons, after an information has been laid,
  - a promise to appear,
  - a recognizance, or
  - an undertaking, in conjunction with a promise to appear or recognizance.

d) No.

e) Yes. A decision may be made not to charge him while he is at the police station.

f) No. If RICE is fulfilled, continued detention is not justified. The accused **must** be released.

PROBLEM 64

a) Yes. The offence is dual procedure and RICE is fulfilled. Release is **mandatory**.

b) No.

c) The OIC or any police officer.

PROBLEM 65

a) Yes. "Robbery" is an indictable offence with a maximum penalty of life imprisonment. No mandatory release exists for this type of offence.

b) Yes. The OIC or any police officer has discretion to release and may release if RICE is fulfilled.

c) No. This document cannot be used to release at the police station.

d) Yes.

e) Only if Wally lives in another province or beyond 200 km from the place of arrest. Otherwise, no cash deposit can be taken.

f) Yes, if the undertaking is served in conjunction with a promise to appear or a recognizance. The undertaking cannot be served alone. Any one or all four specific conditions may be imposed at the officer's discretion.

g) Yes. These conditions are included in the four specified by the *Criminal Code*. Wally may be prohibited from communicating with a specific person and from attending a specific place.

h) No. This type of condition cannot be imposed by the OIC or any police officer. Only a justice may impose a curfew.

PROBLEM 66

a) Yes. Either the OIC or any police officer has discretionary authority to release and may release if RICE is fulfilled, regarding any warrant except in the case of a sec. 469 C.C. offence.

b) Yes. No mandatory obligation exists to release a person arrested with an endorsed warrant. Therefore, the accused may be brought directly to a justice for a bail hearing.

c) Yes. Either the OIC or any police officer has discretionary authority to release and may release if RICE is fulfilled, regarding any warrant except in the case of a sec. 469 C.C. offence (new provision—sec. 503(2) and (3) C.C.).

d) Yes. No mandatory obligation exists to release a person arrested with an unendorsed warrant. Therefore, the accused may be brought directly to a justice for a bail hearing.

PROBLEM 67

a) Yes. Either the OIC or any police officer has discretionary authority to release and may release if RICE is fulfilled, regarding any warrant except in the case of a sec. 469 C.C. offence (new provision — sec. 503(2) and (3) C.C.).

b) Yes. No mandatory obligation exists to release a person arrested with an unendorsed warrant. Therefore, the accused may be brought directly to a justice for a bail hearing.

PROBLEM 68

Yes. Ward cannot be released by OIC or any other police officer.

PROBLEM 69

Eddie's signature represents his promise to appear in court. Refusal to sign it represents reasonable grounds that he may fail to appear in court. RICE is not fulfilled. The accused may be detained and brought before a justice for a bail hearing.

PROBLEM 70

The officer may impose any of the four conditions on an undertaking, in order to release Wally by means of a promise to appear or a recognizance. Wally cannot be forced to agree to this condition or any other, but failure to agree to and sign the undertaking authorizes the patrol officer to continue detention of Wally and bring him to a justice for a bail hearing.

PROBLEM 71

No. The undertaking with conditions may be given to Ward only in addition to a promise to appear or a recognizance.

PROBLEM 72

a) Yes.
b) Without unreasonable delay and within 24 hours of the arrest, if a justice is available. If no justice is available within 24 hours of the arrest, as soon as possible.
c) No. If an adjournment is required to prepare for the bail hearing, Ward must still be brought to a justice without unreasonable delay and within 24 hours. The prosecutor must make an application for a three-day adjournment. The justice has discretion to grant the adjournment or reject it.

PROBLEM 73

- Before a justice. The justice must detain Ward and cannot release him.
- Ward must apply for a bail hearing.
- A judge of the superior court of criminal jurisdiction, e.g., in Ontario, a General Division Court judge.
- Ward.

PROBLEM 74

a) Prosecutor. No reverse onus situation exists.
b) No.
c) In provincial court or at the police station in a JP's office.
d) Yes. The bail hearing must be conducted at the police station if the police officer is the prosecutor.
e) No. June must be present or may appear by any suitable telecommunication device, including a telephone, if the justice deems it to be suitable and both the prosecutor and June agree.
f) Yes.
g) • The justice must release by means of an undertaking without conditions.
   • No.
h) Prosecutor.
i) No. Hearsay evidence is admissible. The investigating officer may read witness statements during testimony. However, the prosecutor has the option of calling the actual witnesses.
j) • Yes, to show a probability of conviction.
   • Yes.
   • Yes. It is relevant to primary and secondary grounds.
   • Yes. It is relevant to primary and secondary grounds.
k) Yes.
l) No. June decides whether she will testify.

m) No. Not unless she testifies about the offence.

n) No.

o) No. The information is laid before the bail hearing. Only the Crown attorney may withdraw an information.

p) Yes.

q) Yes.

r) The justice must release June on an undertaking or recognizance, with or without conditions.

s) Unlimited. The justice may impose any reasonable condition.

PROBLEM 75

Eddie. He has been charged with an indictable offence while awaiting trial for another indictable offence.

PROBLEM 76

The prosecutor. Wally was arrested for an indictable offence while awaiting trial for a summary conviction offence. This does not constitute a reverse onus situation.

PROBLEM 77

George. He was charged today with "fail to appear" while awaiting trial for a criminal offence. The same applies for "breach of undertaking."

PROBLEM 78

Sam. He committed an indictable offence and does not live in Canada. If Sam had been charged with a summary conviction offence, the onus would have been on the prosecutor.

PROBLEM 79

The prosecutor. This is not a reverse onus situation; the accused lives in Canada.

PROBLEM 80

Walter.

PROBLEM 81

a) Eleanor.

b) Eleanor must be held in custody.

PROBLEM 82

Yes. Any person, citizen, or police officer may lay an information if the person has a belief based on reasonable grounds that a specific person has committed a criminal offence. Wally can prove reasonable grounds in this case. "Assault" is a dual procedure offence, which is temporarily classified as indictable at the time of offence. No time limit exists to charge.

PROBLEM 83

No. The informant (applicant) must be named on the information.

PROBLEM 84

a) As soon as practicable afterward and before the court date specified on the promise to appear.

b) A justice, defined as a justice of the peace (JP), or a provincial court judge. A JP is most commonly used.

c) Anywhere other than open court. An information is usually laid in a JP's office at a police station.

d) You must swear under oath that the contents are true.
e) No.
f) Yes. An *ex parte* hearing is mandatory.
g) To prove reasonable grounds that Ward committed "fraud over $5000.00" on the date(s) specified.
h) Yes. Hearsay evidence is allowed. However, the witnesses may be called to testify if the JP considers it necessary.
i) Yes. Unsworn evidence is not permitted.
j) No. The accused is absent from all *ex parte* hearings.
k) The JP will not sign the information, and the promise to appear will be cancelled.
l) The JP will sign the information, and will confirm the promise to appear.
m) When the JP signs the information.
n) The Crown attorney.
o) No. An information must be laid to commence the proceedings. A police officer cannot prefer an indictment; only a Crown attorney can.

PROBLEM 85

Yes. An information may be laid to charge an offender with any classification of offence. The information commences proceedings regarding any criminal offence.

PROBLEM 86

No. One wording must allege only one count. However, both counts may be joined on one information.

PROBLEM 87

a) No. The Crown would then have to prove that the offence occurred exactly at midnight, which is the time between those dates.
b) "Between March 22nd and March 25th"; the border dates must represent dates when the offence definitely did not occur. Consequently, the offence date may be March 23rd or March 24th.
c) No. Only the "city of Hamilton" must be alleged.
d) No. The informal short-form name of the offence does not constitute a valid wording because it does not contain all the facts-in-issue.
e) "did break and enter a certain place TO WIT: a dwelling-house situated at 1000 E. 200th St., and did commit the indictable offence of theft therein, contrary to sec. 348 (1)(b) *Criminal Code*.
f) No. An information cannot be altered after it is signed by a justice. Another information must be laid to charge Eddie with the second break and enter.

PROBLEM 88

a) Yes. However, the counts must be separated by using the phrase "and further" between the wordings.
b) Yes.
c) No. Wally and Eddie are co-accused persons by being joined on the same information. Co-accused persons cannot be compelled by the Crown attorney to testify against each other.
d) They must be charged separately. If separate informations are laid, they are not co-accused persons and may be compelled by the prosecution to testify against each other.

PROBLEM 89

a) By laying an information.
b) No. The hearing is mandatory.
c) No. A preliminary hearing is never conducted before a provincial court trial.
d) Yes.
e) Provincial court.

f) Yes.

g) To determine whether sufficient evidence exists for Ward to stand trial.

h) The prosecutor.

i) No. The prosecutor may introduce only an amount of evidence that proves a *prima facie* case.

j) No.

k) Yes. The attorney general must first personally consent in writing.

l) Yes. The attorney general must first personally consent in writing.

m) It is sent to a clerk at the superior court of criminal jurisdiction. It will not be used at the trial.

n) A prosecutor completes one and signs it. It is not sworn before a justice.

o) Yes. The prosecutor could have preferred an indictment with the attorney general's consent. Ward would be caused to stand trial without the preliminary hearing being conducted.

PROBLEM 90

a) No. Admissibility of evidence is determined only during a trial, by the judge. The jury, if one exists, does not determine admissibility of evidence.

b) No. Sec. 24(2) *Charter* is used to determine admissibility of evidence that was obtained *after the commission* of a *Charter* violation.

c) No. The trial judge must determine whether the admission of the knife would bring the administration of justice into disrepute.

d) According to the *Collins* case, it will likely be admitted because it is a physical item that did not emerge or originate from the accused person and existed before the *Charter* violation occurred. However, a possibility exists that the knife may be excluded.

e) No. No type of evidence obtained after a *Charter* violation has been committed is automatically inadmissible. The trial judge must determine if the admission of the confession would bring the administration of justice into disrepute.

f) It will likely be excluded because a confession is evidence that emerged or originated from the accused, constituting self-incriminating evidence that did not exist before the violation occurred. However, a possibility does exist that the confession may be admitted.

PROBLEM 91

a) Yes. A motor vehicle is a place for the purpose of a search. This means that all the search and seizure laws must be followed relating to the search of the car. A motor vehicle is not a place in relation to break and enter offences only. This means that a person cannot be charged with a break and enter offence if the offender breaks into a car, but must instead be charged with an offence such as "theft" or "mischief."

b) Yes. There is no requirement to prove that reasonable grounds exist that the stolen property is in the car in order to ask for consent.

c) No. You must obtain consent only from one person who has lawful authority to give consent. Since Eddie's father is the owner, and he is not present, obtain consent from the driver, Eddie. The driver has control of the car and can regulate access into the car.

d) Yes. You must prove that he has knowledge of the specific act to be conducted and what the target of the search is. You must also distinguish what you want to search. In this case, there is one car and two people.

e) Yes. No law compels him to consent. Eddie must know he has a choice. You may simply inform him, "you don't have to consent" or "you have a choice to let me search or not."

f) Yes. He must know that he may stop the search at any time.

g) No. Because he is not compelled to give consent, he is simply exercising his right to refuse. Refusing to do something that one is not legally obliged to do is not incriminating evidence and cannot be used against him.

h) No. There is no offence for refusing to consent.

i) No. Search of a person is an act separate from search of a vehicle; therefore, separate consent is needed. If there is more than one person, separate consent is needed for each person.

j) No. Eddie can end the search at any time. However, you may try to obtain consent by using effective communication skills to regain consent. His refusal to open the trunk does not prevent you from trying to obtain his consent. A final alternative is to continue investigating and gather additional evidence that will allow you to obtain a search warrant later.

k) No. Obtaining consent improperly constitutes a sec. 8 *Charter* violation. The trial judge must then determine whether to admit or exclude the evidence, using the guidelines created by the Supreme Court of Canada, in the *Collins* case. The evidence in this case is physical items, and according to the guidelines, that type of evidence is usually admitted.

l) No. Both Eddie and Wally are adults. No requirement exists for you to obtain consent in writing. You may obtain verbal consent, which should be recorded verbatim in your notebook. Alternatively, you may write a consent form on a statement or in your notebook and ask Eddie to sign it.

PROBLEM 92

No. The Supreme Court of Canada, in *R. v. Edwards (1996)*, agreed with the Ontario Court of Appeal, in *R. v. Pugliese (1992)*, that the tenant alone may grant or refuse permission to enter the premises. Walter is not a lawful occupier of the apartment.

PROBLEM 93

No. Eddie is not a lawful occupier as defined by the Supreme Court of Canada. He does not contribute to the household expenses, does not control the premises, and cannot regulate access. Wally, in the absence of his parents, is the lawful occupier because he has control of the premises. Additionally, Wally has a reasonable expectation of privacy whereas Eddie does not. Therefore, consent should be obtained from Wally if you intend to search without first obtaining a search warrant. Finally, it should be noted that if consent is improperly obtained, any evidence found will not be automatically inadmissible despite the commission of a sec. 8 *Charter* violation. If the item seized is a physical item, it may be admissible.

PROBLEM 94

a) Yes. A sec. 487 C.C. search warrant authorizes the search of a building, receptacle, or place. A motor vehicle is a place for this purpose.

b) Obtain valid consent.

PROBLEM 95

Yes, it can be obtained to search for evidence that proves the commission of any classification of criminal offence.

PROBLEM 96

a) Yes. Police are authorized to use a sec. 487 C.C. search warrant to search for and seize any evidence that proves the whereabouts of a person who is believed to have committed any criminal offence.

b) No. You must obtain a "*Feeney*" warrant.

PROBLEM 97

a) No. Sec. 487 C.C. does not have an exception that permits the police to search for this type of evidence without first obtaining a search warrant.

b) No. An Information to Obtain must always be completed before a search warrant may be issued. No circumstances allow you to bypass this step.

PROBLEM 98

a) No. Only one specific place may be named on one Information to Obtain. Multiple places cannot be named.
b) No. If the items may be in any of three places, mere suspicion exists that the items are in one of those places. Therefore, reasonable grounds do not exist that the items are in one of those places. The search warrants will likely be denied.

PROBLEM 99

No. You must list specific items that will be evidence to that offence. Broad terms cannot be used because this prevents the recognition and identification of items that may be found. Each item must be described in detail, to allow you to positively recognize and identify items when they are found.

PROBLEM 100

a) No. That description is general and prevents recognition and identification. Additional general information such as make, and model if known, must be included. Afterward, specific descriptions that are unique features, such as serial number, damage, or any marks unique to that TV, must be added.
b) Yes. You cannot omit this information. You may name "break, enter, and theft" as the offence. If you were not certain that Reg committed that offence, you could name "possession of stolen property under $5000.00." Do not use the short-form name. Use the formal wording that would be used on an information.
c) Summarize the facts of the break and enter to prove that the offence actually occurred.
d) No. The warrant is directed to the place. If you know who the owner is, that fact will elevate the credibility of your reasonable grounds for belief. The important fact is to describe the place specifically on the Information to Obtain and on the appendix B, which will explain your grounds for belief.
e) Yes. The option is yours to refer to Marg as an anonymous informant or to name her. The Supreme Court of Canada has recognized the need to protect the identity of informants. In this case, you should not divulge Marg's identity. Keep her anonymous because she has given you information in the past and is associated with known criminals, which indicates that she will probably be a long-term valuable informant. Additionally, the public may have access to the Information to Obtain if the items are found.
f) No. This simple conclusory statement is insufficient. The written grounds must include the basis for Marg's information. In this case, you should specify
  - the time that Marg was at the house,
  - the fact that she was in the living room,
  - her exact observations about the TV, e.g., the location of the TV and the fact that it was operating,
  - a specific description of the TV,
  - Reg's remarks about the TV, the break and enter, and his attempt to sell it,
  - Marg's familiarity with Reg,
  - all persons present, and
  - Marg's past accuracy regarding information provided.
g) Yes, it should. She is an eyewitness regarding the possession of the stolen property and a recipient of a confession regarding the break and enter. Additionally, she has a degree of reliability based on past incidents.
h) Explain the connection between the TV and the offence named.
i) No. The JP must be a neutral, unbiased evaluator and cannot participate in the investigation. Advice from the JP would constitute a serious sec. 8 *Charter* violation.
j) Anywhere but in open court. Usually, it would be the JP's office, but any place will suffice.
k) No. Advice from the JP would constitute a serious sec. 8 *Charter* violation.

l) Present the information to obtain. The JP evaluates the written grounds and decides whether reasonable grounds exist. Avoid verbal, unsworn communication with the JP.

m) The JP does; you should not have possession of it.

n) You, the applying officer must be named on the warrant. All other officers who will be executing the warrant with you do not have to be named. However, there is no requirement that you participate in the search. Your presence is desirable because it is likely that you will have more knowledge about the investigation.

o) No, the JP must specifically authorize night hours. The JP must write the authorized night hours on the warrant.

p) Any number of officers are authorized. You are not restricted to a certain number.

q) No, unless exigent circumstances exist.

r) Your decision depends on the reasonableness of the circumstances. The warrant does not stipulate that someone must be home; however, to prevent a sec. 8 *Charter* violation, you must prove that you executed the warrant to prevent loss or destruction of the property.

s) Show him the warrant and let him read it. Do not give him a copy.

t) No. The search warrant does not authorize either the search or arrest of persons.

u) No. The search is complete once all the named items are found.

v) No. You must re-apply for another warrant, and use Marg's new information as your grounds for belief.

w) Yes. You have reasonable grounds to arrest Reg without an arrest warrant. Marg was the recipient of a confession. This constitutes reasonable grounds.

PROBLEM 101

A sec. 487 C.C. search warrant only, which can be used to search any place for narcotics. A C.D.S.A. search warrant cannot be used to search a place that is not a dwelling-house.

PROBLEM 102

a) A C.D.S.A. or a sec. 487 C.C. search warrant.

b) No. The same rules apply.

c) At least one officer must be named on a C.D.S.A. search warrant to ensure that a specific officer is responsible for the control and conduct of the search. Naming two officers is acceptable, but not an entire drug unit.

d) Yes, and that officer must closely supervise the search.

e) Any number may participate, but seized evidence must be taken into the possession of the named officer.

f) Yes.

References

CASES

Canada Post Corp. v. Canada (Attorney General) (1995) 95 C.C.C. (3d) p. 568 (Ont. Gen. Div.)

Church of Scientology and the Queen (No. 6) (1987) 31 C.C.C. (3d) p. 449 (Ont. C.A.)

Cloutier v. Langlois (1990) 53 C.C.C. (3d) p. 257 (S.C.C.)

Eccles v. Bourque (1974) 19 C.C.C. (2d) p. 129 (S.C.C.)

Hick v. Faulkner (1882) 8 QBD. 167 at 171, 172; DC.

Hunter v. Southam Inc. (1984) 14 C.C.C. (3d) p. 97 (S.C.C.)

R. v. Akey (1990) 1 O.R. (3d) p. 693 (Ont. Gen. Div.)

R. v. Anderson (1984) 10 C.C.C. (3d) p. 204 (Ont. C.A.)

R. v. B.(G.) (1990) 56 C.C.C. (3d) p. 200 (S.C.C.)

R. v. Bartle (1994) File #23523 (S.C.C.)

R. v. Beare (1988) 45 C.C.C. (3d) p. 57 (S.C.C.)

R. v. Belliveau (1985) 58 A.R. 334 (Alta. C.A.)

R. v. Belnavis (1997) 118 C.C.C. (3d) p. 405 (S.C.C.)

R. v. Bennet (1996) 108 C.C.C. (3d) p. 175 (Que. C.A.)

R. v. Black (1998) 50 C.C.C. (3d) p. 1 (S.C.C.)

R. v. Borden (1994) 92 C.C.C. (3d) p. 404 (S.C.C.)

R. v. Brydges (1990) 53 C.C.C. (3d) p. 380 (S.C.C.)

R. v. Burlingham (1995) Doc. #23966 (S.C.C.)

R. v. Burtasson (1982) 64 C.C.C. (2d) p. 268 (Ont. H.C.J.)

R. v. Caslake (1998) 121 C.C.C. (3d) p. 97 (S.C.C.)

R. v. Charlton (1992) 27 W.A.C. 272, 15 B.C.A.C. 272, 16 W.C.B. (2d) 423 (B.C.C.A.)

R. v. Clarkson (1986) 25 C.C.C. (3d) p. 207 (S.C.C.)

R. v. Clements (1996) Doc. #24932 (S.C.C.)

R. v. Cline (1956) 115 C.C.C. p. 18 (Ont. C.A.)

R. v. Colarusso (1994) Doc. #22433, 1 S.C.R. p. 20 (S.C.C.)

R. v. Colgan (1987) 38 C.C.C. (3d) p. 576 (S.C.C.)

R. v. Collins (1987) 33 C.C.C. (3d) p. 1 (S.C.C.)

R. v. Corcoran (1995) 24 O.R. (3d) p. 558 (Ont. Gen. Div.), at p. 562

R. v. Cote (1977) 33 C.C.C. (2d) p. 353 (S.C.C.)

R. v. Cunningham and Richie (1979) 49 C.C.C. (2d) p. 390 (Man. Co. Ct.)

R. v. Daviault (1994) Doc. #23435 (S.C.C.)

R. v. Dean (1965) Vol. 3 C.C.C. p. 228 (Ont. C.A.)

R. v. Debot (1989) 30 C.C.C. (3d) p. 207 (Ont. C.A.)

R. v. Debot (1989) 52 C.C.C. (3d) p. 93 (S.C.C.)

R. v. Dedman (1985) 20 C.C.C. (3d) p. 97 (S.C.C.)

R. v. Dyment (1988) 45 C.C.C. (3d) p. 207 (S.C.C.)

R. v. Edwards (1996) Doc. #24297 (S.C.C.)

R. v. Eng (1995) 56 B.C.A.C. 18

R. v. Evans (1991) 63 C.C.C. (3d) p. 289 (S.C.C.)

R. v. Feeney (1997) 115 C.C.C. (3d) p. 129 (S.C.C.)
R. v. Fegan (1993) 80 C.C.C. (3d) p. 356 (Ont. C.A.)
R. v. Ferris (1998) 126 C.C.C. (3d) p. 298 (B.C.C.A.)
R. v. Ferron (1989) 49 C.C.C. (3d) p. 289 (B.C.C.A.)
R. v. Fulton (1972) 10 C.C.C. (2d) p. 120 (Sask. Q.B.)
R. v. Genest (1989) 45 C.C.C. (3d) p. 385 (S.C.C.)
R. v. Gimson (1991) 69 C.C.C. (3d) p. 552 (S.C.C.)
R. v. Godoy (1999) File #26078
R. v. Golub (1997) 117 C.C.C. (3d) p. 194 (Ont. C.A.)
R. v. Grant (1991) 67 C.C.C. (3d) p. 268 (S.C.C.)
R. v. Grant (1993) Doc. #23075 (S.C.C.)
R. v. Gray (1993) 81 C.C.C. (3d) p. 174 (Man. C.A.)
R. v. Grenier (1991) 65 C.C.C. (3d) p. 76 (Que. C.A.)
R. v. Herbert (1990) 57 C.C.C. (3d) p. 1 (S.C.C.)
R. v. Hermanus (1993) (B.C. Prov. Ct.)
R. v. Hollis (1992) 76 C.C.C. (3d) p. 421 (B.C.C.A.)
R. v. Jackson (1993) 15 O.R. (3d) p. 709 (Ont. C.A.)
R. v. Jobin (1995) 97 C.C.C. (3d) p. 97 (S.C.C.)
R. v. Knowlton (1973) 10 C.C.C. (2d) p. 377 (S.C.C.)
R. v. Kokesch (1990) 61 C.C.C. (3d) p. 207 (S.C.C.)
R. v. Lal (1998) 130 C.C.C. (3d) p. 570 (B.C.C.A.)
R. v. Laramee (1972) 9 C.C.C. (2d) p. 433 (N.W.T. Mag. Ct.)
R. v. Laundry (1986) 25 C.C.C. (3d) p. 1 (S.C.C.)
R. v. Lepage (1986) 32 C.C.C. (3d) p. 171 (N.S.S.C.A.D.)
R. v. Lerke (1986) 24 C.C.C. (3d) p. 129 (Alta. C.A.)
R. v. Lim (No. 2) (1990) 1 C.R.R. (2d) p. 136 (Ont. H.C.J.)
R. v. MacKenzie (1991) 64 C.C.C. (3d) p. 336 (N.S. C.A.)
R. v. MacKenzie (1991) 64 C.C.C. (3d) p. 336 (S.C.C.)
R. v. Macooh (1993) 82 C.C.C. (3d) p. 481 (S.C.C.)
R. v. Manninen (1987) 34 C.C.C. (3d) p. 385 (S.C.C.)
R. v. McGregor (1985) 23 C.C.C. (3d) p. 266 (Man. Q.B.)
R. v. McKane (1987) 35 C.C.C. (3d) p. 481 (Ont. C.A.)
R. v. Mercer (1992) 70 C.C.C. (3d) p. 180 (Ont. C.A.)
R. v. Moran (1987) 36 C.C.C. (3d) p. 225 (Ont. C.A.)
R. v. Neilsen (1988) 43 C.C.C. (3d) p. 548 (Sask. C.A.)
R. v. Nicholls (1986) (Ont. Dist. Ct.)
R. v. Nolan (1987) 34 C.C.C. (3d) p. 289 (S.C.C.)
R. v. Noseworthy (1995) 101 C.C.C. (3d) p. 447 (Ont. Gen. Div.)
R. v. O'Brien (1954) 110 C.C.C. p. 1 (S.C.C.)
R. v. Pavel (1989) 53 C.C.C. (3d) p. 296 (Ont. C.A.)
R. v. Polashek (1999) File #C28667 (1999) (Ont. C.A.)
R. v. Primeau (1995) 97 C.C.C. (3d) p. 1 (S.C.C.)
R. v. Prosper (1994) Doc. #23178 (S.C.C.)
R. v. Pugliese (1992) 71 C.C.C. (3d) p. 295 (Ont. C.A.)
R. v. Purdy (1972) 8 C.C.C. (2d) p. 52 (N.B. S.C.)
R. v. Rao (1984) 12 C.C.C. (3d) p. 97 (Ont. C.A.)
R. v. Sandhu (1993) 82 C.C.C. (3d) p. 236 (B.C.C.A.)
R. v. Schmautz (1990) 53 C.C.C. (3d) p. 556 (S.C.C.)
R. v. Scott (1990) 61 C.C.C. (3d) p. 300 (S.C.C.)
R. v. Shea (1982) 1 C.C.C. (3d) p. 316 (Ont. H.C.J.)
R. v. Silveira (1995) Doc. #24013 (S.C.C.)
R. v. Simpson (1993) 79 C.C.C. (3d) p. 482 (Ont. C.A.)
R. v. Smellie (1994) 95 C.C.C. (3d) p. 9 (B.C.C.A.)
R. v. Smith (1992) 75 C.C.C. (3d) p. 257 (S.C.C.)
R. v. Smith (1989) 50 C.C.C. (3d) p. 308 (S.C.C.)
R. v. Speid (1991) 8 C.R.R. (2d) p. 383, 13 W.C.B. (2d) p. 659 (Ont. C.A.)
R. v. Spezzano (1977) 34 C.C.C. (2d) p. 87 (Ont. C.A.)
R. v. Storrey (1990) 53 C.C.C. (3d) p. 316 (S.C.C.)
R. v. Strachan (1988) 46 C.C.C. (3d) p. 479 (S.C.C.)
R. v. T.(E.) (1993) 86 C.C.C. (3d) p. 289 (S.C.C.)
R. v. Therens (1985) 18 C.C.C. (3d) p. 481 (S.C.C.)

R. v. Top (1989) 48 C.C.C. (3d) p. 493 (Alta. C.A.)
R. v. Waterfield (1964) 1 Q.B. 164 (C.C.A.)
R. v. West (1915) 24 C.C.C. 249 (Ont. H.C.) AFFD 25 C.C.C. 145 (S.C. App. Div.)
R. v. Whalen (1974) 17·C.C.C. (2d) p. 217 (Ont. Co. Crt.)
R. v. Whitfield (1969) 1 C.C.C. p. 129 (S.C.C.)
R. v. Wijesinha (1995) 100 C.C.C. (3d) p. 410 (S.C.C.)
R. v. Wills (1992) 70 C.C.C. (3d) p. 410 (S.C.C.)
R. v. Wise (1992) 70 C.C.C. (3d) p. 193 (S.C.C.)
R. v. Wong (1993) 60 C.C.C. (3d) p. 460 (S.C.C.)
R. v. Yamanaka (1998) 128 C.C.C. (3d) p. 570 (B.C.C.A.)
R. v. Zammit (1993) 81 C.C.C. (3d) p. 112 (Ont. C.A.)

STATUTES

Canadian Charter of Rights and Freedoms, Part 1 of the *Constitution Act, 1982*	
The Criminal Code	R.C.C. 1985, Chap. C–46
Young Offenders Act	R.S.C. 1985, c. Y–1
Canada Evidence Act	R.S.C. 1985, Chap. C–5
Police Services Act of Ontario	Bill 107 1989
Controlled Drugs and Substances Act	R.S.C. 1996, Chap. 19
Landlord and Tenant Act of Ontario	R.S.O. 1980, c. 232

BOOKS

Dukelow, Daphne A., and Betsy Nuse. *Pocket Dictionary of Canadian Law.* Toronto: Carswell, 1991.

Erhlich, Eugene et al. *Oxford American Dictionary.* New York: Oxford University Press, 1980.

Greenspan, Edward L., Q.C. *Martin's Annual Criminal Code.* Aurora: Canada Law Book, 1999.

Lawyer's Weekly, Feb. 12, 1993, vol. 12, no. 38. Toronto: Butterworths.

Lecture on "Powers of Arrest" at Ontario Police College, 1977.

Minister of Solicitor General of Ontario. *A Police Learning System for Ontario—Final Report and Recommendations.* Strategic Planning Committee on Police Training and Education, 1992.

Powers of Arrest, Ministry of the Solicitor General of Ontario. Ontario Police College, 1986.

Salhany, Roger E. *Canadian Criminal Procedure,* 5th ed. Aurora: Canada Law Book, 1989.

Ministry of the Solicitor General of Ontario. *Statute Search Powers, Search Warrants.* Ministry of the Solicitor General of Ontario. Ontario Police College, 1986.

Watt, David, and Michelle Fuerst. *Tremeear's Criminal Code.* Toronto: Carswell, 1998.

Endnotes

PREFACE

1   *R. v. Lerke (1986)* 24 C.C.C. (3d) p. 129 (Alta. C.A.), at p. 138.
2   Ministry of the Solicitor General, *A Police Learning System for Ontario* (Toronto, 1992), p. 175.
3   Ibid.

UNIT ONE

Chapter 1

1   Section 786(2) C.C.
2   Section 787(1) C.C.
3   Section 266 C.C.
4   *R. v. West (1915)* 24 C.C.C. 249 (Ont. H.C.) affd. 25 C.C.C. 145 (S.C. App. Div.).
5   Section 536(2) C.C.
6   Section 536(2) C.C.
7   Section 2 C.C.
8   Section 536(2) C.C.
9   Ibid.
10   Sections 798 and 785 C.C.
11   Sections 468 and 471 C.C.
12   Section 473(1) C.C.

Chapter 2

13   Section 9 *Charter.*
14   Section 279(2) C.C.
15   Dukelow and Nuse, p. 35.
16   *Canadian Criminal Justice System,* Ontario Police College (1977), p. 3.
17   *R. v. Therens (1985)* 18 C.C.C. (3d.) p. 481 (S.C.C.).
18   Section 495(1) C.C.
19   Section 495(1)(b) C.C.
20   Section 495(1)(a) C.C.
21   Section 495(a) C.C.
22   Section 495(1)(c) C.C.
23   Section 495(1) C.C.
24   Roger E. Salhany, *Canadian Criminal Procedure 5th ed.* (Aurora: Canada Law Book, 1989), p. 44.
25   *R. v. Dean (1965)* Vol. 3 C.C.C. p. 228 (Ont. C.A.).
26   Ibid.
27   Salhany, p. 43.

28 Eugene Ehrlich et al., *Oxford American Dictionary* (New York: Oxford University Press, 1980), p. 138.

29 *Frey v. Fedoruk, Stone and Watt (1950)* 3 D.L.R. at p. 527, as in *R. v. Dean (1965)*.

30 Information received by the writer by attending classes on "Arrest Procedures" at the Ontario Police College, 1977 and 1986.

31 *Hicks v. Faulkner (1882)* 8 QBD. 167 at 171, 172; DC.

32 *R. v. Debot (1989)* 30 C.C.C. (3d) p. 207 (Ont. C.A.).

33 *R. v. Storrey (1990)* 53 C.C.C. (3d) p. 316 (S.C.C.).

34 *R. v. Godoy (1999)*, File #26078.

35 *R. v. Debot (1989)* 30 C.C.C. (3d) p. 207 (Ont. C.A.).

36 *R. v. Bennett (1996)* 108 C.C.C. (3d) p. 175 (Que. C.A.).

37 *R. v. Golub (1997)* 117 C.C.C. (3d) p. 194 (Ont. C.A.).

38 Section 503(4) C.C.

39 Section 265(1)(b) C.C.

40 Section 264.1(1)(a) C.C.

41 Section 463(a) C.C.

42 Section 24(1) C.C.

43 *R. v. Cline (1965)* 115 C.C.C., p. 18 (Ont. C.A.).

44 Section 24(2) C.C.

45 Section 465(a)(c) C.C.

46 *R. v. O'Brien (1954)* 110 C.C.C., p. 1 (S.C.C.).

47 Ibid.

48 Section 495(1)(c) C.C.

49 Section 29(1) C.C.

50 Section 2 C.C.

51 Dukelow and Nuse, p. 251.

52 Section 496 C.C.

53 Section 507(4) C.C.

54 Dukelow and Nuse, p. 57.

55 Section 31(1) C.C.

56 Section 175(1) C.C.

57 *R. v. Simpson (1993)*, 79 C.C.C. (3d) p. 482 (Ont. C.A.).

58 *R. v. Ferris (1998)*, 126 C.C.C. (3d) p. 298 (B.C.C.A.).

59 *R. v. Yamanaka (1998)*, 128 C.C.C. (3d) p. 570 (B.C.C.A.).

60 *R. v. Lal (1998)*, 130 C.C.C. (3d) p. 570 (B.C.C.A.).

61 *R. v. Godoy (1999)*, File #26078 (S.C.C.).

62 *R. v. Dedman (1985)*, 20 C.C.C. (3d) p. 97 (S.C.C.).

63 *R. v. Waterfield (1964)*, 1 Q.B. 164 (C.C.A.).

64 *R. v. Knowlton (1973)*, 10 C.C.C. (2d) p. 377 (S.C.C.).

65 *R. v. Stenning (1979)*, 3 C.C.C. p. 145 (S.C.C.).

66 Ibid.

67 Supra, at note 60.

68 Supra, at note 43.

69 Supra, at note 57.

70 Supra, at note 58.

71 *R. v. Yamanaka (1998)* 128 C.C.C. (3d) p. 570 (B.C.C.A.).

72 *R. v. Lal (1998)* 130 C.C.C. (3d) p. 413 (B.C.C.A.).

73 *Police Services Act of Ontario*, Section 2.

74 Section 494(1)(a) C.C.

75 Section 494(2) C.C.

76 Section 494(1)(b) C.C.

77 Section 30 C.C.

78 Section 494(3) C.C.

79 *R. v. Grant (1991)* 67 C.C.C. (3d) p. 268 (S.C.C.), and *R. v. Cunningham and Ritchie (1979)* (2d) p. 390 (Man. Co. Ct.).

80 Section 139(2) C.C.

81 *R. v. Wijesinha (1995)* 100 C.C.C. (3d) p. 410 (S.C.C.), and *R. v. Whalen (1974)* 17 C.C.C. (2d) p. 217 (Ont. C. Ct.), and *R. v. Spezzano (1977)* 34 C.C.C. (2d) p. 87 (Ont. C.A.).

Chapter 3

82   Section 2 C.C.
83   Section 493 C.C.
84   Section 841 C.C.
85   Sections 507 and 788 C.C., and *Canadian Criminal Justice System,* Ontario Police College précis (1977), p. 16.
86   Section 512 C.C., and *Canadian Criminal Justice System,* Ontario Police College précis (1986), p. 17.
87   Section 507 C.C.
88   Section 507(4) C.C.
89   Sections 504 and 789 C.C.
90   Sections 507 and 789 C.C.
91   Section 507(4) C.C.
92   *Canadian Criminal Justice System,* Ontario Police College précis (1977), p. 17.
93   Sections 512(2)(a) and 512(b) C.C.
94   Section 512(2) C.C.
95   Section 512(1)(b) C.C.
96   Section 512(2)(c) C.C.
97   Section 524(1) C.C.
98   *R. v. Fulton (1972)* 10 C.C.C. (2d) p. 120 (Sask. Q.B.).
99   Sections 502 and 510 C.C.
100   Section 145(5) C.C.
101   Section 698(2)(a) C.C.
102   Section 698(2)(b) C.C.
103   Section 705(1) C.C.
104   Section 511(1) C.C.
105   Section 507(5) C.C.
106   Section 513 C.C.
107   Section 511(2) C.C.
108   Section 20 C.C.
109   Section 29(1) C.C.
110   Section 507(6) C.C.
111   Section 528 C.C.
112   Sections 503(3) and 503(1)(a) C.C.
113   Section 503(3) C.C.
114   Ibid.
115   Section 503(3)(a) C.C.
116   Section 503(3)(b) C.C.
117   Section 528(1) C.C.
118   Ibid.
119   Section 528(1)(a) C.C.
120   Section 528(2) C.C.
121   Ibid.

Chapter 4

122   Section 2 C.C.
123   *R. v. Wills (1992)* 70 C.C.C. (3d) p. 529 (Ont. C.A.).
124   *R. v. Borden (1994)* 92 C.C.C. (3d) p. 404 (S.C.C.).
125   *R. v. Wills (1992)* 70 C.C.C. (3d) p. 529 (Ont. C.A.).
126   *R. v. Edwards (1996)* Doc. #24297 (S.C.C.).
127   *Eccles vs. Bourque (1974)* 19 C.C.C. (2d) p. 129 (S.C.C.).
128   *R. v. Landry (1986)* 25 C.C.C. (3d) p. 1 (S.C.C.).
129   *R. v. Feeney (1997)* 115 C.C.C. (3d) p. 129 (S.C.C.).
130   *R. v. Macooh (1993)* 82 C.C.C. (3d) p. 481 (S.C.C.).
131   Section 26 C.C.
132   *R. v. Shea (1982)* 1 C.C.C. (3d) p. 316 (Ont. H.C.J.); *R. v. Nielsen (1988)* (Sask. C.A.).
133   *Cloutier v. Langlois (1990)* 53 C.C.C. (3d) p. 257 (S.C.C.).
134   *R. v. Smellie (1994)* 95 C.C.C. (3d) p. 9 (B.C.C.A.).
135   Ibid.
136   *R. v. Godoy (1997)* 115 C.C.C. (3d) p. 272 (Ont. C.A.).

Chapter 5

137   Section 24(2) *Charter*.
138   *R. v. Collins (1987)* 33 C.C.C. (3d) p. 1 (S.C.C.).
139   *R. v. Lerke (1986)* 24 C.C.C. (3d) p. 129 (Alta. C.A.), at p. 138.
140   Ibid.
141   1 C.C.C. p. 129 (S.C.C.).
142   18 C.C.C. (3d) p. 481 (S.C.C.).
143   Section 129 C.C.
144   Section 145(1)(a) C.C.
145   Supra, at note 125.
146   Ibid.
147   Ibid, p. 134.
148   *Cloutier v. Langlois (1990)* 53 C.C.C. (3d) p. 257 (S.C.C.).
149   *R. v. Charlton (1992)* 27 W.A.C. 272 (B.C.C.A.); *R. v. Speid (1991)* 8 C.R.R. (2d) p. 383 (Ont. C.A.); *R. v. Smellie (1994)* 95 C.C.C. (3d) p. 9 (B.C.C.A.).
150   63 C.C.C. (3d) p. 289 (S.C.C.).
151   Section 24(2) *Charter*.
152   Section 29(1) C.C.
153   Section 10(b) C.C.
154   53 C.C.C. (3d) p. 556 (S.C.C.).
155   *Young Offenders Act*, Section 11(1).
156   *R. v. Anderson (1984)* 10 C.C.C. (3d) p. 204 (Ont. C.A.).
157   Ibid.
158   Section 56(2)(c) Y.O.A.
159   Section 56(2)(d) Y.O.A.
160   Section 56(2) Y.O.A.
161   *R. v. Brydges (1990)* 53 C.C.C. (3d) p. 380 (S.C.C.).
162   *R. v. Hermanus (1993)* (B.C. Prov. Ct); as in *Lawyer's Weekly*, 12, no. 35 (1993).
163   Section 24(2) *Charter*.
164   *R. v. Bartle (1994)* File no. 23623 (S.C.C.).
165   Supra, at note 137.
166   *R. v. Jackson (1993)* 15 O.R. (3d) p. 709 (Ont. C.A.).
167   Ibid.
168   *R. v. Evans (1991)* 63 C.C.C. (3d) p. 289 (S.C.C.).
169   Ibid.
170   Ibid.
171   Ibid, p. 305.
172   *Canadian Criminal Justice System*, Ontario Police College précis (1986).
173   *R. v. Hollis (1992)* 76 C.C.C. (3d) p. 421 (B.C.C.A.).
174   *R. v. Burlingham (1995)* Doc. 23966 (S.C.C.).
175   Supra at note 173.
176   *R. v. Manninen (1987)* 34 C.C.C. (3d) p. 385 (S.C.C.).
177   Ibid.
178   *R. v. Smith (1989)* 50 C.C.C. (3d) p. 308 (S.C.C.).
179   *R. v. Hebert (1990)* 57 C.C.C. (3d) p. 1 (S.C.C.).
180   *R. v. Pavel (1989)* 53 C.C.C. (3d) p. 296 (Ont. C.A.).
181   *R. v. McKane (1987)* 35 C.C.C. (3d) p. 481 (Ont. C.A.), and *R. v. LePage (1986)* 32 C.C.C. (3d) p. 171 (N.S.S.C.C.A.D.).
182   64 C.C.C. (3d) p. 336 (N.S.C.A.).
183   57 C.C.C. (3d) p. 1 (S.C.C.) at pp. 41–42.
184   *R. v. Ferron (1989)* 49 C.C.C. (3d) p. 296 (B.C.C.A.).
185   *R. v. Top (1989)* 48 C.C.C. (3d) p. 493 (Alta. C.A.).
186   *R. v. T.(E.) (1993)* 86 C.C.C. (3d) p. 289 (S.C.C.).
187   Supra, at note 179.
188   Ibid.
189   Section 56(2)(b)(iv) Y.O.A.
190   Supra, at note 162.
191   Doc. #23178 (S.C.C.) at p. 6.
192   Ibid., and *R. v. Clarkson (1986)* 25 C.C.C. (3d) p. 207 (S.C.C.).
193   Supra, at note 161.
194   *R. v. Clarkson (1986)* 25 C.C.C. (3d) p. 207 (S.C.C.).
195   Supra, at note 161.
196   *R. v. Nicholls (1986)* (Ont. Dist. Ct.).

UNIT TWO

Chapter 6

1   Sections 495(2)(a) C.C. and 498(1)(i) C.C.
2   Sections 495(2) C.C. and 497 C.C.
3   Sections 498 C.C., 499 C.C. and 503 C.C.
4   Sections 503(1) C.C. and 515 C.C.

Chapter 7

5   Sections 501(1) C.C. and 509(1) C.C.
6   Sections 501(3) C.C. and 509(5) C.C., and Sec. 2 *Identification of Criminals Act.*
7   Sections 145(2) C.C., 145(4) C.C. and 145(5) C.C.
8   Section 498(1)(h) C.C.
9   Section 515(2)(a) C.C.
10   Section 505 C.C.
11   Section 9(2) Y.O.A.
12   Sections 9(3) Y.O.A. and 9(4) Y.O.A.
13   Section 9(2) Y.O.A.

Chapter 8

14   Section 497(1) C.C.
15   Section 497(1)(e) C.C.
16   Section 505 C.C.
17   Section 497(1)(d) C.C.
18   Section 503(1)(d) C.C.
19   Section 495(2) C.C.
20   Section 509(2) C.C.
21   Section 509(3) C.C.

Chapter 9

22   Section 493 C.C.
23   Sections 498(1)(a), (b), (c), (d), (i), (j) C.C., and 498(2) C.C.
24   Section 498(1)(e) C.C.
25   Section 498(1)(f) C.C.
26   Section 498(1)(g) C.C.
27   Section 503(1)(d) C.C.
28   Section 499(1) C.C.
29   Section 499(1)(a) C.C.
30   Section 499(1)(c) C.C.
31   Section 499(2) C.C.
32   Section 145(5) C.C.

Chapter 10

33   Sections 515(1) C.C. and 518(2) C.C.
34   Section 503(1) C.C.
35   Supra at note 33.
36   Section 515(11) C.C.
37   Section 522 C.C.
38   Section 27(1) *Interpretation Act.*
39   Section 516 C.C.
40   Section 2 C.C.
41   Section 11(7) Y.O.A.
42   Section 11(3)(a) Y.O.A.
43   Section 515(10)(a) C.C.
44   Section 515(10)(b) C.C.
45   Supra, at note 43.
46   Supra, at note 44.
47   Section 515(10) C.C.
48   Section 515(10)(b) C.C.
49   Section 515(2) C.C.

50	Section 515(6) C.C.
51	Section 515(6)(a) C.C.
52	Section 515(6)(b) C.C.
53	Section 515(6)(c) C.C.
54	Section 515(6)(d) C.C.
55	Section 515(6)(a)(ii) C.C.
56	Section 515(1) C.C.
57	Ibid.
58	Section 518(1)(e) C.C.
59	Section 518(1)(c)(iv) C.C.
60	Section 518(1)(c)(i) C.C.
61	Section 518(1)(c)(i)(iii) C.C.
62	Section 518(1)(c)(ii) C.C.
63	Section 518(1)(b) C.C.
64	Section 515(2) C.C.
65	Sections 515(2)(b), (c), (d), (e) C.C. and 841 C.C.
66	Sections 515(2)(a) C.C. and 841 C.C.
67	Section 515(4) C.C.
68	Section 515(5) C.C.
69	Section 520(1) C.C.
70	Section 525(1) C.C.
71	Section 525(4) C.C.
72	Sections 7.1(1) and 7.1(2) Y.O.A.
73	Sections 7.1(3) and 7.1(4) Y.O.A.
74	Section 7.1(5) Y.O.A.
75	Section 515(6) C.C.

UNIT THREE

Chapter 11

1	Section 841 C.C. (Form 2) (Part XXVIII).
2	Section 504 C.C.
3	*R. v. Akey (1990)* 1 O.R. (3d) p. 693 (Ont. Gen. Div.), and *R. v. Corcoran (1995)* 24 O.R. (3d) p. 558 (Ont. Gen. Div.), at p. 562.
4	Sections 504 C.C. and 788(1) C.C.
5	Supra, at note 1.
6	Sections 504 C.C., 788(2) C.C. and 2 C.C.
7	Section 504 C.C.
8	Section 786(2) C.C.
9	Section 505 C.C.
10	*R. v. Cote (1977)* 33 C.C.C. (2d) p. 353 (S.C.C.).
11	*R. v. B.(G.) (1990)* 56 C.C.C. (3d) p. 200 (S.C.C.).
12	Section 2 C.C.
13	Section 581(1) C.C.
14	Section 581(3) C.C.
15	Section 581(2)(b) C.C.
16	Section 581(2)(a) C.C.
17	38 C.C.C. (3d) p. 576 (S.C.C.).
18	56 C.C.C. (3d) p. 200 (S.C.C.).
19	Ibid., p. 218.
20	*Martin's Annual Criminal Code,* Canada Law Book (Aurora, Ontario; 1997), appendix A/39.
21	*Martin's Annual Criminal Code,* Canada Law Book (Aurora, Ontario; 1997), appendix A/37.
22	*Martin's Annual Criminal Code,* Canada Law Book (Aurora, Ontario; 1997), appendix A/32.
23	Sections 591(1) C.C. and 789(1)(b) C.C.
24	Section 789(1)(b) C.C.
25	Section 591(1) C.C.
26	Supra, at note 23.

27   *R. v. Primeau (1995)* 97 C.C.C. (3d) p. 1 (S.C.C.), and *R. v. Jobin (1995)* 97 C.C.C. (3d) p. 97 (S.C.C.).

28   Section 4(1) C.E.A.

Chapter 12

29   Sections 507(1) C.C. and 508(1) C.C.

30   Ibid.

31   Sections 507(1)(a) C.C. and 508(1)(a) C.C.

32   Ibid.

33   Sections 507(3)(a) C.C. and 508(2)(a) C.C.

34   Section 566(1) C.C.

Chapter 13

35   Section 2 C.C.

36   Section 574(1) C.C.

37   Section 548(1) C.C.

38   Section 536(4) C.C.

39   Section 549 (1) C.C.

40   Section 537 C.C.

41   Section 548(1)(b) C.C.

42   Sections 577(b) C.C. and 577(c) C.C.

43   Section 548(1)(a) C.C.

44   Section 548(1)(a) C.C.

45   *R. v. Caccamo (1975)* 29 C.R.N.S. 78 (S.C.C.).

46   Ibid.

47   Section 540(1)(a) C.C.

48   Ibid.

49   Section 541 C.C.

50   *R. v. Mills (1986)* 26 C.C.C. (3d) p. 481 (S.C.C.).

51   Section 549(1) C.C.

52   Section 551 C.C.

53   Sections 566(1) C.C. and 574(1) C.C.

54   Section 577 C.C.

UNIT FOUR

Chapter 14

1   *R. v . Sandhu (1993)* 82 CCC (3d) 236 (B.C.C.A.).

2   *R. v. Dyment (1988)* 45 CCC (3d) 207 (S.C.C.).

3   Section 2 C.C.

4   *R. v. Grant (1993)* Doc. #23075 (S.C.C.); *R. v. Kokesch (1990)* 61 C.C.C. (3d) p. 207 (S.C.C.).

5   *R. v. Grant (1993)* Doc. # 23075 (S.C.C.).

Chapter 15

6   *Hunter v. Southam Inc. (1984)* 14 C.C.C. (3d) p. 97 (S.C.C.).

7   Ibid. and *R. v. Colarusso (1994)* Doc. #22433, 1 S.C.R. p. 20 (S.C.C.).

8   14 C.C.C. (3d) p. 97 (S.C.C.).

9   *R. v. Collins (1987)* 33 C.C.C. (3d) p. 1 (S.C.C.).

10   Ibid.

11   Ibid.

12   Ibid.

13   *R. v. Stillman (1997)* 113 C.C.C. (3d) p. 321 (S.C.C.).

14   *R. v. Black (1998)* 50 C.C.C. (3d) p. 1 (S.C.C.).

15   Ibid.

16   *R. v. Burlingham (1995)* 97 C.C.C. (3d) p. 385 (S.C.C.).

Chapter 16

17 The Law Reform Commission of Canada. Working Paper 30: "Police Powers—Search and Seizure in Criminal Law Enforcement (1983)," at p. 52; as in *R. v. Mercer (1992)* 70 C.C.C. (3d) p. 180 (Ont. C.A.), at p. 187.
18 Ibid.
19 Ibid.
20 *R. v. Wills (1992)* 70 C.C.C. (3d) p. 529 (Ont. C.A.).
21 Ibid.
22 *R. v. Borden (1994)* 92 C.C.C. (3d) p. 404 (S.C.C.).
23 Ibid.
24 Ibid.
25 *R. v. Clements (1996)* Doc. #24932 (S.C.C.) and (1995) 100 C.C.C. (3d) p. 103 (Ont. C.A.).
26 *R. v. Edwards (1996)* Doc. #24297 (S.C.C.).
27 Ibid.
28 *R. v. Pugliese (1992)* 71 C.C.C. (3d) p. 295 (Ont. C.A.).
29 *R. v. Mercer (1992)* 70 C.C.C. (3d) p. 180 (Ont. C.A.).
30 Supra at note 26.
31 Supra at note 28.

Chapter 17

32 *R. v. B.(J.E.) (1989)* p. 224 (N.S.C.A.).
33 *R. v. Purdy (1972)* 8 C.C.C. (2d) p. 52 (N.B.S.C.).
34 *Church of Scientology and the Queen (No. 6) (1987)* 31 C.C.C. (3d) p. 449 (Ont. C.A.).
35 Ibid.
36 Ibid.
37 Supra at note 33.
38 Supra at note 34.
39 Ibid.
40 Supra at note 33.
41 *R. v. Scott (1990)* 61 C.C.C. (3d) p. 300 (S.C.C.).
42 Bisaillon v. Keable (1983) 7 C.C.C. (3d) p. 385 (S.C.C.) at pp. 411–12.
43 *R. v. Zammit (1993)* 81 C.C.C. (3d) p. 112 (Ont. C.A.).
44 *R. v. Debot (1989)* 52 C.C.C. (3d) p. 193 (S.C.C.).
45 Ibid.
46 Ibid.
47 Ibid.
48 Ibid.
49 Ibid., at p. 195.
50 *R. v. Kelly (1995)* 90 C.C.C. (3d) p. 367 (B.C.C.A.).
51 Ibid.
52 Ibid.
53 *R. v. Gray (1993)* 81 C.C.C. (3d) p. 174 (Man. C.A.).
54 Ibid.
55 Ibid. and Hunter v. Southam Inc. (1984) 14 C.C.C. (3d) p. 97 (S.C.C.).
56 *R. v. Gray (1993)* 81 C.C.C. (3d) p. 174 (Man. C.A.).
57 *R. v. Eng (1995)* 56 B.C.A.C. 18.
58 Part XXVIII *Criminal Code.*
59 Section 488 C.C.
60 Section 2 C.C.
61 Section 487.01(7) C.C.
62 Section 487.05(3) C.C.
63 Section 487.09(4) C.C.
64 Section 529.5 C.C.
65 Section 487.1 C.C.
66 *Eccles v. Bourque (1974)* 19 C.C.C. (2d) p. 129 (S.C.C.), at pp. 133–4; *R. v. Genest (1989)* 45 C.C.C. (3d) p. 385 (S.C.C.).
67 *R. v. Genest (1989)* 45 C.C.C. (3d) p. 385 (S.C.C.).
68 Ibid.
69 *R. v. Grenier (1991)* 65 C.C.C. (3d) p. 76 (Que. C.A.).
70 *R. v. McGregor (1985)* 23 C.C.C. (3d) p. 266 (Man Q.B.).
71 Section 29(1) C.C.

72	*R. v. Silveira (1995)* Doc. #24013 (S.C.C.).
73	Section 495(1)(a) C.C.
74	Section 101(1) C.C.
75	Section 11 N.C.A.
76	Section 489 C.C.
77	*R. v. Moran (1987)* 36 C.C.C. (3d) p. 225 (Ont. C.A.).
78	Section 489.1(2) C.C.
79	Ibid.
80	Sections 490(1)(b) C.C. and 490(2)(b) C.C.
81	Section 490(2)(a) C.C.
82	Section 490(9.1) C.C.
83	Section 490(1)(a) C.C.
84	Section 489.1(a) C.C.
85	Section 491.2 C.C.
86	Sections 491.2(2) and 491.2(3) C.C.
87	Section 491.2(5) C.C.
88	*MacIntyre v. Nova Scotia (A.G.) (1982)* 65 C.C.C. (2d) p. 129 (S.C.C.).
89	Section 11(1) C.D.S.A.
90	Section 11(6) C.D.S.A.
91	*R. v. Scott (1990)* 61 C.C.C. (3d) p. 300 (S.C.C.), at p. 313–14.
92	Section 12 N.C.A.
93	*R. v. Strachan (1988)* 46 C.C.C. (3d) p. 479 (S.C.C.).
94	Supra, at note 67.
95	*R. v. Gimson (1991)* 69 C.C.C. (3d).
96	Supra, at note 67.
97	Supra, at note 70.
98	Section 29(1) C.C.
99	Section 11(5) C.D.S.A.
100	Section 11(6) C.D.S.A.
101	Section 11(8) C.D.S.A.
102	Sections 13(4) and 13(5) C.D.S.A.
103	*R. v. Wong (1993)* 60 C.C.C. (3d) p. 460 (S.C.C.).
104	Section 487.01(4) C.C. and *R. v. Noseworthy (1995)* 101 C.C.C. (3d) p. 460 (Ont. Ct. Gen. Div.).
105	*Canada Post Corp. v. Canada (Attorney General) (1995)* 95 C.C.C. (3d) p. 568 (Ont. Ct. Gen. Div.).
106	Section 487.01(4) C.C.
107	Section 487.01(3) C.C.
108	Section 492.1(4) C.C.
109	*R. v. Wise (1992)* 70 C.C.C. (3d) p. 193 (S.C.C.).
110	Section 492.1(2) C.C.
111	Section 492.1(3) C.C.
112	Section 492.2(4) C.C.
113	*R. v. Fegan (1993)* 80 C.C.C. (3d) p. 356 (Ont. C.A.), at pp. 363–64.
114	Ibid.
115	Ibid.
116	Ibid.
117	Ibid.
118	Section 492.2(1) C.C.
119	Section 492.2(3) C.C.
120	Ibid.
121	Section 487.04 C.C.
122	Ibid.
123	Section 487.05(1) C.C.
124	Ibid.
125	Section 487.05(2) C.C.
126	Section 487.06(1) C.C.
127	Section 487.06(2) C.C.
128	Sections 487.07(1) and 487.07(4) C.C.
129	Section 487.07(2) C.C.
130	Section 487.07(5) C.C.
131	Section 487.09(1) C.C.
132	Section 487.09(2) C.C.

Chapter 18

133   *Cloutier v. Langlois (1990)* 53 C.C.C. (3d) p. 257 (S.C.C.).
134   Ibid.
135   Ibid.
136   Ibid. at p. 278.
137   *R. v. Caslake (1998)* 121 C.C.C. (3d) p. 97 (S.C.C.).
138   Supra, at note 138.
139   *R. v. Speid (1991)* 8 C.R.R. (2d) p. 383, 13 W.C.B. (2d) p. 659 (Ont. C.A.);
       R. v. Charlton (1992) 27 W.A.C.272, 15 B.C.A.C.272, 16 W.C.B.(2d) 423(B.C.C.A.).
140   *R. v. Charlton (1992)*, supra, at note 441.
141   *R. v. Smellie (1994)* 95 C.C.C. (3d) p. 9 (B.C.C.A.).
142   *R. v. Lim (no. 2) (1990)* 1 C.R.R. (2d) p. 136 (Ont. H.C.J.).
143   Ibid. at p. 145.
144   Supra, at note 146.
145   *R. v. Golub (1997)* 117 C.C.C. (3d) p. 194 (Ont. C.A.).
146   *R. v. Lerke (1986)* 24 C.C.C. (3d) p. 129 (Alta. C.A.).
147   *R. v. Shea (1982)* 1 C.C.C. (3d) p. 316 (Ont. H.C.J.).
148   Ibid.
149   *R. v. Grenier (1991)* 65 C.C.C. (3d) p. 76 (Que. C.A.).
150   Canadian Firearms Centre; Department of Justice. *Firearms Officer Desk Manual.*
       Vol. 2 1998.
151   Ibid.
152   Section 117.04(4) C.C.
153   Section 117.02(2) C.C.
154   *R. v. Golub (1997)* 117 C.C.C. (3d) p. 194 (Ont. C.A.).
155   Section 117.03(3) C.C.
156   Ibid.
157   Supra, at note 103.
158   Ibid.
159   Ibid.
160   Ibid.
161   Ibid.
162   Ibid.
163   *R. v. Debot (1989)* 52 C.C.C. (3d) p. 193 (S.C.C.).
164   Sections 11(7) and (6) C.D.S.A.
165   *R. v. Polashek (1999)*, File #C28667 (1999) Ont. C.A.
166   *R. v. Silveira (1995)* Doc. #24013 (S.C.C.).
167   *R. v. Godoy (1999)*, File #26078.
168   Ibid.
169   *R. v. Belnavis.*
170   Supra, at note 168.

Index